STATE SUPREME COURTS
IN STATE AND NATION

G. ALAN TARR AND MARY CORNELIA ALDIS PORTER

YALE UNIVERSITY PRESS   NEW HAVEN AND LONDON

Designed by Sally Harris
and set in Meridien type by
TCSystems, Shippensburg, Penn.
Printed in the United States of America by
Halliday Lithograph, West Hanover, Mass.

Library of Congress Cataloging-in-Publication Data

Tarr, G. Alan (George Alan)
    State supreme courts in state and nation.

    Includes index.
    1. Courts of last resort—United States—States.
I. Porter, Mary Cornelia. II. Title.
KF8736.T37 1988   347.73'36   87-2303
ISBN 0–300–03912–3 (alk. paper) 347.30735

The paper in this book meets the guidelines for
permanence and durability of the Committee on
Production Guidelines for Book Longevity
of the Council on Library Resources.

10   9   8   7   6   5   4   3   2   1

To Susan and Roy

CONTENTS

PREFACE

The title of this volume calls to mind V. O. Key's classic account *Southern Politics in State and Nation*—and designedly so.[1] In that study, Key demonstrated how both intrastate factors and broader national developments—and their interplay over time—shape the character of state politics. Equally important, he showed how a series of well-constructed case studies, focusing on politics in individual states over an extended period, can provide the basis for generalizations about the dynamics of state politics and state political development. Thus, in addition to being intrinsically interesting, Key's analysis is valuable as a model for conducting comparative research in state politics. In this book we seek to adapt this model to a comparative analysis of state supreme courts and of their roles in the political lives of the American states.

The claim that state supreme court rulings are influenced by events and legal developments beyond state borders is hardly surprising. In cases that raise federal questions, state supreme courts must give precedence to federal law over state law and must conform their interpretation of the federal law to the authoritative pronouncements of the United States Supreme Court. Even in the absence of hierarchical authority, the decisional trends among sister courts provide direction for the resolution of common legal problems, particularly in the common law area. More subtly, national political phenomena, fashions in judicial role and legal interpretation, and patterns of court reform may likewise influence the operations of state supreme courts.

These factors, as well as the common responsibilities shared by state high courts—for example, elaborating common law principles and interpreting the statutory and constitutional law of the state—promote a degree of uniformity in state supreme court rulings and

1. New York: Vintage, 1949.

activities. Yet, even a passing familiarity with state supreme courts reveals marked differences in jurisprudence and in the roles they play both nationally and within their states. Some courts have tended to defer to other state political institutions and to eschew independent policy development, whereas others have aggressively seized opportunities to define policy for the state. Still others have followed a more complex course, embracing activism in one period and judicial restraint in another or adopting different postures depending upon the substance of the issue or the type of law involved. Thus legal, political, and historical factors peculiar to the state affect the orientation of a state high court.

This initial recognition of both variety and uniformity and continuity and change in the operations of state supreme courts suggests the utility of comparative research along the lines of Key's comparative case study approach. In this volume we examine the activities of three distinctive courts—the Alabama, Ohio, and New Jersey supreme courts—from the end of World War II to the mid-1980s. By focusing on more than a single court, we can identify the range of variation in state supreme court activity and begin to explore the causes and consequences of that variety. By examining the activities of those courts over several decades, a focus facilitated by our comparative case study approach, we can explore those factors that have precipitated changes in the roles played by particular courts as well as those broader factors producing change on all courts. By restricting our focus to a limited number of courts, we can investigate in depth the developments we uncover. Finally, by structuring our analysis of each court along similar lines, we can produce research that is truly comparative and provide generalizations applicable to courts beyond those directly under examination.

Chapter 1 explores how the American system of judicial federalism affects the work of state supreme courts. Chapter 2 describes the interaction between state supreme courts and other state political institutions. Chapters 3, 4, and 5 examine the activities of the Alabama, Ohio, and New Jersey courts, respectively. Chapter 6 draws upon our case studies and upon the available research on other state high courts to offer generalizations and conclusions about the legal and political roles that state supreme courts play both within their states and in the nation more generally.

ACKNOWLEDGMENTS

In undertaking a project of this sort, we have incurred debts to a host of people who have shared their time and insights with us.

We extend our thanks to the justices of the Alabama Supreme Court for responding to the questionnaire and for lengthy and wide-ranging interviews with one of the authors: Chief Justice Clement Clay Torbert, Jr., and Justices Hugh Maddox, James H. Faulkner, Richard L. Jones, Reneau P. Almon, Janie L. Shores, Samuel A. Beatty, Oscar W. Adams, Jr., and retired Justice Pelham Merrill. We are also grateful to the following, who provided information crucial to understanding the Alabama high court: Arthur Briskman, Francis H. Hare, Larry Yackle, Timothy Hoff, John Payne, Tinsley Yarbrough and Howard Mandell. Robert A. Martin read and made suggestions for chapter 3, coordinated the interviews, and, during a four-year period, generally assisted our endeavors. We owe him a special debt of gratitude.

The justices of the Ohio Supreme Court responded fully and thoughtfully to our questionnaire and gave generously of their time in interviews: A. William Sweeney, Ralph S. Locher, Robert E. Holmes, Andy Douglas, Craig Wright, and Chief Justice Frank D. Celebrezze. Justice Clifford Brown facilitated the interviewing process and supplied us with extensive and invaluable documentation of political and legal developments in the state. We also appreciate Mrs. William Brown's response to the questionnaire sent to her husband, who was then very ill and had retired from the bench. Several experts on the Ohio judiciary contributed valuable insights, including David Goldberger, Bruce Campbell, Louis Jacobs, Leslie W. Jacobs, Joseph Krabach, Stewart Jaffy, Dennis Hale, Jim Underwood, Sharon Crook West, Thomas Schwartz, Duke Thomas, John Thomas, and Jeffrey A. Hennemuth. (In chapter 4, interviews with the Ohio justices are generally so designated. Other interviews, since we promised anonymity, make no reference to the occupation or the position of the person interviewed.) We are particularly indebted to Kathleen L. Barber for sharing her storehouse of information with us and for her painstaking and helpful critique of chapter 4. We also thank the editors of the Ohio State Law Journal for permitting us to use portions of a previously published article.

Robert Williams, Stanley Friedelbaum, and Stewart Pollock read an earlier version of the chapter on the New Jersey Supreme Court and offered valuable criticism and suggestions.

Walter Murphy undertook a close reading of several chapters and provided many helpful suggestions for improvements.

The New Jersey Administrative Office of the Courts and Arthur Vanderbilt III generously provided us with pictures of New Jersey justices.

The authors' initial research on this volume was aided by a grant from Project '87. Subsequent research by Alan Tarr was facilitated by grants from the Rutgers University Research Council.

We also gratefully acknowledge the assistance and support of Marian Ash, the political science editor at Yale University Press; the diligent copy-editing of Lawrence Kenney; and the useful suggestions of several anonymous reviewers. Any errors of commission and omission are, of course, ours.

In conclusion, we have special thanks for Bobby, Andy, and Mary, as well as for Susan and Roy, to whom this book is dedicated.

ONE

JUDICIAL FEDERALISM AND STATE SUPREME COURTS

State supreme courts decide over ten thousand cases each year. In the vast majority of these cases, their rulings are determinative: most litigants do not seek to appeal the decisions, and should they wish to do so, often the United States Supreme Court either lacks jurisdiction or declines to hear the appeals.[1] Some of these rulings by state high courts define the allocation of powers among the branches of state government or between state and local governments. Others structure legal relations among residents in such areas as family relations, contracts, and torts, at times establishing new legal principles in the course of resolving private disputes. Still others may clarify the scope of individual rights, vindicate those rights when they are infringed by government or by private parties, or announce broad policy mandates.

Despite the intrinsic importance of these responsibilities, state supreme courts tend to operate in relative obscurity, and public knowledge about the courts is at best rudimentary. As Preble Stolz has observed, "Americans love the law and have long paid close attention to the U.S. Supreme Court, but they have tended to overlook the state supreme court."[2] This volume seeks to remedy this oversight by

1. During its 1985 term, for example, the United States Supreme Court either denied certiorari or dismissed appeals for want of a substantial federal question in 3,999 of the 4,289 instances in which review was sought. Altogether, it decided with full opinion only 26 cases on appeal from state supreme courts. Figures are drawn from the annual review of the Supreme Court's rulings published in *Harvard Law Review* 100 (November 1986): tables II and III.

2. Preble Stolz, *Judging Judges* (New York: Free Press, 1981), p. 4. For empirical verification of Stolz's claim, see "The Public Image of the Courts: Highlights of a National Survey of the General Public, Judges, Lawyers, and Community Leaders," in *State Courts: A Blueprint for the Future* (Williamsburg, Va.: National Center for State Courts, 1978).

demonstrating the significant roles played by state high courts within their states and nationally.

Underlying our analysis are several premises that will be elaborated and documented in the course of the book. First, the role that a state supreme court plays within a state and in American federalism more generally can be defined in terms of three sets of relationships: (1) the state high court's relations with federal courts (vertical judicial federalism), which entails a division of labor and patterns of interaction; (2) its relations with courts in other states, particularly other state supreme courts (horizontal judicial federalism); and (3) its relations with other institutions of state government, which again involve a division of labor and patterns of interaction.[3] Second, these relationships are defined, to a greater or lesser extent, by legal and extralegal factors. No element of the relationships is either totally determined by legal considerations nor altogether immune from them. Third, these relationships are dynamic, changing over time in response to legal and extralegal factors, to changes on the court and to changes outside its control. Fourth, although the similarities among state supreme courts impose a degree of uniformity in the relationships with other actors that define their legal and political roles, the considerable diversity among state supreme courts also has a pronounced effect on the character of those relationships. Because there is no typical state supreme court, there can be no typical role for a state supreme court in either the state or national arenas.

We emphasize these initial premises because they direct us away from the paths typically followed by previous studies of state supreme courts. One approach, particularly prevalent among legal scholars, has been to view state supreme courts primarily as participants in the system of vertical judicial federalism and to emphasize the legal aspects of their relations with federal courts, particularly the U.S. Supreme Court.[4] This research has accordingly described how law

3. In earlier research we distinguished between "vertical federalism," which pertains to the relations between national and state governments, and "horizontal federalism," which refers to patterns of communication and interaction among the states. See "Editors' Introduction," in Mary Cornelia Porter and G. Alan Tarr, eds., *State Supreme Courts: Policymakers in the Federal System* (Westport, Conn.: Greenwood Press, 1982), pp. xix–xxii. We continue to employ this terminology in the present study.

4. Much of the recent research on the development of state civil liberties law by state supreme courts, usually referred to as the "new judicial federalism," has followed this approach. See, for example, Peter J. Galie and Lawrence P. Galie, "State Constitutional Guarantees and Supreme Court Review: Justice Marshall's

creates separate spheres for state and federal courts and structures their areas of concurrent responsibility.

Valuable as these studies are, the picture of state supreme courts they paint is incomplete and, consequently, misleading. Most obviously, by viewing state supreme courts in terms of the roles they play in vertical judicial federalism, these studies ignore a host of other relationships, such as those with other state courts and with state political institutions, that are crucial for understanding state high courts. Moreover, even within their chosen parameters, these studies seriously oversimplify the nature of vertical judicial federalism. For one thing, these studies tend to depict the legal relationships within vertical judicial federalism as static, whereas in fact the governing law may—and often does—change as a result of developments within or outside of the legal system. For another thing, by focusing exclusively on the influence of legal factors in vertical judicial federalism, these studies slight the influence of extralegal factors. Legal factors are unquestionably significant in channeling the activities of state supreme courts, but by themselves they cannot fully explain the patterns of behavior found among these courts. Many aspects of judicial activity are not governed by legal principle. Where legal principles do apply, they may merely circumscribe the leeways legitimately available to judges rather than foreclose judicial choice, and extralegal factors may decisively affect choices within those legal parameters. Certainly, legal principles cannot preclude the development of patterns of conduct and influence beyond those which they prescribe. Indeed, as the contemporary literature on American federalism has shown, patterns of reciprocal influence are common even in legally hierarchical relationships.[5] And as has been documented in the

---

Proposal in Oregon v. Hass," *Dickinson Law Review* 82 (1978): 273–93; "Developments in the Law—-The Interpretation of State Constitutional Rights," *Harvard Law Review* 95 (April 1982): 1324–1502; and Harold J. Spaeth, "Burger Court Review of State Court Civil Liberties Decisions," *Judicature* 68 (February–March 1985): 285–91.

It is also revealing that the preeminent legal treatise on judicial federalism looks at the topic from the perspective of the federal courts and treats state courts as secondary. See Paul M. Bator, Paul J. Mishkin, David L. Shapiro, and Herbert Wechsler, *Hart and Wechsler's The Federal Courts in the Federal System*, 2d ed. (Mineola, N.Y.: Foundation Press, 1980).

5. The classic account remains Morton Grodzins, *The American System*, ed. Daniel J. Elazar (Chicago: Rand McNally, 1966). Other noteworthy studies from this perspective include Carl J. Friedrich, *Trends of Federalism in Theory and Practice* (New York: Praeger, 1968), and Daniel J. Elazar, *The American Partnership:*

literature on judicial impact, judges may at times act contrary to the legal principles that govern them.[6]

Finally, as a result of their excessive emphasis on the legal structure of vertical judicial federalism, these studies tend to ignore both variations in the roles played by specific state courts and changes in those roles over time. As a result, they present an account of state supreme courts that is unduly narrow in focus and simple in description.

Other studies have sought to avoid this narrow perspective through a case study approach, intensively examining the work of a single state supreme court.[7] The advantage of this focused approach lies in the opportunity it provides for detailed consideration of judicial behavior over time in relation to the full range of other actors who help define its scope and character. As our survey of the legal and extralegal factors influencing state supreme courts will show, however, there are substantial differences in the legal and political contexts in which these courts operate. Thus case studies run the risk of being merely studies of particular courts that do not permit generalizations applicable to other courts.

Some political scientists, recognizing the opportunities for comparative research provided by fifty state supreme courts, have undertaken quantitative analyses based on data drawn from all the state high courts.[8] Obviously, this approach avoids the problem that

Intergovernmental Co-operation in the Nineteenth-Century United States (Chicago: University of Chicago Press, 1962).

6. Among these students are G. Alan Tarr, *Judicial Impact and State Supreme Courts* (Lexington, Mass.: Lexington Books, 1977); Jerry K. Beatty, "State Court Evasion of the United States Supreme Court Mandates During the Last Decade of the Warren Court," *Valparaiso University Law Review* 6 (Spring 1972): 260–85; Bradley C. Canon, "Reactions of State Supreme Courts to a U.S. Supreme Court Civil Liberties Decision," *Law & Society Review* 8 (Fall 1973): 109–34; Neal T. Romans, "The Role of State Supreme Courts in Judicial Policymaking—Escobedo, Miranda, and the Use of Judicial Impact Analysis," *Western Political Quarterly* 27 (March 1974): 38–59; and Kenneth N. Vines, "Southern State Supreme Courts and Race Relations," *Western Political Quarterly* 18 (March 1965): 5–18.

7. Representative studies include Thomas R. Morris, *The Virginia Supreme Court* (Charlottesville, Va.: University Press of Virginia, 1975); Robert J. Frye, *The Alabama Supreme Court* (University, Ala.: Bureau of Public Affairs, University of Alabama, 1961); Kenneth N. Vines, "Political Functions of a State Supreme Court"; and Charles H. Sheldon, *A Century of Judging: A Political History of the Washington Supreme Court* (Seattle: University of Washington Press, 1987).

8. As Gregory Caldeira has remarked, "For the empirical social scientist, political and legal institutions in the American states have the singular virtue of encompassing intriguing peculiarities within a range of contexts that is sufficiently

plagues the case study approach, namely, the nongeneralizability of findings. Yet this advantage is purchased at considerable cost. Often these studies present a snapshot of state supreme courts, when a moving picture would be more revealing. In addition, the scope of these studies prevents them from providing the richly textured perspective necessary to delineate the range of legal and political roles played by various state supreme courts.

The comparative case study approach we employ represents a fundamental departure in the analysis of state supreme courts. To place our case studies in perspective, however, it is necessary to begin with an overview of state supreme courts' relationships with federal courts (vertical judicial federalism), with their sister courts in other states (horizontal judicial federalism), and with other governmental institutions within the state. For each set of relationships, we look first to the legal factors structuring them, then to the extralegal factors influencing them, and finally—where appropriate—to significant developments in substantive law.

Vertical Judicial Federalism

THE LEGAL CONTEXT

Federal law is extremely influential in structuring the relations between state supreme courts and federal courts.[9] First of all, it defines the jurisdiction of the federal courts. For although Article III of the United States Constitution grants the federal judicial power to the national government, it does not create a separate system of federal courts (save for the U.S. Supreme Court), leaving Congress free to

---

invariable to be essentially comparable" (Gregory A. Caldeira, "Review Essay: Departures in the Study of State Supreme Courts," *Judicature* 67 [April 1984]: 459). Examples of this approach include Burton M. Atkins and Henry R. Glick, "Environmental and Structural Variables as Determinants of Issues in State Courts of Last Resort," *American Journal of Political Science* 20 (February 1976): 97–115, and Dean Jaros and Bradley C. Canon, "Dissent on State Supreme Courts: The Differential Significance of Characteristics of Judges," *Midwest Journal of Political Science* 15 (May 1971): 322–46. The approach used in these studies was pioneered in Thomas R. Dye, *Politics, Economics, and the Public* (Chicago: Rand McNally, 1966).

9. This section draws upon the excellent general treatments of vertical judicial federalism from the federal perspective in Bator et al., *Federal Courts in the Federal System;* Martin H. Redish, *Federal Jurisdiction: Tensions in the Allocation of Judicial Power* (Indianapolis: Michie, 1980); and Richard A. Posner, *The Federal Courts: Crisis and Reform* (Cambridge: Harvard University Press, 1985).

Table 1. Comparing the Business of State Supreme Courts (SSC)
and Federal Courts of Appeals (FCA) (in percent)

	SSC (1940–70)	FCA (1935–55)	FCA (1960–75)
Real Property	11	3	1
Business Cases	16	30	16
Criminal Justice	18	16	21
Public Law	19	37	38
Torts	22	13	15
Family Law/Estates	12	—	—

establish inferior federal courts and to assign them the jurisdiction it
deems appropriate. Historically Congress has not vested in the courts
it created the full range of judicial power that might be assigned to
them. Prior to 1875, for example, the federal district courts did not
have general original jurisdiction in cases raising federal questions,
that is, cases arising under the Constitution, laws, and treaties of the
United States. And although the federal judicial power extends to all
civil cases between citizens of different states (the so-called diversity-
of-citizenship jurisdiction), the Judiciary Act of 1789 permitted initiation of such suits in federal court only when the amount in dispute
exceeded $500, in order to prevent citizens from being summoned
long distances to defend small claims. (With the passage of time and
the effects of inflation, the minimum amount has been raised to
$10,000.) Furthermore, in conferring diversity jurisdiction on federal
courts, Congress has also determined what restrictions shall be placed
on the removal of a suit from a state court to a federal district court.
Lastly, it is Congress alone that decides whether federal jurisdiction is
to be exclusive, thereby precluding initiation of actions in state court,
or concurrent.

By determining what sorts of cases may be initiated in federal courts
and what sorts may not be initiated in state courts, federal law does
more than affect the business of federal and state trial courts. Since
state supreme courts serve as appellate tribunals within state judicial
systems, the mix of cases they receive is vitally affected by the mix of
cases at the trial level. Perhaps not surprisingly, then, comparative
analysis of the dockets of federal courts of appeals and state supreme
courts reveals major differences in the sorts of issues each addresses.
Generally speaking, state supreme courts are much more likely to
address issues of state law, and federal courts to address issues of
federal law, especially federal statutory law. In more substantive

terms, state supreme courts issue many more rulings involving tort law, family law and estates, and real property than do federal courts of appeals (table 1).[10] On the other hand, federal appellate courts confront public law issues much more frequently—indeed, they compose the single largest category of business for those courts.

Despite these differences, each system of courts may have occasion to rule on issues of both federal and state law. For example, at least since the United States Supreme Court's decision in *Erie Railroad Co.* v. *Tompkins* (1938), federal courts have been required to apply state law in deciding diversity cases.[11] And since federal constitutional or statutory claims may be advanced in a state proceeding, a state court may need to resolve issues of both state and federal law in reaching its decisions. Three legal principles govern the exposition and interrelation of these two bodies of law. First is the supremacy of federal law. Under the Supremacy Clause of the United States Constitution, all inconsistencies between federal and state law are to be resolved in

10. Data for this table were drawn from Robert A. Kagan, Bliss Cartwright, Lawrence M. Friedman, and Stanton Wheeler, "The Business of State Supreme Courts, 1870–1970," *Stanford Law Review* 30 (November 1977): 121–256, esp. 133–36, and Lawrence Baum, Sheldon Goldman, and Austin Sarat, "The Evolution of Litigation in Federal Courts of Appeals, 1895–1975," *Law & Society Review* 16 (1981–82): 291–309. Although these data represent the best available estimates of the business of state high courts and federal appeals courts during the period, they should be viewed with due consideration of their limitations. First, the data are drawn from samples of courts. The Kagan study collected data on sixteen state supreme courts selected to furnish a cross-section of state high courts, and the Baum study collected data on three courts of appeals. Second, both studies drew samples of cases rather than surveying all decisions of the courts under scrutiny. For the Kagan study, eighteen cases were randomly selected from each court every five years. For the Baum study, it was fifty cases per court every five years. Third, because the Baum study failed to aggregate the findings from the various appeals courts, we have undertaken this task, and thus the composite figures in this table represent estimates based on data reported for the various courts, among whom there was at times considerable variation, rather than computations by the Baum research team. Finally, although Baum and his fellow researchers readily acknowledged their debt to the Kagan study, some questions must remain about differences in coding and other potential disparities in approach between the two research groups.

For somewhat different approaches to cataloguing the business of state supreme courts and of federal courts of appeals, see Atkins and Glick, "Environmental and Structural Variables," and J. Woodford Howard, Jr., *Courts of Appeals in the Federal Judicial System: A Study of the Second, Fifth, and District of Columbia Circuits* (Princeton, N.J.: Princeton University Press, 1981), app. 2, pp. 315–18.

11. 304 U.S. 64 (1938). This landmark decision overruled *Swift* v. *Tyson,* 16 Pet. (41 U.S.) 1 (1842).

favor of the federal law. Indeed, the Constitution expressly mandates that "the Judges in every State" are bound by this principle and requires that they take an oath to support the Constitution. Second is the authority of each system of courts to expound its own body of law: state courts must not only give precedence to federal law over state law but also interpret that law in line with the current rulings of the U.S. Supreme Court. As the Mississippi Supreme Court put it in striking down a state law prohibiting the teaching of evolution in public schools, "In determining this question we are *constrained* to follow the decisions of the Supreme Court of the United States wherein that court has construed similar statutes involving the First Amendment to the Constitution of the United States."[12] Conversely, in interpreting state law, the federal courts are obliged to accept as authoritative the interpretation of the highest court of the state. Third is the so-called autonomy principle, that is, when a case raises issues of both federal and state law, the U.S. Supreme Court will not review a ruling grounded in state law unless the ruling is inconsistent with federal law.[13] The legal basis for this principle is somewhat unclear. Some legal scholars have insisted that it is a constitutionally mandated jurisdictional requirement grounded in the Case-or-Controversy provision of Article III of the U.S. Constitution. Other scholars have contended that the principle lacks a firm legal base, viewing it as a matter of congressional policy or judicial self-restraint.[14] The Supreme Court's own pronouncements on the matter have varied over time and contributed to the confusion on the subject, although recent cases have taken the position that the principle is jurisdictional.[15] More important is the variation in the Court's willingness to assume, when the matter is disputed, that state rulings are in fact

12. *Smith* v. *State*, 242 So.2d 692, 696 (Miss. 1970).

13. For discussion of this principle, see "Developments—Interpretation of State Constitutional Rights," pp. 1332–47.

14. The relevant literature is surveyed in Daniel Kramer, "State Court Constitutional Decisionmaking: Supreme Court Review of Nonexplicit State Court Judgments," *Annual Survey of American Law* (1983): 277–302, and in Stewart G. Pollock, "Adequate and Independent State Grounds as a Means of Balancing the Relationship Between State and Federal Courts," *Texas Law Review* 63 (1985): 977–94. According to some authors, a proper respect for the principles of American federalism requires that the United States Supreme Court should overturn state judgments only when their reliance on federal law is undeniable. See, for example, Robert C. Welsh, "Reconsidering the Constitutional Relationship Between State and Federal Courts: A Critique of *Michigan v. Long,*" *Notre Dame Lawyer* 59 (1984): 1118–44.

15. *Herb* v. *Pitcairn*, 324 U.S. 117, 126 (1945).

grounded in state law.[16] Yet whatever the disagreements about the source and application of the principle, when a state ruling rests on an "independent state ground," it is immune from review by the U.S. Supreme Court.[17]

As this reference to review by the Supreme Court implies, Congress has established mechanisms to ensure the accuracy and faithfulness of state interpretations of federal law. Foremost among these is the provision for review by the Supreme Court of state rulings that present issues of federal constitutional or statutory law. Originally, under the Judiciary Act of 1789, the Supreme Court was empowered to review state rulings involving federal constitutional claims only if the state judges rejected the constitutional claim and upheld the challenged state law. Underlying this limitation was the assumption that whereas state courts might be prone to favor state law against federal claims, they would be unlikely to expand federal restrictions on the governing power of the states. During the early twentieth century, however, state courts began striking down state economic regulations as violations of the Due Process Clause of the Fourteenth Amendment; and following the invalidation of the first American workers' compensation act in *Ives* v. *South Buffalo Railway* (1911), Congress in 1914 extended the Supreme Court's appellate jurisdiction to encompass all state rulings that rest on federal law.[18] The result, as the Supreme Court has recently noted, is that "a State [court] may not impose greater restrictions [on state powers] as a matter of *federal constitutional law* when this Court specifically refrains from imposing them."[19] This augmentation of the Supreme Court's authority to supervise the development of federal constitutional law by state courts has become increasingly important in recent years. According to one account, between 1972 and 1980,

16. See, in particular, *Michigan* v. *Long*, 463 U.S. 1032 (1983).

17. Although state supreme court rulings premised on independent and adequate state grounds may escape direct appellate review by the United States Supreme Court, they are not immunized from federal habeas corpus review. Thus even if a petitioner has not met state procedural requirements, he may seek federal collateral review. *See Fay* v. *Noia*, 372 U.S. 391, 399 (1963). But cf. *Engle* v. *Issac*, 456 U.S. 107 (1982); *Wainwright* v. *Sykes*, 433 U.S. 72 (1977); and *United States* v. *Frady*, 456 U.S. 152 (1982).

18. 201 N.Y. 2712 (1911). For discussion of the aftermath of *Ives*, see Felix Frankfurter and James M. Landis, *The Business of the Supreme Court* (New York: Macmillan, 1928), pp. 193–98.

19. *Oregon* v. *Hass*, 420 U.S. 714, 719 (1975).

the Court reversed twenty state supreme court decisions that ruled in favor of the individual on federal constitutional grounds.[20]

Rulings by state supreme courts in criminal cases are subject not only to direct review on appeal but also to collateral review when state prisoners petition federal courts for a writ of habeas corpus. In construing federal courts' authority to issue the writ, an authority granted by the Judiciary Act of 1789, the U.S. Supreme Court initially held that the purposes for which the writ could be used were controlled by the common law.[21] This meant that "only challenges to nonjudicial detentions undertaken without proper legal process or of confinement by the judgment of a court without competence in the matter could be heard on federal habeas corpus."[22] During Reconstruction, Congress's well-founded suspicion that state courts would be unwilling to vindicate federal rights led to an expansion of habeas corpus protection. Under the Habeas Corpus Act of 1867, the writ was made available to all persons in custody "in violation of the constitution, or of any treaty or law of the United States." Before this act could have much effect, however, Congress withdrew the Supreme Court's appellate jurisdiction in habeas corpus cases arising under the act in order to forestall a ruling that might have threatened its Reconstruction program.[23] When jurisdiction was restored in 1885, the Court initially read the enactment very narrowly. However, in 1953 the Court dramatically expanded the scope of federal collateral review, holding that federal courts could consider all federal constitutional questions raised by petitioners, even if the issues had previously been adjudicated in the state court, and that district court judges might hold evidentiary hearings if the state's fact-finding process had been inadequate.[24] A decade later it completed the transformation of the writ from a device for policing jurisdictional irregularities to a mechanism for de novo consideration of claims

20. Hans A. Linde, "First Things First: Rediscovering the States' Bill of Rights," *University of Baltimore Law Review* 9 (Spring 1980): 389, n. 42. See also, more generally, Spaeth, "Burger Court Review."

21. Surveys of the development of federal habeas corpus include William F. Duker, *A Constitutional History of Habeas Corpus* (Westport, Conn.: Greenwood Press, 1980), and "Developments in the Law—Federal Habeas Corpus," *Harvard Law Review* 83 (1970): 1038–1280. For more recent concerns, see "Symposium: State Prisoner Use of Federal Habeas Corpus Procedures," *Ohio State Law Journal* 44 (1983): 269–445.

22. "Developments—Federal Habeas Corpus," p. 1045.

23. *Ex Parte McCardle*, 7 Wall. (74 U.S.) 506 (1869).

24. *Brown* v. *Allen*, 344 U.S. 443 (1953).

that federal rights had been violated.[25] This change in the character of collateral review, in conjunction with the expansion of federal due process rights and the elimination of prison rules preventing the filing of habeas corpus petitions, has had dramatic effects.[26] The numbers speak for themselves: only 560 habeas corpus petitions were filed in 1950 and 871 in 1960, but in 1970 filings jumped to 9,063.[27] From the perspective of judicial federalism, the increased availability of habeas corpus has had several effects. One has been to shift the primary locus for federal scrutiny of state supreme courts' rulings from a multimember national court to individual judges on federal district courts within the states. Another has been to increase substantially the number of state rulings subjected to federal review and thereby to reduce the autonomy of state high courts and the finality of their rulings. A third effect, perhaps inevitable in light of the previous two, has been to aggravate tensions between federal and state courts.

Although institutional means have long been available for ensuring that state courts faithfully apply federal law, until recently there were no comparable procedures for ensuring that federal courts properly interpreted state law. In 1967 Florida took the lead in attempting to remedy this situation, authorizing its supreme court to rule on questions of state law certified to it by either the United States Supreme Court or federal courts of appeals. During the next decade and a half, twenty-three other states followed Florida's example by permitting certification of questions of state law to their supreme courts, and in 1983 the American Bar Association adopted a resolution urging that all states adopt certification procedures.[28] Federal

25. *Fay* v. *Noia,* 372 U.S. 391 (1963), and *Townsend* v. *Sain,* 372 U.S. 293 (1963).

26. On the importance of changes in prison rules governing the preparation of habeas corpus petitions, see Walter Schaefer, "Federalism and State Criminal Procedure," *Harvard Law Review* 70 (1956): 21. The incorporation of the Bill of Rights is discussed on pages 22–27 of the text.

27. Data are drawn from *Annual Report of the Director* (Washington, D.C.: Administrative Office of the United States Courts, various years).

28. The perceptions of federal judges regarding the success of certification are reported in Caroll Seron, *Certifying Questions of State Law: Experience of Federal Judges* (Washington, D.C.: Federal Judicial Center, 1983). For both positive and critical assessments, see John R. Brown, "Certification—Federalism in Action," *Cumberland Law Review* 7 (1977): 455–65; Brian Mattis, "Certification of Questions of State Law: An Impractical Tool in the Hands of the Federal Courts," *University of Miami Law Review* 23 (1969): 717–35; and Larry M. Roth, "Certified Questions from the Federal Courts: Review and a Proposal," *University of Miami Law Review* 34 (1979): 1–22.

judges have lauded this procedure as a means of securing authoritative pronouncements on previously unconsidered issues of state law and building "a sense of proper relationship and respect between federal and state courts."[29] Yet despite this praise, certification is not widely used, and in its absence, state high courts have no means for reviewing federal courts' interpretations of state law. On the other hand, they are not bound by federal interpretations of state law that they consider erroneous, and by their rulings in subsequent cases they may seek to correct these errors.

Several observations can be made on the legal context of state supreme courts' relations with federal courts.

First, it is emphatically federal law rather than state law that structures these relationships.

Second, whereas the legal principles governing these relationships have not changed over time, the institutional arrangements and procedures designed to vindicate those principles clearly have, affecting both the division of responsibilities between state and federal courts and the avenues for interaction between them.

Third, although some changes in the applicable federal statutory law have resulted from a concern for more efficient or rational judicial administration, more frequently they have reflected substantive policy concerns, in particular a dissatisfaction with or suspicion of rulings by state courts. Congress's expansion of the U.S. Supreme Court's appellate jurisdiction after *Ives* v. *South Buffalo Railway* and its expansion of habeas corpus relief for state prisoners after the Civil War are prime examples of policy-based jurisdictional reforms. Efforts during the 1980s to limit the power of federal courts to hear abortion and school prayer cases likewise reflected the injection of policy concerns into jurisdictional issues, although these proposals were of course premised on the assumption that state courts would be more likely to rule in line with their sponsors' wishes.[30]

Fourth, despite these recent proposals, the trend has been toward an increased availability of federal forums, which—when combined with decisional and statutory limitations on the powers of state courts—has affected the sorts of cases brought to state supreme courts

29. Quoted in Seron, *Certifying Questions*, p. 11.

30. See e. g., S. 26, 98th Cong., 1st Sess. (1983), which would have deprived lower federal courts of jurisdiction in cases involving state or local abortion laws, and S. 88, 98th Cong., 1st Sess. (1983), which would have deprived all federal courts, including the U.S. Supreme Court, of jurisdiction in cases involving voluntary prayer in the public schools.

and the finality of their rulings. Thus congressional expansion of the types of issues that can be litigated in federal court, as exemplified by the extension of the courts' jurisdiction over federal questions in 1875, has in effect diverted some types of cases to federal forums that might otherwise have been brought to state supreme courts on review. And the expansion of habeas corpus has transformed federal review of state supreme courts' criminal justice rulings from occasional intervention to a more regularized and consistent oversight.

THE BROADER CONTEXT

Federal Constitutional Law

Although the legal principles governing the relationships between state supreme courts and federal courts emphasize hierarchy and—-to a lesser extent—autonomy, in actuality these relationships are often characterized by reciprocity and interdependence. Among the basic legal principles governing these relations is the supremacy of federal law over conflicting state law, with the United States Supreme Court assigned ultimate responsibility for vindicating this principle through its authoritative interpretation of federal law. Judicial practice, however, often departs from this hierarchical model. First of all, as the literature on judicial impact has documented, state supreme courts do not invariably follow authoritative pronouncements of the U.S. Supreme Court. Rather, in areas as diverse as race relations and police interrogations, search and seizure and church-state relations, state supreme courts have on occasion refused to accept the constitutional principles enunciated by the Supreme Court. And such noncompliance has not been confined to a few recalcitrant courts sharing a common ideology or isolated in a single geographic area. Whereas Kenneth Vines discovered noncompliance with the Court's desegregation decisions among southern state supreme courts, Neal Romans found that southern courts were more willing than those in other regions to give appropriate scope to important Supreme Court rulings governing police interrogations and the right to counsel.[31] And whereas Bradley Canon found that failure to observe the exclusionary rule was more frequent among southern and midwestern supreme courts, a finding he attributed to "regional differences in politico-legal culture," Alan Tarr's study of response to Establishment Clause

31. Vines, "Southern State Supreme Courts," and Romans, "Role of State Supreme Courts."

decisions uncovered noncompliance by supreme courts in ten states that differed markedly in region, political culture, and ideological complexion.[32] One survey has suggested that although state supreme courts typically do comply with Supreme Court rulings, noncompliance occurs when compliance would require invalidation of important and long-standing state policies and practices.[33] This conclusion, if correct, means that intrastate factors are decisive in promoting this departure from the legal requirements of vertical judicial federalism and that therefore the Supreme Court, short of altering the substance of its rulings, cannot force state supreme courts to comply with its decisions. It also suggests that even in the presence of clear and authoritative legal principles, noncompliance can be expected to be a continuing, though infrequent, feature of the relations between state supreme courts and the U.S. Supreme Court.

State supreme court noncompliance, however, is hardly the sole departure from a strictly hierarchical relationship in the exposition of federal law. As Daniel Kramer and Robert Riga have observed, the leeways legitimately available to—and exploited by—state supreme courts in dealing with Supreme Court rulings make it impossible to "conclude simply that the Supreme Court is the commanding officer and that a major state's highest tribunal is a usually obedient but occasionally recalcitrant private."[34] Rather, the patterns of interaction are frequently complex, with state high courts actively seeking to shape federal law. Even without directly challenging the authority of the Supreme Court, state supreme courts may affect the development of federal decisional law by employing various interpretive techniques to limit the effective scope of the Court's rulings. They may, for example, refuse to extend a right recognized by the Court to other individuals or groups in analogous, but not identical, factual situations. Thus eight years after the Supreme Court ruled that evidence obtained as a result of an illegal warrantless search of a private residence could not be introduced in a criminal prosecution, the California Supreme Court held that that decision did not require the exclusion of

32. Canon, "Reactions of State Supreme Courts," and Tarr, *Judicial Impact and State Supreme Courts.*

33. G. Alan Tarr, "State Supreme Courts and the U.S. Supreme Court: The Problem of Compliance," in Porter and Tarr, *State Supreme Courts.*

34. Daniel C. Kramer and Robert Riga, "The New York Court of Appeals and the U.S. Supreme Court, 1960–1976," in Porter and Tarr, *State Supreme Courts,* p. 196.

evidence obtained in a warrantless backyard search.[35] And after the Supreme Court extended the right to counsel to suspects being interrogated by the police, several state supreme courts continued to distinguish the Court's rulings on factual grounds.[36]

Alternatively, a state supreme court may qualify a decision of the Supreme Court by carving out exceptions. Thus after the Court in 1956 ruled that Congress had preempted the sedition field through passage of the Smith Act, several state supreme courts continued to enforce state sedition statutes, maintaining that the Court's ruling applied only to sedition against the national government, not to sedition against the state.[37] And in 1939, two years after the Supreme Court struck down provisions of the Oregon Criminal Syndicalism Law that forbade peaceful assembly by organizations that espoused prohibited doctrines, the Illinois Supreme Court granted a permanent injunction against labor picketing, noting that such picketing implicated property rights and that the Supreme Court's decision did not indicate the construction to be given in cases of "conflicting constitutional rights."[38]

State supreme courts' use of permissible leeways to restrict the effective scope of Supreme Court rulings does not, of course, end the matter. Because of the continuous character of interactions between federal and state courts, the Supreme Court can in those very cases or in subsequent cases respond to restrictive rulings by state supreme courts. Several options are available to the Court. First, it may reaffirm its earlier ruling and further specify the substance and application of the right it granted, thereby restricting the leeways available to state courts in applying the federal constitutional principle. For example, after state supreme courts had exploited the ambiguities in *Escobedo* v. *Illinois* to minimize its effect, the Court in *Miranda* v. *Arizona* reaffirmed its commitment to the constitutional principle announced in that case and issued detailed guidelines governing the conduct of police interrogations.[39] Second, the

35. The relevant cases—*Mapp* v. *Ohio*, 367 U.S. 643 (1961), and *People* v. *Edwards*, 458 P.2d 713 (1969)—are discussed in Canon, "Reactions of State Supreme Courts," pp. 109 and 131, n. 11.

36. *Escobedo* v. *Illinois*, 378 U.S. 478 (1964); Romans, "Role of State Supreme Courts," pp. 45–48.

37. *Pennsylvania* v. *Nelson*, 350 U.S. 497 (1956); Carol E. Jenson, *The Network of Control: State Supreme Courts and State Security Statutes, 1920–1970* (Westport, Conn.: Greenwood Press, 1982), pp. 81–84.

38. *DeJonge* v. *Oregon*, 299 U.S. 353 (1937); *Meadowmoor Dairies* v. *Milk Wagon Drivers' Union*, 21 N.E.2d 308 (1939).

39. *Escobedo* v. *Illinois*, 378 U.S. 478 (1964); *Miranda* v. *Arizona*, 384 U.S. 436 (1966).

Supreme Court may ignore state judicial decisions restricting the
scope of its rulings, thereby *sub silentio* allowing those courts to
participate in defining the operational meaning of the federal constitutional right. Although the constraints imposed by a heavy caseload
may at times explain the Court's failure to respond to state court
rulings, considerations of judicial policy may also be involved. By
permitting some (perhaps temporaiy) erosion of unpopular rulings,
the Court may reduce the pressures upon it to reverse its course
without repudiating the constitutional principles it has established.
Alternatively, continually denying certiorari in cases where state
courts have eroded a constitutional principle enunciated by the Court
may signal a lack of support for the earlier decision announcing the
principle without directly overruling the decision. Finally, restrictive
rulings by state supreme courts, if accompanied by convincing arguments regarding the theoretical or practical problems they pose, may
prompt the Supreme Court to reconsider and modify or abandon its
earlier ruling. In such circumstances dialogue has altogether replaced
hierarchy as the defining characteristic of vertical judicial federalism.

A reluctance to accept the Supreme Court's mandates is most
frequently the basis for departures from a strictly hierarchical arrangement. Because state courts share with federal courts an obligation "to
guard, enforce, and protect every right granted or secured by the
Constitution of the United States," they also may take the lead in
protecting those rights and thereby guide federal courts through their
expansion or elaboration of federal constitutional principles.[40] When
the U.S. Supreme Court's rulings have established the basic constitutional principles governing an area of the law, the state supreme court
may nonetheless provide direction regarding how those principles
apply in new factual contexts. A considerable literature has documented state supreme courts' sympathetic expansion of Supreme
Court rulings according rights to defendants in criminal case.[41] Their
activity is not confined to the criminal justice realm. For example,
although the U.S. Supreme Court had developed a two-tiered approach in interpreting the Equal Protection Clause and indicated
considerations that might trigger "strict scrutiny" of legislative classifi-
cations, it was the California Supreme Court that, anticipating the

40. *Robb* v. *Connolly*, 111 U.S. 624, 637 (1883).
41. See, in particular, Donald E. Wilkes, Jr., "The New Federalism in Criminal
Procedure: State Court Evasion of the Burger Court," *Kentucky Law Journal* 62
(1974): 421–51; Wilkes, "More on the New Federalism in Criminal Procedure,"

U.S. Supreme Court, first ruled that alienage was to be considered a suspect classification under the Fourteenth Amendment.[42] Furthermore, when the U.S. Supreme Court has not previously addressed a constitutional question, a state supreme court may consciously attempt to channel the development of constitutional principle. A prime example of such an effort, albeit an ultimately unsuccessful one, was the California Supreme Court's ruling in *Bakke* v. *Regents of the University of California*.[43] The court's exhaustive treatment of the issue of affirmative action, as well as its decision to base its ruling on the federal rather than the state constitution, reflects a clear attempt to affect the Supreme Court's thinking on the issue.

On other issues state supreme courts have fared better. For example, in upholding a state law banning the sale of certain sexually provocative materials to minors, the Supreme Court relied heavily on an earlier New York Court of Appeals's ruling that had developed the notion of "variable obscenity."[44] And in *Terry* v. *Ohio* the Court expressly accepted the rationale articulated by the New York Court of Appeals in legitimating stop-and-frisk searches by police officers.[45] Indeed, Justice William Brennan, who sat on the New Jersey Supreme Court before being elevated to the U.S. Supreme Court, has acknowledged that his own opinions in "such important and controversial areas as reapportionment, obscenity, the first amendment's guarantee of religion, the rights of criminal suspects and the application to the states of the fifth amendment's privilege against self-incrimination have drawn much from trail-blazing state court opinion."[46]

Thus far, for the sake of convenience, we have focused on patterns of interaction between state supreme courts and the United States Supreme Court in the exposition of federal constitutional law. However, the interaction between state high courts and federal district courts in habeas corpus cases likewise has important nonhierarchical

---

Kentucky Law Journal 63 (1975): 873–94; and Wilkes, "The New Federalism in Criminal Procedure Revisited," *Kentucky Law Journal* 64 (1976): 729–52.

42. *Purdy & Fitzpatrick* v. *State*, 456 P.2d 649 (1969).

43. Compare *Bakke* v. *Regents of the University of California*, 553 P.2d 1152 (1976) with *Regents of the University of California* v. *Bakke*, 438 U.S. 265 (1978).

44. *Ginsberg* v. *New York*, 390 U.S. 629 (1968); *Bookcase, Inc.* v. *Broaderick*, 218 N.E.2d 668 (1966); discussed in Kramer and Riga, "New York Court of Appeals," pp. 180–81.

45. *Terry* v. *Ohio*, 392 U.S. 1 (1968); *People* v. *Rivera*, 201 N.E.2d 32 (1964); discussed in Kramer and Riga, "New York Court of Appeals," pp. 184–85.

46. William J. Brennan, Jr., "Some Aspects of Federalism," *New York University Law Review* 39 (1964): 947.

dimensions. In their treatment of the "dialectical federalism" that characterizes habeas corpus proceedings, Robert Cover and Alexander Aleinikoff note that state supreme court justices and federal district judges initially bring rather different perspectives to criminal cases.[47] The federal judges generally share what Cover and Aleinikoff term a "utopian" perspective on the criminal law, which elevates due process considerations over concern for public safety, whereas state judges typically have a "pragmatic" perspective, which is more sympathetic to the requirements of effective law enforcement. Although federal judges' power to overturn state convictions might suggest that the utopian perspective uniformly prevails, in practice the situation is considerably more complex. Even if federal opinions, especially circuit court rulings, set the parameters for decision, state supreme courts respond to the federal guidelines in a variety of ways:

> Sometimes they choose a utopian federal rule (even when not the rule of their circuit), usually quite aware that they do so out of choice not duty. At other times, state courts explicitly reject the utopian rule, even if it is the rule of their circuit. This act is often accompanied by explicit avowal of the power to reject the rule of an inferior federal court. And state courts may acquiesce in a utopian rule out of a practical sense that it is the lesser of two evils—the alternative being federal collateral attack of many convictions.[48]

Indeed, in their review of cases involving alleged denials of effective assistance of counsel and claims of a right to counsel for probation and parole revocation hearings, Cover and Aleinikoff found that state courts presented each of these responses, and they concluded that this same range of responses would probably occur with "any issue of complexity." Moreover, federal district judges do not necessarily insist that the state courts fully adopt the utopian federal perspective. Instead, they "sometimes respond to persuasive articulation of practical constraints upon state criminal justice, either by explicitly shaping rules to those constraints or by simply not pressing forward with demands."[49] What emerges, once again, is a sort of dialogue, in which possession of authority does not preclude a willingness to listen and

---

47. Robert M. Cover and T. Alexander Aleinikoff, "Dialectical Federalism: Habeas Corpus and the Court," *Yale Law Journal* 86 (1977): 1035–1102.
48. Ibid., p. 1054.
49. Ibid., p. 1065.

learn and in which the duty of obedience does not eliminate all say over how that authority will be exercised.

The impact of this dialogue on the development of federal constitutional law is not, of course, confined to the district court level. The Supreme Court's rulings precipitate the dialogue, which proceeds in a decentralized fashion among the various federal circuits, often yielding diverse decisions reflecting a broad range of opinions and perspectives. This very diversity, however, provides an impetus for the Supreme Court to undertake review of these rulings and impose some uniformity. Yet in once again addressing the issue, the Court can (and does) draw upon the range of experience and opinion that its earlier decision had provoked. For example, between the Court's ruling in 1967 that counsel must be provided to indigent persons at a proceeding for revoking probation and its reconsideration of the issue six years later, federal district courts had decided dozens of cases on the issue and state courts literally hundreds.[50] The Court in 1973 thus returned to the issue enlightened by an extended dialogue that pointed to serious practical concerns and revealed ambivalence on the federal level and resistance to the broadest interpretation of the Court's precedent on the state level. The Court's willingness to temper its extension of the precedent in light of the states' pragmatic objections can be seen as reflecting the impact of state perspectives on the development of federal constitutional law.

State Law

Although legal principle provides that state supreme courts are the authoritative expositors of state law, in practice the autonomy of state courts is far from complete. Rather, federal courts contribute to the development of state law at least as much as state courts do to the development of federal law. This occurs most obviously when federal courts are called upon to decide issues of state law, usually under their diversity-of-citizenship jurisdiction. For if state courts have not already addressed an issue of state law, they may well be persuaded by a prior federal court ruling on the matter, even though the federal ruling is not authoritative precedent.

Where the federal court is not called upon to interpret the law of a state, its rulings can nonetheless affect how a state supreme court interprets its own law. This fact holds true even when one focuses on

50. *Mempa v. Rhay,* 389 U.S. 128 (1967); *Gagnon v. Scarpelli,* 411 U.S. 778 (1973); discussed in Cover and Aleinikoff, "Dialectical Federalism," pp. 1065–66.

the body of law that is usually regarded as the exclusive preserve of the states, namely, the common law. During the latter part of the nineteenth century, federal courts expanded *Swift* v. *Tyson* far beyond its initial commercial law focus to develop virtually a federal equivalent of state common law, thereby providing legal principles that state courts might draw upon in developing the common law within their borders.[51] Despite the U.S. Supreme Court's decision in 1938 overruling *Swift*, the impact of federal courts on the common law has continued.[52] A prime example involves the claim of wives to recover for negligent invasion of consortium. In 1950, at a time when no state permitted recovery, the U.S. Court of Appeals for the District of Columbia ruled that wives in the District could recover for negligent invasion of consortium. This federal ruling provided the impetus for supreme courts in several states to reconsider their traditional position, and those which chose to allow wives to recover expressly relied on the federal court's analysis to justify their change in position.[53] What occurred in this instance is somewhat unusual but hardly unique: because federal courts confront common law issues, they contribute to the development of the common law, and state courts may draw upon their rulings in enunciating common law principles.[54]

Federal courts have made their greatest contribution to state jurisprudence, however, in the field of state constitutional law and particularly in the field of civil liberties. Prior to the 1920s, the provisions of the Bill of Rights served to limit only the federal government (except for the "takings" clause of the Fifth Amendment), and only a minuscule proportion of federal cases, even at the Supreme Court level, concerned civil liberties. As a result, federal judges did not produce a large body of doctrine upon which state judges could draw in elaborating their own constitutional guarantees, and typically these courts did not look to the Supreme

51. *Swift* v. *Tyson*, 16 Pet. (41 U.S.) 1 (1842). The implications of this ruling for American federalism are detailed in Tony Freyer, *Harmony & Dissonance: The Swift and Erie Cases in American Federalism* (New York: New York University Press, 1981).

52. *Erie Railroad Co.* v. *Tompkins*, 304 U.S. 64 (1938).

53. *Hitaffer* v. *Argonne Co.*, 183 F.2d 811 (D.C. Cir.) cert. denied, 340 U.S. 852 (1950). For a more detailed discussion, see G. Alan Tarr and Mary Cornelia Porter, "Gender Equality and Judicial Federalism: The Role of State Appellate Courts," *Hastings Constitutional Law Quarterly* 9 (1982): 937–42.

54. For another example of federal court leadership, see *Bonbrest* v. *Katz*, 65 F. Supp. 138 (D.D.C. 1946), in which the right of a child to sue for injuries incurred before birth was first recognized.

Court for guidance.[55] With the incorporation of the various guarantees of the Bill of Rights, which began in 1925 and accelerated enormously in the 1960s, the business of the Supreme Court—and to a lesser extent that of other federal courts—was transformed. Civil liberties came to dominate the Supreme Court's agenda, leading it to elaborate constitutional doctrine on issues such as freedom of speech, equality, and the rights of defendants.

The effects of this transformation on state constitutional law have been dramatic. Initially, the elaboration of federal law served to retard the development of state constitutional law because, faced with a choice between developed federal standards and inchoate and/or inhospitable state constitutional doctrines, civil liberties claimants increasingly relied on federal guarantees in pressing their claims. Even after the advent of the Burger Court in the early 1970s, which encouraged rights claimants to turn their attention to state constitutional protections, the effects of federal dominance in civil liberties law continued to be felt.[56] Some state supreme courts, inexperienced in interpreting state bills of rights and accustomed to accepting federal civil liberties rulings as dispositive, assumed without serious consideration that their own constitutional provisions were mere analogues of the federal guarantees and therefore afforded no independent protection. Those courts that were more receptive to state constitutional claims were likewise mindful of federal constitutional rulings. Because the protection of civil liberties law had been ceded for so long to the federal courts, their decisions furnished the intellectual baggage,

55. For examples of independent state development of constitutional standards in the realm of freedom of expression, see Margaret A. Blanchard, "Filling in the Void: Speech and Press in State Courts Prior to *Gitlow*," in B. F. Chamberlin and C. J. Brown, eds., *The First Amendment Reconsidered: New Perspectives on the Meaning of Freedom of Speech and Press* (New York: Longman, 1982). State supreme courts anticipated the United States Supreme Court's rulings on the provision of counsel to indigent defendants—*Carpenter v. Dane*, 9 Wis. 249 (Wis. 1859) and *Cogdill v. State*, 246 S.W.2d 5 (Tenn. 1951)—and on the exclusionary rule—*State v. Sheridan*, 96 N.W. 730 (Iowa, 1903). On the other hand, drawing upon a broad data base of state supreme court decisions from 1870 to 1970, Peter K. Harris has found that the presence of a state constitutional issue was strongly associated with the number of citations to federal court decisions, "The Communication of Precedent Among State Supreme Courts" (Ph.D. diss., Yale University, 1980), p. 145.

56. For a discussion of state judicial rulings on the freedoms of religion, speech, and the press, which seem to confirm this, see G. Alan Tarr, "State Constitutionalism and 'First Amendment Freedoms,'" in Stanley Friedelbaum, *Human Rights in the States* (Westport, Conn.: Greenwood Press, 1987).

the doctrines and precedents, that state court judges brought with them in confronting state constitutional guarantees. Thus, when state judges turned their attention to their own charter, it was only natural for them to look to Federal precedents as a way to invigorate their long dormant state provisions.[57] As a result, the categories and conceptions of federal constitutional law have decisively influenced developments on the state level.

SELECTIVE INCORPORATION

Thus far we have focused on how legal and extralegal factors have had an effect on the operation of vertical judicial federalism. Substantive legal developments, however, may also be important in defining the legal context of state high court activity. Since 1945, the most important of these developments for vertical judicial federalism has been the U.S. Supreme Court's adoption of the doctrine of selective incorporation, under which certain provisions of the federal Bill of Rights are deemed fully applicable to state governmental action, and its incorporation under that doctrine of most criminal justice guarantees of the Bill of Rights.

One begins with the recognition that substantive criminal law in the United States is overwhelmingly state law and that prior to 1960 state law played the decisive role as well in defining the rights of defendants in trials in state courts. Initially, the federal Bill of Rights placed no restrictions on state prosecutions, since it was understood to apply only against the national government.[58] Even the Fourteenth Amendment, which clearly sought to alter the relative responsibilities of the state and national governments for the protection of individual rights, initially produced little change. When defendants appealed their convictions in state courts, claiming that they were denied rights

57. Robert Welsh, "Whose Federalism? The Burger Court's Treatment of State Civil Liberties Judgments," *Hastings Constitutional Law Quarterly* 10 (1983): 819–76. State judges' inexperience in interpreting state constitutional provisions is matched, if not surpassed, by the inexperience of their law clerks. Because law school has given the clerks extensive exposure to federal constitutional law and usually none to state constitutional law—less than a dozen schools in 1983 offered courses in state constitutional law—they also tend to cast state constitutional issues in terms of federal constitutional categories and concepts. Insofar as they play a role in drafting opinions, the result once again is to contribute to the federalization of state constitutional law. See Charles G. Douglas III, "State Judicial Activism—The New Role for State Bills of Rights," *Suffolk University Law Review* 11 (1978): 1147.

58. *Barron* v. *Baltimore*, 7 Pet. (32 U.S.) 243 (1833).

guaranteed by the Bill of Rights, the Supreme Court rejected their assumption that either the Due Process or Privileges and Immunities clauses of the Fourteenth Amendment incorporated those rights as limitations on the states.[59] State divergence from the requirements of the Bill of Rights, the Court maintained, was not decisive. As long as state procedures accorded with fundamental fairness, they satisfied the requirements of the Fourteenth Amendment.

In refusing to impose uniform procedures on the states, the Court sought to ensure room for growth and vitality, for adaptation to shifting necessities, for wide differences of opinion over aims and methods.[60] Implicit in the position adopted by the Court was the assumption of a division of labor: the states—and state courts in particular—would continue to have primary responsibility for the protection of the rights of defendants, with federal intervention limited to those infrequent situations in which states failed to meet their responsibilities. In fact, however, the states all too frequently failed to protect defendants' rights. Although isolated examples of initiative by the states can be found—Iowa, for example, adopted the exclusionary rule prior to *Weeks* v. *United States*, and Wisconsin required that counsel be provided for indigent defendants over a century before *Gideon* v. *Wainwright*—it is safe to say that state constitutional guarantees played little role in the cases before state courts, and those courts did little to develop state civil liberties law.[61]

The Supreme Court's adoption of the fundamental fairness standard for reviewing convictions in state courts ultimately frustrated its efforts to supervise those courts effectively. Because of its inherent vagueness, the fundamental fairness standard offered state judges little guidance in resolving specific cases. And such guidance was not provided either by the Supreme Court's decisions in those cases in which it reversed state rulings. For since the Court struck down the actions of state authorities without elaborating concrete standards for

59. See, e.g., *Hurtado* v. *California*, 110 U.S. 516 (1884), and *Twining* v. *New Jersey*, 211 U.S. 78 (1908).

60. Felix Frankfurter, "Memorandum on 'Incorporation' of the Bill of Rights into the Due Process Clause of the Fourteenth Amendment," *Harvard Law Review* 78 (1965): 74–83. See also, Henry J. Abraham, *Freedom and the Court* (New York: Oxford University Press, 1977), chap. 2.

61. The Iowa Supreme Court anticipated the U.S. Supreme Court in adopting the exclusionary rule in *State* v. *Sheridan*, 96 N.W. 730 (Iowa 1903), eleven years before *Weeks* v. *United States*, 232 U.S. 383 (1914). The Wisconsin Supreme Court required provision of counsel to indigent defendants in *Carpenter* v. *Dane*, 9 Wis. 249 (Wis. 1859), over a century before *Gideon* v. *Wainwright*, 372 U.S. 335 (1963).

distinguishing permissible from impermissible conduct, state judges had considerable difficulty determining when state policies and practices violated defendants' rights. Thus any reversal by the Supreme Court came like a bolt from the blue. Moreover, in seeking to promote flexibility and state initiative, the Court actually may have discouraged decisive efforts by state judges to protect defendants' rights. According to one observer,

> local law-enforcement officials found their authority diminished. The final decision in any cases could [be]—and sometimes was—made elsewhere. . . . Since the Supreme Court took upon itself the burden of deciding what is fair and did so in a way that ignored the notions of local judges and officials, the slighted judges and officials sometimes felt free to shirk their own legal and traditional responsibility to make moral judgments and to consider the fairness of their own actions.[62]

Whatever the validity of this charge, clearly the Court's rulings did not promote the desired development of state civil liberties law.

In a series of decisions in the 1960s, the U.S. Supreme Court initiated a "due process revolution" that altered the legal landscape of criminal justice and imposed new responsibilities on state courts. The Court never accepted the argument that the Fourteenth Amendment incorporated the entire Bill of Rights, making its provisions fully applicable to the states. But its rulings selectively incorporating various criminal justice provisions had much the same effect. In *Mapp* v. *Ohio* (1961), the Court ruled that "all evidence obtained by searches and seizures in violation of the Constitution is, by that same authority [the Fourth Amendment] inadmissible in a state court."[63] By the end of the decade, the Court had further significantly extended the rights of state defendants.[64] In so doing, it not only applied existing federal law to the states for the first time but often simultaneously expanded the range of

62. Paul Lermarck, *Rights on Trial: The Supreme Court and the Criminal Law* (Port Washington, N.Y.: Associated Faculty Press), p. 32.

63. *Mapp* v. *Ohio*, 367 U.S. 643, at 655 (1961).

64. Relevant cases include *Robinson* v. *California*, 370 U.S. 660 (1962) (cruel and unusual punishment); *Gideon* v. *Wainwright*, 372 U.S. 335 (1963) (right to counsel); *Murphy* v. *Waterfront Commission*, 378 U.S. 52 (1964) (self-incrimination); *Pointer* v. *Texas*, 380 U.S. 400 (1965) (confrontation of witnesses); *Klopfer* v. *North Carolina*, 386 U.S. 213 (1967) (speedy trial); *Duncan* v. *Louisiana*, 391 U.S. 145 (1968) (trial by jury); and *Benton* v. *Maryland*, 392 U.S. 784 (1969) (double jeopardy).

conduct covered by the constitutional provisions.[65] The effects of these changes on state courts were enormous.

Some of the effects were immediate and obvious. As a result of the U.S. Supreme Court's decisions, which effectively federalized the rights of defendants, state judges were presented with a new body of law to apply and a new set of rights to protect. Often the federal rulings gave more expansive readings to constitutional protections than had occurred under state law. Prior to *Mapp,* for example, only twenty-three states had exclusionary rules, and except in capital cases, few furnished counsel to indigent defendants before *Gideon* v. *Wainwright.*[66] Moreover, the rights of defendants in state courts were frequently more extensive in theory than in practice, for many states had been lax in enforcing state constitutional guarantees. Fidelity to the Court's mandates thus typically required state supreme courts to protect rights beyond those that had traditionally been recognized under state law. And the Court's aggressive oversight of state courts' implementation of its rulings left little doubt that it was serious about securing compliance with its mandates.[67]

The Supreme Court's criminal justice rulings also altered the mix of cases coming before state supreme courts by promoting an increase in appeals by defendants. For defendants, the Court's rulings either held out the possibility of vindication directly, since the decisions were immediately applicable to their cases, or indirectly, since the Court's evident sympathy toward defendants' claims seemed to hold out the prospect of eventual success if their cases were reviewed by the Court. Taken altogether, the necessity of applying new legal requirements in large numbers of cases, with the very real threat of review on appeal or under habeas corpus, forced many state judges to consider defendants' rights seriously for the first time.

Other effects on state supreme courts, although less obvious, were

65. Standard sources charting the process of selective incorporation and the expansion of defendants' rights include Ronald Mykkeltvedt, *The Selective Incorporation of the Bill of Rights: Fourteenth Amendment Due Process and Procedural Rights* (New York: Kennikat, 1982), and Richard C. Cortner, *The Supreme Court and the Second Bill of Rights* (Madison: University of Wisconsin Press, 1981).

66. Canon, "Reactions of State Supreme Courts," p. 126; and Lawrence Baum, "Lower Court Response to Supreme Court Decisions: Reconsidering a Negative Picture," *Justice System Journal* 3 (1978): 208–19.

67. Data on the frequency of appellate review by the United States Supreme Court of state rulings on criminal justice during the 1960s and on the frequency of the Court's reversal of those rulings can be found in the annual statistical reviews of the Court's work, published in *Harvard Law Review.*

likewise important. In addition to their immediate effects on the outcomes of cases, the Court's rulings changed legal thinking about the rights of defendants. The decisions provided state judges with a body of legal principles and an approach for dealing with issues of defendants' rights. Over time some state judges not only became adept at applying these principles but also accepted them as appropriate interpretations of constitutional guarantees. This experience and change in attitude became important in the 1970s, when the Burger Court sought to curtail various rulings of the Warren Court.[68] Defendants who had previously sought federal review or relied on federal law began, under the rubric of "the new judicial federalism," to raise issues of defendants' rights under state bills of rights.[69] For these litigants, the Warren Court's rulings provided a starting point for interpreting state provisions protecting analogous rights. Thus, for at least some members of state supreme courts, experience applying the Warren Court's rulings gave them confidence in dealing with rights claims and affected the approaches that they brought to the interpretation of state provisions.[70]

Second, over time, as new justices were recruited to state high courts, many brought with them a perspective on issues of defendants' rights which had been shaped in law school and thereafter by the Warren Court's rulings. As one state justice put it, "When I was in law school, Warren and Brennan were my heroes."[71] Thus when they turned to the interpretation of state bills of rights, these judges also automatically turned for guidance to the rulings of the Warren Court.

This experience suggests that the process of selective incorporation, in addition to its immediate effects in terms of vertical judicial

68. For comparisons of Warren Court and early Burger Court rulings, see Leonard Levy, *Against the Law: The Nixon Court and Criminal Justice* (New York: Harper & Row, 1974). For more recent cases, see Yale Kamisar, "The Warren Court (Was It Really So Defense-Minded?), the Burger Court (Is It Really So Prosecution-Oriented?), and Police Investigatory Practices," in Vincent Blasi, ed., *The Burger Court: The Counter-Revolution That Wasn't* (New Haven: Yale University Press, 1983).

69. The literature on the new judicial federalism is vast and constantly expanding. Useful overviews include Bradley D. McGraw, ed., *Developments in State Constitutional Law* (St. Paul: West, 1985), and Ronald K. L. Collins and Peter J. Galie, "Models of Post-Incorporation Judicial Review: 1985 Survey of State Constitutional Individual Rights Decisions," *Publius* 16 (1986): 111–39.

70. See, in particular, Mary Cornelia Porter, "State Supreme Courts and the Legacy of the Warren Court: Some Old Inquiries for a New Situation," in Porter and Tarr, *State Supreme Courts*.

71. The quote is from Chief Justice William Richardson of the Hawaii Supreme Court, quoted in "Better than Burger," *The New Republic*, March 4, 1985, p. 10.

federalism, also promoted cooperation and borrowing between state supreme courts and federal courts, along the lines of the horizontal judicial federalism that obtains among state supreme courts. (We shall address this theme in greater detail below.) Paul Lermack's conclusion about the effects of selective incorporation thus seems persuasive:

> When the Supreme Court began its activist tinkering, the power of the states was not lessened; federal activities provided the opportunity for the exercise of state power. After the Supreme Court ended its activism, state initiative continued. Eventually the balance between state and federal courts was restored, with the courts on both levels exercising far more power than formerly.[72]

Horizontal Judicial Federalism

THE LEGAL CONTEXT

Law plays a comparatively minor role in structuring relations among state supreme courts. In resolving questions under state law, a state supreme court characteristically looks first to the legal capital of the state—to the state's constitution, statutes, and/or legal precedents. Although in expounding these legal materials a court in one state may recur to rulings or doctrines developed in another state, it is not obliged to do so. Rather, when a state supreme court justifies a ruling by referring to the decisions of sister courts, as it often does, the authority of those decisions derives from their persuasiveness rather than from the legal position of the court that announced them. Even when a state supreme court is called upon to enunciate common law principles, the decisions of other courts are relevant simply as evidence of the content of those principles. Put simply, conformity with the decisions of other state supreme courts is always a matter of choice.

Yet even though there is no obligation for a state supreme court to rely on the decisions of other state courts, various legal factors, taken together, do promote such reliance. Chief among these is the positive orientation toward precedent that characterizes the American system of law.[73] This orientation creates an expectation—one shared, it might be added, by judges, the legal community, and the general public—that judges will consult prior rulings in arriving at their

---

72. Lermarck, *Rights on Trial*, p. 93.
73. This orientation toward precedent is, of course, not confined to the American context but rather is characteristic of common law systems generally.

decisions. It likewise produces a tendency to give weight to those rulings even when they are not strictly controlling.[74] Thus the basic character of the American legal system encourages state supreme courts to consult and borrow from the decisions of sister courts. The fact that all state supreme courts confront, as part of their work loads, certain basic sorts of legal issues (see table 1 above) likewise promotes reliance on sister courts' decisions. In saying this, we of course acknowledge that there are important differences as well in the issues addressed by various state supreme courts and in the frequency with which certain types of issues come before them.[75] But the essential similarity in the policy concerns of state governments and the limited scope of federal law together ensure basic similarities in the types of legal issues that state courts face. And because state supreme courts deal with common legal problems, judges in one state can usefully look to their colleagues in another state for instruction.

Basic similarities in the substantive law of the various states constitute a final factor promoting reliance on the decisions of sister courts; for if the law is the same in two states, it is only natural that a court in one state will look beyond its borders for instruction on how to handle problems in its interpretation and application. What comes to mind most immediately, of course, is how state supreme courts deal with issues of the common law. Yet important uniformities can also be found in the constitutions and statutes of the various states. Sometimes these similarities reflect a deliberate borrowing. During the nineteenth century, groups of settlers in new states, seeking to devise constitutions that reflected the institutional and cultural patterns back home, often adopted provisions directly from their previous charters.[76]

74. As Martin Shapiro has aptly put it in "Toward a Theory of Stare Decisis," *Journal of Legal Studies* 1 (1972): 131: "Under the rules of the game, the lawyer-communicator has the highest chance of winning if he can show a court that his client must prevail if the court keeps doing exactly what it has been doing; the next highest chance if he can persuade the court that it should do exactly what some other court has been doing."

75. For a survey of the business of each state supreme court that clarifies the character and extent of differences in the issues they address, see Atkins and Glick, "Environmental and Structural Variables." Our discussion of the Alabama, Ohio, and New Jersey supreme courts in chapters 3–5 will also point out important differences.

76. On the implications of such borrowing for constitutional patterns among the American states, see Daniel J. Elazar, "The Principles and Traditions Underlying State Constitutions," *Publius* 12 (1982): 11–25, and Donald S. Lutz, "The Purposes of American State Constitutions," *Publius* 12 (1982): 27–44.

Throughout American history, moreover, common political concerns during various constitution-making periods have prompted those drafting state constitutions to consult the experience of other states.[77]

In statutory law, a similar pattern of borrowing may also be seen. Several studies have documented the diffusion of policy innovations across state lines, and often states have adopted not merely the policy in other states but the very legislation in which it is couched.[78] This tendency toward statutory uniformity has been encouraged by various groups that have proposed uniform solutions for the common problems confronting the states. Thus the National Conference of Commissioners on Uniform State Laws has succeeded in securing broad adoption of model laws such as the Uniform Commercial Code and the Uniform Child Custody Act.[79] Other nonpartisan groups, such as the American Law Institute and the National Municipal League, have also proposed laws and ordinances for nationwide adoption. From a more self-interested perspective, various industry-wide groups and trade associations have developed model laws, regulations, and guidelines as a means of providing a stable and uniform environment for corporate planning. Many of these groups, such as the National Association of Insurance Commissioners, have been quite successful in persuading state legislatures to adopt their recommendations.[80] Taken altogether, the factors promoting convergence in state laws may be seen

77. These historical dimensions of state constitution making are explored in Albert L. Sturm, "The Development of American State Constitutions," *Publius* 12 (1982): 57–98.

78. Major contributions to the policy diffusion literature include Jack L. Walker, "The Diffusion of Innovations Among American States," *American Political Science Review* 63 (1969): 880–89; Virginia Gray, "Innovation in the States: A Diffusion Study," *American Political Science Review* 67 (1973): 1174–85; and Robert L. Savage, "Policy Innovativeness as a Trait of American States," *Journal of Politics* 40 (1978): 212–24. Recently a social science journal has devoted an entire issue to the subject—see "Symposium: Policy Diffusion in a Federal System," *Publius* 15 (1985).

79. Data on the substantial success of efforts by the National Conference of Commissioners on Uniform State Laws are presented in *The Book of the States, 1982–1983* (Lexington, Ky.: Council of State Governments, 1982), pp. 86–90.

80. The activity and success of such a group is documented in Benn Prybutok, "Federalism Without Washington: The Insurance Regulatory Environment in the United States," *Publius* 12 (1982): 79–97.

as simultaneously promoting increased reliance by state courts on the decisions of sister courts.

THE BROADER CONTEXT

Even though they have no legal authority beyond state borders, the decisions of a state supreme court may nonetheless influence the rulings of sister courts. Most obviously such decisions may serve as precedents in factually similar cases, at times persuading a court of the wisdom or propriety of a particular outcome, and at other times affording justification for a step which it might otherwise have been reluctant to take. In addition, the decisions of sister courts might announce legal doctrine that a court can incorporate into its own law, thus not only resolving the particular case but also establishing new legal standards that will be applied in analogous situations in the future. The revolution in tort law that has occurred since World War II, which will be discussed in detail below, exemplifies such intercourt influence in doctrinal development.

Rather than developing doctrine for resolving a particular set of issues, a state supreme court may pioneer an approach for addressing a broad range of issues. The prime contemporary example of this phenomenon is the "state law first"approach championed by Justice Hans Linde of the Oregon Supreme Court and adopted by that court.[81] According to Linde, the structure of the federal system obliges state supreme courts, when confronted with claims based on both state and federal law, to resolve the question of state law first and to address the federal question only if the issue cannot be resolved on the basis of state law. As a result of Linde's persuasive sponsorship of this position, both in judicial opinions and in off-the-bench writings and addresses, three state supreme courts during the early 1980s followed Oregon's lead in accepting the state law first approach.[82] Such initiatives have, in turn, partially reversed the trend toward the

---

81. Justice Hans E. Linde initially presented his position in "Without 'Due Process': Unconstitutional Law in Oregon," *Oregon Law Review* 49 (1970): 125–87. For a more recent formulation, see Linde, "E Pluribus—Constitutional Theory and State Courts," in Bradley D. McGraw, ed., *Developments in State Constitutional Law.* Decisions of the Oregon Supreme Court exemplifying his approach include *Sterling* v. *Cupp,* 625 P.2d 123 (1981); *State* v. *Kennedy,* 666 P.2d 1316 (1983); and *Hewitt* v. *SAIF,* 653 P.2d 970 (1982).

82. The states are Washington (*State* v. *Coe,* 679 P.2d 353 [Wash. 1984]); Maine (*State* v. *Cadman,* 476 A.2d 114 [Me. 1984]); and Vermont (*State* v. *Badger,* 450 A.2d 336 [Vt. 1982]).

federalization of civil liberties law and encouraged state courts to be more creative in their approach to constitutional issues.

For such intercourt influence to occur, it is essential that a state supreme court be aware of and have access to the relevant rulings of sister courts. This precondition, however, has not always been met. Until the 1840s and 1850s there were no official reports of state decisions, and this typically prevented a state supreme court from recurring to the precedents of other states—and sometimes even to its own decisions.[83] The publication of state supreme courts' decisions since then has changed the problem but has not altogether eliminated it. Given the thousands of decisions reported annually, justices characteristically rely on counsel to locate relevant out-of-state rulings and to demonstrate their applicability. Although the adversarial system offers incentives for such diligence, and although there are dramatic examples of counsel successfully drawing upon rulings from other states, attorneys do not always perform this function adequately. As a result, the justices themselves on occasion seek out applicable precedent from other states. But in doing so, they face serious jurisprudential and practical problems. From a practical standpoint, state supreme court justices may lack ready access to libraries holding judicial decisions from outside their reporter area, particularly if the justices do not remain in residence at the court. Their search for pertinent case law is thus necessarily restricted. From a jurisprudential perspective, there are questions about the propriety of ruling on the basis of arguments not presented in court, and judges may therefore be reluctant to seek out legal authorities beyond those cited by counsel.[84]

Even if this precondition of knowledge and access is met, it does not necessarily follow that a state supreme court will look to the rulings of other courts in reaching a decision. As we have noted, legal factors are not decisive on this matter. Peter Harris concluded in his study of intercourt citations that state supreme courts typically look beyond their borders when confronting novel legal

83. Frederick G. Kempin, Jr., "Precedent and Stare Decisis: The Critical Years, 1800 to 1850," *American Journal of Legal History* 3 (1959): 28–54. It is interesting to note that the creation of the state reporter system coincides with the development of a new approach to judicial decision making that emphasized stare decisis and a deductive approach to legal reasoning. See Karl Llewellyn, *The Common Law Tradition: Deciding Appeals* (Boston: Little, Brown, 1960).

84. Stolz, *Judging Judges*, pp. 403–05.

problems or when contemplating legal change.[85] Intuitively, this seems persuasive. Conservation of judicial resources, as well as a respect for *stare decisis,* disposes judges to look first to state precedents in deciding a case. Only when these precedents prove inadequate, because they furnish no guidance or the wrong guidance, is there reason for a court to look beyond its borders for legal authority.

The more difficult task is to explain in what direction a state supreme court looks, and why—more precisely, to identify and explain patterns of intercourt interaction and influence in horizontal judicial federalism. One approach has been to examine patterns of intercourt citation, proceeding on the assumption that because no state supreme court is obliged to cite another's rulings, citation indicates that it has found the cited court's opinion persuasive. In a historical analysis that drew upon a sample of cases from selected courts, Peter Harris found that the willingness of state supreme courts to cite other courts increased significantly from 1870 to 1970.[86] Shared experiences and perspectives among state populations were important in determining patterns of citation throughout the period: a state high court was particularly likely to cite decisions from states that were geographically proximate or that had contributed substantially to the native white in-migration into the state. So too was the accessibility of legal materials: state high courts tended to cite the decisions of courts whose rulings were contained in the same West regional reporter as its own decisions, and this tendency has increased over time. And the availability of state legal authority, often referred to as legal capital, likewise affected patterns of citation throughout the period: the number of cases a court decided (and hence the body of citable decisions it produced) affected the frequency of citations to its decisions, although this factor has declined in importance over time. Nonetheless, despite these uniformities, Harris discovered major changes in the patterns of intercourt citation from 1870 to 1970:

> [t]he trend in this communication network over the last century has been from a hierarchy dominated by a few Eastern courts, through a homogeneous phase of widespread growth and communication, to a pattern of decentralization and, to some degree disintegration,

85. Peter Harris, "Difficult Cases and the Display of Authority," *Journal of Law, Economics and Organization* 1 (1985): 209–21.

86. Harris, "Communication of Precedents," pp. 124–25.

with diffuse centers of authority and no overall national "pecking order" in prestige.[87]

Gregory Caldeira's study of the transmission of legal precedent, based on an analysis of all references each state supreme court made to the decisions of other state high courts in 1975, provides a complementary perspective.[88] Like Harris, Caldeira found that geographic proximity, patterns of migration, legal capital, and legal reporting regions all influenced patterns of citation. Even more important, however, were various characteristics of the cited court: "a supreme court's prestige, professionalism, societal diversity, and, to a lesser extent, progressivism and the size of caseload—all can and do incline the highest courts of the several states to invoke its decisions more often."[89] Caldeira's analysis also suggests the emergence of a new leading court: even after controlling for other relevant factors, he discovered that the California Supreme Court's decisions were cited far in excess of what might have been predicted.

The findings reported by Harris and Caldeira should be treated with some caution, for they rest on the assumption that one can ascribe influence merely on the basis of citations. This assumption, however, is open to challenge: a court might as readily cite another court's ruling to register disagreement with it, to justify or bolster a decision reached on other grounds, or to complete a string of citations put together by an industrious law clerk. At best, then, reliance on these findings must await confirmation through more direct tests of influence.

An alternative means of assessing intercourt influence is to trace patterns in the adoption of doctrinal innovations among state supreme courts. At present Bradley Canon and Lawrence Baum's pioneering study of the adoption of plaintiff-oriented innovations in tort law represents the only attempt to employ this approach.[90] Where comparison is possible, their findings contrast with Harris's and Caldeira's. Region, which played an important role in patterns of citation, was considerably less significant in determining patterns of

87. Peter Harris, "Structural Change in the Communication of Precedent Among State Supreme Courts, 1870–1970," *Social Networks* 4 (1982): 210.

88. Gregory A. Caldeira, "The Transmission of Legal Precedent: A Study of State Supreme Courts," *American Political Science Review* 79 (1985): 178–93.

89. Ibid., p. 190.

90. Bradley C. Canon and Lawrence Baum, "Patterns of Adoption of Tort Law Innovations: An Application of Diffusion Theory to Judicial Doctrines," *American Political Science Review* 75 (1981): 975–87.

tort innovation, leading Canon and Baum to conclude that "state appellate courts are open to influence by other courts regardless of location."[91] Indeed, the adoption of tort law innovations followed no consistent pattern: although some courts were on the whole more innovative than others, no single court or set of courts either claimed national leadership in all tort law reforms or invariably lagged behind the others. (Canon and Baum attributed this "idiosyncratic" pattern of adoption to the reactive position of judges, that is, their reliance on litigants to raise issues for resolution, and suggested that "it is doubtful that this idiosyncracy is peculiar to one branch of the law.")[92] In addition, whereas Caldeira found that the California Supreme Court had assumed a role of national leadership, Canon and Baum discovered that the California court's national ranking in terms of tort law innovativeness did not change substantially after World War II and that the New Jersey Supreme Court was the most innovative state supreme court of the postwar era.

THE TORT LAW REVOLUTION

The innovations in tort law that Canon and Baum examined constitute state courts' most important substantive contribution to legal development during the postwar era. Writing in 1969, Robert Keeton observed that "[t]he most striking impression that results from reading the weekly outpouring of torts opinions handed down by appellate courts across the nation for the decade commencing in 1958 is one of candid, openly acknowledged, abrupt change."[93] The tort law revolution that Keeton chronicled almost two decades ago has continued unabated to the present, with virtually all state supreme courts participating in the process of reform.[94] As a result of these rulings, standards for determining liability have been transformed, long-standing immunities abolished, and other barriers to plaintiffs' recovery either reduced or eliminated. In this section we shall summarize these changes and assess how the processes of horizontal

91. Ibid., p. 984.

92. Ibid., p. 985.

93. Robert E. Keeton, *Venturing to Do Justice: Reforming Private Law* (Cambridge: Harvard University Press, 1969), p. 3.

94. For an extremely useful overview of more recent developments, see Lawrence Baum and Bradley C. Canon, "State Supreme Courts as Activists; New Doctrines in the Law of Torts," in Porter and Tarr, *State Supreme Courts.* We rely heavily on their account in the succeeding discussion.

judicial federalism in this field have affected state judges' views on the legitimacy of judicial initiation of reform in the common law.

Immunities

Among the most dramatic developments in tort law has been the erosion or elimination of long-standing immunities that shielded various persons and institutions from liability for injuries caused by their negligence.[95] Under the doctrine of sovereign or governmental immunity, which originated in medieval England and became part of American common law during the colonial period, governmental bodies could not be sued without their consent. Over twenty states expressly incorporated the state's immunity from suit in their constitutions, and state high courts consistently recognized state and municipal immunity in their rulings.[96] As the initial justification for the doctrine, rooted in the notion that "the king can do no wrong," lost its cogency in America, various functional justifications were offered for its retention.[97] Although these justifications too came under increasing attack in the legal literature during the twentieth century, the doctrine of sovereign immunity survived largely intact into the postwar era. In the late 1950s, however, the Florida Supreme Court abrogated immunity for municipalities, and in 1961 the California Supreme Court abolished the doctrine at both the state and local levels.[98] These decisions sparked a reconsideration of the doctrine, and by the late 1970s, thirty-three states had abolished governmental immunity at the municipal level, and roughly half that number had done so at the state level as well.

These rulings by state high courts on sovereign immunity reveal that once a few seminal decisions challenged established doctrine, most other courts moved rapidly to erode or abrogate traditional governmental immunities. Judicial rulings on charitable immunity

95. See generally Jethro K. Lieberman, *The Litigious Society* (New York: Basic Books, 1981), chap. 6.

96. Baum and Canon, "State Supreme Courts as Activists," p. 86.

97. It was argued, for example, that imposing liability on government would require it to divert resources to the settlement of individual claims that might otherwise be devoted to the pursuit of the public good. Thus it was better that one party suffer as a result of governmental action than that the larger public be deprived of the good government might do. A similar argument was advanced in support of charitable immunity.

98. *Hargrove* v. *Town of Cocoa Beach*, 96 So.2d 130 (Fla. 1957), and *Muskopf* v. *Corning Hospital District*, 359 P.2d 457 (Cal. 1961).

present a similar pattern of consensus, challenge, and rapid reform.[99] Until the early 1940s, the doctrine of charitable immunity prevailed in all American jurisdictions. After a ruling in 1942 by Judge (later Justice) Wiley Rutledge effectively demolished every argument for the doctrine, state courts began to reconsider their support, with most expressly relying on Rutledge's arguments.[100] By 1960, fourteen state supreme courts had abandoned the doctrine, and by 1980 their number had swelled to forty-two.

In addition to their intrinsic importance, the rulings eliminating these immunities reflect a more general shift in thinking about tort law. During the nineteenth century, "the central purpose of tort law" was seen as "admonishing blameworthy persons," and thus the law focused on negligence, determining whether the person causing the injury was at fault.[101] By the mid-twentieth century, the primary concern had shifted to compensating injured persons, with government intervening "to distribute losses among society generally, with the criteria for distribution being prevailing notions of efficiency or fairness."[102] This shift in thinking transformed tort law into a type of public law and courts into policy analysts. The question facing the courts became whether abrogation of these immunities would prevent governments and charitable institutions from achieving their socially important aims. Seizing upon the emergence of liability insurance, which permitted these institutions to socialize risk, most courts concluded that it would not.

Obstacles to Recovery

If the central purpose of tort law is viewed as compensating injuries, it also follows that courts should remove unwarranted obstacles to recovery, and during the postwar era state supreme courts mounted a campaign to remove such obstacles. One set of obstacles was posed by

99. For a discussion of the abrogation of charitable immunity and its impact, see Bradley C. Canon and Dean Jaros, "The Impact of Changes in Judicial Doctrines: The Abrogation of Charitable Immunity," *Law and Society Review* 13 (1979): 969–86.

100. *Georgetown College* v. *Hughes,* 130 F.2d 810 (1942).

101. G. Edward White, *Tort Law in America: An Intellectual History* (New York: Oxford University Press, 1980), p. 148.

102. Ibid. Lieberman traces the change to the rise of a "fiduciary ethic" that influenced doctrinal development in all areas of the law. See Lieberman, *The Litigious Society,* chap. 1.

legal doctrines that prevented recovery for injuries.[103] Perhaps the most important of these was the requirement of privity of contract, which prevented consumers from suing manufacturers for defective products unless they had purchased the products directly from them. In a mass production economy, in which consumers typically purchased products from distributors, this requirement effectively shielded most manufacturers from liability for injuries caused by their defective products. Although some courts early in the twentieth century developed exceptions to the privity requirement, it remained the rule in the states until the 1960s.[104] But once a pioneering decision of the state supreme court abolished the privity requirement in New Jersey, other courts quickly followed suit.[105]

Another set of obstacles arose from common law limitations on causes of action, among which might be included prohibitions on suits for wrongful death and on recovery by wives for negligent invasion of consortium, as well as interspousal and interfamilial immunity.[106] Some of these limitations had long existed in the common law—the ban on wives' recovering for loss of consortium, for example, had its roots in the outmoded notion that the husband had no duties toward his wife, and thus his injury deprived her of nothing to which she was entitled.[107] Other limitations, such as

103. Among these doctrines were privity of contract, contributory negligence, the fellow servant rule, assumption of risk, and standard of care.

104. The most famous case carving out an exception is *MacPherson* v. *Buick Motor Co.*, 111 N.E. 1050 (N.Y. 1916). For discussion of judicial decisions that created exceptions to the doctrine, see Edward H. Levi, *An Introduction to Legal Reasoning* (Chicago: University of Chicago Press, 1949), pp. 8–27.

105. *Henningsen* v. *Bloomfield Motors*, 161 A.2d 69 (N.J. 1960). This case is discussed in greater detail in chapter 5.

106. The prohibition on suits for wrongful death prevented relatives of the deceased from suing for damages, based on the notion that a tort suit must be personal to the victim. As William Prosser has observed, this ban made it "more profitable for the defendant to kill the plaintiff than to scratch him." (William Prosser, *Handbook on the Law of Torts*, 3d ed. [St. Paul: West, 1964], p. 924; quoted in Lieberman, *The Litigious Society*, p. 38.

The prohibition on recovery by wives for negligent invasion of consortium meant that only husbands could recover for the loss of the company, affection, and aid of their spouses caused by the negligent actions of a third party.

Interspousal immunity refers to the tort law ban on suits by one spouse against another, and interfamilial immunity to the ban on suits by one family member against another (usually suits by children against parents for injuries resulting from automobile accidents).

107. See Tarr and Porter, "Gender Equality and Judicial Federalism," pp. 937–42.

interfamilial immunity, were of more recent vintage. Whatever their
bases, these limitations on causes of action came under increasing,
and increasingly successful, attack in the postwar era. Interspousal
immunity, for example, which obtained in all but eleven states prior
to World War II, had been abrogated in thirty states by 1980.[108] And
the bar on recovery for negligent invasion of consortium, recognized
in all states until 1953, was lifted in thirty-seven states by 1980.[109]

The fate of the privity requirement and these other obstacles to
recovery in many ways typifies developments in the postwar era.
Once successfully challenged in a single jurisdiction, the legal doctrines that prevented recovery soon found themselves under attack in
other jurisdictions and quickly fell by the wayside. Part of the
explanation can be found in changing social relations, part in the
emerging notion of a right to redress, part in extralegal developments
such as the spread of liability insurance, and part in altered judicial
attitudes toward initiating change in the common law. Although the
pace and extent of change varied according to the particular issue,
what characterized the performance of state supreme courts was a
new willingness to entertain challenges to established doctrines and to
pave the way for plaintiffs to obtain redress for injuries.

Products Liability

Because of their unusual substantive importance, the changes that
have occurred in the area of products liability deserve special consideration. During the nineteenth and early twentieth centuries, manufacturers were liable for the injuries that their goods produced only if
they had sold the product directly to the injured party (the privity-of-
contract requirement) and if the product's defect could be traced to
negligence on the part of the manufacturer. The effect of these
requirements was to shield manufacturers from liability in the vast
majority of cases. However, the recognition of a right to redress
produced a revolution in products liability law. We have already
noted the elimination of the privity-of-contract requirement. Another
major development was the substitution of strict liability for negligence as the standard for determining liability. Over the thirteen-year
period from its initial acceptance in California in 1963, the supreme
courts in thirty-seven states adopted the strict liability standard, and

108. Baum and Canon, "State Supreme Courts as Activists," p. 89.
109. Tarr and Porter, "Gender Equality and Judicial Federalism," pp. 959–62,
table D.

another four states did so by statute.[110] A third development was the increasing judicial receptivity to plaintiffs' claims based on defects in products' design. Under the new regime in products liability, then, plaintiffs could sue manufacturers for all products-related injuries, and they would emerge victorious if they could show that the injuries they received were tied to some defect in either the construction of the item they had purchased or in the design of the overall product line.

Effects of the Tort Law Revolution

The pioneering rulings of state supreme courts have, of course, produced major changes in the substantive law, extending the scope of liability and removing obstacles that barred plaintiffs from recovery. Their implications for the political and legal roles of state supreme courts, however, may be just as important. For one thing, the example of judicially initiated change presented by leading courts, as well as the proliferation of similar claims for redress in other states, has altered judicial attitudes about the appropriate role of courts in common law policy making.[111] Despite mounting criticism by commentators, many courts remained reluctant to initiate basic changes in common law doctrines. This reluctance reflected less an attachment to established doctrine than either a general unwillingness to take a leadership role or a belief that when settled common law principles were involved, the legislature was the appropriate organ of reform. When activist courts initiated changes in the common law, however, the situation changed dramatically. Principles that had previously appeared settled were settled no longer, and indeed the movement appeared to be away from previously established positions. Moreover, rulings in other states had appeared to vindicate the legitimacy of court-initiated change. Finally, although most state supreme courts were reluctant to take a leadership role, they were equally reluctant to defend doctrines that had been repudiated by the majority of their

110. As Baum and Canon have observed, "Never before had such a momentous change in tort law swept the American states so rapidly" ("State Supreme Courts as Activists," p. 88). For a more general discussion of the changes in products liability, albeit from a highly critical perspective, see Richard A. Epstein, *Modern Products Liability Law* (Westport, Conn.: Quorum Books, 1980).

111. Thus Robert Keeton has concluded, "As important and interesting as particular reforms of substantive law achieved during this period may be, they are less significant in the long run than changes that occurred in processes and attitudes" (*Venturing to Do Justice,* pp. 3–4). See also Baum and Canon, "State Supreme Courts as Activists," pp. 97–102.

sister courts. In sum, by challenging established legal doctrines, a few courts created a momentum that carried less adventurous courts along the path of reform.

Once state supreme courts had become involved in the process of tort law reform in one area, however, they could no longer deny the legitimacy of judicially initiated legal change. Thus involvement in tort law reform in one area produced a greater receptivity to plaintiffs' claims in other areas. At the same time, the success of earlier claims prompted new efforts by the plaintiffs' bar to secure redress, thereby creating further opportunities for activism by state supreme courts in tort law.

This process of tort law reform illustrates the dynamics of horizontal judicial federalism and underlines its importance. At the same time, it directs attention to the contributions that state supreme courts make to the governance of their states.

TWO

STATE SUPREME COURTS AND STATE GOVERNANCE

Thus far we have examined the relations between state supreme courts and other legal institutions beyond their borders. Yet to understand how state supreme courts participate in governance, one must also look at them as institutions of state government, interacting with and both influencing and being influenced by other political actors in the state.

State Supreme Courts as Institutions of State Government

THE INTRASTATE LEGAL CONTEXT

The roles that a state supreme court plays within the state political system and nationally depend in large measure on the distribution of political power among the various institutions of state government. This distribution of power, in turn, is often decisively influenced by state constitutional and statutory law. More particularly, state law affects the roles a state supreme court plays by (1) regulating the sorts of claims that can be adjudicated in state courts and thus brought to the state supreme court on appeal, (2) determining the authority of the state supreme court to regulate its work load and focus on important cases, and (3) providing most of the legal requirements the state high court is to apply and enforce.[1]

---

[1]. Although they are of somewhat lesser importance, for the sake of completeness one must also mention constitutional and statutory provisions that affect the nondecisional powers allocated to the states' high courts. The most significant of these include the power to make rules governing court procedures and the legal profession, the power to discipline members of the bar, and "inherent powers" to mandate expenditures necessary to carry out court operations. For a recent survey

Direct Regulation of Access to Courts

Justiciability   State constitutions and statutes regulate the claims that
can be initiated in state courts most directly through provisions
governing litigants' standing to sue. To have standing in a federal
court, the party invoking judicial power must show "not only that the
[challenged] statute is invalid, but that he has sustained or is
immediately in danger of sustaining some direct injury as the result of
its enforcement."[2] Relying on this standard, which is derived from the
Case-or-Controversy requirement in Article III of the federal Constitution, the U.S. Supreme Court has ruled that mere payment of taxes
does not ordinarily provide a taxpayer with standing to challenge
governmental programs.[3] Although some states have adopted a
similarly restrictive approach, most have been far more liberal in
awarding standing to taxpayers and to private attorneys general. As
early as 1847, for example, a New York trial court recognized a
taxpayer's right to sue a municipality, and other state courts during
the nineteenth century went beyond the New York court, permitting
taxpayer suits against state as well as local governments.[4] During the
twentieth century the trend has continued, and several courts that had
previously denied standing to state taxpayers have now overruled
those decisions.[5] In part, the differences in taxpayers' access to state
and federal courts may be traced to differences in federal and state
constitutions—the Louisiana Constitution of 1974, for example, does
not limit jurisdiction to cases and controversies but instead extends it
to "all civil and criminal matters."[6] In addition, a number of states
have enacted statutes authorizing taxpayers' actions, at least in some

---

of the scope of judicial rule making power in the states, see Donna J. Pugh, Chris A.
Korbakes, James J. Alfini, and Charles W. Grau, *Judicial Rulemaking* (Chicago:
American Judicature Society, 1984). For a discussion of "inherent powers," see
Carl Baar, "Judicial Activism in State Courts: The Inherent Powers Doctrine," in
Mary Cornelia Porter and G. Alan Tarr, eds., *State Supreme Courts: Policymakers in the
Federal System* (Westport, Conn.: Greenwood Press, 1982).

   2. *Frothingham* v. *Mellon,* 262 U.S. 447, 488 (1923).

   3. *Flast* v. *Cohen,* 392 U.S. 83 (1968).

   4. *Adriance* v. *Mayor of New York,* 1 Barb. 19 (N.Y. Sup. Ct. 1847). The
development of state taxpayer actions is reviewed in, "Taxpayers' Suits: A Survey
and Summary," *Yale Law Journal* 69 (April 1960): 895–924.

   5. See, e.g., *Borden* v. *Louisiana State Board of Education,* 123 So. 655 (La. 1929),
overruling *Sutton* v. *Buie,* 66 So. 956 (La. 1914).

   6. Louisiana Constitution, Article V, section 16. For commentary on the
implications of this departure from the language of the Louisiana Constitution of

circumstances. But whatever the bases, the differences between federal and state jurisdiction, and among the jurisdictions of court systems in various states, are dramatic: according to one survey, thirty-four states permit taxpayers' suits to challenge state governmental action, and "virtually every jurisdiction" permits such suits against municipalities.[7] The obvious effect of these liberal standing requirements has been to increase the range of governmental action susceptible to judicial scrutiny.

Other limits on justiciability that circumscribe the activities of federal courts are absent, or present in only attenuated form, in many states, with discernible effects on both the frequency and timing of judicial involvement in controversial policy issues. Whereas federal courts cannot render advisory opinions, again as a result of the Case-or-Controversy requirement, seven state constitutions expressly impose on their state supreme courts a duty to render advisory opinions, usually upon request by the legislature or executive. In two other states courts have upheld statutes permitting advisory opinions even in the absence of constitutional authorization, and in North Carolina the power to issue advisory opinions is the product of judicial decisions.[8] Although such opinions are not legally binding, they are characteristically viewed as authoritative by all parties and thus play an important part in governance. A recent study reveals that advisory opinions most frequently address issues pertaining to the mechanics of state government, so the duty to render opinions often involves the judges directly in day-to-day political issues.[9] In addition, the availability of the justices' legal expertise results in their confronting issues of federal constitutional law during legislative deliberations that might be litigated in federal court if the bill were enacted. For example, during the decade following the United States Supreme Court's "one-man-one-vote" ruling in 1964, state supreme courts issued advisory opinions on state reapportionment plans on fifteen different

---

1921, see Lee Hargrave, "The Judiciary Article of the Louisiana Constitution of 1974," *Louisiana Law Review* 37 (1977): 765–849.

7. "Taxpayers' Suits," p. 895.

8. Colorado, Florida, Maine, Massachusetts, New Hampshire, Rhode Island, and South Dakota provide for advisory opinions by constitutional mandate, Alabama and Delaware by statute, and North Carolina by court decision. For a general treatment, see "The State Advisory Opinion in Perspective," *Fordham Law Review* 44 (1975): 81–113.

9. Ibid., pp. 94–98.

occasions.[10] Thus the power to issue advisory opinions clearly affects the range and character of the issues that state supreme courts confront and the timing of their involvement.

In addition, whereas federal courts have developed the "political questions" doctrine to avoid impinging on coordinate branches of the national government, such separation-of-powers concerns seldom affect state courts.[11] Perhaps this is because in construing state constitutions, which are designed to limit and structure the exercise of governmental power rather than to confer power, there is less justification for relying on the good faith of the other branches of government to produce conformity with constitutional mandates. Not all state judges, surely, would echo the New Jersey justice who declared that "no thicket [is] too political for us."[12] Yet the fact remains that state law seldom poses a barrier to the adjudication of delicate constitutional issues. Last, limitations such as comity and abstention, which federal courts have developed in deference to the federal character of the American polity, play no role at the state court level.[13] Thus, the access limitations that circumscribe the involvement

10. *Reynolds* v. *Sims*, 377 U.S. 533 (1964). Listings of advisory opinions by state supreme courts in reapportionment cases can be found in "State Advisory Opinion," p. 93 and pp. 85–91.

11. Hans A. Linde, "E Pluribus—Constitutional Theory and State Courts," in Bradley D. McGraw, ed., *Developments in State Constitutional Law* (St. Paul: West, 1985), p. 289. On the other hand, one author has maintained that in several instances state courts have relied on a variant of the political questions doctrine. These cases, however, seem to reflect primarily prudential considerations rather than separation-of-powers concerns. See Nat Stern, "The Political Questions Doctrine in State Courts," *South Carolina Law Review* 35 (1984): 405–23.

12. Quoted in Richard Lehne, *The Quest for Justice: The Politics of School Finance Reform* (New York: Longman, 1978), p. 43.

13. Abstention is the doctrine under which the U.S. Supreme Court and other federal courts choose not to rule on state cases, even when empowered to do so, so as to allow the issue to be decided on the basis of state law. Comity refers to the respect which federal courts give to the decisions of state courts. Some commentators have maintained that this results in the underenforcement of federal constitutional guarantees and have suggested that state courts, because they are not subject to federalism concerns, can ensure full enforcement. See Lawrence G. Sager, "Fair Measure: The Legal Status of Under-enforced Constitutional Norms," *Harvard Law Review* 91 (1978): 1212–64, and Sager, "Foreword: State Courts and the Strategic Space Between the Norms and Rules of Constitutional Law," *Texas Law Review* 63 (1985): 959–76. The leading abstention case is *Railroad Commission* v. *Pullman Co.*, 312 U.S. 496 (1941); for a more recent elaboration of abstention doctrine, see *Colorado Water Conservation District* v. *United States*, 424 U.S. 800 (1976). An important comity case that is representative of the current Supreme Court approach is *Younger* v. *Harris*, 401 U.S. 37 (1971).

of federal courts in policy disputes are generally weaker at the state level, although differences in state law produce considerable variation in the range of cases that may be initiated in various state judicial systems.

Class-Action Suits   Class-action suits facilitate access to the courts by permitting large numbers of potential litigants with individually small claims to join together, thereby reducing or eliminating altogether the financial costs of seeking redress. State law governs the initiation and conduct of class-action suits in state forums, and a survey of the law in the various states indicates substantial interstate diversity as well as considerable deviation from the prevailing federal law on class actions. New York adopted the first state statute governing class actions in 1849, and a number of states followed New York's lead in permitting class actions but imposing strict and rather arbitrary limits on their initiation.[14] When the United States Supreme Court in 1938 promulgated the "old" Rule 23 of the Federal Rules of Civil Procedure, which established procedures for commencing and maintaining class-action suits in federal courts, several states followed the federal lead and modeled their laws on the federal rule. When the "new" Rule 23 was adopted in 1966, facilitating class-action suits in federal courts, some states again responded to the federal initiative by modifying their own law. During the 1970s, rulings by the U.S. Supreme Court restricted the initiation of class actions in federal courts by enforcing stringent jurisdictional requirements in diversity cases and saddling the plaintiff class with burdensome notification costs.[15] However, not all states have followed the Court's lead. North Dakota and Iowa adopted the Uniform Class Action Act, which was developed in 1976 to make state courts more receptive to class-action suits. Other states, either through legislation or court decisions, have developed guidelines on class actions that are considerably more liberal than those prevailing in the federal courts.[16]

14. This historical survey is derived from Adolf Homburger, "State Class Actions and the Federal Rule," *Columbia Law Review* 71 (1971): 609–59; "State Class Action Suits: A Comparative Analysis," *Iowa Law Review* 60 (1974): 93–121; "Developments in the Law—Class Actions," *Harvard Law Review* 89 (1976): 1318–1644; and "The Iowa Uniform Class Actions Rule: Intended Effects and Probable Results," *Iowa Law Review* 66 (1981): 1241–75.

15. *Snyder* v. *Harris*, 394 U.S. 332 (1969); *Zahn* v. *International Paper Co.*, 414 U.S. 291 (1973); and *Eisen* v. *Carlisle & Jacquelin*, 417 U.S. 156 (1974).

16. See, for example, Jonathan P. Hayden, "The California State Courts and Consumer Class Actions for Antitrust Violations," *Hastings Law Journal* 33 (1982): 689–726.

Thus the law on class-action suits varies from state to state. Some states, such as Nebraska, continue to be governed by a modified version of the Field Code. Others have modeled their law on federal law and operate under law derived from either the old or new versions of Rule 23. Still others have developed their own class-action law, which is often receptive to such suits. Insofar as the likelihood of some issues being litigated depends upon their presentation in a class action, these differences in state law affect the range of issues litigated in state courts. Moreover, given differences in the receptivity of state and federal courts to class-action suits, litigants who have a choice of forum in which to initiate their cases can be expected to choose the more receptive forum, again affecting the division of business between federal and state courts.

Hospitality of State Forums Because the jurisdiction of state and federal courts is in part concurrent, litigants may at times have the option of filing suit in either a state or a federal court. In such circumstances state procedural requirements, usually the result of state legislation, may influence the willingness of plaintiffs to pursue constitutional claims in state courts and thereby affect the range of issues coming before state supreme courts. According to Burt Neuborne, three procedural concerns—uniformity, familiarity, and hospitality—are crucial in determining counsel's choice of a forum.[17] For the national civil rights–civil liberties bar, "which is called upon to litigate constitutional cases in numerous states, often simultaneously," procedural uniformity is essential because it obviates the need "to respond to complex cases in unfamiliar procedural settings." Consequently, the decision to use a state forum may depend upon whether the state has adopted the Federal Rules of Civil Procedure. Conversely, "a state that insists on maintaining a parochial system of procedure should not expect a substantial influx of constitutional cases."[18] Closely related to this concern for uniformity is a concern for familiarity of procedure. Clearly, it is easier to master a single federal rule than to learn the various procedural requirements found in state courts. Yet more is involved: because national law schools require courses in federal civil procedure but not in state procedure, the training that lawyers receive typically orients them to forums in which federal procedural rules are applied. Thus once again divergence from

---

17. "Toward Procedural Parity in Constitutional Litigation," *William and Mary Law Review* 22 (1981): 725–87.

18. Ibid., p. 734.

the federal rules is likely to deter constitutional litigation. And by establishing burdensome pleadings requirements, discouraging class actions, limiting discovery, and imposing restrictive notions of immunity, states may signal an inhospitality to constitutional litigation and thus deflect cases raising such claims to federal courts.

Legal provisions governing who will pay attorneys' fees may also affect potential litigants' judgments about the hospitality of a court system and thus about whether to initiate actions in it. Historically the American practice has been to require each party to reimburse its own attorney.[19] However, in the last decade, legislatures have begun to authorize awarding attorneys' fees to plaintiffs serving as private attorneys general. Generally, a party's chances of obtaining a fee award are greater in federal than in state court. Since 1975, when the U.S. Supreme Court ordered lower federal courts to cease awarding attorneys' fees in the absence of statutory authorization, Congress has enacted several laws—most notably the Civil Rights Attorneys' Fees Award Act and the Equal Access to Justice Act—that have created strong incentives for conducting "public interest litigation" in federal courts.[20] State legislatures, on the other hand, generally have been less willing to encourage such litigation, and even when they have acted, they have usually been less comprehensive in their approach. The two states that have actively promoted such litigation are California and New Jersey. The California Supreme Court in 1977 endorsed the payment of attorneys' fees to private attorneys general, and a few days later the California General Assembly confirmed the court's ruling by incorporating an even broader provision in the California Code of Civil Procedure.[21] Taking a rather different approach, the New Jersey

19. Two limited exceptions to the traditional "American rule" allowed the awarding of attorneys' fees when the court could assess the fees against funds that had been created, increased, or protected by successful litigation (the "common fund" exception) or when the losing party had acted in bad faith. For an overview of the American rule and recent departures from it, see Karen O'Connor and Lee Epstein, "Bridging the Gap Between Congress and the Supreme Court: Interest Groups and the Erosion of the American Rule Governing Awards of Attorneys' Fees," *Western Political Quarterly* 38 (1985): 238–49.

20. The Supreme Court's decision is *Alyeska Pipeline Service Co.* v. *Wilderness Society*, 421 U.S. 240 (1975). The statutes may be found at 42 U.S.C. sec. 1988 (1982) and 90 Stat. 2641 (1976), as amended by 94 Stat. 2330 (1980).

21. The California court decision is *Serrano* v. *Priest* (*Serrano* III), 569 P.2d 1303, 1312–15 (Cal. 1977). The legislature's endorsement of attorneys' fees for private attorney general may be found at California Civil Procedure Code, sec. 1021.5 (1978). For an overview of the California law, see John E. McDermott and Richard

Assembly in 1974 established the Department of the Public Advocate, which is authorized to determine what the public interest is and to decide whether to represent that interest in ongoing proceedings or to institute proceedings on its own.[22]

The effect of laws governing the recovery of attorneys' fees can be dramatic. If state and federal courts have concurrent jurisdiction, these provisions may influence where a suit is initiated. If a state court has exclusive jurisdiction, litigation costs may affect the vigor with which an action is pursued or even whether it is commenced at all. Perhaps it is not coincidental that the two states that have been most receptive to "public interest litigation," California and New Jersey, have state supreme courts with national reputations for activism.

REGULATION OF THE JURISDICTION OF STATE SUPREME COURTS

State law, both statutory and constitutional, also influences the part that a state supreme court plays in governing by prescribing the court's appellate jurisdiction. It is now commonly accepted that litigants have a right to appellate review of trial-court rulings. In states that have not instituted intermediate courts of appeals, the responsibility for appellate review falls directly on the state supreme court.[23] Particularly in populous states, the absence of intermediate courts of appeals, which could share the appellate work load, imposes an overwhelming burden of cases on state high courts.[24] In such circumstances the state supreme court finds itself relegated to dealing with a succession of relatively minor disputes, devoting its energies to error correction rather than to more time-consuming efforts to shape the law of the state. On the other hand, by diverting routine cases to intermediate appellate courts, a state allows its high court to devote more attention to cases that raise important policy questions. Thus a study of the effects of instituting an intermediate court of appeals in

---

Rothschild, "Foreword: The Private Attorney General Rule and Public Interest Litigation in California," *California Law Review* 66 (1978): 138--77.

22. "The Private Attorney General and the Public Advocate: Facilitating Public Interest Litigation," *Rutgers Law Review* 34 (1982): 350–77.

23. In several states appeals from rulings of trial courts of limited jurisdiction go to trial courts of general jurisdiction for trial de novo.

24. Data on how caseload pressures overwhelmed state supreme courts in populous states during the early decades of the twentieth century are presented in Robert A. Kagan, Bliss Cartwright, Lawrence M. Friedman, and Stanton Wheeler, "The Evolution of State Supreme Courts," *Michigan Law Review* 76 (1978): 961–1001.

North Carolina concluded that it enabled the state supreme court to assume "a position of true leadership in the legal development of the state."[25]

However, not all states that have introduced intermediate courts of appeals have witnessed a transformation like North Carolina's. Many state supreme courts have experienced only a temporary reduction in caseload pressures. The key variable here is whether the institution of an intermediate appellate court is accompanied by a reduction in the mandatory jurisdiction of the state's high court. States such as Arizona, which continue to require their high courts to hear appeals from appellate-court rulings in a wide variety of cases, or such as Alabama, which impose a burdensome original jurisdiction on their high courts, have found that the establishment of new courts has not solved caseload problems.[26] On the other hand, states such as Florida, which have granted their supreme courts broad discretion in case selection, have thereby allowed them to keep their caseloads within manageable bounds.[27]

Yet the effects of this reform may go beyond mere alleviation of caseload pressures. Granting a state high court control over its docket can also influence how the court views its responsibilities:

> Discretionary review at the highest level . . . transforms the nature of the judicial process. The high court is no longer merely reacting to disputes brought to it by adversaries; it is selecting those disputes in which it chooses to participate. Almost surely this has affected the self-perception of the judges of the high courts, who tend to view themselves primarily as policy-makers and secondarily as conflict-resolvers, thus reversing the traditional relationship between those dual functions and taking leave of a fundamental assumption of the Common Law. In sum . . . [t]he architecture of the system tells the judges of the top court to be creative.[28]

25. Roger D. Groot, "The Effects of an Intermediate Appellate Court on the Supreme Court Work Product: The North Carolina Experience," *Wake Forest Law Review* 7 (1971): 548–72.

26. Victor Eugene Flango and Nora F. Blair, "Creating an Intermediate Appellate Court: Does It Reduce the Caseload of a State's Highest Court?" *Judicature* 64 (1980): 74–84.

27. John M. Scheb and John M. Scheb II, "Making Intermediate Appellate Courts Final: Assessing Jurisdictional Changes in Florida's Appellate Courts," *Judicature* 67 (1984): 474–85.

28. Paul D. Carrington, Daniel J. Meador, and Maurice Rosenberg, *Justice on Appeal* (St. Paul: West, 1976), p. 150.

Assuredly, encouraging or discouraging state high courts from pursuing an active course in policy development was not a salient concern for those debating structural reform: alarm about supreme courts' increasing caseloads dominates debate on the issue. Yet as the North Carolina experience suggests, it may be among the most important consequences of these attempts to introduce structural reforms.

THE SUBSTANCE OF STATE LAW

Because a prime function of courts is to enforce existing legal norms, the sorts of issues that a state supreme court confronts depend in large measure on the substantive law of the state. More is involved here than the obvious point that each state supreme court enforces the law of a specific state. These bodies of law differ in ways that affect a court's opportunities to participate in policy development and thereby help to define the role that the court plays in governing.

State Constitutions

In identifying these basic differences, one turns first to state constitutions. According to traditional legal theory, the state government inherently possesses all governmental power not ceded to the national government, and thus a state constitution does not grant governmental power but merely structures and limits it.[29] Perhaps because of this, state constitutions tend to be longer and more detailed than their federal counterpart—only Vermont's is shorter, and the average state constitution is over three times as long—with many "legislative matters" enshrined in constitutional provisions.[30] Yet state constitutions vary enormously in the range and detail of the limitations they impose on state governments. These differences are important because, generally speaking, the more extensive the substantive and procedural limitations a state constitution imposes, the greater the opportunity for a litigant to oppose governmental policy on constitutional grounds, and thus the greater the likelihood of participation by

29. For a comprehensive discussion of the character of state constitutions, see Robert F. Williams, "State Constitutional Law Processes," *William and Mary Law Review* 24 (1983): 169–228.

30. Article 19, section 22 of the Louisiana Constitution, for example, established Huey Long's birthday as a state holiday in perpetuity. For a more general treatment, see Albert L. Sturm, "The Development of American State Constitutions," *Publius* 12 (1982): 57–98.

the state supreme court in determining the ultimate policy in the state.[31]

Yet is is not merely the length or detail of state constitutions but also the substance of the limitations they impose that is important in determining the policy-making roles of state supreme courts. This can be seen most clearly by focusing on state bills of rights. Some state bills of rights afford relatively narrow protection, entailing little more than a reiteration of the constitutional guarantees of the federal Bill of Rights. Others, however, offer more detailed and extensive protections. For example, seventeen state constitutions contain "little ERA's," ten expressly protect privacy rights, and several others in some form guarantee a right to environmental quality.[32] As we stated in another context, "Construing documents that reflect such lively topical issues virtually requires state supreme courts, whatever their inclinations, to engage in broad policymaking."[33] Moreover, even when a category of rights is similar to rights protected under the federal Constitution, some state constitutions contain more detailed language or afford more extensive protection, thereby inviting more vigorous judicial intervention. Thus differences among state constitutions may well lead to different roles for state supreme courts in policy development and hence in American federalism generally.

State Statutory Law

The scope of state statutory law profoundly affects the role state supreme courts play in governing. The limited output of state legislatures in the nineteenth century afforded state supreme courts an opportunity to shape state law through their enunciation of the common law, and they made the most of this opportunity. During the first half of the nineteenth century, they used the freedom conferred by legislative inaction to transform common law conceptions of property, contracts, and negligence, thereby providing the legal underpinning for the emergence of an industrial society. As Morton

31. See Robert F. Williams, "State Constitutional Limits on Legislative Procedure: Legislative Compliance and Judicial Enforcement," *Publius* 17 (1987): 91–114.

32. G. Alan Tarr and Mary Cornelia Porter, "Gender Equality and Judicial Federalism: The Role of State Appellate Courts," *Hastings Constitutional Law Quarterly* 9 (1982): 919–73; "Toward a Right of Privacy as a Matter of State Constitutional Law," *Florida State University Law Review* 5 (1977): 633–745; and A. E. Dick Howard, "State Constitutions and the Environment," *Virginia Law Review* 58 (1972): 193–229.

33. "Editors' Introduction," in Porter and Tarr, *State Supreme Courts*, p. xv.

Horwitz has observed, prior to the Civil War "the common law performed at least as great a role as legislation in underwriting and channeling economic development. In fact, common law judges regularly brought about the sort of far-reaching changes that would have been regarded earlier as entirely within the power of the legislature."[34] When state legislatures began to pass regulatory statutes in the latter half of the century, state courts characteristically subjected them to "strict interpretation" if they were in derogation of the common law in order to safeguard the legal edifice they had created.

During the twentieth century the American legal system was transformed from one "dominated by the common law, divined by courts, to one in which statutes, enacted by legislatures, have become the primary source of law."[35] Through an "orgy of statute making"[36] beginning in the Progressive Era and reaching fruition during the New Deal, legislatures at both the state and national levels assumed the dominant policy-making role (even if ultimately they delegated much of this responsibility to the myriad agencies created to administer their enactments). This transformation meant more than merely the substitution of state legislative policy for judicial policy, although this of course occurred.[37] For even when state legislative policy did not displace judicial policy, it often changed the legal landscape within which courts operated, requiring them to "take into account the gravitational pull of statutes in doing their traditional job of updating the common law" and thereby circumscribing the range of judicial creativity.[38] In addition, because legislatures had assumed primary

34. Morton J. Horwitz, *The Transformation of American Law, 1780–1860* (Cambridge: Harvard University Press, 1977), pp. 1–2. Other historical studies documenting the opportunities for state court policy making presented by legislative inaction include William E. Nelson, *Americanization of the Common Law* (Cambridge: Harvard University Press, 1975), and Stephen Skowroneck, *Building a New American State: The Expansion of National Administrative Capacities* (Cambridge: Cambridge University Press, 1982).

35. Guido Calabresi, *A Common Law for the Age of Statutes* (Cambridge: Harvard University Press, 1982), p. 1, and more generally, Roscoe Pound, "Common Law and Legislation," *Harvard Law Review* 21 (1908): 383–407.

36. Grant Gilmore, *The Ages of American Law* (New Haven: Yale University Press, 1977), p. 94.

37. For an authoritative overview of the movement from judge-made law to statutory and administrative law, see James Willard Hurst, *Law and Social Order in the United States* (Ithaca: Cornell University Press, 1977), especially chap. 2.

38. Calabresi, *A Common Law*, p. 44, and Robert F. Williams, "Statutes as Sources of Law Beyond Their Terms in Common-Law Cases," *George Washington Law Review* 50 (1982): 554–600.

responsibility for instituting legal change, some courts concluded that all major legal change should come from the legislature and refused to reconsider even outmoded common law doctrines.[39] And when state supreme courts did undertake to reform common law rules, they found at times that statutory developments virtually wiped out the effects of their doctrinal innovations.[40]

It would be a mistake to view the expansion of state legislative activity as simply eclipsing opportunities for state supreme courts to participate in governing. For one thing, contraction of some policy-making opportunities may lead to increased opportunities in other areas. Thus although expanding legislative and administrative output curtailed common law policy making, it has increasingly involved state supreme courts in the tasks of statutory interpretation and oversight of administrative activity, and they have seized the opportunities presented by this involvement to put their imprint on state law. A study of supreme courts in four populous states, for example, found that judicial review of the rulings of administrative agencies accounted for almost 20 percent of the courts' caseloads in the early 1970s and that they were not reluctant to substitute their judgments for those of the agencies, ruling against the agencies in almost half the cases they heard.[41] Moreover, even though the expansion of legislative policy making has reduced the scope of the common law, state courts continue to make important policy within this narrowed scope, as evidenced by the revolution in tort law that has occurred since World War II. Last, although statutification has been a national phenomenon, the pace and extent of the process has varied among the states, affecting the division of policy-making responsibilities among the branches of state government.

Three major points emerge from our survey of how state law affects the relations between state supreme courts and other branches of state government. First, procedural and structural elements of state law, just as much as its substantive content, affect a state supreme court's

39. Tarr and Porter, "Gender Equality," pp. 937–42, and Lawrence Baum and Bradley C. Canon, "State Supreme Courts as Activists: New Doctrines in the Law of Torts," in Porter and Tarr, *State Supreme Courts*, pp. 93–97.

40. See, for example, Gregory A. Caldeira, "Changing the Common Law: Effects of the Decline of Charitable Immunity," *Law & Society Review* 16 (1981–82): 669–93.

41. Stephen Frank, "The Oversight of Administrative Agencies by State Supreme Courts: Some Macro Findings," *Administrative Law Review* 32 (1980): 477–500.

opportunities to participate in policy development. State law governing the initiation and conduct of litigation, for example, influences the sorts of cases filed in state courts by encouraging or discouraging the transformation of disputes into legal conflicts and by facilitating or impeding the use of state forums for policy-oriented litigation. And state law creating appellate courts and defining their jurisdictions affects not only caseload pressures on state supreme courts but also the justices' perceptions of their responsibilities for the development of substantive law. Second, both general and state-specific legal factors may affect state supreme courts' contributions to public policy. Some developments, such as the statutification of state law, have occurred nationwide and have had a uniform effect on all state supreme courts, even though the extent of statutification has varied from state to state. Other developments, such as the institution of intermediate courts of appeals, although widespread, have not been uniform in their character, timing, or results. Still others, such as the adoption of constitutional protections for privacy rights, have occurred in relatively few states. Moreover, some developments, such as the establishment of the Department of the Public Advocate in New Jersey, are peculiar to a single state, and their effects have been confined within its borders. Third, with the exception of legislative preemption of judicial policy making in certain substantive areas, the effect of law on the function of a state high court is largely facilitative or permissive rather than mandatory. Institutional reforms, such as the development of intermediate courts of appeals, may create opportunities for courts to assume a more active policy role, but they do not demand it. The same may be said for the adoption of broad constitutional limitations on state government. Conversely, the absence of such spurs to judicial activity does not necessarily preclude judicial participation in policy making. In other words, whereas state law may invite or discourage judicial involvement in policy development, it frequently neither demands nor prevents it; and thus for a full explanation of state supreme courts' relations with other branches of state government, we must look beyond the legal context.

THE BROADER INTRASTATE CONTEXT

Although state law channels and influences the division of policy-making responsibility within state government, state supreme courts retain considerable discretion in defining the policy role they will play. Various courts have used this discretion to develop diverse policy roles, and over time the policy roles of particular courts have changed dramatically.

Within the range of available discretion, the particular policy role adopted by a court depends in large part on the state's political and legal climate. Among the relevant factors here is, first of all, the state's political culture, that is, "the particular pattern of orientation to political action in which each political system is embedded."[42] Judicial backgrounds and experiences help to account for the influence that political culture exerts on judicial activity. Over 90 percent of the justices on state high courts were born and/or educated in the state in which they serve.[43] Often the justices are the products of politically active families and were themselves involved in state and local politics before their elevation to the state bench. Over half of the justices have had prosecutorial experience, almost 20 percent have served in the state legislature, and almost 20 percent have served in the state attorney general's office. Altogether, over 70 percent have held at least one nonjudicial political office prior to selection, and most had held two or more such offices.[44] Even these figures probably underestimate the level and intensity of pre-judicial political activity, and this involvement may not cease with elevation to the bench, particularly in systems employing partisan selection methods. Justice Richard Neely of the West Virginia Supreme Court has suggested that frequently judgeships serve as "consolation prizes for those who fail in big-time elected politics," and there is undoubtedly some truth to the

42. Daniel J. Elazar, *American Federalism: A View from the States*, 3d ed. (New York: Harper & Row, 1984), p. 109.

43. Data on judicial backgrounds and experience are derived from Bradley C. Canon, "Characteristics and Career Patterns of State Supreme Court Justices," *State Government* 45 (1972): 34–41, and from Henry R. Glick and Craig F. Emment, "Stability and Change: Characteristics of State Supreme Court Judges," *Judicature* 70 (1986): 107–12. For single-state studies that are consistent with these national data, see Francis H. Heller, "The Justices of the Kansas Supreme Court, 1861–1975: A Collective Portrait," *University of Kansas Law Review* 24 (1975–76): 521–35, and Walter A. Borowiec, "Pathways to the Top: The Political Careers of State Supreme Court Justices," *North Carolina Central Law Review* 7 (1976): 280–85. Interestingly, the backgrounds of justices do not depend much on differences in modes of judicial selection. See Bradley C. Canon, "The Impact of Formal Selection Processes on the Characteristics of Judges—Reconsidered," *Law & Society Review* 6(1972): 579–93, and Henry R. Glick, "The Promise and Performance of the Missouri Plan: Judicial Selection in the Fifty States," *University of Miami Law Review* 32 (1978): 509–41.

44. Henry R. Glick and Kenneth N. Vines, *State Court Systems* (Englewood Cliffs, N.J.: Prentice-Hall, 1973), p. 48, table 3–4, and pp. 49–50.

characterization.[45] Yet the failure that these politicians-turned-judges experienced was relative rather than absolute, and their considerable political success could not have been achieved without adherence to the prevailing political norms in the state. Thus state justices' backgrounds and experiences dispose them to accept the state political culture, and this in turn influences the orientations they bring to the judicial task.

The influence of political culture on judicial activity does not, however, prevent sharp differences in perspective within state high courts. For one thing, many states do not share a homogeneous political culture, and the orientations of judges on a single court may reflect the various political cultural strains in a state. In addition, although political culture establishes orientations toward political life, it does not determine particular outcomes in policy disputes—otherwise there would be no political conflict in the state. Ultimately, although political culture is important, it is hardly the only factor affecting the policy role adopted by state supreme courts.

The political ideologies and partisan affiliations of the judges may also influence what policy role a court adopts. In one-party states, political elites (which would include the justices) characteristically share an ideological consensus, oftentimes supporting institutions and practices that diverge from prevailing national norms. In such circumstances the state's elites undertake to defend the divergent institutions and practices against attempts from outside the state to impose national standards. The southern states, at least until the 1970s, are a prime example. This combination of ideological consensus and external "threat" promotes supportive rather than conflictual relations among state governmental institutions. Rather than seeking to develop an independent policy role, the state supreme court typically serves an important but subordinate role in defending state values.

In states where political parties are competitive, political ideology and partisan affiliation can be expected to produce rather different effects on the policy roles of the state supreme court. Because there are two viable political parties, a citizen's choice of party serves as a rough indicator of political ideology and as an implicit selection of a reference group.[46] This initial partisan perspective is reinforced by the

45. Richard Neely, *Why Courts Don't Work* (New York: McGraw-Hill, 1983), p. 41.

46. See Tarr, *Judicial Impact*, pp. 68–69: "According to this view, an individual initially chooses a party on the basis of a conjunction between his political attitudes

political activity that judges engage in before their elevation to the bench. Where parties participate in selecting judicial candidates, those selected tend to be not merely candidates with party ties but partisans. Systems that provide for a limited tenure for judges and require them to run for reelection on partisan ballots may reinforce the partisan perspective that a judge has brought to the bench.

The sorts of cases that state supreme courts decide may render the justices' partisan and ideological attachments particularly important. As we have noted, the detail and specificity of state constitutions, the absence of limitations on justiciability, and (in some states) the duty to render advisory opinions all serve to involve state supreme courts in day-to-day governmental operations, where divisions along party lines are common. Other issues addressed by state supreme courts may also furnish opportunities for judges' partisan views to come to the fore. When a state supreme court rules on a workers' compensation case, for example, its decision depends largely on how sympathetically it views workers' claims.[47] Similarly, the absence of a legal text to interpret in common law cases may tempt justices to advance their personal conceptions of proper policy.

Yet neither party affiliation nor political ideology offers a complete explanation for the policy roles adopted by state supreme courts. For one thing, not all cases present issues that lend themselves to resolution along party or ideological lines. Whatever their partisan composition, most state supreme courts register considerably lower levels of dissent than are found on the U.S. Supreme Court, and the dissent that occurs does not invariably reflect partisan or ideological divisions.[48] Moreover, as David Adamany's study of the Wisconsin Supreme Court has shown, even cases that raise issues with strong

(ideology) and the policies supported by the party, with subsequent group interaction serving to confirm and clarify these attitudes. Over time, further political issues arise on which the individual may take positions, and his policy choices are influenced in large measure by the positions taken by the like-minded individuals who comprise the political party and to whose arguments he is particularly susceptible."

47. Studies that have found partisan divisions in workers' compensation cases include Glendon Schubert, *Quantitative Analysis of Judicial Behavior* (New York: Free Press, 1959), pp. 132–34, and S. Sidney Ulmer, "The Political Party Variable in the Michigan Supreme Court," *Journal of Public Law* 11 (1962): 352–62.

48. On dissent in state supreme courts, see Dean Jaros and Bradley C. Canon, "Dissent on State Supreme Courts: The Differential Significance of Characteristics of Judges," *Midwest Journal of Political Science* 15 (1971): 322–46, and John W.

ideological components, like workers' compensation, do not always divide a court or divide it along partisan lines.[49] And although partisan affiliation and political ideology may influence the members of a court, they do not dictate whether the court should be an active or self-restrained participant in policy making.

If state supreme court justices were formerly partisans, they are currently judges, and thus legal factors can likewise be expected to influence their views of the role they should play in governing. Perhaps the most important of these factors is the state's legal culture, that is, the norms and expectations that govern the legal processes in the state and guide the behavior of participants in the process. For the judge, this legal culture is communicated and reinforced through legal training, experience in legal practice, and interactions with other participants in the legal process.[50] Although the legal cultures of the various states are similar in many respects, they differ in their perspectives on the proper role for judges and on the legitimacy of judicial policy making, and these differences help to explain the policy roles adopted by various state supreme courts.

The influence of state legal cultures can be seen in both the attitudes and behavior of state court judges. In separate sets of interviews with justices on eight state supreme courts, Henry Glick and John Wold found considerable variation in the judges' views regarding their function but, significantly, general intracourt agreement on the issue.[51] Lawrence Baum and Bradley Canon found that although no state supreme court was perfectly consistent in its response to tort law

Patterson and Gregory J. Rathjen, "Background Diversity and State Supreme Court Dissent Behavior," *Polity* 9 (1976): 610–22. For discussion of the limitations of studies emphasizing party affiliation as a determinant of judicial voting behavior, see Malcolm M. Feeley, "Another Look at the 'Party Variable' in Judicial Decision-Making: An Analysis of the Michigan Supreme Court," *Polity* 4 (1971): 91–104, and Tarr, *Judicial Impact*, pp. 78–82.

49. "The Party Variable in Judges' Voting: Conceptual Notes and a Case Study," *American Political Science Review* 63 (1969): 57–73.

50. For a more detailed treatment of state legal cultures, see "Editors' Introduction," in Porter and Tarr, *State Supreme Courts*, pp. xiv–xvi. It should be emphasized that legal culture is not merely a subcategory of political culture but a distinct element, and states with similar political cultures may have divergent legal cultures.

51. Henry R. Glick, *Supreme Courts in State Politics: An Investigation of the Judicial Role* (New York: Basic Books, 1971), p. 41, table 2-3, and John T. Wold, "Political Orientations, Social Backgrounds, and Role Perceptions of State Supreme Court

innovations, most courts assumed characteristic postures of activism or restraint.[52] Other studies have found that the policy roles courts adopt may be even more variegated: whereas some courts are consistently active or passive, others embrace activism in some legal fields (for example, common law) while eschewing it in others (for example, constitutional law).[53] Yet whatever the patterns of activism or restraint, intervention or deference, the main point is that courts do develop consistent patterns, reflecting coherent judgments about the circumstances under which judicial involvement in policy making is appropriate. These patterns—and the judgments underlying them— in large part reflect the influence of legal culture.

THE INFLUENCE OF JUDICIAL REFORM

Among the most important of the broader contextual factors affecting state supreme courts in the postwar era has been the movement to reform state judicial systems. The modern movement for court reform originated with Roscoe Pound's famous speech in 1906 before the American Bar Association, in which he attributed popular dissatisfaction with the administration of justice to the byzantine structure of state judicial systems and to outmoded legal procedures that produced delays and expense, confusion and injustice.[54] To remedy these problems, Pound proposed a radical simplification of court structure, the standardization of procedure within states, and the adoption of managerial practices designed to promote greater efficiency and coordination.

Although Pound envisioned that the legal profession would take the lead in promoting reform, the immediate response to his proposals was decidedly negative—a resolution to print four thousand copies of

---

Judges," *Western Political Quarterly* 27 (1974): 239–41. A study of the Rhode Island Supreme Court likewise found a consensus regarding the court's policy role. See Edward N. Beiser, "The Rhode Island Supreme Court: A Well-Integrated Political System," *Law & Society Review* 8 (1974): 167–86.

52. "State Supreme Courts as Activists," pp. 97–102.

53. See especially Tarr and Porter, "Gender Equality and State Courts," pp. 949–52.

54. Roscoe Pound, "The Causes of Popular Dissatisfaction with the Administration of Justice," in A. Leo Levin and Russell R. Wheeler, eds., *The Pound Conference: Perspectives on Justice in the Future* (St. Paul: West, 1979).

his speech was defeated at the ABA convention, and speaker after speaker mounted the podium to defend the American judicial system and attack his recommendations.[55] This initial rejection was short-lived, and judicial reformers, including in their number some of the nation's most renowned lawyers, soon rallied around a set of specific proposals derived from Pound's address.[56] These reform proposals, usually denominated as court unification, included consolidation of trial courts; centralized management of the court system by the chief justice (with the assistance of an administrative office of the courts); centralized rule making vested in the state high court; a unitary (centrally prepared) judicial budget; and full state financing of the state judicial system.[57] With the waning of the Progressive movement, however, interest in court reform flagged, and not until the postwar era did proponents of court unification begin to make inroads in transforming state judicial systems.[58]

Since World War II, judicial reformers have succeeded in achieving many of their objectives; and although the timing and extent of reform have varied, no state has been unaffected by the reform movement. Since 1945, the vast majority of states have undertaken to consolidate their trial courts, often closely approximating the simplified structure espoused by reformers.[59] Although efforts to centralize managerial authority in the chief justice's hands have been less

55. R. Stanley Lowe, "Unified Courts in America: The Legacy of Roscoe Pound," *Judicature* 56 (1973): 316–17.

56. Discussions of the development of support for court unification and of the groups now favoring it are found in Larry Berkson and Susan Carbon, *Court Unification: History, Politics and Implementation* (Washington, D.C.: National Institute for Law Enforcement and Criminal Justice, 1978), chap. 1, and Henry R. Glick, "The Politics of State-Court Reform," in Philip L. Dubois, ed., *The Politics of Judicial Reform* (Lexington, Mass.: Lexington Books, 1982).

57. This definition of court unification is derived from Berkson and Carbon, *Court Unification*. For an alternative formulation, see Allan Ashman and Jeffrey Parness, "The Concept of a Unified Court System," *DePaul Law Review* 24 (1974): 1–41.

58. Frank Munger, "Movements for Court Reform: A Preliminary Interpretation," in Dubois, *Politics of Judicial Reform*.

59. Larry Berkson has developed rankings of the states based on both individual components of court unification and their levels of overall unification through 1976, and our conclusions about levels of trial court consolidation, as well as about other components of court unification, are based in large part on his data. See Berkson, "Unified Court Systems: A Ranking of the States," *Justice System Journal* 3 (Spring 1978): 264–80. The discussion and tabulation by Berkson and Carbon, *Court Unification*, pp. 208–09, are also useful.

successful, most state court systems have taken steps in this direction. All states but Mississippi have institutionalized systemwide planning efforts, and many have authorized their supreme courts to prescribe rules for the operations of state courts and to supervise their operations.[60] Few states have introduced centralized budgeting or taken over the financing of the courts, yet reformers have achieved some partial successes.[61] Other reform proposals such as merit selection of judges have been widely adopted.[62] In essence, during the postwar period, reformers have experienced considerable success in restructuring and reforming state judicial systems.

The adoption of these reforms has coincided with the dissolution of the scholarly consensus about their efficacy.[63] But whatever its contributions to a more effective administration of justice, judicial reform has had a significant impact. Most obviously, with its emphasis on managerial centralization, court unification has enhanced the administrative control exercised by state supreme courts over lower courts.[64] In many states the chief justice can reassign judges from one court to another to combat delay and to distribute caseloads more evenly. In some the chief justice can establish budgetary priorities and determine the allocation of funds to courts throughout the state. In addition, through vigorous use of their rule-making power, state high

60. For discussion of centralized management and centralized rule making and for rankings of the states on these factors, see Berkson, "Unified Court Systems," and Berkson and Carbon, *Court Unification,* pp. 210–13. The Mississippi experience with centralized management is analyzed in John W. Winkle, "Judicial Planning and the Politics of Nonrenewal," in Dubois, *Politics of Judicial Reform.*

61. Again the basic source of data is Berkson, "Unified Court Systems." Other important sources on centralized budgeting and state financing include Carl Baar, "The Limited Trend Toward Court Financing and Unitary Budgeting in the States," in Larry Berkson, Steven Hays, and Susan Carbon, eds., *Managing the State Courts* (St. Paul: West, 1977), and Baar, "The Scope and Limits of Court Reform," *Justice System Journal* 5 (Spring 1980): 274–90.

62. See the discussion in Glick, "Promise and Performance of the Missouri Plan."

63. Studies critical of the claims for court unification include G. Alan Tarr, "The Effects of Court Unification on Court Performance: A Preliminary Assessment," *Judicature* 64 (March 1981): 356–68; Carl Baar and Thomas Henderson, "Alternative Models for the Organization of State-Court Systems," in Philip L. Dubois, ed., *The Analysis of Judicial Reform* (Lexington, Mass.: Lexington Books, 1982); and Geoff Gallas, "The Conventional Wisdom of State Court Administration: A Critical Assessment and an Alternative Approach," *Justice System Journal* 2 (Spring 1976): 35–56.

64. As we shall see, this is true of both Alabama and New Jersey.

courts can exert control over the legal profession and over the operations of lower courts.

Judicial reform has also enhanced the independence of the state judiciary. By vesting the rule-making power in the state supreme court, reformers forestalled legislative intervention in a field of particular concern to the judiciary, and even "restraintist" supreme courts have been vigilant in protecting their institutional prerogatives. Centralizing managerial and budgetary authority has also limited the intrusion of local political concerns into the operations of the courts. And by assigning chief justices major responsibility for the administration of justice in their states, reformers have enhanced their ability to speak with authority for the entire judicial branch.

Yet in many states the indirect effects of judicial reform have been far more crucial. Enactment of the reform agenda has usually required state legislative action, constitutional amendments, or both. Typically reformers have had to combat both the force of inertia—judicial reform is not an issue that immediately commands either popular or legislative attention—and the opposition of groups that either benefited from the old system or feared the effects of centralization. In some states legal professionals have quietly engineered reforms without making major changes in the personnel or perspectives of the bench. In others, however, judicial reformers have succeeded only after carefully mounted political campaigns conducted outside the usual partisan politics of the state and spearheaded by a single leader or small coterie of reformers.

The success of these campaigns has often led to legal changes that went far beyond the concern for administrative reforms that initially prompted them. For one thing, the critical analysis of the workings of the state's judicial system necessary to create a movement for reform has prompted a reexamination of the substantive law. In addition, opening the judicial system to change in one sphere can have a catalytic effect in other spheres.

To understand why, one must examine the impact that movements for judicial reform can have on the composition of high courts. Successful reform campaigns catapult their leaders to statewide prominence; their stature and demonstrated concern for the administration of justice have made them obvious candidates to fill vacancies on state high courts. Often these reformers have brought to the court a jurisprudential perspective decisively different from that which had previously prevailed, and thus court reform has begotten reform in the law. Their elevation to the bench signals a changed legal environment, which itself is a factor in the recruiting of new and different types of people to the court. In essence the battle for judicial reform, where successful, has often brought the reformers to power.

Comparing State Supreme Courts

Our decision to focus on a limited number of courts raises basic questions, such as: How representative are the courts we have selected for examination? and to what extent can we generalize from our findings about those courts' roles in state and nation?

In the selection of courts for our study, two considerations were paramount. First, the states selected had to have established an intermediate court of appeals prior to the beginning of our investigation. The presence of an intermediate court of appeals does not by itself guarantee a state supreme court a manageable caseload, relieve it of routine appeals, or ensure opportunities for active policy involvement. On the other hand, the absence of an intermediate court of appeals virtually ensures that a state supreme court will face tremendous caseload pressures. Thus the institution of an intermediate appellate court may be a necessary, if not sufficient, condition for a state supreme court to undertake more than error correction. Equally important, if the institution of an intermediate appellate court can make a major difference, it is probably inappropriate to compare high courts in states that have such courts to supreme courts in states that do not. If this is correct, then there is ample justification for restricting our attention to states with intermediate appellate courts. Since most states have established such courts and the trend to do so seems to be accelerating, such a focus is necessary to ensure the contemporary applicability of our findings. Moreover, since intermediate appellate courts are almost invariably found in the most populous and diverse states, the broader generalizability of our findings requires that we concentrate on states that have such courts.

Second, the states chosen from those that had intermediate appellate courts in 1945 must display political, legal, cultural, and demographic diversity. Needless to say, no set of three courts can be completely representative, nor is that our claim. The supreme courts of Alabama, Ohio, and New Jersey operate in sufficiently different political and

Table 2. Legal and Political System Characteristics: Alabama, Ohio, and New Jersey

	Alabama	Ohio	New Jersey
Legal System			
Number of justices	9	7	7
Mode of initial selection	Partisan election	Nonpartisan election; partisan primary	Gubernatorial appointment
Tenure of justices	6 years	6 years	7 years; to retirement age after reappointment
Mode of subsequent selection	Partisan election	Nonpartisan election	Gubernatorial appointment
Year intermediate court of appeals established	1911	1851	1844
Year state judiciary article adopted	1901	1851	1947
Type of state supreme court*	2	2	3
Population of state (1980)	3,900,000	10,800,000	7,400,000
Percentage nonwhite population (1980)	25	11	16
State cluster†	3	2	2
Party competition‡	One-party Democratic	Two-party	Two-party
Political culture (dominant strain)§	Traditionalistic	Individualistic	Individualistic

* *Type of state supreme court* refers to the typology developed by Robert Kagan et al., "The Evolution of State Supreme Courts," *Michigan Law Review* 76 (1978): 981–87. Type 2 states are medium-sized (over one million people) and large states in which the state supreme court has little case-selecting discretion or has a heavy

legal contexts that we can expect them to reveal the sorts of uniformity and diversity characteristic of American judicial federalism (table 2).

Alabama is the self-proclaimed heart of Dixie. Until recently, it was a one-party state—based on data from 1962 to 1973, only Mississippi was more thoroughly one-party Democratic. Thus although judges are elected on a partisan ballot, the major contest takes place in the Democratic primary. According to Daniel Elazar, a traditionalistic political culture has dominated the state, and the high court itself for many years reflected the dominant conservative (rather than populist) element of the state's politics. For the most part it devoted its greatest attention to coping with the case pressures generated by its broad mandatory jurisdiction, emphasizing error correction and deferentially avoiding policy initiation. When presented with political issues, it followed the lead of the state's legislative and executive branches, and in the 1950s and 1960s it aided and abetted the state's "massive resistance" to desegregation. Since reform of the state ju-

---

caseload. Type 3 states are medium-sized or large states in which the supreme court exercises substantial control over its caseload.

† *State cluster* refers to a demographic/socioeconomic categorization of states based on "data for population, industrialization, urbanization, per capita income, and racial composition . . . as well as evaluations of legislative innovations and other variables that seemed to bear some relation to the legal business of a state court system." See Robert Kagan, et al., "The Business of State Supreme Courts," *Stanford Law Review* 30 (1977): 125. Cluster 2 refers to "the most urban industrialized states," and cluster 3 to "the Southern states."

‡ Rankings on levels of interparty competition are derived from Austin Ranney, "Parties in State Politics," in Herbert Jacob and Kenneth N. Vines, eds., *Politics in the American States; A Comparative Analysis*, 3d ed. (Boston: Little, Brown, 1976), p. 61, table 4, which measures levels of interparty competition from 1962 to 1973.

§ The *political culture* categorizations are drawn from Daniel J. Elazar, *American Federalism: A View from the States* (New York: Thomas Y. Crowell, 1966), p. 97, fig. 3, and p. 108, fig. 4. The individualistic political culture views politics as a means for individuals to advance themselves rather than to pursue conceptions of the public good. It emphasizes limiting community intervention into private affairs, and thus politicians undertake political innovations only when prompted by overwhelming public demand. The moralistic political culture encourages government intervention into the economic and social life of the community as a means of promoting the good society. It spawns a politics dominated by issue-concerns and deprecates strong party ties. The traditionalistic political culture is rooted in a paternalistic conception of the commonwealth. It seeks to sustain rule by an established elite and the maintenance of social order by emphasizing family and social ties in political recruitment.

dicial system in the 1970s, however, the Alabama Supreme Court has sought to steer a somewhat different course, ceasing its overt defiance of the United States Supreme Court and showing an unprecedented willingness to consider innovations in tort law and to overturn past rulings. The appointment and subsequent election of the state's first black justice symbolize the changes taking place in the state and on the court.

Ohio is a heavily industrialized and unionized midwestern state but also has a significant agricultural sector. As befits the state's individualistic political culture, politics in Ohio is neither issue-oriented nor intensely ideological. On the other hand, its two political parties do compete on fairly even terms; and because the Democratic party maintains strong ties to the labor movement and the Republican party to business and farming interests, political conflicts can be intense. Judges in Ohio are elected on nonpartisan ballots after winning nomination in party primaries—this system, unique to Ohio, gives a strongly partisan flavor to judicial recruitment. The limited research on the Ohio court has found that partisanship carries over into judicial deliberations and decisions—the justices often divide along party lines, especially in cases involving politically volatile issues such as reapportionment and workers' compensation, and dissent on the court is frequent and rancorous. Yet the Ohio court has rarely been in the forefront of doctrinal innovation, and when confronted with civil liberties claims, it has shown a marked tendency to defer to the legislature.

Like Ohio, New Jersey is a heavily urbanized northern state with a highly competitive two-party system. Although an individualistic political culture predominates in the state, the New Jersey Supreme Court operates in a unique legal culture that reflects the reform efforts of Chief Justice Arthur Vanderbilt in the late 1940s. The court currently enjoys a national reputation for progressivism, innovation, and solicitude for individual rights. Justices are appointed by the governor with the consent of the senate and, after reappointment, may serve until mandatory retirement at age seventy, thereby ensuring stability in the membership of the court. Narrow partisan concerns appear to play little role in the selection process, and the court's active policy role has not prevented a high degree of consensus among the justices. Thus far, the court's far-reaching and politically controversial decisions have not produced determined efforts to undermine its independence.

Because of the diversity of these courts and of the political and legal environments in which they operate, our study documents the full variety of roles played by state supreme courts and the regularities that may be found even among diverse courts. By itself, of course, this analysis does not permit definitive statements about how representative any of these courts are, and in the final chapter we shall draw upon the extant literature on other state supreme courts to offer some conclusions on this issue.

A historical perspective is essential for analyzing the activities of state supreme courts, and the four decades since World War II should be sufficient to incorporate this dimension. The decades since World War II also coincide with what the literature on judicial federalism has identified as three distinct periods in the relations between state supreme courts and the U.S. Supreme Court. The first period, which began prior to 1945 and lasted until the early 1960s, involved a rough division of labor between state and federal courts, with state courts exercising the primary responsibility for the protection of individual liberties, particularly the rights of defendants. The second period, from the early 1960s to the early 1970s, involved intensified interaction between the Supreme Court and state high courts, as those courts responded to the innovative decisions of the Warren Court, particularly its decisions incorporating various procedural guarantees of the Bill of Rights and expanding their scope. The third period, which began in the early 1970s, involved a reinvigoration of state constitutional law by state supreme courts (the new judicial federalism), as some courts sought to provide more extensive protection for individual liberties in the wake of retrenchment by the Burger Court. By focusing on the work of state supreme courts throughout these three periods, we can determine the validity of the proclaimed shifts in the roles played by state supreme courts in vertical judicial federalism.

Initially we assumed that the appropriate approach for this study was to collect and analyze data on all cases decided by our three courts during selected years within each time period. It soon became apparent, however, that these case data, by themselves, could tell us relatively little about the roles our three courts have played within their states and nationally. Therefore, instead of focusing on these data in the aggregate, we have used them to identify cases that deserved more detailed consideration, and we have also culled legal sources to identify other leading rulings of the postwar era. In addition, we have looked to newspapers, legal journals, and political histories to furnish background information about the states and the rulings of their supreme courts. We have supplemented our case data and other materials with interviews, both of former and current justices of the Alabama and Ohio supreme courts and of other authorities on the three courts and their operations.[65]

---

65. The rules of the New Jersey Supreme Court precluded formal interviews of the sitting justices. However, we have had some informal contacts with members of the court, and our inability to conduct interviews was less serious for the New Jersey court, since its prominence has ensured full legal and periodical coverage of its rulings and activities.

THREE

ALABAMA: THE COURT THAT CAME IN FROM THE COLD

"When I went to national conferences," an Alabama judge once confessed, "I would kind of mumble about where I came from."[1] And for good reasons. Alabama's judicial system had remained virtually intact in its nineteenth-century form, "largely immunized" from the institutional, organizational, and administrative changes occurring in other states. "[O]ur court system was one of the nation's worst," candidly admits a current justice,

> with its justices of the peace; no age limit for judicial tenure; no mechanism for the disciplining of judges; nonuniformity of court structure; noncurrent court calendars; and a salary and retirement system that discouraged new judicial talent. [And] the executive and legislative branches seemed perfectly content to accept with aloofness the system's inefficiency, waste, and mediocrity.[2]

The state ranked among the three states least affected by bar professionalism.[3] Its highest court, "in total control of old men" operating under "antiquated," "petty," and "ludicrous" rules, held something of a national record for the length of time it took to decide cases. The court's reputation outside the state was further diminished by its eager participation in Alabama's fierce resistance to the civil rights movement, especially as the movement entered the federal judicial arena.

1. Quoted in Robert Martin, "Alabama Courts—Six Years of Change," *Alabama Lawyer* 38 (1977): 21
2. Robert J. Frye, *The Alabama Supreme Court: An Institutional View* (University, Ala.: University of Alabama Press, 1969), p. 3. Richard L. Jones, "Reflections from the Bench," *Alabama Lawyer* 40 (1979): 163.
3. Kenneth N. Vines and Herbert Jacob, "State Courts and Public Policy," in Jacobs and Vines, eds., *Politics in the American States* (Boston: Little, Brown, 1976), p. 250.

"Among state supreme courts," wrote Anthony Lewis, "Alabama's was considered to have a particularly notable record for cynical disregard of the law."[4] In the American judicial system, which by its nature allows for considerable diversity among state and federal courts, the Alabama judiciary was at best an embarrassment, at worst a pariah.

By the 1970s all of this would change. Under the leadership of Howell Heflin the judicial system was modernized. A virtually complete turnover brought a new breed of justices to the high court, including a new chief justice, Howell Heflin, all determined to create respect for Alabama courts and for their court in particular.[5] The extent, significance, and drama of the transformation, cannot be appreciated without a detailed understanding of what some of the current justices refer to as the "old court"[6] and its largely discredited and repudiated works.

"THE OLD COURT"

The Justices

For the better part of the twentieth century the Alabama Supreme Court's membership "reflected a remarkable degree of cultural and social homogeneity." The justices—white, male, Protestant (Baptist, Methodist, and Presbyterian), identified in some degree with the

---

4. Neil R. Peirce, *The Deep South States of America* (New York: Norton, 1972), p. 238. Frye, *The Alabama Supreme Court*, p. 3; Charles D. Cole, "Judicial Reform in Alabama: A Survey," *Cumberland-Samford Law Review* 4 (1973–74): 50; "Push But Not Shove," *Time Magazine*, September 27, 1976, p. 88, col. 2. "Alabama Court Congestion: Observations and Suggestions from an Empirical Study," *Alabama Law Review* 21 (1968): 150. Whatever the court's post–World War II problems, it was ranked, according to various indicia, sixteenth among the high courts of the forty-eight states. Rodney Q. Mott, "Judicial Influence," *American Political Science Review* 30 (1936): 295–315. A more recent rating places it in twenty-sixth place of the fifty states. Gregory A. Caldeira, "On the Reputation of State Supreme Courts," *Political Behavior* 5 (1983): 83–108. Anthony Lewis, quoted in Frye, *The Alabama Supreme Court*, p. 88, n. 7.

5. Howell Heflin, "The Dawning of a New Era," *Cumberland-Samford Law Review* 3 (1972): 1–7.

6. The phrase was frequently employed by members of the Alabama Supreme Court. Interviews, March 9–12, 1982, Montgomery, Ala. "We just sat on our behinds and followed *Plessy*," said one of the justices, "and didn't redistrict as we should." *Plessy* v. *Ferguson*, 163 U.S. 537 (1896), established the racial doctrine of separate-but-equal.

Democratic party—received their legal training in the South, for the most part at the University of Alabama Law School. One-half were initially appointed, subsequently winning, along with the rest of their colleagues, easy and usually uncontested elections.[7] Roughly half arrived on the bench with either prior judicial experience or public service in a legal capacity, such as attorney general or legal adviser to the governor.[8] Two-thirds came from and represented the most reactionary region and elements of the state, the so-called black-belt counties. The disproportionate representation of these counties on the court followed the pattern in the state legislature, where counties containing less than 14 percent of the state's population elected almost 30 percent of the legislature.[9] Among the old court's most noteworthy members was Thomas Lawson, whose tenure spanned thirty years (by no means an unusual term for an Alabama justice),[10] and who is best remembered for handling the state's case when the

7. Frye, *The Alabama Supreme Court*, p. 29 and chap. 3 passim.

8. Justice Hugh Maddox's term spans the old and new courts. He served as Governor George Wallace's legal adviser and was described by an unsympathetic news reporter as a "Baptist boy with an aversion to alcohol and the theory of evolution," "wearing a dour houndlike expression with a stitched brow . . ." and "cultivating the careful gloom of a funeral director." Marshall Frady, *Wallace* (New York: New American Library, 1968), p. 215. When told of the description Justice Maddox was amused and stated that he could not recall Frady. Alcohol and evolution were not discussed in our interview, and the interviewer found the justice to be a thoughtful, scholarly conservative with an open and inquiring mind who was extraordinarily generous with his time. His demeanor is dignified, gently humorous—and hardly funereal.

9. Frye, *The Alabama Supreme Court*, p. 33; James L. Larson, *Reapportionement in Alabama* (University, Ala.: University of Alabama Press, 1955), pp. 24–25. As a prominent civil rights attorney explained, "Alabama's supreme court justices are elected. During the 1950s and 1960s, there was no way an individual could have been elected to the supreme court, or appointed by Governor Wallace to any vacancies which might arise, who did not espouse a states rights, segregationist anti-federal government philosophy. Thus, lawyers who were willing to handle civil liberties cases quickly saw the futility of attempting to vindicate rights in state courts. This realization was amply borne out on those few occasions when federal questions were raised on appeal (including criminal cases): the issues were either not dealt with (see *New York Times* v. *Sullivan*) or were resolved adversely to the defendant." Letter from Howard Mandell, Montgomery, Alabama, Feb. 1, 1982.

10. For the tenure of the justices, see *Alabama Appellate Courts*, 7th ed. (Montgomery, Ala.: Alabama Supreme Court and State Law Library, 1983). Among the justices was F. Scott Fitzgerald's father-in-law. Zelda Fitzgerald's obituary, *Chicago Tribune*, June 19, 1986.

Scottsboro Boys appealed their death sentences for rape to the United States Supreme Court.[11]

Race and Criminal Appeals Cases

The racist view of the Alabama justices had long been evident in criminal appeals. The Alabama high court consistently sustained the convictions of blacks, even if obtained by all-white juries amid expressions of public hostility at the trial.[12] Some of those convictions, including those of the Scottsboro defendants, were successfully appealed to the United States Supreme Court. In one such case, remanded by the Court, an all-black jury was selected and returned a

11. *Powell* v. *State*, 131 So.2d 201 (Ala. 1932); rev'd. and remanded, 287 U.S. 45 (1932). The case became a cause célebre and had significant political connotations. The Court's opinion provides a graphic description of the events surrounding the arrest, pretrial procedures, and the trial. The ruling established the principle that the federal Constitution commands that effective counsel be provided in capital cases.

12. *Ball* v. *State*, 42 So.2d 626 (Ala. 1949) raised questions about racial exclusion from the jury, public hostility at the trial, and inadequate counsel; cert. denied, 339 U.S. 959 (1950). *Arrington* v. *State*, 43 So.2d 644 (Ala. 1949) cert. denied 339 U.S. 950 (1950), was appealed on grounds not only of racial exclusion from the jury, but also of involuntary confession and denial of counsel. *Fikes* v. *State*, 81 So.2d 303 (Ala. 1951), was reversed not on grounds of jury composition, but coerced confession, 352 U.S. 191 (1958). The case has been aptly described as follows: "Detained, after his arrest, in a prison far from home, denied a preliminary hearing required under Alabama law, and without counsel or visits from friends, except one from his father, defendant was interrogated intermittently over a period of eleven days, and made his first confession on the fifth after arrest and the second on the tenth day, whereupon he was arraigned." *The Constitution of the United States* (Washington, D.C.: U.S. Government Printing Office, 1964), p. 1247. *Reeves* v. *Alabama*, 68 So.2d 14 (Ala. 1953), was reversed on grounds of coerced confession, not jury composition. 348 U.S. 891 (1954). Some jury selection cases made the rounds of the state appellate and federal courts in protracted litigation. See, for example, *Washington* v. *Alabama*, 112 So.2d 179 (Ala. 1959), 148 So.2d 206 (Ala. 1962), 227 So.2d. 805 (Ala. App. 1969), 245 So.2d 842 (Ala. App. 1971), 245 F. Supp. 116 (M.D. Ala. 1965), rev'd. on other grounds, 364 F.2d 618 (5th Cir. 1966). Another defendant did not fare as well. *Aaron* v. *State*, 122 So.2d 360 (Ala. 1969), *Ex Parte Aaron*, 155 So.2d 334 (Ala. 1962), cert. denied, 375 U.S. 898 (1963), 214 So.2d 327 (Ala. 1968); *Aaron* v. *Capps*, 507 F.2d. 685 (5th Cir. 1975). In *Swain* v. *Alabama*, 156 So.2d 368 (Ala. 1963) the U.S. Supreme Court agreed with the Alabama high court that there was no proof of systematic and "purposeful discrimination on race alone," 380 U.S. 202, 208 (1968). Critical commentary on *Swain* includes "Swain v. Alabama: A Constitutional Blueprint for the Perpetuation of the All-White Jury," *Virginia Law Review* 52 (1966): 1157–75. *Swain* was overruled in *Batson* v. *Kentucky*, 54 U.S.L.W. 4425 (1986).

verdict of not guilty. (This is thought to be the first time since Reconstruction that an all-black jury tried a black for murder.) What is perhaps most remarkable is that *any* of these cases were appealed. As noted by a federal appellate court, few lawyers were willing to risk careers and social position by raising the issue of black exclusion from juries. In addition "[c]onscientious southern lawyers often reason[ed] that the prejudicial effects on their clients of raising the issue far outweigh[ed] any practical protection in the particular case." And the court's obdurate insistence that the exclusion of blacks from juries was coincidental, not systematic, indicates that such attorneys were, from the start, faced with an all but hopeless task. In one case, which also involved the question of a confession obtained under egregious circumstances from a mentally ill black, the court blandly asserted that black defendants whose victims were black did not want black jurors, and that, furthermore, the most "intelligent" and "competent" blacks in the county could generally be found only among occupational groups excluded from jury service. The remainder were, by the court's lights, not qualified, for "[t]he evidence shows that a large majority of the Negroes are ignorant, with little or no education and low moral character, and there is much venereal disease among them and a large percentage of illegitimacy."[13]

In cases involving black defendants and white victims, the court unfailingly highlighted the race issue. Thus it upheld imposition of the death penalty on " 'Big Time' Coleman, a Negro tried and convicted in the first degree murder of John D. 'Screwdriver' Johnson, a white mechanic." Convictions were regularly affirmed for "men of the colored race" and "Negroes" accused of raping "white" women and girls. One such defendant, Samuel Taylor, alias "Iron Man," had, according to (later repudiated) trial testimony referred to in the court's opinion, made known his plan "to go hunting for some white stuff."[14]

13. *Norris* v. *State*, 156 So.2d 556 (Ala. 1934), 294 U.S. 587 (1935). *Coleman* v. *State*, 195 So.2d 800 (Ala. 1965), rev'd and remanded, 389 U.S. 22 (1967). *United States* v. *Harpole*, 263 F.2d 71, 82 (5th Cir. 1959); *Aaron* v. *Capps*, 507 F.2d 685 (5th Cir. 1975). *Harpole* quoted in "Constitutional Law. Right to Be Tried Before Jury From Which Members of One's Race Have Not Been Systematically Excluded," *Alabama Law Review* 16 (1963–64): 119. *Fikes* v. *State*, 81 So.2d 303, 306 (Ala. 1951)

14. *Coleman* v. *State*, 164 So.2d 704, 705 (Ala. 1963). *Arrington* v. *State*, 43 So.2d 644, 654 (Ala. 1949), cert. denied, 339 U.S. 950 (1950); *Swain* v. *Alabama*, 156 So.2d 368 (Ala. 1963). *Taylor* v. *State*, 97 So.2d 802, 803 (Ala. 1957). Here a new trial was not ordered despite a prosecution witness's repudiation of his trial testimony.

One case, in which the court sustained the death sentence for a black man accused of a $1.98 robbery, is particularly telling. Here, in addition to the robbery charge, it was alleged that "the Negro" had attempted to rape the "white" victim. Although her testimony was exceedingly vague and contradictory, the court had no difficulty with the trial court's refusal to permit a sexual assault claim.[15] And considering that "when in Alabama a Negro was accused of rape he was on his way to the electric chair," it may be surmised that the alleged rape attempt, not the robbery, accounted for the severity of the sentence.[16] Although the case brought national and international opprobrium to the Alabama Supreme Court, to a great extent it represented business as usual.

Civil Rights Cases

The Alabama high court's response to the civil rights movement, to federal rights legislation, and to *Brown* v. *Board of Education* and its implementation by lower federal courts echoed that of the state's political leadership.[17] The court advanced the cause of the "Dixiecrat

15. *Wilson* v. *State*, 105 S.2d 66 (Ala. 1958); Frye, *The Alabama Supreme Court*, p. 88. "[I]t is not entirely clear what the evidence of the attempted rape tended to prove in connection with the crime of robbery which was the only crime for which the defendant was tried and which was, by the state's own evidence, complete before the assault took place." *Alabama Law Review* 11 (1958): 172.

16. Peirce, *The Deep South States of America*, p. 248. There is no record of an execution in this case. It is likely that Governor Jim Folsom commuted the sentence, as he often did when blacks received the death penalty. That capital punishment was meted out disproportionately to blacks is borne out by statistics that coincide with the days of various old courts. Between 1927 and 1969, 151 executions took place in Alabama. Of those electrocuted 124 were black males and 1 a white woman. At least three were seventeen-year-olds. Ira De Ment, "A Plea for the Condemned" *Alabama Lawyer* 29 (1969): 450. De Ment prevailed on occasion for a gubernatorial commutation. For a discussion of his role in the movement to reform Alabama's mental institutions, see Tinsley E. Yarbrough, *Judge Frank Johnson and Human Rights in Alabama* (University, Ala.: University of Alabama Press, 1981), pp. 161–63. Bad as things were for black defendants in Alabama, even that state's high court, during this disgraceful period, occasionally redeemed itself. In *Smith* v. *State*, 24 So.2d 546 (Ala. 1945), it was held that a black defendant's rights were violated when he was asked to stand up in the courtroom so that he could be identified by the white woman whom he was accused of raping.

17. 347 U.S. 483 (1954), holding that the Equal Protection Clause of the Fourteenth Amendment prohibits de jure racial segregation. *Brown* acted as something of a catalyst in the Deep South, reviving the racial animosities and resentment of the federal government that had somewhat subsided after President Truman's electoral victory in 1948 and the failure of the "Dixiecrat revolt" within

revolt" of 1948, providing "another jolt" for Democratic party loyalists, when it invalidated, on Twelfth Amendment grounds, a state law requiring candidates for presidential elector in the primary election to support the party's nominee.[18] Electors, said the court, were "free agents," and neither laws nor party directives could demand a so-called "loyalty pledge."[19] The court played an absolutely indispensable role in the state's "counterattack" late in the 1950s against the National Association for the Advancement of Colored People (NAACP), the organization directly responsible for successful federal court challenges to segregationist policies in the Deep South.[20] The state's tactics included a demand that the NAACP produce its

---

the Democratic party. William D. Barnard, *Dixiecrats and Democrats: Alabama Politics 1942–1950* (University, Ala: University of Alabama Press, 1974), pp. 144–45.

18. Ibid., p. 131.

19. *Ray v. Blair*, 57 So.2d 795 (Ala. 1948), rev'd. 343 U.S. 154 (1952). An address by the president of the Alabama state bar association captures the flavor of the times and gives a fair indication of the attitudes of bench and bar:

> In our State, even after the people of Alabama in the Democratic Primaries of 1948 had spoken with a thunderous voice in opposition to all efforts of would-be dictators in Washington to direct our purely local affairs, there were those,— some holding high office,—who almost raised Heaven and Earth to see that the will of the people was thwarted and who tried to force our eleven Presidential Electors who were nominated by the people of Alabama in our Democratic Primaries by an overwhelming avalanche of votes, to violate the solemn pledge which they had given to the people of our State that under no circumstances would they even consider for the office of President of the United States, Harry S. Truman, or any other man who advocated his unthinkable Anti-Southern Hate Program, frequently referred to as a "Civil Rights" Program.
>
> Be it said to the glory of the lawyers of Alabama that when those who had trampled under foot the wishes and instructions of the people of this State, and endeavored to force our Presidential Electors to violate their most solemn oath, lawyers in all parts of Alabama sprang up and offered their services to our Presidential Electors to fight any such immoral plan as that proposed by some of those in high official position. These lawyers, without a single exception, refused to accept any compensation whatsoever for their services and it is to the credit of the bar of this State that through their efforts each and everyone of the almost countless suits filed against our Presidential Elector in Circuit Courts throughout Alabama, in the Supreme Court of Alabama, in the District Courts of the United States and even in the Supreme Court of the United States, were thrown out of Court by just and fair Judges. The will of the people was then carried out, as it should have been. [Gessner T. McCorvey, "Annual Address President State Bar 1949," *Alabama Lawyer* 10 (1949): 374–75].

20. For a discussion of the NAACP's difficulties throughout the South, see Walter F. Murphy, "The South Counter-Attacks: The Anti-NAACP Laws," *Western Political Quarterly* 11 (1959): 371–89.

membership list, a routine requirement for foreign corporations doing business in the state, but one that would have exposed NAACP members to harassment, economic reprisals, and probably worse. Failure to comply carried with it expulsion from the state, which was, of course, the state's objective. The court's maneuvers are strikingly illustrative of its eagerness to align itself with the most resistant and extreme elements in the state.[21]

The Alabama high court initially refused to stay a circuit court's temporary injunction against further NAACP activities in the state. In three subsequent rulings, based on procedural grounds, it sustained the lower court's contempt citation and $100,000 fine for failure to produce membership lists—despite the fact that all other requests for information had been complied with and despite the efforts of NAACP lawyers, as one despairingly noted, to follow requisite legal procedures: "First they tell us a motion for stay of execution is improper, and we should have brought certiorari; then we are told the certiorari petition is insufficient; and finally they tell us that certiorari has been the wrong remedy all along—we should have brought mandamus."[22]

With all avenues of state relief thereby closed, the NAACP went on to win a partial victory in the U.S. Supreme Court. The Court held that the federal constitutional guarantee of freedom of association protected against membership disclosure, that the Alabama high court could not trifle with its own rules of procedure and long-standing precedent ("novelty in procedural requirements cannot be permitted to thwart review in this court . . . applied for by those who, in justified reliance on previous decisions, seek vindication in state courts of their rights"), and that the Alabama Supreme Court must remand the case to the circuit court.[23] The Alabama high court, engaging in numerous delaying tactics, not only refused to forward the U.S. Supreme Court's mandate, but sustained the contempt

21. The account and case citations are based on George R. Osborne, "The NAACP in Alabama," in C. Herman Pritchett and Alan F. Westin, eds., *The Third Branch of Government* (New York: Harcourt Brace and World, 1963); "Freedom of Association: Constitutional Right or Judicial Technique?," *Virginia Law Review* 46 (1969): 730–55; "The Supreme Court, 1957 Term," *Harvard Law Review* 72 (1958): 193–95; Murphy, "The South Counter-Attacks;" Michael Meltsner, "Southern Appellate Courts: A Dead End," in Leon Friedman, ed., *Southern Justice* (New York: Random House, 1965).

22. *Ex Parte NAACP*, 91 So.2d 214 (Ala. 1956); 91 So.2d 220 (Ala. 1956); 91 So.2d 221 (Ala. 1956). The NAACP attorney is quoted in Osborne, "The NAACP in Alabama," pp. 169–70.

23. *NAACP* v. *Alabama*, 357 U.S. 449, 457–58 (1958).

citation, chiding the Court for its "mistaken premise" that failure to produce the membership lists constituted the sole basis of the contempt citation.[24] Following a second order to remand from the U.S. Supreme Court, the Alabama Supreme Court continued to find ways of not forwarding the mandate.[25] After litigation at all three levels of the federal courts, the circuit court held a hearing and made the temporary injunction permanent.[26] On appeal, the Alabama Supreme Court dismissed the petition on the ground that the NAACP, by combining arguments with and without merit in the same brief, had again failed to follow proper procedures. For anyone should know that the Alabama high court "had a rule of long-standing and frequent application that where unrelated assignments of error are argued together and one is without merit, the other will not be considered." To which an increasingly exasperated U.S. Supreme Court retorted: "The consideration of asserted constitutional rights may not be thwarted by the simple recitation that there has not been compliance with a procedural rule with which there has been compliance both in substance and form in every real sense."[27] By the time the U.S. Supreme Court (and the NAACP) prevailed,[28] eight years had elapsed. Legally, the NAACP remained in business in the state. In actuality, thanks to the protracted litigation and the uncertainty surrounding its continued existence, the association's effectiveness had come to an end in Alabama. For this achievement the Alabama Supreme Court could claim a major share of the credit.

In the early and mid-1960s Alabama, like other southern states, was confronted with the phenomenon of civil rights demonstrations and marches. And once again the Alabama high court performed yeoman's service. It sustained convictions against Martin Luther King, Jr., among others, for the Good Friday and Easter Sunday marches

24. Osborne, "The NAACP in Alabama," pp. 186–87; 109 So.2d 138 (Ala. 1959).

25. 360 U.S. 240 (1959); Osborne, "The NAACP in Alabama," pp. 188–90.

26. *NAACP* v. *Gallion*, 190 F. Supp. 583 (M.D. Ala.); 290 F.2d 337 (5th Cir. 1961); 368 U.S. 19 (1961); Meltsner, "Southern Appellate Courts," pp. 141–45.

27. *NAACP* v. *State*, 150 So.2d 677 , 679 (Ala. 1961). *NAACP* v. *Alabama ex rel. Flowers*, 377 U.S. 288, 297 (1961).

28. Alabama complied with the U.S. Supreme Court's orders, 167 So.2d 171 (Ala. 1964), realizing, no doubt, that the Court meant business. ("Should we unhappily be mistaken in our belief that the Supreme Court of Alabama will not implement this disposition, leave is given the Association to apply to this court for further appropriate relief.") *NAACP* v. *Alabama ex rel. Flowers*, 377 U.S. 288, 310 (1961).

held in Birmingham.[29] The first case, *Walker* v. *Birmingham*, involved defiance of a court-ordered injunction against proceeding with the planned marches. The second, *Shuttlesworth* v. *Birmingham*,[30] involved parading without a permit. In *Walker* the court, employing skills honed in the NAACP cases, managed to hold off its decision for two years after the appeal was filed, a period considered "unusually long" "even for the court's standards," as well as for Justice James Coleman, to whom the opinion had been assigned on a random basis, and who was "famous for . . . long delays" in completing his tasks.[31] When the court finally got around to acting, it rested its ruling on the fact that the march leaders had neither sought to dissolve the injunction (which would understandably have failed) nor had complied with the law by requesting a permit to hold the march (which would not have been granted).[32] The U.S. Supreme Court, in a 5-4 ruling, agreed that the First Amendment issue could not be litigated until the circuit court's order, which had sustained the validity of the permit ordinance, had been subject to the processes of orderly review.[33]

While *Walker* was pending before the Alabama Supreme Court, the Alabama intermediate appellate court held in *Shuttlesworth* that the parade permit ordinance was overly broad in that it gave officials administering it unfettered discretion, and that it had indeed been administered in a racially discriminatory manner—a judgment with

29. For background, an account of events, the strategies of the civil rights leaders and Birmingham officials, and the reaction of the U.S. Department of Justice to the proposed marches, see Alan F. Westin and Barry Mahoney, *The Trial of Martin Luther King* (New York: Crowell, 1974).

30. 180 So.2d 377 (Ala. App. 1965); rev'd., 206 So.2d 348 (Ala. 1965); rev'd., 394 U.S. 147 (1969). 181 So.2d 493 (Ala. 1965); aff'd., 388 U.S. 307 (1967).

31. Westin and Mahoney, *The Trial of Martin Luther King*, pp. 83–88.

32. *Walker* v. *Birmingham*, 181 So.2d 493 (Ala. 1965).

33. *Walker* v. *Birmingham*, 388 U.S. 307 (1967). For a discussion of *Walker* from the perspective of the views and propensities of the individual Supreme Court justices, see Alice Fleetwood Bartee, *Cases Lost Causes Won* (New York: St. Martin's Press, 1984), chap. 3. In essence, as the author argues, *Shuttlesworth* vindicated the position of the four *Walker* dissenters. In *Carroll* v. *President and Commissioners of Princess Anne*, 393 U.S. 175 (1968) the Court held that an *ex parte* injunction, such as that sustained in *Walker*, violated First Amendment rights in situations where it was possible to notify the opposing parties and give them an opportunity to be heard. For an approving view of *Walker* see, Sheldon Tefft, "Neither Above the Law Nor Below It: A Note on Walker v. Birmingham," *The Supreme Court Review* (1967): 181–92.

which the U.S. Supreme Court, holding that the ordinance violated First Amendment norms, essentially agreed. The Alabama high court, overruling the appellate court in *Shuttlesworth,* and aware that the U.S. Supreme Court would, in this case, reach the First Amendment issue, sought to save the day by insisting that the ordinance was, in accord with other U.S. Supreme Court holdings, narrowly drawn and meant to be administered in an evenhanded fashion.[34] This, since the ordinance provided that a permit could be denied whenever public authorities deemed that "the public welfare, peace, safety, health, decency, good morals or convenience required that it be refused," was too much for the Supreme Court: "It would have taken extraordinary clairvoyance for anyone to perceive that this language meant what the Alabama Supreme Court was destined to find that it meant four years after its enactment." Indeed, in its zeal to affirm the convictions (which carried a penalty of 138 days at hard labor for the city) of the black pastors who had organized the march, the Alabama high court had, as the U.S. Supreme Court acidly commented, "performed a remarkable job of plastic surgery on the ordinance."[35]

Another aspect of the civil rights movement, northern sympathy and support for the black cause in the South, also engaged the attention of the Alabama high court. In *New York Times* v. *Sullivan*[36] it sustained a $500,000 libel judgment against the *Times* (which had virtually no circulation within the state) for publishing a minor error about police mistreatment of civil rights activists. Here, the court's policy concerns were less blatant, and the legal issue, at least on the surface, was straightforward, unencumbered by the sorts of machinations that accompanied the NAACP and Easter Week cases. The state libel law at issue was similar to those of other states, and the First Amendment had until then never been viewed as affording protection from libelous publications. In reversing the Alabama Supreme Court the U.S. Supreme Court held that public officials could sue for libel under only the most circumscribed of conditions—and this was not one of them. This aside, both the Alabama and the U.S. high courts were operating in a charged atmosphere, impelled by events taking place in the state, the region, and the nation.

34. 180 So.2d 377 (Ala. App. 1965); rev'd. 206 So.2d 384 (Ala. 1965).
35. 394 U.S. 147, 156, 153 (1969).
36. 144 So.2d 25 (Ala. 1963); rev'd. on grounds that First Amendment protects against libel suits by public officials unless "actual malice" proven, 376 U.S. 254 (1964).

The inescapable impression is that although Alabama law on libel and defamation had not been distorted to achieve the result, Alabama had somehow pounced on the *Times* for its role in supporting the civil rights movement in the South. The judgment . . . represented a powerful blow in the South's counterattack. In the civil war that is being waged in the courts as elsewhere, the political importance of the case could not be ignored.[37]

Taken altogether, the Alabama Supreme Court's record in civil rights cases reflected a consistent animosity against black claimants and a willingness to align itself with the resistance initiated by other state political institutions. Indeed, its record was conspicuously worse than that of other state high courts in the South, ruling in favor of blacks in only 7.7 percent of all cases between 1954 and 1963, as compared with 33.3 percent, 54.5 percent, 29.1 percent, 23.8 percent, and 28.6 percent for the courts of Arkansas, Georgia, Louisiana, Mississippi, and South Carolina, respectively.[38] Such cases included, for example, in addition to those discussed above, a ruling that the action of a personnel review board that refused to administer police examinations to blacks was not reviewable—thereby foreclosing the possibility of review by the U.S. Supreme Court—and a ruling that determined that the necessary papers had not been filed in time to dissolve an injunction against placing a black political organization on the election ballot.[39] Insisting that court records identified a witness as "Mary Hamilton" and not "Miss Mary Hamilton," the Alabama high court sustained a contempt citation against a black woman who refused to respond when addressed by her first name. It denied certiorari when a state senator appealed his disorderly conduct citation for efforts to test segregation laws.[40]

37. Harry Kalven, Jr., "The New York Times Case: A Note on the Central Meaning of the First Amendment," *The Supreme Court Review* (1964): 194.

38. Kenneth N. Vines, "Southern State Supreme Courts and Race Relations," *Western Political Quarterly* 18 (1965): 5, 11.

39. *Johnson* v. *Yielding*, 100 So.2d 29 (Ala. 1958), refused on procedural grounds, 165 F. Supp. 76 (N.D., So. Div. Ala. 1958). *Herndon* v. *Lee*, 199 So.2d 74 (Ala. 1967).

40. *Ex Parte Hamilton*, 156 So.2d 926, 927 (Ala. 1963), rev'd., 376 U.S. 650 (1964). Said the Alabama court, "The record conclusively shows that petitioner's name is Mary Hamilton, not Miss Mary Hamilton. . . . Many witnesses are addressed by various titles, but one's own name is an acceptable appellation at law. This practice is almost as universal in the written opinions of courts." A commentator noted that the "supreme court of Alabama upheld the contempt conviction in

The court also legitimized the segregationist cause in ways other than holding the line in cases and controversies. At Governor Wallace's request, it obligingly provided advisory opinions sustaining the validity of his closing of the public schools instead of obeying federal court integration orders. It helped the state find a way around the Supreme Court's invalidation of the Boswell Amendment to the state constitution, which for all intents and purposes denied the ballot to blacks.[41] In response to a legislative request, the court drew up a set of questions to be asked of prospective voters, a test that blacks, at the discretion of the registrars, would surely "fail." Applicants, for instance, "had to demonstrate ability to spell and understand individual words from the dictation of the registrar. Applicants in Selma were required to spell such difficult and technical words as 'emolument,' 'capitation,' 'impeachment,' 'apportionment,' and 'despotism.' "[42]

And last, but far from least, in off-the-bench remarks the justices proclaimed their fervent support for massive resistance. Chief Justice Livingston, who presided over the court during the NAACP Cases, was "for segregation in every phase of life . . . and would close every school before he went to school with colored people." One of his

---

such a manner as to suggest that the issue did not exist. [T]he United States Supreme Court subsequently reversed Miss Hamilton's contempt conviction, finding it as offensive to the Constitution as segregation in the courtroom." Meltsner, "Southern Appellate Courts," p. 140. *Taylor* v. *Birmingham*, 45 So.2d 53 (Ala. App. 1950), cert. denied, 45 So.2d 60 (Ala. 1960), cert. denied, 340 U.S. 832 (1950).

41. *Opinion of the Justices*, 156 So.2d 639 (Ala. 1963); 160 So.2d. 648 (Ala., 1964); Yarbrough, *Judge Frank Johnson*, p. 94. Alabama, like most southern states, employed various means to keep blacks from voting, all of which ultimately were either invalidated by U.S. Supreme Court rulings or superseded by federal legislation. The Boswell Amendment, adopted in 1948, was passed in response to the fact that the property qualifications to vote established in the state constitution of 1901 were no longer high enough to restrict the franchise, and to the U.S. Supreme Court's invalidation of the White Primary in *Smith* v. *Allwright*, 321 U.S. 649 (1944). The amendment required prospective voters to pass a literacy test and to read, write, and demonstrate satisfactory understanding of the constitution. As one of its sponsors pointed out, "A small parrot could be taught to recite a section of our Constitution," quoted in Barnard, *Dixiecrats and Democrats*, p. 61. Governor Folsom, as well as other progressives, opposed the amendment, and it was invalidated by the U.S. Supreme Court in *Davis* v. *Schnell*, 336 U.S. 933 (1949).

42. Donald S. Strong, *National Voting Rights Legislation in the Federal Courts* (University, Ala.: University of Alabama Press, 1968), pp. 64–67. Testimony of Attorney General Katzenbach before the Senate Committee on the Judiciary, *Hearings, Voting Rights*, 89th Congress, Last Session, 1965, p. 11.

colleagues, denouncing "forced integration," prayed "to God that Southerners might yet save their land from the 'abomination of desolation.' "[43] Along with the most strident voices in the Deep South, the members of the Alabama Supreme Court cried, "Never!"

Deference to the Legislature—The Common Law and Judicial Rules of Procedure

The old court's role during the period of reaction to civil rights initiatives represented just one aspect—albeit an uncharacteristically flamboyant one—of its habitual posture of deference and passivity vis-à-vis the other branches of state government. It performed for the state the useful (and, as far as many state supreme courts are concerned, the not untypical) judicial function of "legitimizing decisions made elsewhere in the political system."[44] Its insistence that courts had no business ordering reapportionment, the legislature's failure to redistrict every ten years in accordance with constitutional mandate notwithstanding, provides just one example. The court's basic passivity was further manifested by its rigid adherence to precedent and by its tendency to reaffirm lower court rulings (unless, as in the case of *Shuttlesworth,*[45] a decision flew in the face of state and local policies).

43. Quoted in Jack W. Peltason, *Fifty-eight Lonely Men: Southern Judges and School Desegregation* (New York: Harcourt Brace and World, 1961), p. 61. Quoted in *Alabama Lawyer* 21 (1960): 410.

44. See, for example, Edward N. Beiser, "The Rhode Island Supreme Court: A Well Integrated Political System," *Law & Society Review* 8 (1974): 167–86; Thomas R. Morris, *The Virginia Supreme Court: An Institutional and Political Analysis* (Charlottesville, Va.: University of Virginia Press, 1975). Frye, *The Alabama Supreme Court,* p. 87.

45. *Opinion of the Justices,* 81 So.2d 697 (Ala. 1955). This situation was not unique to Alabama. *Baker* v. *Carr,* 369 U.S. 186 (1963), culminated a successful challenge by urban voters in Tennessee. A series of federal rulings, including the U.S. Supreme Court's famous "one man one vote" apportionment standard, ordered the reapportionment of both houses of the Alabama legislature, as well as the state's congressional districts and local units of government. Apportionment schemes that were racially discriminatory and that sought to dilute the black vote were also invalidated. *Reynolds* v. *Sims,* 377 U.S. 533 (1964); *Sims* v. *Amos,* 366 F. Supp. 924 (M.D. Ala., 1972); *Moody* v. *Flowers,* 256 F. Supp. 195 (M.D. Ala., 1966); *Avery* v. *Midland County,* 390 U.S. 474 (1968); *Driggers* v. *Gallion,* 308 F. Supp. 632 (M.D. Ala., 1969); *Sullivan* v. *Alabama State Bar,* 295 F. Supp. 1216 (M.D. Ala., 1969); *Sims* v. *Bagget,* 247 F. Supp. 96 (M.D. Ala., 1965); *Smith* v. *Paris,* 257 F. Supp. 901 (M.D. Ala., 1968); *Yelverton* v. *Driggers,* 370 F. Supp. 612 (M.D. Ala., 1947). The challenges were initially heard by Judge Frank Johnson, see

Indeed, the reports of the Alabama cases are replete with such classic expressions of judicial self-restraint as "all reasonable intendment must be indulged in favor of the validity of legislative acts," and "the court has only the power to declare, not amend state law."[46] There is, of course, nothing remarkable about judicial abnegation and buck-passing. What was noteworthy was the court's self-effacement in areas of the law in which even the most modest courts characteristically show some signs of life. These include the development of the common law and the assertion of inherent judicial power to conduct judicial business. But as one justice was fond of saying when such questions arose, "[T]he legislature is just down the street."[47]

One of Alabama's most active plaintiffs' lawyers has complained that the court showed a "marked disinclination to overrule [its] former [tort] decisions." Such rigidity was patent in its refusal, despite decisional trends in other states and "law review lobbying," to abrogate the doctrines of sovereign immunity, contributory negligence, and privity. The beleaguered tone of many of the court's opinions suggests that it was uncomfortable with accusations that it was outside the mainstream, "aligned," in the words of one critic, "with a dwindling number of states," "digress[ing] toward the 19th century." The court, for instance, acknowledged that it was indeed "mindful of the general disrepute of the principle" of sovereign immunity, but reiterated, as it had over and over again, that the

---

Yarbrough, *Judge Frank Johnson*, p. 143. *Shuttlesworth*, 180 So.2d 377 (Ala. App. 1965), rev'd., 206 So.2d 348 (Ala. 1965).

46. *Thomas* v. *Ferguson*, 102 So.2d 220, 223, (Ala. 1958). This court was not invariably self-effacing. Weary of its contribution to the state's attraction as a divorce mill, it finally refused to put its imprimatur on the terms of a "quickie" nonresident divorce in *Hartigan* v. *Hartigan*, 128 So.2d 725 (Ala. 1961). See generally, "Migratory Divorce: The Alabama Experience," *Harvard Law Review* 75 (1962): 568–75. And, like many other state courts, it did not follow the U.S. Supreme Court's lead in abandoning substantive due process as regards taxing and regulatory measures and policies. *Morgan* v. *State*, 194 So.2d 820 (Ala. 1967); *Estelle* v. *Birmingham*, 286 So.2d 872 (Ala. 1973). For a discussion of state court supervision of economic legislation, see James C. Kirby, Jr., "Expansive Review of Economic Regulations Under State Constitutions," *Tennessee Law Review* 48 (1981): 241–83.

47. Francis H. Hare and Francis H. Hare, Jr., "Stare Decisis," *Alabama Law Review* 31 (1970): 273–82; and "Principal Alabama Actions in Tort," *Alabama Law Review* 21 (1960): 619–64. James Duke Cameron, "The Place for Judicial Activism on the Part of a State's Highest Court," *Hastings Constitutional Law Quarterly* 4 (1977): 278–95. Quoted in Frye, *Alabama Supreme Court*, p. 84.

responsibility for change rested with the legislature, not the judiciary.[48] This attitude did not preclude the court from carving out significant exceptions that, it has been argued, exacerbated the situation by creating serious inequities.[49] Nonetheless, "the protection of the public treasure [was] the most consistent thread running through the case law."[50] Language employed in a products liability case is similarly illustrative of the court's posture:

> In effect, we are asked to overturn the long-existing rule in this jurisdiction that there must be privity of contract between a buyer and a seller and a person injured by a defect in the article sold. . . . Although this is a "judge-made" rule which could be changed by another "judge-made" rule, we entertain the view, that because of its long existence as part of the jurisprudence of the state, it would be most appropriate, for its demise to be effectuated by legislative action.[51]

Whatever the options in other jurisdictions, whatever for that matter the judicial preference for change, the court, as it stated, considered itself compelled "to follow the common law on *any* subject when the same has not been changed by the legislative branch of . . . government."[52]

We can only speculate about the extent to which the court was motivated by reluctance to effect the sort of change a legislature might also bring about or by reluctance to take cues from courts in sister states. There is no suggestion in the opinions that the court disap-

48. Hare and Hare, "Stare Decisis," p. 620. "Torts—Wrongful Death—*Geohagen* v. *General Motors Corp.*, 279 So.2d 436 (Ala. 1973)—Wrongful Death—Breach of Implied Warranty," *Cumberland-Samford Law Review* 4 (1973–74): 663–64. *Decatur* v. *Parham*, 109 So.2d 668, 669 (Ala. 1970).

49. Timothy McMahon, "The State as Defendant: The Doctrine of Sovereign Immunity in Alabama," *Alabama Lawyer* 41 (1980): 583–99; "To Catch the Elusive Conscience of the King: The Status of the Doctrine of Sovereign Immunity in Alabama," *Alabama Law Review* 26 (1973–74): 463–84.

50. "To Catch the Elusive Conscience of the King," p. 463.

51. *Harnishferger Corp.* v. *Harris*, 190 So.2d. 286, 288 (Ala. 1966).

52. *Smith* v. *United Construction Workers*, 122 So.2d. 153, 154 (Ala. 1960). The ruling sustained the common law doctrine, now generally abrogated, that only husbands may sue for loss of consortium. In *Swartz* v. *United States Steel Corporation*, 304 So.2d. 881 (Ala. 1974), the court held that wives might sue for loss of their husband's consortium. Alabama was one of the last states to retain the doctrine; for a listing, see G. Alan Tarr and Mary Cornelia Porter, "Gender Equality and Judicial Federalism: The Role of State Appellate Courts," *Hastings Constitutional Law Quarterly* 9 (1982): 919–73, table D, pp. 959–62.

proved of tort law innovations in other jurisdictions, and, as a matter of fact, it did not entirely disregard them. Studies of post–World War II tort law development indicate that the Alabama court, while hardly an enthusiastic emulator, slowly succumbed to the tides of doctrinal change. It is in the areas mentioned above, sovereign immunity, products liability, and privity, to which we would add the doctrine of charitable immunity[53]—all of which, if altered, would affect public as well as substantial private economic interests—that the court shied away from initiating policy changes.

There need be no speculation as concerns the court's approach to its own authority. Not only was it willing to accept the legislature's authority to formulate judicial rules of procedure—only Chief Justice Livingston ever raised the question of separation of powers[54]—but it went out of its way to render the already unworkable rules (which might be regarded as the legislature's means of "controlling" the judiciary) even more unworkable.[55]

The Alabama rules of civil and criminal procedure were first promulgated in 1852 and underwent a number of legislative revisions before the high court was granted the rule-making power in 1971. But as late as 1967, one of the court's most respected and hardest-working justices complained that the court was operating with "1915

---

53. Bradley C. Canon and Lawrence Baum, "Patterns of Tort Law Innovations: An Application of Diffusion Theory to Judicial Doctrines," *American Political Science Review* 75 (1981): 975–87; Robert E. Keeton, *Venturing to Do Justice* (Cambridge: Harvard University Press, 1969).

"[T]he change in tort law was gradual and not a sudden flip-flop. Most of the plaintiff's lawyers lost their first cases but the Court gradually in a ten year period, became more favorable to their position." Letter from a member of the Alabama Supreme Court, April 16, 1982.

By the mid-1970s Alabama retained a doctrine of only partial charitable immunity, and was thus neither a leader nor a laggard. Bradley C. Canon and Dean Jaros, "The Impact of Changes in Judicial Doctrine: The Abrogation of Charitable Immunity," *Law & Society Review* 13 (1979): 973.

54. "Our Supreme Court has held many times over that the 'rule-making power' resides in the Legislature, and it is my opinion that the Legislature will have to grant us that power if we are to have it." Justice Pelham J. Merrill, "The Facts About Alabama Courts and Judges Today," *Alabama Lawyer* 28 (1967): 145. Justice Livingston, dissenting in *Ex Parte Foshee*, 21 So.2d 827 (Ala. 1945).

55. For a discussion of the old rules, see "The Alabama Appellate Process, Part I," *Cumberland-Samford Law Review* 5 (1975): 451–99, and ibid., Part II, 6, 63–107; Cole, "Judicial Reform in Alabama: A Survey," pp. 48–53. Richard H. Gill, "The Proposed Alabama Appellate Rules: An Overview," *Alabama Law Review* 46 (1974): 639–54; Frye, *Alabama Supreme Court*, pp. 15–18.

tools."[56] This is not to say that the situation was accepted with equanimity. One chief justice, albeit as a minority of one, maintained that the court had inherent power to formulate the rules. A president of the state bar association, acknowledging that he was "a voice crying in the wilderness," urged adoption of federal rules.[57] During the 1950s the entire bar association addressed itself to the problem, and in 1957 new rules of procedure were passed by the lower house of the state legislature; but, having been labeled as "federal rules" by opponents (anything federal being anathema at that point), they never came to a vote in the senate.[58]

That the rules were applied stringently even in cases of "mistake, inadvertence, accident or misfortune" was generally recognized, as was the fact that many cases, at least 9 percent, turned on technicalities rather than resulting in a decision on the merits.[59] Serious injustices were done, particularly to the most vulnerable—those with few resources and those convicted of crimes. A widow with a young child to support, for instance, was denied recovery for the wrongful death of her husband not on a point of fact or law but because her inexperienced attorney failed to post sufficient security for the costs of the appeal. In another case, an appeal from a ninety-nine-year sentence for murder was dismissed because the transcript had been filed one day beyond the deadline.[60]

Nonetheless, the old rules did serve a dual purpose for the court. They provided a means of disposing of cases—a boon for a court hopelessly in arrears. Appeals were dismissed, among other reasons, because transcript pages were incorrectly numbered, because margins were not of requisite width, because the knot of the "inevitable red ribbon" girding the transcript was not arranged according to specifi-

56. Merrill, "Facts about Alabama Courts," p. 140.

57. *Ex Parte Foshee*, 21 So.2d 827 (Ala. 1945). Quoted in *Alabama Lawyer* 4 (1943): 409.

58. Reported in *Alabama Lawyer* 16 (1955): 115–30. Cole, "Judicial Reform in Alabama," p. 50.

59. "The Alabama Appellate Process, Part I," pp. 474, 463. "Simple forms for many actions have been provided, but . . . as is so often the case, the practitioner must draw his complaint within the rigid requirements of our . . . system and thus set off the fireworks for the usual endless pleading extravaganza. He is met at the threshold by the mandate of the procedural slave of strict construction." Quoted in Frye, *The Alabama Supreme Court*, p. 4.

60. *Gray* v. *Alabama*, 185 So.2d 125 (Ala. 1966), cited in "The Alabama Appellate Process, Part I," p. 212. *Hornbuckle* v. *Alabama*, 105 So.2d 864 (Ala. 1966).

cation (and some time, it seems, was spent examining the knot), because counsel had failed to include in the brief the "ritual incantations about the organization of the circuit courts."[61] Further, because of their complexity and the general uncertainty about how they might be applied, the rules lent themselves to manipulation by the court; and this came in handy as a means of achieving such politically desired ends as thwarting the civil rights movement (as in the NAACP Cases)[62] and the almost equally unpopular labor movement.[63] In one labor case, for example, a request for a declaratory judgment about the constitutionality of a statute prohibiting public employees from joining a union was dismissed not only for failing to raise a case or controversy, but also because "the ends of the cord with which the transcripts were bound were not fastened with the clerk's seal." On both matters the court could hardly be expected to "make shipwreck of well-known rules of procedure" merely "to accommodate a case."[64]

Finally, whatever the views of individual members of bench and bar about the necessity for change, the rules had the advantages that accompany familiarity. It is reasonable to speculate that alterations, emanating either from the legislature or the judiciary, would not only entail judicial time and energy, but would demand alterations in

61. Gill, "Alabama Appellate Rules," p. 94.

62. See notes 21–30 and accompanying text.

63. For the difficulties encountered by unions in the South, see generally John Samuel Ezell, *The South Since 1865* (New York: Macmillan, 1964), chap. 11. For many years, of course, courts throughout the nation, by issuing injunctions against strikes and picketing, were an important part of the antiunion political and economic establishment. In *International Union of Operating Engineers* v. *Waterworks Board of Birmingham*, 163 So.2d 619 (Ala. 1964), the court held that a state public agency lacked authority to engage in collective bargaining or enter into a union contract. In *U.S. Steel Workers Union, AFL-CIO* v. *Manely*, 104 So.2d 306 (Ala. 1957), it was held that nonunion employees may be awarded damages for wages lost due to their being unable to cross picket lines. In *Taggart* v. *Weinrackers, Inc.*, 214 So.2d 913, 915 (Ala. 1968), the court justified an injunction against picketing in a shopping center on the grounds that "trespass" was a "potential cause of violence." In *Kinard Construction Co.* v. *Building Trades Council*, 64 So.2d 400 (Ala. 1953), an employer was held entitled to enjoin picketing in a state court; rev'd. on grounds that the National Labor Relations Board had exclusive jurisdiction, 346 U.S. 933 (1954). Earlier, however, the court reversed on First and Fourteenth Amendment grounds a decree enjoining picketing. *Hotel and Restaurant Employees International Alliance* v. *Greenwood*, 30 So.2d 696 (Ala. 1947), cert. denied, 332 U.S. 847 (1948).

64. *American Federation of City and Municipal Employees* v. *Dawkins*, 104 So.2d 827, 834 (Ala. 1958).

judicial work habits. (Some justices were not known for their diligence.) Lawyers who had long since learned to make the rules work to their advantage would have to evolve new legal strategies should new rules be adopted.[65] And it is possible, over time, that different rules would entail different sorts of case outcomes—the plaintiffs' bar was undoubtedly frustrated by the ease with which appeals involving arguments for tort law change were dismissed, while the defendants' bar was probably far more comfortable with the rules.

In sum, the Alabama high court, even at the risk of appearing ridiculous in the eyes of the wider legal community,[66] was unwilling either to "lobby" for or initiate change in the rules of procedure. It would not rock the boat even to the extent of finding some way to do its job more efficiently. The old rules and the old court, and for that matter the old legislatures, coexisted in perfect harmony and understanding.

Relations with the United States Supreme Court

The cases involving race, the rights of defendants, and civil liberties discussed earlier paint a picture of a court at war with the U.S. Supreme Court, with the federal Constitution, with a social movement whose time had come, and with prevailing opinion throughout the country. And in fact the Alabama Supreme Court's record vis-à-vis the U.S. Supreme Court might have been unparalleled. A study of appeals to the Supreme Court between 1925 and 1953 disclosed that the Court reversed in 45.8 percent of the cases coming from Alabama appellate courts as compared with a 20.7 percent reversal rate for cases coming from all state appellate courts. Of the Alabama cases, over one-third constituted criminal appeals.[67]

---

65. "Thus while there are some within the legal system in the state who are profoundly distressed by the cumbersome and wasteful appellate system, it is probably accurate to assume that in weighing the utilities associated with a complicated legal system, many lawyers have opted in favor of its retention, on the assumption that the system helps them more than it hurts (winning cases on procedural points to which they know the court is particularly solicitous)." Frye, *The Alabama Supreme Court*, p. 80.

66. In arguing one of the NAACP Cases before the U.S. Supreme Court, the lawyer for the State of Alabama "found himself embarrassedly trying to explain his own court's ruling." Anthony Lewis, *Portrait of a Decade: The Second American Revolution* (New York: Random House, 1964), pp. 292–93.

67. Daniel J. Meador, "Alabama Cases in the Supreme Court of the United States—1925–1953," *Alabama Lawyer* 19 (1955): 341–67. Some of these cases went directly from either the Alabama criminal or civil court of appeals after the top

Between 1954 and 1972, when the new court came into place, the patterns continued.[68] There was, however, a major difference. Before *Brown* and the advent of the civil rights movement, U.S. Supreme Court reversals, however unhappily received, were not regarded as having an ideological component. For that matter the U.S. Supreme Court, when given a choice, gave the impression of preferring to reverse a conviction on grounds *other* than racial exclusion from the jury,[69] thus indicating that the differences between the highest state and federal appellate courts did not always appear to be over matters of racial justice. After 1954 the lines, at least according to the Alabama high court, were drawn. Earlier disagreement turned into contempt for and fear and hatred of the federal judiciary. Indeed, whatever the tenor of the relations between the highest Alabama and federal courts over the years, "many Alabama cases," as one of the current justices ruefully noted, "made law in the United States Supreme Court." The Alabama Supreme Court may well enjoy the dubious distinction of having provided a particularly singular catalyst for the fashioning of federal constitutional principles.[70]

---

court denied certiorari; e.g., *Taylor* v. *Birmingham*, 45 So.2d 53 (Ala. App. 1950), cert. denied 45 So.2d 60 (Ala 1960), cert. denied, 340 U.S. 832 (1950). Some landmark U.S. Supreme Court rulings establishing important constitutional principles concerning religious liberty, the concept of "state action," and symbolic speech came directly from the Alabama court of civil appeals. *Jones* v. *Opelika*, 7 So.2d 503 (Ala. App. 1942), cert. denied 7 So.2d 503 (Ala. 1942), aff'd., 316 U.S. 584 (1942), rehearing granted, 318 U.S. 796 (1943), rev'd., 319 U.S. 103 (1943) (religious liberty). *Marsh* v. *Alabama*, 21 So.2d 558 (Ala. App. 1945); cert. denied, 21 So.2d. 564 (Ala. 1945), rev'd., 326 U.S. 501 (1946) (state action). *Thornhill* v. *Alabama*, 189 So.2d 913 (Ala. App. 1939), cert. denied, 189 So.2d. 913 (Ala. 1939), rev'd., 310 U.S. 88 (1940) (symbolic speech). Some criminal appeals denied review by the Alabama high court went directly to the Supreme Court, which likewise allowed the convictions to stand. Meador, "Alabama Cases," pp. 349–51. One involving prolonged questioning of a black mentally ill defendant was reversed. *Blackburn* v. *State*, 109 So.2d 736 (Ala. App. 1958), cert. denied, 109 So.2d 738 (Ala. 1958); rev'd., 361 U.S. 199 (1960).

68. See cases in notes 12–15.

69. Ibid.

70. *Powell* v. *Alabama*, 287 U.S. 47 (1932); *Norris* v. *Alabama*, 294 U.S. 587 (1935) (right to an unbiased jury); *NAACP* v. *Alabama*, 337 U.S. 288 (1964) (right of association). *New York Times* v. *Sullivan*, 376 U.S. 254 (1964) (libel laws restricted by First Amendment); *Boykin* v. *Alabama*, 395 U.S. 238 (1969) (standards for determining voluntariness of guilty plea). Also, see cases cited in note 67. Interview, March 12, 1982.

"I often state, somewhat humorously, that the Alabama supreme court's treatment of controversial cases which came before it during the 1950s and 1960s was responsible, in great part, for the liberal and expansive decisions of the United States Supreme Court." Letter from Howard Mandell.

"THE NEW COURT"

The National Reputation

By 1976 Alabama had modernized and reformed its judicial system,
and the revitalized Alabama Supreme Court and its new chief justice
had become objects of attention and admiration. A national magazine
put it this way:

> Armed with a passionate belief in business-type supervision of the
> operations of courts and a native sense of how to push without
> shoving, [Chief Justice Howell] Heflin has transformed Alabama's
> antique judiciary into one of the most modern and efficient in the
> U.S. As soon as he had assumed office he began sweet-talking the
> legislature and electorate into reforming the state's briarpatch of
> conflicting jurisdictions and ludicrous rules. It was a five year
> campaign and he won it. . . . While lobbying through his reforms,
> the chief justice was also wielding his official and personal power to
> chop into a horrifying backlog of cases. He drafted 55 retired or
> underworked judges to dispose of hundreds of appeals. . . . Since
> 1973 the appellate docket has been "current," a rarity for state
> courts.[71]

In recognition of his accomplishments, Heflin was in 1976 elected
chairman of the Conference of Chief Justices. Alabama civil rights
activists, while hardly anticipating a liberal court, were satisfied that
Heflin's court would be fair-minded—one went so far as to say that he
would "rather take [his] chances with the supreme court of Alabama
than with the Supreme Court of the U.S."[72] Clearly, an era had come
to an end.

The Justices

The Alabama high court of the 1980s includes its first woman, a black
who had been identified with the legal aspects of the civil rights
movement, and the attorney who had represented the *New York Times*
in *New York Times* v. *Sullivan*.[73] All of the justices now serving were

71. "Push But Not Shove," p. 88.
72. Ibid.
73. Janie Ledlow Shores. Oscar W. Adams, Jr., was appointed by Governor
"Fob" James and was elected without primary opposition in 1982. When asked
why a black had been appointed, a court official responded with a nonchalant,
"Oh, the governor just thought it was time." (One of Justice Adams's law partners,
U. W. Clemon, upon the recommendation of Senator Howell Heflin, became

elected or appointed after the civil rights movement had peaked,[74] after racial tensions had somewhat abated, after blacks had begun to participate in a meaningful way in the political affairs and processes of the state,[75] and after the shock waves generated by federal court intervention and legislation, such as the Civil Rights Act of 1964 and the Voting Rights Act of 1965, had subsided. One of the current

---

Alabama's first black federal district judge. Heflin, it is said, "caught hell," but not to the extent that his political career was in any jeopardy. Alabama's other black federal district judge, Myron Herbert Thompson, was appointed to fill the vacancy left by Judge Frank Johnson's appointment to the then-Fifth [now Eleventh] Circuit Court of Appeals.) Thomas Eric Embry was counsel for the *New York Times*. He is a Roman Catholic, in all likelihood the first to serve on the Alabama Supreme Court. *Alabama Lawyer* 56 (1970): 450. "[T]o the writer's knowledge, there have been no justices of either the Jewish or Catholic faith" on the court. Frye, *The Alabama Supreme Court*, p. 34. *New York Times* v. *Sullivan*, 44 So.2d 25 (Ala. 1963).

74. Alva Hugh Maddox, 1969; James H. Faulkner, 1972; Richard L. Jones, 1972; Reneau P. Almon, 1975; Eric Embry, 1975; Janie L. Shores, 1975; Samuel A. Beatty, 1976; Clement Clay "Bo" Torbert, Jr., C. J., 1977; Oscar W. Adams, 1980; J. Gorman Houson, 1985 (replacing Justice Embry); Henry P. Steagall, 1986 (replacing Justice Faulkner).

75. For a general discussion, see Jack Bass and Walter DeVries, *The Transformation of Southern Politics: Social Change and Political Consequences Since 1945* (New York: Basic Books, 1977), chap. 4, and M. Elizabeth Sanders, "New Voters and New Policy Priorities in the Deep South: A Decade of Political Change in Alabama," presented at the Annual Meeting of the American Political Science Association, 1979. In 1968 Alabama had 24 black elected officials; by 1981 the figure had risen to 247, including the mayor of Birmingham. "In the 10 counties of Alabama with black majorities . . . , 55 percent of all elective offices are held by blacks," William E. Schmidt, "Selma 20 years after the Rights March," *New York Times*, Mar. 1, 1985, pp. 1, 6, col. 1. Charles S. Bullock III and Charles M. Lamb, *Implementation of Civil Rights Policy* (Monterey, Cal.: Brooks/Cole, 1984, p. 45. Political practices, formal and informal, that discriminate against blacks and other minorities persist, however, in Alabama as elsewhere. For a discussion, see *The Right to Vote* (New York: Rockefeller Foundation, 1981). The state's mood is well described in the following letter: "Toward the middle of the 1970s, the sentiments of the masses in Alabama had begun to change. George Wallace no longer wielded the power he once did. Judge Johnson's name was no longer an anathema; to the contrary he was finally receiving the credit and respect he had always merited. A Southerner, with a basically liberal, populist philosophy had been elected President. Probably more important than anything else, however, black citizens of the state were now registered in sufficient numbers to influence the outcome of elections. All elected officials, especially those elected on a state-wide basis could no longer be insensitive to the needs and wants of the large black minority." Letter from Howard Mandell. "Blacks make up 25 percent of the state's population and 35 percent of its registered Democrats. . . . [In 1985 enough blacks were] elected to form a majority in the Birmingham City Council for the first time." *New York Times*, Jan. 26, 1986, p. 16, col. 3.

justices, while speaking only for himself in off-the-bench remarks, probably sums up the prevailing judicial attitude toward a deplored past and a more sanguine future:

> While the modern day Blacks of our nation may justly point to the *Brown* decision as their Exodus from bondage to freedom, equally important is the liberation of the human mind—particularly the southern White mind. I believe that [in] its unleashing of our mental captivity, one of *Brown*'s ultimate victories will emerge in the form of renewed intellectual contributions from southern writers, business leaders, educators, lawyers, jurists, theologians, and scientists—free at last "to follow the truth wherever it may lead."[76]

Surprising as all this may appear, it must be remembered that the attitudes of today's justices, while perhaps more "advanced" than those of a substantial number of officials and citizens, are not aberrational in Alabama politics. Alabama has, after all, a strong populist/progressive tradition personified by statewide officeholders such as Senators Lister Hill, John Sparkman, and Hugo Black and Governor "Big Jim" Folsom, whose belief in the equality of the races was matched by his devotion to the New Deal.[77] Another governor,

---

76. Jones, "Reflections from the Bench," p. 172.

77. For the classic description of Alabama's dual, indeed schizophrenic, political tradition and the ultimate triumph of racism and the economically powerful Big Mules, see V. O. Key, *Southern Politics in State and Nation* (New York: Knopf, 1949), chap. 3. Other useful insights are provided by Barnard, *Dixiecrats and Democrats,* and Peirce, *The Deep South States of America,* chap. 5. Lister Hill's obituary summed up the dilemma faced by southern liberals: "Among the bills he directed in his 45 years in Congress were the Tennessee Valley Authority Act and the Hill Burton Hospital Act. His slow, persistent efforts in behalf of social legislation which included the Rural Telephone Act, the Rural Housing Act, the G.I. Bill of Rights . . . Medicare and Social Security made Mr. Hill, as much as any legislator of his generation, a key figure in bringing modern medical care and adequate educational facilities to every region of the United States. . . . Like many of the 'progressive' Southern Democrats who came to Washington in the New Deal era, Senator Hill became an opponent to change as the civil rights movement swept the South in the early 1960s, and he opposed the Civil Rights Act of 1965. . . . In an interview in 1977, Mr. Hill said he considered himself a progressive and was apologetic about his segregationist role. 'I had to do that to get elected,' he said. 'We all did.' " *New York Times,* Dec. 22, 1984, p. 13, col. 4. Senator Sparkman was Adlai Stevenson's vice-presidential running mate in the election of 1952; for his subsequent accommodation to racist sentiment in the state, see Peirce, p. 201. The "ambiguity of the Populist" and progressive "legacy on race has appeared time and time again

George Wallace, symbol of the archsegregationist, harkened back to his earlier populist convictions and brushed up on his populist rhetoric when he courted *and won* black votes on his return to public office in 1982.[78] And while native-born southern federal judges have been deservedly honored for their enforcement of the *Brown* decree, not one has matched the overall reformist zeal and activism of Alabama's native son, Frank Johnson.[79] The members of the new court not only reflect what has been described as the new south, but also represent a viable, however long dormant, political culture.

Judicial Reform

Generally, the Alabama judicial reform experience conformed to the patterns described in chapter 2; reform movements are, after all, championed by professionals who are engaged in what has become a national enterprise. Each movement, however, as may be expected in a federal system, has its indigenous and atypical aspects. In Alabama these were provided by the vagaries of the state's political culture and the leadership of Howell Heflin.

Heflin began the campaign for reform from his position as president of the state bar association, a group he transformed from a "social club into a lobby for reform." Next, in 1966 he put together a broadly based Citizens' Conference on State Courts, whose proposals became

---

in the course of Southern history. . . . The progressive economic programs of the Populists" were often "coupled with a virulent racism. . . . Some champions of the Southern masses, however, retained and never abandoned the Populist liberalism on race, including . . . Hugo Black and 'Big Jim' Folsom." Barnard, *Dixiecrats and Democrats*, p. 161. "In Alabama, many viewed Black as pariah, a traitor to the white Southern cause. Through most of the 1950s and 1960s, he was never invited back to Alabama to address any group—a bitter exile that did not end until the last years of his life, when various lawyers' groups invited him back for appearances. There was a climactic dinner sponsored by the state bar association in Birmingham, when 500 Alabama lawyers raised their glasses in tribute to the old man. It must have been an immensely gratifying moment for Black, for those who know him well said he never lost any feeling of kinship for and loyalty to the Southern soil that nurtured him." Peirce, *The Deep South States of America*, p. 265.

78. Wallace managed Senator Hill's reelection campaign in 1962. Black voters gave Wallace the 20 percent support critical to his primary victory in 1982. Michael Hirsley, "A weaker Wallace ponders one more last hurrah," *Chicago Tribune*, Mar. 19, 1985, p. 5, col. 1.

79. Frank Johnson, a Republican from northern Alabama, was appointed to Alabama's Middle District by President Dwight Eisenhower in 1955. For an account of his rulings and his remarkable role as the "real governor of Alabama," see Yarbrough, *Judge Frank Johnson and Human Rights in Alabama*.

the basis for measures eventually adopted by the legislature and the constitutional commission that drew up the judicial article of 1973.[80] The conference functioned in spite of the distractions of the civil rights agitations; and there is strong evidence that Heflin saw to it that blacks were represented.[81] In 1970, when it appeared that former governor John Patterson, an outspoken advocate of segregation, was the leading candidate, Heflin determined to "take him on"—and won by a 2-1 margin.[82]

Patterns of support and opposition to reform did not follow the patterns characteristic in other states. The state bar association provided remarkably solid backing; no member would, considering Heflin's power and prestige, have had the temerity to protest. Since Alabama was still largely a one-party state, political resistance did not form around party lines as such but manifested itself in other ways. Governor Wallace, for example, took a dim view of reform, and although his opposition was (uncharacteristically) muted, "his people" were considered a serious threat. From the left of the Democratic spectrum, ex-governor Folsom voiced what were undoubtedly diffuse suspicions when he dubbed the judicial article presented to the voters for ratification a "lawyer-judge amendment." Alabama's mayors,

80. "Push But Not Shove," p. 88. For descriptions of the reform movement, see William D. Stewart, Jr., *The Alabama Constitutional Commission: A Pragmatic Approach to Constitutional Revision* (University, Ala.: University of Alabama Press, 1975), chap. 4; M. Ronald Nachman, "Alabama's Breakthrough for Reform," *Judicature* 56 (1972): 112–14; Charles D. Cole, "Judicial Reform in Alabama: A Survey;" "Citizens' Conference on State Courts," *Alabama Lawyer* 28 (1967): 131–36; Larry Berkson and Susan Carbon, *Court Unification: History, Politics and Implementation* (Washington, D.C.: National Institute of Law Enforcement and Criminal Justice 1978), pp. 47–49.

81. The following opaque, oblique account of the conference's beginnings can mean little else: "From the outset there was no question that every segment of the population of Alabama should be represented for if any particular group was denied its right to participate, then could it truly be called a 'Citizens' Conference'? So the rather delicate question of what individuals should be invited to attend . . . was presented and resolved by designating Committee Chairman Robert T. Cunningham, Justice Pelham Merrill and Ronald Nachman to act as a Committee of Three to seek the services of Mr. Douglas Arant of the Birmingham Bar in the performance of this vital and most important function.

"The manner and method that Mr. Arant employed in solving his delicate task have not been recorded but that he performed his duties in an outstanding way is indicated by listing the names and addresses of those Alabama citizens who registered for and attended the . . . Conference, "Citizens' Conference on Alabama State Courts," pp. 133. The listing is on pp. 134–36.

82. "Push But Not Shove," p. 88.

faced with the specter of court unification, fought hard to retain the independence of the municipal courts, which had long been the source of partronage and political power.[83] The legislature had earlier signaled its contempt for reform by routing changes recommended by the citizens' conference to a highway safety commission.[84] Some opponents sought to capitalize on lingering resentments against the federal government and the rest of the country (outside the South) generally, contending that the proposed new rules of procedure, because they largely followed the federal model, would "federalize" the state courts. The creation of a department of court administration headed by a court administrator raised apprehensions about "some liberal New York professor" riding herd over judges elected by the people of the sovereign state of Alabama. Indeed, Heflin himself was a target, accused by some as being engaged in a "personal power grab."[85]

Schooled in the ways of Alabama politics, Heflin had little difficulty juggling, deflecting, and doing end runs around the opposition. He also knew when to compromise. Merit selection of judges, although high on the citizens' conference list, was jettisoned by the constitutional commission. In keeping with its populist tradition, Alabama prefers to elect judges on partisan ballots. Their terms, however, were extended from four to six years. The constitutional commission placated the mayors by permitting local courts to retain a degree of autonomy. Since the support of judges on the criminal and civil courts of appeals was crucial, their objections to the merging of the two courts carried the day. One way or another, as one justice succinctly noted, Heflin managed to "outfox them all."[86] Additionally, Heflin's immense energy, personal charisma, and dedication were also decisive. He was a constant goad to the thirty-five-odd groups working for voter approval of the judicial article referendum; and he himself, in just a two-month period, made more than fifty speeches and television appearances.[87] Working with and for him was, it seems, regarded as a privilege; one hears him referred to as a "hero."[88]

83. Berkson and Carbon, p. 82. Stewart, *The Alabama Constitutional Commission,* pp. 109, 82–93.
84. Nachman, "Alabama's Breakthrough for Reform," p. 113.
85. Stewart, *The Alabama Constitutional Commission,* pp. 97 and 96; 82–93.
86. Interview, March 9, 1982.
87. Stewart, *The Alabama Constitutional Commission,* pp. 105–11.
88. Interview, March 9, 1982. An Alabama justice has aptly described Heflin's powers of persuasion: "He can presume on your friendship to extract more from

Howell Heflin chose to serve just one six-year term on the bench. In 1978 he was elected to the U.S. Senate and in 1984 reelected.[89] He was succeeded by Clement Clay "Bo" Torbert, a highly respected state representative and senator, and one of the handful of state legislators who worked for reform. Torbert was widely regarded as Heflin's choice for the job. On the court Chief Justice Torbert continues to press for changes designed to improve the quality of justice in Alabama.[90] In 1987 he assumed the chairmanship of the Conference of Chief Justices.

Once the movement for reform was under way, progress was unusually swift; and whatever the assessment of reform in other states,[91] in Alabama it did make a difference. While one can only speculate about the extent to which the success should be attributed to Howell Heflin alone or to his role in conjunction with the more moderate social and political climate that followed the turbulent fifties and sixties, we believe that credit is largely due to Heflin. The critical first steps were taken at a time when black protests, federal intervention, and massive resistance dominated the public agenda. During this period Heflin managed, quietly and persistently, to divert attention to another issue. Furthermore, when Heflin came on the bench in 1971, the old fires had not yet died out: he was confronted with at least one justice eager to find ways to "get around" the Supreme Court of the United States.[92] In 1975, when the new judicial article and new rules of procedure were operative, when new blood came on the court, when Heflin had assumed the leadership of the Conference of Chief Justices, times had changed in Alabama and aspects of her "other" culture emerged from the shadows. But Heflin laid the groundwork for reform and won some of the major battles *before* the ancien regime was toppled by the full effects of the legislative redistricting decisions[93]

---

you than any person alive. When you are ready to draw the line and cry, 'Halt, no more,' you don't, for you realize that he asks of you only a fraction of that which he imposes on himself. He is a man with a sense of mission—a doer, a driver." Jones, "Reflections from the Bench," p. 159.

89. Senator Heflin's voting record is considered "moderately conservative." Among his assignments are the Judiciary and Ethics committees. *New York Times,* Dec. 17, 1986, p. 9, col. 1.

90. Interview, March 9, 1982. "Alabama's chief justice in spotlight as directors report on court improvements," *Judicature* 67 (1984): 511.

91. For discussion, see chap. 2.

92. "Push But Not Shove," p. 88.

93. For Alabama cases, see note 45.

and the Voting Rights Act of 1965. He took on what, by any lights, might be regarded as a hopeless task in a period of turmoil. In this sense, his achievements, even when compared with those of other chief justices who have been reform leaders,[94] are the more remarkable.

The Judicial Perspective

When Howell Heflin arrived on the Alabama Supreme Court he was, as one of the current justices bluntly put it, "saddled with some status quo justices," at least one of whom "was no longer in charge of all his faculties."[95] These encumbrances shed, the court's attitude toward its responsibilities, the legislature, other state high courts, and the U.S. Supreme Court and lower federal courts changed appreciably. This is not to say that the court joined the ranks of liberal, activist courts. It is to say that the court, like most state high courts, is not regarded as remarkable.[96] And that, considering its repute in days gone by, is remarkable in itself. The justices, however, articulate rather broad concerns, regard the court as having a policy-making role, and, on the whole, characterize their rulings as liberal and progressive. We do not mean that the justices claim more for their court than is due. We do suggest that this is a very self-conscious court—painfully sensitive about a painful past and anxious to leave a mark as a positive force in the state.

To begin with, all the justices are frustrated because the court does not, despite the reform measures of the seventies, have total discre-

94. For discussion of another celebrated reformer, Chief Justice Arthur Vanderbilt, see chap. 5.

95. This section draws upon interviews with the justices of the Alabama Supreme Court, March 9–12, 1982, Montgomery.

96. The court receives bad reviews from at least one long-time observer: "A major matter, about which you would hesitate to say anything in public, is that the Alabama court is not very sophisticated legally and is miserably briefed by counsel. As a consequence it struggles along as best it can and falls into all sorts of vagaries and inconsistencies. These are of much greater concern to practitioners than to those outside the legal profession and disturb us much more than whether the court is following a progressive party line. We do not have a strong court and there is little likelihood that we will get one. Of course, I should prefer not to be quoted on that point." Letter, Oct. 14, 1982. This represents just one view and it should be put in perspective. Today's court is very different from that of yore, and according to one national ranking it is considered about average. Gregory Caldeira, "The Reputation of State Supreme Courts." Further, we surmise that the same sort of comment might be made about many other state high courts by those who have studied or done business with them.

tionary control over its docket. It is still obliged to hear cases in which the amount in dispute is at least $10,000, as well as appeals from the Public Service Commission. It also has original jurisdiction in boundary line disputes. The justices feel bogged down by the number of cases in which they address only factual questions and would prefer that theirs were a "cert. court" that could, with a lighter caseload, "devote more time to disputes presenting significant legal, constitutional and policy issues" and "handle important issues as they should be."

Second, the current justices take pride in what they perceive as the court's increased activism in a number of areas and, whatever their differences on specific issues and questions, are agreed that they should "no longer leave all change to the legislature." Rather, they recognize that impatience with the failure of the legislative and executive branches to act with sufficient dispatch invites judicial activism. Such challenges and assertions of rights, the justices believe, reflect the increasing litigiousness of Americans, which may, in turn, be attributed to an increasingly sophisticated citizenry.

All the justices emphasized recent changes in the court's common law jurisprudence. Not only has the court applied "the philosophical and historical heritage of the common law to make changes when changes are in order," but it has developed the sort of "innovative" doctrines that occasion "surprise among other courts." The court "has adopted most, if not all," of the post–World War II "common law changes;" but the pace, according to one justice, has been "a little slow and gradual." This is just fine, he added, for "the law should move slowly with one progressive decision, then one step backward. Courts should not jump on the bandwagon, 'the life of the law has been experience,' and the law learns from experience." Conversely, one justice noted that there are those who think that the court "has gone too far."

Third, the justices *say* that they look to Alabama precedent before casting their nets wider and *say* that they are comfortable with precedent from other southern courts because of shared concerns and, being more interested in substance than in a court's reputation, *say* that they do not seek out the more prestigious courts for guidance. Still, they acknowledge that they find precedent from New York and Massachusetts, particularly in commercial cases, to be persuasive and valuable. As for the California high court, some justices felt that its rulings, however constructive, are too "radical" for Alabama law. In other words, the Alabama justices, whatever their rationales, appear to keep a close approving or disapproving watch on activist courts in urban, industrialized, and heavily populated states.

One justice, illuminating this point, provided extensive and candid insights into his court's, as well as his own, somewhat aberrant attitudes toward precedent from sister states:

> If the law in a particular area is well-developed in Alabama, we would be less apt to look to other states. The exception to this would be if there is a strong trend in other states, for example, "wrongful life" claims. Then the cases would be collected and the hope would be that other lawyers had done the work for you. Through the years, off and on, Alabama has followed New York precedent, depending on the time and the questions. California tends to be discounted with the phrase that this is "just one of those California cases." This is not fair as fine work has been done in California abrogating guest statutes.[97] The California Supreme Court ruled there that guest statutes violated equal protection because they were contrary to basic state policy on guest liability. This illustrates how important it is to determine the basis for a court's ruling and not just to go by general reputation in a line of cases.

Fourth, with one exception, the justices expressed enthusiasm for developing state constitutional civil liberties law. The Burger Court's invitation to state courts to develop state civil liberties law is "welcome" "absolutely." The justices should be "sensitive to using the state constitution because it is broader and can go further." The Alabama high court "frequently uses the Alabama constitution to protect civil liberties," indeed, "state supreme courts should be most competent to determine what the will of the people is as expressed in their own constitutions."

For one justice, one of the "most notable advances" made by the Alabama judiciary "is the rediscovery of . . . the Alabama State constitution.

> No longer is our state constitution ignored or viewed as an obstacle to be sidestepped; rather with due deference to the supremacy clause of the United States Constitution, it is accorded its rightful position of pre-eminence—the polestar by which all other laws are tested. The minimum standards of the Federal Constitution serve

97. As of 1981 the Alabama Supreme Court had not abrogated the state's guest statute. For discussion, see "Alabama's Automobile Guest Statute: The Edsel Lives!" *Alabama Law Review* 33 (1981): 143–79.

only as a floor, not as a ceiling, upon the operative effect of our own Declaration of Human Rights–broader in scope and more eloquent in expression than the Bill of Rights.

Another claimed that since three hundred thousand blacks are now registered to vote in the state and since judges are elected, it stands to reason that courts will be receptive to protecting civil liberties. This justice reports that he advised Jack Greenberg of NAACP-LDF that more cases should be filed in state courts rather than federal courts— for "it is a new ball game" for civil liberties in Alabama.

In the final analysis, views about the federal judiciary are probably not too different from those held by other state justices, but there is evidence that those held by Alabama justices reflect the court's past stormy relationships with federal courts and the stunning legacy of Judge Frank Johnson, whose supervision of mental institutions, prisons, school desegregation programs, and political districting earned him the title of "the other Governor of Alabama." What emerges clearly from conversation is that the justices are eager that their "respect" for the U.S. Supreme Court be known. And for the most part this respect animates a sense of obligation to obey the U.S. Supreme Court, no matter how great the distress over its rulings, as well as a reluctance to express disagreement publicly. More than one justice acknowledged that the court had been "ready for leadership from the federal judiciary; the Alabama justices had known what was wrong." "The 1960s was a period ripe for judicial action and leadership. . . . As a result of inaction at the state level, many Alabama cases made significant law in the U.S. Supreme Court," said another. Yet another noted, "once leadership and the people of the state got over the shock of social change by judicial decrees they accepted the mandates and went about their business. This state and its judiciary took to heart their obligation to uphold the federal Constitution. Once the gavel was down that was that as far as public officials were concerned."

This docility is less apparent where specifics are concerned; however desirous of putting distance between itself and its predecessor, the Alabama high court has more than one bone of contention to pick with the federal judiciary. A major substantive concern centers on the Warren Court's search-and-seizures rulings, particularly because the Fourth Amendment claims have frequently been raised in habeas corpus petitions. Here Chief Justice Torbert has been particularly vocal. Testifying before a subcommittee of the Senate Committee on the Judiciary, he complained that "overextension" of federal court authority to issue the writ "denigrates" state high courts, reducing them to little more than lower courts "[s]ubservient to Federal district courts and Federal magistrates."[98] In an interview one justice said that the Warren Court's "basic error" of "not trusting state courts" had yet "to be corrected," adding that federal court oversight of state judiciaries is one reason "why good people are unwilling to serve on state courts."

Another area of discontent has less to do with substance and more with process. Whether a justice believed that the Supreme Court should do more to balance the rights of "victims of crime" against those of criminal defendants or that many of the Warren Court rulings "were long overdue," there was some agreement that the Warren Court was "at least logical" in extending rights to defendants, but that the Burger Court, by reversing the Warren Court "by degrees," was often "illogical." Rather than "doing away with the exclusionary rule" (which would have been this particular justice's preference), the Court, it was contended, is "chipping away at it in such a way that state courts are often left with little guidance. . . . State courts should be dealt with in a cleaner and surer fashion."

The role federal district courts play in such "local" matters as habeas corpus petitions and demands for social and economic change elicited strong responses. Most justices had serious reservations about the "expansion of federal district court jurisdiction which has unduly caused conflicts with state supreme courts and the elected branches of government." Another responded more cautiously that "federal court intrusion should be more careful in requiring the exhaustion of state remedies." Reaction to Judge Johnson himself is mixed. One justice "admires" him and "accepts what he is doing. There is a special need for the rulings, particularly [concerning] prisons, which are dangerous places for the inmates." Another said that he thought Judge Johnson had "intruded in areas which should be left to state courts . . . courts should not be involved in prison management," but that tensions had lessened since Judge Johnson had gone on to the federal appellate bench. He then offered an assessment of Judge Johnson's motives and intellectual capabilities: "Johnson's decisions," he said, "may be

98. Clement Clay Torbert, Jr., "Statement to the Subcommittee on Courts of the U.S. Senate Committee on the Judiciary in Support of S. 653," undated.

explained as part of his reaction to his rejection by the social leadership of Montgomery. Montgomery is an aristocratic town, and Johnson didn't fit in. Johnson is not as intelligent as he is made out to be; Justice Department briefs provided the basis for his opinions." Then he added, almost as an afterthought, "Maybe on balance what Johnson did was not so bad."[99]

Post-*Brown* rulings that mandated busing as a means of achieving integration in the public schools and judicially mandated affirmative action programs do not sit well with Alabama justices:[100] "The mandate to integrate the schools was inevitable, but the federal courts went overboard with busing as a remedy." Another had given the matter considerable thought:

"The federal courts made two basic errors. The first concerns the question of enforcing decrees. The available remedy is the use of the contempt power, but judges consider this too extreme. In failing to avail themselves of this means of enforcement the judges made a mistake—they took over the legislative and executive functions in the remedies they fashioned. To compel integration the courts should only have used the contempt power and put recalcitrant officials in jail. If judges are afraid to use the contempt power, afraid to see if it is effective, then this is an admission that the political/judicial system does not work the way it is supposed to. The second basic error concerns reverse discrimination, which is just as wrong as segregation. When Justices Stewart and Black said the Constitution is 'color-blind,' they were correct. Reverse discrimination is an instance of the judiciary going too far in attempting to fashion remedies. The courts should enunciate principles that are consistent

99. The reactions to Judge Johnson are certainly ambivalent. The author of the definitive work on Judge Johnson has written, "Judge Johnson observed several years ago that he could 'borrow flour' from any of the court's members. In my judgment, the change in the court's reaction to issues of judicial federalism reflects a variety of factors, including massive increases in black voter registration and a gradual moderation of Alabama racial politics, personnel changes, the healing propensities of time, and a changing legal climate created in part by Judge Johnson's decisions." Letter from Tinsely Yarbrough, Jan. 20, 1982.

100. E.g., *Swann* v. *Charlotte-Mecklenburg Board of Education*, 402 U.S. 1 (1971). In *Arrington* v. *Associated General Contractors*, 403 So.2d 893 (Ala. 1981); cert. denied, 455 U.S. 913 (1981), the court invalidated a Birmingham ordinance that provided that contractors doing business with the city must have 10 percent participation of minority business enterprises.

and that constitute a body of law. The country, for precedential purposes, will 'reap a whirlwind' from reverse discrimination for centuries. The minorities will, in my opinion, be the ultimate victims of these transitory policies of affirmative action."

An Overview

Once in place in the mid-1970s, the court's role within the state changed dramatically. Where the old court performed a legitimating, supportive, even sycophantic function vis-à-vis the other branches of government and the dominant political, social, and economic forces within the state,[101] the new court is far more independent, far more willing to take initiatives, far more mindful and respectful of the federal judiciary, more interested in utilizing precedent from other states, and certainly more sympathetic to civil liberties claims. The unanimous holding in a police brutality case that Section 1983 claims are cognizable in the state's courts provides evidence that the court has fully repudiated the events and attitudes of the past.[102]

This does not mean that the court has precipitated a tort law revolution in the state, that it has discarded long-standing precedent,

101. "Generally speaking, the court is one of conservative character, providing reinforcement for many of the conservative points of view within the state. . . . The membership of the court would probably not willingly concede the notion that they are part of the political system of Alabama, if by political is meant involvement in activities of a policy-making variety. To be sure, many of the cases adjudicated by the court are devoid of policy significance or involve very minute policy questions. Yet, in some measure, virtually every case will involve a cluster of values which are in conflict, and which call for settlement by invocation of precedent or otherwise. Accordingly, within David Easton's formulation of politics and policy-making as the 'authoritative allocation of values' it is quite appropriate to view the court as involved in policymaking.

"Furthermore, it is apparent that the court has a political function in terms of legitimating decisions made elsewhere within the political system. Evidence of this lies in the authority of the court to issue advisory opinions. . . . Decisions involving the validity of bond issues, for example, may have an influence upon the timing and other factors incidental to the implementation of bond issues." This able summation is by Robert Frye, *The Alabama Supreme Court,* p. 87.

102. *Terrell* v. *Bessemer,* 406 So.2d 337 (Ala. 1981). Section 1983 provides the following: "Civil action for deprivation of rights. Every person who, under color of any statute, ordinance, regulation, custom, or usage of any State or Territory, subjects, or causes to be subjected, any citizen of the United States or other persons within the jurisdiction thereof to the deprivation of any rights, privileges or immunities secured by the Constitution and laws, shall be liable to the person injured in an action of law, suit in equity, or other proper proceedings for redress."

that it seeks out doctrines promulgated elsewhere, that it bends with whatever winds may blow from federal benches, or that it has, in the light of Burger Court retrenchments, rushed the state constitution to the rescue.[103] Changes in tort law have not occurred at a steady pace and have not always been consistent.[104] While citations from other jurisdictions have increased, the rise has not been overwhelming.[105] And, as indicated by the interviews and case law, some members of the court have significant disagreements with the U.S. Supreme Court. Further, as is fairly typical throughout the states, the justices

103. No Alabama cases are cited by Donald E. Wilkes, Jr., in his articles on the new judicial federalism: "The New Federalism in Criminal Procedure: State Court Evasion of the Burger Court," *Kentucky Law Journal* 62 (1974): 421–51; "More on the New Federalism in Criminal Procedure," *Kentucky Law Journal* 63 (1975): 873–94; "The New Federalism in Criminal Procedure Revisited," *Kentucky Law Journal* 64 (1976): 729–52.

104. State law journals have been critical of the court on this point. But, it must be remembered that it is part of the business of law journals to act as Monday morning quarterbacks. Whereas the old Alabama high court was castigated for its passivity, the new court is taken to task for contradicting itself, for not providing clear directives, for failing to develop workable principles, for second-guessing the legislature, for not taking the initiative to formulate coherent policy, and so on. See, for example, "Reforming the Common Law: A Factor Analysis for Alabama Courts," *Alabama Law Review* 34 (1983): 631–56; "Tort Liability for State Officials in Alabama," *Alabama Law Review* 35 (1983): 153–66; "Election and Coemployee Immunity Under Alabama's Workmen's Compensation Act," *Alabama Law Review* 31 (1979): 2–27; McMahon, "The State as Defendant;" "Boone v. Mullendore: Confusion of Actions in Wrongful Life, Wrongful Birth and Wrongful Pregnancy," *Alabama Law Review* 35 (1984): 179–92. For commentary that gives credit for the court's initial efforts, see, for example, Stephen D. Heninger, "Bad Faith in Alabama: An Infant Tort in Intensive Care," *Alabama Law Review* 34 (1983): 563–84, and "Henderson v. Wade Sand and Gravel: A Prototype for Economic Analysis in Strict Liability Cases," *Alabama Law Review* 33 (1981): 199–212. "Section 13: Constitutional Armor for the Common Law," *Alabama Law Review* 35 (1984): 127–39, praised the court for invalidating the portions of the state's workers' compensation act that provided immunity against suits by co-employees. *Grantham v. Denke*, 359 So.2d 785 (Ala. 1979), and *Pipkin v. Southern Electric and Pipefitting Co.*, 358 So.2d 1015 (Ala. 1979), were grounded in Sec. 13 of the Alabama constitution, which provides that "all courts shall be open; and that every person, for any injury done him, in his land, goods, person or reputation shall have a remedy by due process of law." *Grantham* and *Pipkin* thus breathed new life into Article 13, formerly interpreted by the court to "provide little more than ex post facto protection for plaintiffs and their rights of action." "Section 13," p. 127.

105. Our survey of cases decided in 1957–58 indicates that out-of-state quotations occurred in about 8 percent of the cases. A slight increase occurred a decade later.

have their problems interpreting directives from their federal counter-parts.[106]

Tort Law and the Debate about Judicial Policy Making

The Setting The Alabama Supreme Court has adopted many of the tort law innovations initiated since the end of World War II, but has not itself been an initiator. "We break no new ground here," dryly observed one of the justices.[107] Despite this, the growing number of "first impression" cases appearing in the Reports and noted in the law journals[108] attests to changes taking place within the state and to what appears to be an easy acceptance of these changes. This acceptance may be attributed to a number of factors. In the first place, however novel a ruling might be in Alabama, the doctrine followed had been espoused and accepted elsewhere. For another, the overruling of precedent had certainly been long pressed upon the court by members of the plaintiffs' bar and by the law reviews.[109] Further, Alabama's lawyers, whatever their predilections, must surely prefer to operate within rather than outside the mainstream of American law. Finally, the court can hardly ignore or escape from the expectations and demands of an increasingly litigious society.[110] In short, decisions that would have appalled the old court are routinely handed down today. Nonetheless, this sort of judicial policy making does not always meet

106. The justices did not agree concerning the standards established for the regulation of obscenity in *Miller* v. *California*, 413 U.S. 15 (1973). *Pierce* v. *State*, 296 So.2d 218 (Ala. 1974), Justice Jones dissenting, cert. denied, 419 U.S. 1130 (1975); *Ballew* v. *State*, 297 So.2d 206 (Ala. 1974), Justice Jones dissenting, Justices Heflin and Maddox concurring separately, cert. denied, 419 U.S. 1130 (1975), Justices Brennan, Stewart, and Marshall dissenting. In *McKinney* v. *Birmingham*, 296 So.2d 202 (Ala. 1974), Justice Jones dissented on the basis of the protections of the Alabama state constitution, cert. denied, 420 U.S. 959 (1975), Justices Brennan, Stewart, and Marshall dissenting on grounds of *Paris Adult Theater* v. *Slayton I*, 413 U.S. 49 (1973).

107. Alabama ranked thirtieth among states in adopting tort law doctrines. Baum and Canon, "Patterns of Tort Law Innovation." Keeton, *Venturing to Do Justice*, cites no Alabama cases. Interview, March 10, 1982.

108. E.g., *Ex Parte McIntosh*, 443 So.2d 1283 (Ala. 1983) (possession of marijuana for personal use not a crime); *Berdeaux* v. *City National Bank*, 424 So.2d 594 (Ala. 1982) (bank has no special duty to protect customers from third persons who attempt armed robbery of bank); *Byars* v. *Baptist Medical Center*, 361 So.2d 350 (Ala. 1978); see also note 117 and accompanying text.

109. See note 47.

110. See note 95 and accompanying text for justices' views.

with the approval of a unanimous court; in sharp contrast to the
united front presented by the old court,[111] the lively and sometimes
acrimonious debate that takes place among today's justices reflects the
fact that no matter how bland rulings may appear to outsiders, the
court's role within the state is undergoing (by Alabama standards)
almost cataclysmic change.

The Cases: An Overview   A sampling of rulings handed down over the
past ten years provides a measure of the court's orientation and the
scope of the changes that have occurred. For example, the court has
significantly eroded the doctrine of sovereign immunity in the state,[112]
has adopted the doctrine of strict products liability,[113] has established
strict liability for harm resulting from inherently dangerous prod-

111. According to the authors' investigations, dissent on the old court never
exceeded 5 percent during the periods 1957–58 and 1967–68, but occurred in 15
percent of the cases during the 1977–78 period. The increased dissent was regarded
by the court's administrator as a sign of a revitalized court. Robert A. Martin,
"Alabama's Courts—Six Years of Change." One justice attributed rising disagreement on the court to the fact that the justices are no longer required to live in
Montgomery and so do not form the close social ties that encouraged unanimity.
Interview, March 10, 1982.

112. The Alabama constitution protects the state against suits but is silent about
the liability of other governmental bodies. In 1973 Alabama was one of only eight
states that retained sovereign immunity for local government. The change came
suddenly. Within five years the court flung precedent to the winds and held that
counties, municipalities, and school boards were liable: *Cook* v. *County of St. Clair,*
384 So.2d 1 (Ala. 1980); *Jackson* v. *Florence,* 320 So.2d 68 (Ala. 1975); *Board of
School Commissioners* v. *Carver,* 355 So.2d 712 (Ala. 1980). Further, the court has
been ingenious in finding ways to circumvent state immunity: *De Stafney* v.
University of Alabama, 413 So.2d 319 (Ala. 1982); *Bell* v. *Chisholm,* 421 So.2d 1239
(Ala. 1982); *Dampier* v. *Pegues,* 362 So.2d 224 (Ala. 1978); *Horton* v. *Northeast
Alabama Regional Medical Center,* 334 So.2d 885 (Ala. 1976); *Hardin* v. *Fullilove
Construction Company,* 353 So.2d 779 (Ala. 1977). For commentary on this trend,
see McMahon, "The State as Defendant."

113. *Casrell* v. *Altec Industries, Inc.,* 335 So.2d 128 (Ala. 1976), and *Atkins* v.
American Motors Corp., 335 So.2d 134 (Ala. 1976). The court has, for all intents and
purposes, adopted the Restatement (Second) of Torts doctrine on products liability.
Alabama Law Review 29 (1977): 266–68. For the view that the old Alabama high
court was not entirely unsympathetic to strict products liability, see C. B. Arendell,
Jr., "A Review of Alabama Cases on Products Liability," *Alabama Lawyer* 32
(1964): 181–94. On the other hand, it has been claimed that the Alabama high
court stubbornly resisted change. "Few parapets of the citadel of privity have been
more stoutly defended than that portion of the fort assigned to the protection of the
Alabama judiciary." Julian B. McDonnell, "The New Privity Puzzle: Products
Liability Under Alabama's Uniform Commercial Code," *Alabama Law Review* 22
(1970): 455.

ucts,[114] has held corporations responsible for the slanderous utterances of their agents, and has permitted wives to sue for loss of consortium.[115] It has recognized new frontiers of the law by permitting suits for mental anguish and emotional distress,[116] for wrongful interference with employment opportunities, for physician disclosure of information obtained through the doctor/patient relationship, and for wrongful pregnancy.[117] In what might be called environmental cases, the court has, in a manner reminiscent of the New Jersey Supreme Court, creatively employed the common law to effectuate policy concerns. In two instances involving charges of pollution, the court applied the more stringent law of trespass rather than the more usual law of negligence, making it clear that trial courts could no longer "weigh the social utility of defendant's activity against the harm suffered by plaintiffs."[118] Along the way it has, over the protests of some of the

114. *Beloit Corp.* v. *Harrell*, 339 So.2d 922 (Ala. 1976), adhering to "standards established in a majority of jurisdictions," *Alabama Law Review* 33 (1982): 799, n. 90, overturned *Lehigh Portland Cement Co.* v. *Dobbins*, 213 So.2d 246 (Ala. 1968). For discussion of the earlier position, see Hare and Hare, "Principal Alabama Actions in Tort."

115. *Cooper* v. *Alabama Farm Bureau Mutual Casualty Insurance Co.*, 385 So.2d 630 (Ala. 1981), overturned hoary precedent going back to 1907, *Mfg. Co.* v. *Taylor*, 43 So.2d 210, and brought Alabama in line with the majority of jurisdictions, *Alabama Law Review* 32 (1981): 805. *Swartz* v. *United States Steel Corp.* 304 So.2d 881 (Ala. 1974), overruling *Smith* v. *United Construction Workers* 122 So.2d 153 (Ala. 1960), allowed a wife to recover for loss resulting from negligent action.

116. In *American Road Service Co.* v. *Inman*, 394 So.2d 361 (Ala. 1981), the court permitted recovery for suffering of mental anguish stemming from intentional infliction of severe emotional distress, thus bringing Alabama in line "with a growing number of jurisdictions," *Cumberland-Samford Law Review* 12 (1982): 527. Earlier, in *Holcombe* v. *Whitaker*, 318 So.2d 289 (Ala. 1975), the court allowed damages for mental suffering caused by a woman who was fraudulently induced to marry an already married man. The ruling was considered "innovative in light of prior Alabama law," *Alabama Law Review* 28 (1976): 199, and followed a New Jersey ruling that recognized the tort of willful, as contrasted with the more usual negligent, infliction of mental anguish. *Morris* v. *MacNab*, 135 A.2d 657 (N.J. 1957). In *Taylor* v. *Baptist Medical Center*, 400 So.2d 369 (Ala. 1981), the court permitted recovery for negligent infliction of emotional distress. To follow precedent that permitted recovery for physical injury only would, said the court, be to adhere to "procrustean principles having no resemblance to medical realities."

117. *Byars* v. *Baptist Medical Center, Inc.*, 361 So.2d 350 (Ala. 1978) (employment); *Horne* v. *Patton*, 287 So.2d 824 (Ala. 1973) (doctor/patient); *Boone* v. *Mullendore*, 416 So.2d 718 (Ala. 1982) (pregnancy).

118. *Rushing* v. *Hopper McDonald, Inc.*, 300 So.2d 94 (Ala. 1974), and *Borland* v. *Sanders Lead Co.*, 369 So.2d 523 (Ala. 1979). *Alabama Law Review* 22 (1975): 408, and ibid. 31 (1980): 861. In *Henderson* v. *Wade Sand and Gravel Co.*, 338 So.2d 900

justices to be sure, discarded an ancient baggage of precedent and has taken its bearings from the rulings of other state supreme courts.[119]

A different sort of common law issue—one that raises questions of constitutional interpretation—has presented the court with almost unlimited policy-making opportunities.[120] The state constitutional provision in question is Section 13 of the first article, which reads in part that "every person, for any injury done him in his lands, goods, person, or reputation shall have a remedy by due process of law." For years statutes that abridged traditional common law rights and remedies were sustained almost routinely against Section 13 claims on the grounds that the common law was outmoded, as in the case of recovery for alienation of affections, or because the legislature, in the exercise of its police powers, sought to eradicate a "perceived social evil." It is under the latter rationale that automobile guest statutes, despite their alleged desuetude and shrinking number nationwide, continue to be upheld by the Alabama high court.[121]

The plaintiffs' bar obviously chafed under such restrictions and when the Alabama legislature amended the state's workers' compensation law to immunize co-employees from suit, thought the time was

---

(Ala. 1980), nuisance law provided the basis for the conservation of water resources. This sort of situation-oriented use of the common law is considered a "trademark" of the far more innovative New Jersey high court, "Project Report: Toward an Activist Role for States Bills of Rights," *Harvard Civil-Rights-Civil-Liberties Law Review* 8 (1973): 338.

119. See cases cited in notes 112–16. E.g., in *Jackson* v. *Florence,* 320 So.2d 68 (Ala. 1975), the court cited decisions from the following states that had abolished municipal immunity: Arizona, California, Florida, Illinois, Kansas, Kentucky, Michigan, Nebraska, Nevada, New Jersey, Rhode Island, and New Mexico. In *Opelika Production Credit* v. *Lamb,* 361 So.2d 95 (Ala. 1975), the court, permitting recovery for violation of a quasi-contract, "relied on two cases from other jurisdictions and cited no Alabama cases for support." This was considered "noteworthy" by a commentator. "In Equity and Good Conscience: The Requirements for a Quasi-Contractual Recovery in Alabama," *Alabama Law Review* 33 (1982): 492–519.

120. The discussion that follows is based largely on "Section 13: Constitutional Armor for the Common Law," and "Election and Coemployee Immunity Under Alabama's Workmen's Compensation Act." Twenty-six states have similar constitutional provisions.

121. *Pickett* v. *Matthews,* 192 So.2d 261 (Ala. 1939); "Alabama's Automobile Guest Statutes." The rationale behind the guest laws is that host immunity protects against collusive suits. In 1985 such statutes were in effect in only seven states, having been abrogated by courts or rescinded by legislatures. In 1975 three Alabama justices stated that the time had come to repeal "this inherently bad law." *Beasley* v. *Bozeman,* 315 So.2d 570, 571.

ripe to make some practical use of Section 13.[122] In the case of *Grantham* v. *Denke*[123] (1978) the court agreed with the plaintiffs' argument that while the employer's immunity was an exchange for his assumption of liability, there was no such voluntary accommodation among employees. Other than Justice Shores, who later complained that her colleagues had given little thought to the reasons for that immunity, no other justice gave much consideration to the perceived social evil that the law sought to combat, as had been the practice in previous Section 13 litigation. The majority's focus was confined to the withdrawal of a common-law right without the provision of an alternative recourse. *Grantham* opened the floodgates, and since handing down that decision the court has devoted considerable time and energy to explaining it. And, as might be expected considering the novel aspects of the case, the court has wavered between the *Grantham* and guest statute approaches to Section 13.[124]

The Debates The Alabama Supreme Court's more aggressive stance in tort law cases has been accompanied by considerable debate among the justices concerning the proper division of labor between the court and the legislature, the pace at which the court has proceeded in overturning precedent and adopting new doctrines, and the substance of legal and constitutional doctrine. The dissenting position in the landmark sovereign immunity cases provides a good example of the restraintist position. Here Justice Merrill, who would shortly retire after twenty-three years' service on the court, reiterated the old court's objections to judicial abrogation: there was a strong relationship between sovereign immunity and governmental fiscal stability and, further, the court had assumed a prerogative that rightly belonged to the legislature.[125]

Dissents in other cases reflected the same perspective. When the court (finally) got around to holding that wives could sue for loss of

122. *Alabama Trial Lawyers Journal,* July–August 1977, p. 15; "Election and Coemployee Immunity," p. 14. In a telephone conversation with one of the authors, a plaintiff's lawyer said, "The Alabama legislature has by statute exempted certain groups from lawsuits. This is unwarranted 'judicialization,' and, in essence, deprives people of their right to defend their interests in the court. Under this legislation the 'little man' cannot have his day in court." March 25, 1982.

123. *Grantham* v. *Danke.* The companion case is *Pipkin* v. *Southern Electric and Pipefitting Co.,* 359 So.2d 785 (Ala. 1979); 358 So.2d 1015 (Ala. 1979).

124. E.g., *Harris* v. *Montgomery,* 435 So.2d 1207 (Ala. 1983), sustained the immunity provisions of the Child Abuse Reporting Act against Section 13 claims.

125. *Jackson* v. *Florence,* 320 So.2d 68 (Ala. 1975).

consortium, the four dissenters, led by Chief Justice Torbert, insisted that although the rule that wives could not sue was judge-made, it had been incorporated into Alabama law by statute; that the statute provided for legislatively initiated change; that the court had no business in the matter other than to fill the open spaces of the law; and that the decision created a new cause of action—a function traditionally reserved to the legislature.[126] In a case that applied the laws of nuisance in a dispute between a landowner and the owner of a quarry over water diversion, Chief Justice Torbert and Justice Maddox thought that the legislature, not the court, should strike the balance between the rights of one living near a quarry and the right of the quarry owner to do business.[127] In the Section 13 workers' compensation case the dissenters could not claim that the court had usurped a legislative function, since a constitutional question had been raised. Instead, they rested their objections on the familiar judicial self-restraint arguments. Justice Maddox, defending the legislative choice, expressed the view that workers who enjoyed the protections of workers' compensation had, in effect, surrendered their right to sue fellow workers. Chief Justice Torbert, while conceding that "the result reached by the majority has an appeal—that of making an injured party whole,"—admonished his colleagues that "it is the recognized duty of this court to sustain an act unless it is clear beyond a reasonable doubt that it is violative of the fundamental law." The decisions, in his view, did "great violence to the rules which govern how this court has interpreted constitutional provisions."[128]

When the court allowed recovery for mental distress, Chief Justice Torbert joined Justice Almon in objecting to a "departure from the long-standing rule in this jurisdiction." When the majority, overtur-

---

126. *Swartz* v. *United States Steel Corp.* overruled *Smith* v. *United Construction Workers,* 304 So.2d 881 (Ala. 1974); 122 So.2d 153 (Ala. 1960).

127. *Henderson* v. *Wade Sand & Gravel,* 338 So.2d 900 (Ala. 1980).

128. *Grantham* v. *Denke,* 359 So.2d 785, 789, (Ala. 1979). Chief Justice Torbert quoting from *Alabama State Federation of Labor* v. *McAdomy,* 18 So.2d 810 (Ala. 1944). A plaintiffs' attorney told the authors that, in his view, the revolution in tort law was "drawn up short" in the late 1970s and early 1980s. This could be attributed to the chief justice, who, he says, is "situation-oriented," conservative, and has "polarized" the court. The more liberal and innovative justices are, in his view, Jones, Faulkner, and Shores. Justice Adams, because of his background, might also be found there, but there was an insufficient track record (as of 1982). Justice Beatty provides the swing vote. With the chief justice on the "right" are Justices Maddox ("a true scholar"), Almon, and Embry. Telephone interview March 25, 1982.

ning a line of cases antedating the Civil War, held that a lessee might sue for the capricious and unreasonable withholding of consent to sublet, Justices Bloodworth and Almon took issue with what they regarded as the majority's trifling with existing property law without giving proper notice to landlords, tenants, and lawyers. In one case in which the dissenters ostensibly were unhappy about a break with precedent, it seems as though their policy preferences, if not crucial, were a factor. Here the court substituted a strict liability rule for the existing negligence standard when defendants were sued for causing harm resulting from abnormally dangerous activities (blasting). Justices Embry, Torbert, Almon, and Beatty indicated they thought that the social policy of encouraging economic development remained viable.[129]

Disagreement on the court was not confined to objections to or reservations about altering the common law. Some of the justices thought that the court was proceeding too slowly or had not gone far enough. Two cases involving landlord/tenant disputes are instructive. In the first the majority declined to hold exculpatory clauses in residential leases unenforceable. Plaintiffs, relying on California precedent, urged the court to void the clause on public policy grounds: the scarcity of apartments affected the relative bargaining power of tenants and landlords. "A spirited dissent," it was reported, "objected to the majority's reflexive deference to the legislature." Said Justice Jones, joined by Justices Shores and Beatty, "The majority, unfortunately, has opted to skirt the problem by a cleverly phrased dichotomy of issues that in effect does nothing more than pass the buck to the legislature." Two years later the court held that a landlord who had *concealed* a known latent defect was not protected by an exculpatory clause. Justices Faulkner, Jones, and Embry concurring felt, however, that "it was time for the court to announce the invalidity of all exculpatory clauses in residential leases, asserting that the clauses not only invalidated public policy but are *prima facie* unconscionable."[130]

129. *Taylor* v. *Baptist Medical Center*, 400 So.2d 369, 375 (1981) (mental distress); *Homa-Goff Interiors, Inc.* v. *Cowden*, 350 So.2d 1053 (Ala. 1977); *Nave* v. *Berry*, 22 Ala. 382 (1853) (sublet); *Harper* v. *Regency Development Co.*, 399 S.2d 248 (Ala. 1981) (blasting), overruling *Coalite, Inc.* v. *Weeks*, 224 So.2d 251 (Ala. 1969).

130. *Matthews* v. *Mountain Lodge Apartments, Inc.*, 388 So.2d 935 (Ala. 1980). *Henrioulle* v. *Marin Ventures, Inc.*, 573 P.2d 465 (Cal. 1978). The precedent was not, of course, dispositive. The majority indicated that the legislature was in a better position than the court to deal with the "broad socioeconomic ramifications of the

In a dispute that concerned a hospital employee dismissed because she refused to falsify medical records, the court held that it would not depart from precedent to create a new tort for wrongful termination of an employment-at-will contract. Justices Jones, Shores, and Embry dissented, claiming that there should be public policy exceptions to the contracts-at-will rule. For "the law is not unaccustomed to dealing with the 'public policy' concept both in its definition and application." There is a strong public interest in the "accuracy and integrity of hospital records."[131]

Finally, the court's refusal to abolish the doctrine of contributory negligence, while admitting that it certainly had the authority to do so, drew particularly acerbic dissents. Justice Jones pointed out that the court had in the products liability and consortium cases claimed that it *was* the proper body to change judicially created doctrine. The majority's claim that the legislature should enact a comparative negligence law just because other legislatures had done so was not a valid one. To which Justice Faulkner added: "The majority's holding . . . is like shaking the clammy lifeless hand of another man. It has no meaning. If the court has the power to change the rule, a better reason than passing the buck to the legislature should be given."[132]

The Section 13 cases, as might be expected, occasioned fundamental disagreements on the court; indeed, so serious were the doubts surrounding *Grantham* that in *Fireman's Fund American Insurance Co. v. Coleman,* a ruling that extended co-employee immunity to cover supervisory employees, Justices Beatty and Shores changed their minds about the extent of their support of *Grantham.* Justice Beatty's position was the more clear-cut. He simply joined the *Grantham* dissenters in iterating deference to the "plenary power of the legislature," and gave as his reasons "the continuing necessity for explaining

---

existing and proposed rule." "Reforming the Common Law," p. 652. n. 165. *Matthews* v. *Mountain Lodge,* at 940. *Taylor* v. *Leady & Co.,* 412 So.2d 73 (Ala. 1982); Olin L. Browder, "The Taming of a Duty—The Tort Liability of Landlords," *Michigan Law Review* 81 (1982): 99–156. The dissenters would agree with the California Supreme Court's ruling that "rejected the traditional common law rule that landlords are not liable for injuries caused by a defective condition unless there is fraud, concealment or a covenant in the lease." *American Bar Association Journal* 71 (1985): 94, noting *Becker* v. *IBM Corp.,* 698 P.2d 116 (Cal. 1985).

131. *Henrichs* v. *Tranquilaire Hospital,* 352 So.2d 1130, 1133 (Ala. 1977).

132. *Golden* v. *McCurry,* 392 So.2d 815, 819 (Ala. 1980). The Alabama legislature considered but did not adopt a comparative negligence scheme. "Reforming the Common Law," p. 651, n. 160.

the 'judicial tar-baby', *Grantham*, as well as the explanations themselves."[133]

Justice Shores's approach was more subtle. While concurring, she
was clearly troubled by the implications of the case as it pertained to
precedent, constitutional explication, and, most important, legislative/
judicial relations: "It was up to the courts to supply content to
[Section 13] without overstepping their traditional role and legislating
themselves. . . . [T]oo literal a reading of the prohibitions of Section
13 may effectively preclude government action in areas of crucial
public concern; too broad a reading eviscerates the very rights the
section was intended to support."[134]

In addition to the question of the court's proper stance vis-à-vis the
legislature, another Section 13 issue was the mode of analysis to be
utilized in Section 13 cases. In *Lankford* v. *Sullivan, Long & Haggerty,* a
unanimous court invalidated a law limiting the time period in which
products liability claims might be brought. Justice Almon's plurality
opinion adopted a strict scrutiny approach. Applying the two-tiered
standard of review, the court held that it could determine no
relationship between the statute and the goal of preventing higher
consumer and insurance costs; therefore, it failed the "perceived
social evil" test. Put differently, to withstand Section 13 challenges,
the legislature must satisfy the court that it had a good reason for
interfering with common-law rights and/or causes of action. Justice
Almon was joined by Justices Shores, Jones, Embry, and Adams
(Justice Faulkner concurred separately). In his separate concurrence,
Justice Jones indicated that he believed that Section 13 protects all
fundamental rights of action, whatever their source:

A right of such fundamental character as contemplated by Section
13 may have its source in the legislative process, customs or
practices, or in the judicial process. It is the nature and the character
of the right, i.e., its being so ingrained in the fabric of the law as to
acquire a fundamental and basic status, rather than its source, that
dictates Section 13's protective applicability.[135]

133. *Grantham*, 359 So.2d 785 (Ala. 1979). *Fireman's Fund*, 394 So.2d 334 (Ala.
1980). Dissenting in *Fireman's Fund*, at 355–58. Justice Beatty defended his
"switch" for "purist souls" by providing instances of U.S. Supreme Court judicial
changes of heart and the example of a British judge who, confronted by an earlier
and rejected stance, expressed amazement that "a man of his intelligence should
have been guilty of such an opinion."
134. 394 So.2d, 352–54.
135. 416 So.2d 996, 1007 (Ala. 1982).

Chief Justice Torbert, joined by Justices Maddox and Beatty, took issue with both the strict scrutiny and fundamental rights approaches. In their view, since they contended that all possible leeway should be permitted to the legislature, Section 13 invalidated only arbitrary and capricious laws such as the one under review. In a separate concurrence, Chief Justice Torbert would have had the court rest its ruling on the state and federal constitutional guarantees of due process of law and the equal protection of the laws. Thus, even a unanimous court could not agree on the appropriate approach. Five justices (Almon, Shores, Embry, Jones, and Adams) adopted the strict-scrutiny, two-tiered analysis; one (Faulkner) simply registered a concurrence; one (Jones) proposed the fundamental rights approach; three (Torbert, Maddox, and Beatty) found the statute arbitrary and capricious; and one (Torbert) thought that it violated other state and federal constitutional guarantees. Such a display, of course, would never have occurred on the old court, both because the justices would not have dreamed of offending the state legislature and because the old court did not have so many independent-minded, articulate members.

In a subsequent case, *Scott* v. *Dunn*, Justices Shores and Almon joined the *Lankford* dissenters, thus indicating that the court is as much influenced by the facts and policy-making implications of a ruling as it is with searching for standards to guide it in making Section 13 decisions. Here a bare majority sustained a statute that immunized livestock owners against suits when automobiles hit cattle and passengers were injured. The majority thought that cattle owners needed protection against motorists who did not exercise sufficient care. In his dissent Justice Jones pointed out that this particular immunity statute merely reflected interest group pressures, having been adopted by the rural black belt legislators who had for so long dominated politics in the state. Justice Faulkner's opinion, in which all dissenters joined, took a different tack:

> Whether the statute eradicated a social evil in 1939, I cannot say. But clearly it does . . . not today. It abolishes an action for negligence, recklessness, and for failure to secure an animal whose known mischievous propensity is to roam the highways. . . . The safety of those driving automobiles should not be jeopardized by the recklessness of livestock owners.[136]

136. 419 So.2d 1340, 1350 (Ala. 1982).

The dissenters, in other words, sought in the manner of classic judicial activism to find a constitutional remedy for what they regarded as an unjust law enacted in a manner that perverted the democratic process. Perhaps had the issue in the case been of greater interest or had it adversely affected more people, the dissenters might have brought another justice to their side. The fact that they did not succeed is less important than the fact that they came very close to prevailing.

As the tort law cases reveal, there is disagreement on the court concerning the judicial role in formulating public policy. The cases also reveal that there are generally activist and restraintist blocs on the court. But as *Scott* v. *Dunn* illustrates, the blocs do not always hold together. Factual and policy considerations, not to mention doctrinal questions, account for differences between blocs and among justices such as Shores and Jones, who often agree. Divisions aside, the significant point is that the court quite openly discusses the part it should, or should not, play in the governing process. This was unheard of fifteen years ago. And so, while the court has not "broken new ground," it is rather self-consciously carving out for itself a place in the political system that is substantially different from the position it occupied for so many years.

Civil Rights and Liberties

"There is no hesitancy about protecting civil liberties on the Alabama Supreme Court," said one of its justices with evident pride; "indeed there have been massive and extraordinary changes since the days of the 'old court'." The Alabama high court may not be included among the nation's activist, civil libertarian "lighthouse" state courts,[137] but it

137. Interview, March 11, 1982. The literature on state high court civil libertarian activism cites few cases from the Alabama Supreme Court. For representative articles, see G. Alan Tarr, "Bibliographic Essay," in Mary Cornelia Porter and G. Alan Tarr, *State Supreme Courts: Policymakers in the Federal System* (Westport, Ct.: Greenwood Press, 1982), pp. 206–08. A comprehensive survey is found in "Developments in the Law—The Interpretation of State Constitutional Rights," *Harvard Law Review* 95 (1984): 1324–1502, and an assessment in Ronald K. L. Collins, "Reliance on State Constitutions: Some Random Thoughts," *Mississippi Law Journal* 54 (1984): 371–421. In a series of cases presenting challenges to the regulation of obscenity, the court sustained, on the basis of *Miller* v. *California*, convictions obtained for the distribution of pornography. Justice Jones dissented on the ground that the antiobscenity ordinances violated the state constitution. In *McKinney* v. *Birmingham*, Jones, arguing against the majority's quashing of a writ of certiorari as improvidently granted, agreed that United State

may be described as being in the mainstream, responding to U.S. Supreme Court rulings and civil liberties issues generally much as state courts have during the eras of the Warren and Burger courts. That is, the court has followed and distinguished precedent and has relied on the state constitution to guarantee rights as well as to evade restrictive U.S. Supreme Court rulings. It has on occasion creatively adhered to the spirit as well as the letter of Court holdings and has attempted to persuade its federal counterpart to change course.[138]

Supreme Court standards would not afford relief to the appellant. He questioned, however, "the extent to which the United States Supreme Court's interpretation of the minimum safeguards afforded by the United States Constitution" were "controlling where the Alabama Constitution grants like or broader safeguards to personal freedom." He asserted that the Ninth and Tenth Amendments to the federal Constitution allow state constitutions to provide greater protection of civil liberties than that afforded by the federal Constitution. Jones added that while he did not "condone the widespread proliferation of obscenity in society today," he refused to force others to conform to his standards of morality. "[T]he restraint against such inclination is the very essence of the constitutional safeguards of personal liberties." Finally, Jones, calling upon Socrates and St. Thomas Aquinas, added that "controlling crime and safeguarding morals are different things." Cases cited in note 106 above. Jones, at 296 So.2d 237–39.

138. The Alabama justices, like all state justices, consider themselves bound by United States Supreme Court's interpretation of the United States Constitution. There is, of course, often a considerable choice among federal precedents, and a court may select those that are more and those that are less expansive. For instance, in sustaining a law that restricted the inheritance rights of illegitimates, the court distinguished *Trimble* v. *Gordon*, 430 U.S. 762 (1977), and relied instead on *Lalli* v. *Lalli*, 439 U.S. 259 (1978). *Everage* v. *Gibson*, 372 So.2d 829 (Ala. 1979), cert. denied, 445 U.S. 931 (1980). And in *Arrington* v. *Associated General Contractors*, 403 So.2d 893 (Ala. 1981), cert. denied, 455 U.S. 913 (1981), the court relied on Justice Powell's *Fullilove* v. *Klutznick*, 448 U.S. 448, 496–98 (1980), concurrence to void a Birmingham ordinance that required a portion of funds for each city contract to be spent on "minority business enterprises" (MBE). The court determined that the city plan was not tailored specifically to remedy past discrimination and further that it conflicted with state law requiring competitive bids. Justices Jones, Shores, and Beatty dissented on the grounds of the majority opinion in *Fullilove* and on Justice Powell's *Bakke* criteria for constitutionally permissible preferential treatment for minorities. *Regents of the University of California* v. *Bakke*, 438 U.S. 265, 269–324 (1978). In *Davis* v. *State*, 291 So.2d 346 (Ala. 1974), it was held that state constitution guarantees the right to be represented by counsel of one's own choosing. See also, *Peddy* v. *Montgomery*, 354 So.2d 631 (Ala. 1977), and Justice Jones's solitary position in obscenity cases, notes 106 and 137. In *Gilbreath* v. *Wallace*, 292 So.2d 651 (Ala. 1974), the court held, federal precedent notwithstanding, that legislative provision for six-person juries violated the spirit, if not the letter, of the state constitution. *Williams* v. *Florida*, 399 U.S. 78 (1970), held that twelve-person juries are not required by the Constitution. *Hudson* v. *Hudson*, 373

The Warren Court's criminal justice rulings had an immediate and stunning effect on state judiciaries including Alabama's. In the first place, the court was overwhelmed by the new demands on its docket. "Oh, they *swamped* us," recalled one justice, "they really *impacted* on us," adding that the burden that federal right to counsel and search-and-seizure rulings placed on the state courts was in some measure responsible for the impetus to reform the state's judicial system.[139] In the second place, bitterness over federal judicial intervention in the racial cases exacerbated what was early on a typically negative high state court response to the expansion of the rights of defendants.[140] The

---

So.2d 310 (Ala. 1979), held that without statutory authorization courts lacked authority to issue sterilization orders. The case involved a parental request for the procedure to be performed on a sixteen-year-old mentally defective female. While the court's holding was on its face narrow, the court, citing *Roe* v. *Wade,* 410 U.S. 113 (1973), and *Carey* v. *Population Services,* 431 U.S. 678 (1977), iterated that the Constitution protects the fundamental right to procreation, thus suggesting that it would carefully scrutinize any legislative authorization of sterilization. In *Harris* v. *State,* 356 So.2d 623 (Ala. 1978), the court, relying on *Planned Parenthood* v. *Danforth,* 428 U.S. 52 (1976), held that a father had to pay support for an illegitimate child he did not want when the mother refused to have an abortion. The court thus utilized a federal holding that the decision about abortion is solely the mother's up to the twelfth week of pregnancy in order to compel the father of an illegitimate to meet his responsibilities. In *Paschal* v. *State,* 365 So.2d 681 (Ala. 1975), the court held, over the protests of Chief Justice Torbert, whose aversion to the exclusionary rule was clear (see pp. 118–19 below), and Justice Maddox, that a police radio dispatch did not provide probable cause for a warrantless automobile search. In *Taylor* v. *State,* 399 So.2d 881 (Ala. 1981); rev'd. 451 U.S. 67 (1982), the court came within one vote of persuading the United States Supreme Court to adopt a "good faith" exception to the exclusionary rule. Alabama rejected the exclusionary rule in 1984, and prior to *Mapp* v. *Ohio,* 367 U.S. 643 (1961), excluded illegally seized evidence only when the seizure violated state statute. Lee L. Hale, "Searches and Seizures in Violation of an Alabama Statute," *Alabama Lawyer* 40 (1979): 527–34.

139. Interview, March 9, 1982. Our survey of cases indicates a 17 percent increase in the court's criminal docket between 1957–58 and 1967–68.

140. The court's churlishness was evident when it held, federal precedent notwithstanding, that appointed counsel was not required for appeals where no "appealable error" existed, and would "thereby amount to nothing more than a gesture pure and simple." *Caton* v. *State,* 205 So.2d 239, 244 (Ala. 1967). *Douglas* v. *California,* 372 U.S. 353 (1965), addressed precisely this point, holding that counsel *was* required, even when appellate courts considered the appointment useless. Commentary on the Alabama holding was harsh. "It is conceivable that court appointed counsel might, by means of this 'gesture' discover valid grounds for appeal." "Constitutional Law—Criminal Law," *Alabama Law Review* 20 (1967–68): 353. Note 17 listed similar cases in which the Alabama high court distinguished *Douglas* v. *California.* In *Boykin* v. *State,* 207 So.2d 412 (Ala 1968), rev'd.

approach of the Heflin and Torbert courts has, by contrast, been marked by a conscientious effort to be a good, if not always enthusiastic, soldier. The interpretation of federal directives meant that sometimes defendants were winners and sometimes losers.[141] Like courts in sister states, the Alabama high court has had its share of problems in applying the Supreme Court's standards for the administration of the death penalty.[142] Only the exclusionary rule, regarded by

---

395 U.S. 238 (1969), the court sustained the death penalty for five counts of armed robbery. Three justices dissented on the ground that the guilty plea had not been knowingly and intelligently entered. Justice Lawson of *Powell* v. *Alabama* fame, 131 So.2d (Ala. 1932). rev'd 287 U.S. 45 (1932), argued that "[t]he record contains nothing to indicate that Boykin's plea of guilty was not voluntarily and knowingly made or that it was the product of coercion, either mental or physical, or was unfairly obtained or given through ignorance, fear or inadvertence. For aught appearing, the plea was entirely voluntary and Boykin fully realized and was competent to know and understand the possible consequences of such a plea," at 414. In minor criminal cases the Alabama high court almost went out of its way to distinguish federal precedent, ruling that since "trespass is a potential cause of violence," "the right to picket" must be balanced against not only the owner's right to use his property, but also against the state's interest in keeping the peace. *Taggart* v. *Weinrackers*, 214 So.2d 913 (Ala. 1968), distinguishing *Amalgamated Food Employees Union* v. *Logan Valley Plaza*, 391 U.S. 308 (1968). *State* v. *Mills*, 176 So.2d 884 (Ala. 1966), rev'd. on First Amendment grounds, 384 U.S. 214 (1966), sustained the conviction of a newspaper editor who had published an editorial supporting a change to the mayor-council form of government for Birmingham. The statute under which the conviction was obtained prohibited electioneering in favor of or opposition to ballot propositions. The new form of government was understood to be aimed at establishing more moderate racial policies.

141. Winners: **Searches and Seizures**: *Kinard* v. *State*, 335 So.2d 924 (Ala. 1976), following *Coolidge* v. *New Hampshire*, 403 U.S. 443 (1971); *Horzempa* v. *State*, 290 So.2d 220 (Ala. 1974), following *Spinelli* v. *U.S.*, 393 U.S. 410 (1969), and *Aguilar* v. *Texas*, 378 U.S. 108 (1964). **Confrontation of Witnesses**: *Shockley* v. *State*, 335 So.2d 663 (Ala. 1976), following *Douglas* v. *Alabama*, 380 U.S. 415 (1965), which went from the Alabama Court of Criminal Appeals directly to the United States Supreme Court, the Alabama high court having denied certiorari, 163 So.2d 496 (Ala. 1979), following *Barker* v. *Wingo*, 407 U.S. 514 (1972); **Confessions, Miranda standards**: *Garrett* v. *State*, 369 So.2d 833 (Ala. 1979); *Harrison* v. *State*, 358 So.2d 763 (Ala. 1978); *Davis* v. *State*, 389 So.2d 952 (Ala. 1980); **Probation Revocation**: *Armstrong* v. *State*, 312 So.2d 620 (Ala. 1977), following *Morrissey* v. *Brewer*, 408 U.S. 471 (1972); **Prison Discipline**: *Williams* v. *Davis*, 386 So.2d 415 (Ala. 1981), following *Presier* v. *Rodriguez*, 411 U.S. 475 (1973), and *Wolff* v. *McDonnell*, 418 U.S. 539 (1974). Losers: **Searches and Seizures**: *Reid* v. *State*, 338 So.2d 208 (Ala. 1980), following *South Dakota* v. *Opperman*, 428 U.S. 364 (1976), and *Chambers* v. *Monroney*, 399 U.S. 42 (1973); *Rickman* v. *State*, 361 So.2d 28 (Ala. 1978), following *U.S.* v. *Rabinowitz*, 339 U.S. 56 (1950).

142. For a general discussion, see Joseph A. Conquitt, "The Death Penalty Laws of Alabama," *Alabama Law Review* 33 (1982): 213–351. Divided courts and strong

the court's majority as a "crude, heavy-handed sanction of doubtful effectiveness . . . failing to accomplish its stated purpose of deterring unlawful police conduct,"[143] evoked the defiance of the old court. But this view is shared by other state judges as well as federal judges, including some on the Supreme Court, and indeed may become the position of the Rehnquist Court.

In civil liberties areas, such as freedom of expression and gender equality, the Alabama justices evinced considerable support for principles established by the Warren and Burger courts. For example, one justice remarked that libel law in Alabama now goes beyond the *Sullivan* strictures, and cases that have expanded the "public figure" doctrine and strictly construed the "actual malice" doctrine bear this out.[144] After refusing, over the strong protests of Justice Jones, to review an unsuccessful challenge to the state's alimony statute that required support only from ex-husbands, the equality of the sexes shortly became a particular concern of the court.[145] Relying on the

dissents reflect the court's problems and its efforts to do what was correct. In *Harris* v. *State,* 352 So.2d 479 (Ala. 1977), only five justices thought that the state's new capital punishment law followed the U.S. Supreme Court's post-*Furman* guidelines. *Furman* v. *Georgia,* 408 U.S. 238 (1972); *Roberts* v. *Louisiana,* 431 U.S. 633 (1977); *Williams* v. *Oklahoma,* 428 U.S. 907 (1976); *Woodson* v. *North Carolina,* 428 U.S. 280 (1976); *Jurek* v. *Texas,* 428 U.S. 262 (1976); *Gregg* v. *Georgia,* 428 U.S. 153 (1976); *Profitt* v. *Florida,* 428 U. S. 242 (1976). In *Evans* v. *State,* 361 So.2d 666 (Ala. 1978), sentence vacated, 448 U.S. 903 (1980), and *Jacobs* v. *State,* 361 So.2d 640 (Ala. 1978), cert. denied, 439 1122 (1979), the justices were also divided. In *Swaim* v. *State,* 274 So.2d 305 (Ala. 1974), the death sentence was vacated on grounds of *Furman.* In 1980 the U.S. Supreme Court vacated nine Alabama death sentences, among them *Baldwin* v. *State,* 372 So.2d 32 (Ala. 1978), 448 U.S. 903; *Beck* v. *State,* 396 So.2d 645 (Ala. 1978), 448 U.S. 903; on remand the Alabama court "salvaged" the death penalty statute by severing the unconstitutional section from the remainder, 396 So.2d 666, (Ala. 1981), *Alabama Law Review* 33 (1982): 662; *Cade* v. *State,* 375 So.2d 828 (Ala. 1979), 448 U.S. 9903; *Thomas* v. *State,* 373 So.2d 1167 (Ala. 1979), 448 U.S. 903.

143. *Taylor* v. *State,* 399 So.2d 881, 893 (Ala. 1981), rev'd. 451 U.S. 67 (1982).

144. *New York Times* v. *Sullivan,* 376 U.S. 254 (1964). *American Benefit Life Insurance Co.* v. *McIntyre,* 375 So.2d 239 (Ala. 1979), *Mobile Press Register, Inc.* v. *Faulkner,* 372 So.2d 1282 (Ala. 1977), *Fulton* v. *Advertiser Co.,* 388 So.2d 533 (Ala. 1980), cert. denied, 449 U.S. 1125 (1981), *Browning* v. *Birmingham News,* 348 So.2d 455 (Ala. 1977). Citing *Sullivan* and *Gertz* v. *Robert Welch,* 418 U.S. 323 (1979), the court reversed a libel judgement for lack of proof of actual injury by the plaintiffs and the failure of the trial court to instruct the jury about the requirement for proof of "actual malice" for the purpose of awarding punitive damages, *Bryan* v. *Brown,* 339 S.2d 577 (Ala. 1976), cert. denied 431 U.S. 954 (1977).

145. *Orr* v. *Orr,* cert. initially granted, then quashed as improvidently granted, 351 So.2d 906 (Ala. 1977), appealed from Ala. Ct. Civ. App., 351 So.2d 904

state constitution, but grounding its rulings in federal precedent, the court invalidated a statute, the only one of its kind still extant in the United States, that prohibited a married woman from alienating or mortgaging her land without her husband's consent. The decision marked, at that time, one of the relatively rare instances in which a state court struck down a gender-based law or practice on state constitutional grounds—and this includes efforts to reach similar outcomes based on state "little ERA's." The holding also supplied precedent for striking down a law that provided that a woman's marriage operates as a revocation of her will.[146] Continuing the trend, the court held that married women are not required to use their husband's name when registering to vote[147] and that the "tender years presumption," which almost invariably awards custody of very young children to their mothers, reflects outmoded sex-role stereotyping and must be replaced with careful consideration of the facts of each case.[148] And overruling more than ninety years of precedent, the court invalidated a statute proscribing the use of "abusive, insulting or obscene language in the presence or hearing of a woman" as an "unwarranted gender-based classification."[149]

(1977), rev'd. 440 U.S. 268 (1979). For overall discussion of the status of women and family law in Alabama, see Marjorie Fine Knowles, "The Legal Status of Women in Alabama: A Crazy Quilt," *Alabama Law Review* 29 (1978): 427–515. Knowles, "The Legal Status of Women in Alabama, II: A Crazy Quilt Restitched," ibid. 33 (1982): 375–406, and Camille W. Cook, "Family Law: Surveying 15 Years of Change in Alabama," ibid. 36 (1985): 419–71.

146. *Peddy* v. *Montgomery*, 345 So.2d 631 (Ala. 1977), citing *Reed* v. *Reed*, 404 U.S. 71 (1971), *Frontiero* v. *Richardson*, 411 U.S. 677 (1972), and *Stanton* v. *Stanton*, 421 U.S. 7 (1975). Tarr and Porter, "Gender Equality and Judicial Federalism." *Parker* v. *Hall*, 362 So.2d 872 (Ala. 1978) followed *Peddy*.

147. *State* v. *Taylor*, 415 So.2d 1043 (Ala. 1983), indicated that *Forbush* v. *Wallace*, 314 F. Supp. 217 (M.D. Ala. 1971), aff'd. per curiam, 405 U.S. 970 (1972), incorrectly stated Alabama's common law rule. At that time no procedures were available for federal courts to certify questions of state law to the Alabama Supreme Court. As of 1983, Alabama was one of three states in the Eleventh Circuit to which questions of state law may be certified. See generally, Carroll Seron, *Certifying Questions of State Law: Experience of Federal Judges* (Federal Judicial Center, January 1983), and John R. Brown, "Certification—Federalism in Action," *Cumberland-Samford Law Review* 7 (1977): 455–65.

148. *Devine* v. *Devine*, 398 So.2d 686 (Ala. 1981). While Alabama law formally provided for equal rights for both parents, the courts had sustained the maternal preference. *Skipper* v. *Skipper*, 195 So.2d 797 (Ala. 1967); *Thompson* v. *Thompson*, 326 So.2d 124 (Ala. App. 1975), cert. denied, 326 So.2d 129 (Ala. 1976).

149. *Frolick* v. *State*, 392 So.2d 846 (Ala. 1981), overruling *Laney* v. *State*, 17 So.2d 107 (Ala. 1895). The court cited *Craig* v. *Boren*, 429 U.S. 190 (1976), and *Stanton* v. *Stanton*, 421 U.S. 7 (1975).

The Alabama high court, like its counterparts in other states, is not, except for defendants' rights cases, presented with many opportunities to decide civil rights issues. Further, old habits developed by necessity die hard, and federal courts in Alabama, especially the hospitable and extraordinary forum provided by District Judge Frank Johnson, have been considered more sympathetic to federal claims than state courts. And it may be that the Alabama high court has sent mixed signals on some issues such as church/state relations, so that those claiming rights violations continue to shy away from state courts.[150] The point,

150. See generally, Yarbrough, *Judge Frank Johnson.* The famous Tuskegee gerrymandering case was initiated in a federal court. *Gomillion* v. *Lightfoot,* 364 U.S. 339 (1961). An example of a case raising civil liberties issues is *Roe* v. *Conn,* 417 F. Supp. 769 (M.D. Ala.), in which the court invalidated portions of Alabama statutes that established procedures for legitimization on the ground that the laws provided neither for notice to the mother nor protection for the child. In *Hunter* v. *Underwood,* 85 L. Ed. 2d 222 (1985), the United States Supreme Court, in a case initiated in a federal district court struck down a provision of the Alabama constitution that disenfranchised those convicted of crimes of "moral turpitude" and other petty offenses. "The provision was adopted in 1901 by an all-white state constitutional convention that was explicit about its desire to keep blacks from voting." Justice Rehnquist, who gave the Court's opinion, noted that a " 'zeal for white supremacy ran rampant' at the . . . convention," adding that "the delegates chose specific public offenses, such as vagrancy and adultery, of which blacks at that time were more likely to be convicted than whites. In the early years after its enactment, the provision disenfranchised more than 10 times as many blacks as whites; today the ratio is still 1.7 to 1." In its appeal to the United States Supreme Court, Alabama argued that "it had a legitimate interest in disenfranchising those convicted of crimes involving moral turpitude and that, in any event, the 1901 convention had also been interested in disenfranchising poor whites." *New York Times,* Apr. 17, 1985, p. 12, col. 5. Federal court intervention to relieve prison overcrowding remains controversial in Alabama. "Alabama Seeks to Block Order to Free Prisoners," and "U.S. Appeals Court Block Release of 300 From Prisons in Alabama," *New York Times,* Dec. 16, 1981, p. 14, col. 1; ibid., Dec. 22, 1981, p. 1, col. 1. In an advisory opinion the Alabama Supreme Court held that a pending bill to provide state aid to students attending private sectarian as well as nonsectarian colleges and universities would constitute the "excessive entanglement" of church and state that *Lemon* v. *Kurtzman,* 403 U.S. 602 (1971), prohibits. *Opinion of the Justices,* 280 So.2d 547 (Ala. 1973). However, in *Alabama Education Association* v. *James,* 373 So.2d 1076 (Ala. 1979), the student grant program was sustained against claims that it violated state as well as federal constitutional prohibitions against state establishment of religion. The court relied on *Roemer* v. *Maryland Public Works Board,* 426 U.S. 736 (1976), as well as *Lemon.* Religious practices in public schools, which included recitation of the Lord's Prayer, were challenged, initially and unsuccessfully, in a federal court. *Jaffree* v. *Board of School Commissioners,* 554 F. Supp. 1104 (S.D. Ala.), *rev'd. sub nom. Jaffree* v. *Wallace,* 705 F.2d 1526 (11th Cir. 1983), aff'd. 53 U.S.L.W. 5665 (1985), Justices Burger, Rehnquist, and White dissenting. The challenged Alabama statute provided for a one-minute period of

however, is that the Torbert court is receptive as no Alabama high court has been since the 1940s to civil rights arguments and is eager to establish a reputation as a court that respects and guarantees individual rights and liberties. A report of a recent meeting of Alabama appellate and trial judges and federal judges and magistrates in Alabama sums up the current climate well. Eleventh Circuit Chief Judge John C. Goodbold said, "Twenty years ago, many state and federal judges were sharing hostilities; today they are sharing ideas and learning from each other. We are lighting a lot of candles, rather than cursing the darkness. We are pursuing the ends of justice, which is what our jobs are all about." Chief Justice Torbert added, "Our joint discussions of habeas corpus and other issues have pointed out that federal and state judges not only share common problems, but we have a mutual goal—that of enforcing and upholding the Constitution of the United States."[151] Long-dead justices of the old court would regard such words as heresy. Sitting and retired old court justices accept them as a matter of course.

As earlier chapters in this book demonstrate, judicial reform may or may not transform a state supreme court. It did have that effect in Alabama, but whether the change would have been as far-reaching had there not been social and political change as well is a matter of conjecture. The point is that, for whatever reasons, the culmination of reform efforts and the advent of the "new South" coincided, and nothing—nothing—was the same on the Alabama high court after Howell Heflin completed his first and only term as chief justice.

The question, of course, is whether the cluster of practices, jurisprudential trends, and judicial outlooks that characterize the new court will remain viable into the twenty-first century, or whether the Alabama high court will become a court that again takes a back seat to the legislature and the governor, loses interest in developments in other jurisdictions, and no longer feels a sense of obligation to

---

silence for "meditation" or "voluntary prayer" and for the authority of teachers to lead "willing students" in a prescribed prayer to "Almighty God the Creator and Supreme Judge of the World." Alabama, "unlike most other states that have been forced to defend the laws in court . . . , made no effort to defend its law as anything other than an effort to bring religion into the classroom." Linda Greenhouse, "High Court Upsets Alabama Statute on School Prayer," *New York Times*, June 5, 1985, p. 1, col. 5, p. 13, col. 1.

151. *The Third Branch* 17 (1985). Administrative Office of the U.S. Courts and the Federal Judicial Center, Washington, D.C.

compensate for a dubious past. Factors contributing to the development of a passive, status quo court could be an Alabama electorate that turns politically to the right and gubernatorial interim appointments that reflect dissatisfaction with new court jurisprudence.

On the other hand, the respect and recognition accorded the Alabama high court reflect favorably on the state's political and legal elites and opinion-makers who, common sense dictates, would in all likelihood be as distressed by a lackluster high court as they would be by a return to the days of "segregation forever." And, it must be remembered, a new generation of lawyers is attuned to the ways of the new court. Further, the beneficiaries of recent tort law developments have created a constituency, and the court is considered as receptive to a wide range of claims. Additionally, black leaders and black voters, consolidating hard won gains and pursuing further economic, social, and political advances are unlikely to risk "losing" the court. And, since justices continue to be affiliated with the Democratic party and the party receives 35 percent of its support from black voters,[152] it is unlikely that many aspirants to the high state bench would be so reactionary as to offend this significant voting bloc.

Finally, as demonstrated in the chapter on the New Jersey court, fundamental change in a state's legal culture may be sufficient to insulate a court against the vagaries of social and political forces. The pride of place assumed by the new court provides an impressive base for the socialization of newly elected and/or appointed judges; no Alabama judges who attend national conferences will have to "kind of mumble" where they come from but can announce they are "from Alabama."[153] The institutional factors and the public and personal interests that favor the continuation of the new court's traditions far outweigh those that point in the opposite direction.

152. See note 75 above.
153. Martin, "Alabama's Courts."

FOUR

OHIO: PARTISAN JUSTICE

A quiet revolution is afoot. The insurgents are graying men who wear black robes and whose words carry the weight of law—the justices of the Ohio supreme court.—Plain Dealer, *April 22, 1984[1]*

Elections, 1986

On November 4, 1986, the Ohio electorate, having overwhelmingly voted Democratic for all other statewide offices, almost as overwhelmingly defeated its controversial Democratic chief justice, and by the slimmest majorities reelected a Republican justice and selected a moderate Democrat to replace a highly partisan and outspoken retiring Democratic justice.[2] After eight extraordinary years of change

---

1. Mary Anne Sharkey and W. Stevens Ricks, "Frank Celebrezze: A law unto himself," *Plain Dealer*, pp. 20A–21A.

2. For discussion and election results, see notes 113 and 117 below and accompanying text. The Republican challenger for the chief justiceship, Thomas J. Moyer, defeated incumbent Frank D. Celebrezze by 43,372 votes, winning 54.47 percent of the vote to Celebrezze's 45.53 percent. The Democratic candidates for governor, attorney general, auditor, secretary of state, and U.S. Senator won by 60.60 percent, 59.85 percent, 66.46 percent, 59.72 percent and 62.45 percent of the vote, respectively. *Official Report—Statewide Summary Sheet—General Election, November 1986* (compiled by Secretary of State Sherrod Brown). Outgoing Justice Clifford F. Brown has been described as "no shrinking violet," and Celebrezze's "most outspoken defender." He attributed Celebrezze's defeat to Republican Justices Craig Wright and Andy Douglas, who, working "hand in glove" with reporters, he charged, had "been incessant and relentless over the past two years in giving the Ohio supreme court a bad image." The objective of Wright, Douglas, and the press, he continued, was to change "the composition of the Ohio supreme court." Brown predicted that the court, with its 4-3 Republican majority, "will be to the right of the McKinley era where it was dog eat dog." Justice Brown "flatly predicted that Moyer would undo the landmark case of *Blankenship* v. *Cincinnati Milacron*" along with, he added, "many others this court decided in order to give

Howell T. Heflin, Chief Justice of the Alabama Supreme Court,
gives oath of office to his successor, C. C. Torbert, Jr. (January 1977).

Alabama Supreme Court (1980): *front row, l. to r.:* Richard L. Jones, Alva Hugh Maddox, Chief Justice C. C. Torbert, Jr., James H. Faulkner, Reneau P. Almon; *back row, l. to r.:* Samuel A. Beatty, Janie L. Shores, Eric Embry, Oscar W. Adams, Jr.

Ohio Supreme Court (September 1981): *l. to r.:* Clifford Brown, Ralph S. Locher, William Brown, Chief Justice Frank D. Celebrezze, A. William Sweeney, Robert E. Holmes, Blanche Krupansky.

Ohio Supreme Court (January 1987): *front row, l. to r.:* A. William Sweeney, Chief Justice Thomas J. Moyer, Ralph S. Locher; *back row, l. to r.:* Herbert R. Brown, Robert E. Holmes, Andy Douglas, Craig Wright.

Arthur T. Vanderbilt, Chief Justice of the New Jersey Supreme Court (1948–57).

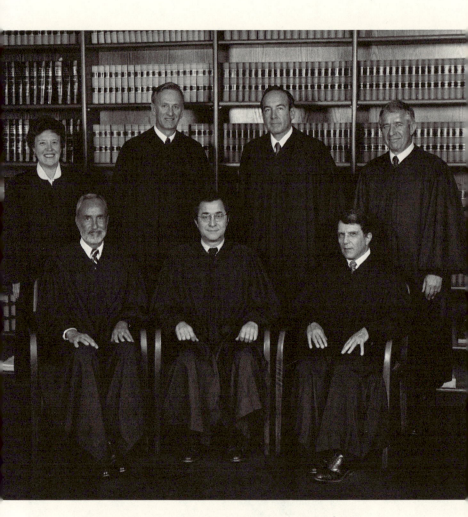

New Jersey Supreme Court (1987): *front row, l. to r.:* Robert L.
Clifford, Chief Justice Robert N. Wilentz, Alan B. Handler; *back
row, l. to r.:* Marie L. Garibaldi, Stewart G. Pollock, Daniel J.
O'Hern, Gary S. Stein.

and ferment under Democratic control, the court was reclaimed, albeit narrowly, by the Republicans, the party that had for so many years been able to count the appellate judiciary as its virtually exclusive preserve. Just the same, the jurisprudential changes initiated by the Democratic majorities should not, in retrospect, be considered aberrational and transitory: the Republican victory was due less to disenchantment with the Democratic court's "quiet revolution" than to a repudiation of the leadership style of its chief. And as this chapter demonstrates, continuity in the face of change has in many respects been a hallmark of Ohio's highest court.

The Setting: Republicans, Democrats, and Chief Justice Frank D. Celebrezze

Like the high courts of Alabama and New Jersey, the Ohio Supreme Court underwent sudden and dramatic transformation in the postwar era. The change did not, as in New Jersey, result from a revamping of the state's judicial system, although the Modern Courts Amendment of 1969 introduced important structural and procedural reforms.[3] Nor

---

Ohioans equal justice." Gary Webb, "Moyer vows to end brawling on Supreme Court," *Plain Dealer*, Nov. 9, 1986, pp. 1B, 6B. For press assessment of election results, see Gary Webb, "Newspapers called key in defeat of Celebrezze," *Plain Dealer*, Nov. 6, 1986, p. 1B, col. 1, 3B.

3. The Modern Courts Amendment, adopted overwhelmingly, constituted the first major revision of the state constitution since 1851. The following pertained to the Ohio Supreme Court: The court was given supervisory power over lower courts and plenary rule making power. The chief justice was authorized to make temporary assignments and utilize emeritus judges. The "all but one rule," a constitutional provision that no appellate court ruling could be overturned without the concurrence of six of the seven justices, was rescinded. Had this rule not been in force, *Mapp* v. *Ohio*, 367 U.S. 643 (1961), would not have been appealed, and another case would have provided the occasion for the holding that states are obliged to observe the Fourth Amendment's guarantee against unreasonable searches and seizures; the Ohio high court, by a four to three vote, would have reversed the conviction on the ground that the statute that prohibited mere "knowing possession" of obscene materials and under which Mapp was convicted, violated the First Amendment of the federal constitution. 166 N.E.2d 387 (Ohio 1960). Four members of the U.S. Supreme Court also found the First Amendment claim to be compelling, among them Potter Stewart, whose father, James Garfield Stewart, served on the Ohio high court from 1947 to 1959. In 1973 a constitutional amendment established a partially unified court system. Chief Justice Celebrezze has urged that courts be fully funded by the state, as does his successor. In 1971 the

was it, as in Alabama, the product of changes in the state's political and legal cultures, brought about in part by federal legislation and judicial action. In Ohio, change resulted quite simply from partisan realignment on the bench.

Despite occasional pressure from the bar and civic groups for merit selection, Ohio has throughout the better part of the twentieth century elected judges in nonpartisan elections following nomination in partisan primaries, a system now unique to Ohio.[4] Although this system has produced its share of voter confusion, frustration, apathy, and irrationality, overall the results of judicial elections have mirrored the Ohio electorate's general preference for Republican officeholders at the legislative and local levels of government. Indeed, with the exception of a brief period in 1959–60, Republicans have prevailed in judicial elections even when the Democrats have captured the gover-

---

Ohio Supreme Court adopted a series of Rules of Superintendence that "asserted the . . . Court's authority to monitor judicial performance and to hold judges responsible for their criminal and civil dockets." For an assessment of the effectiveness and effects of the rules, see Charles W. Grau and Arlene Sheskin, "Ruling Out Delay: The Impact of Ohio's Rules of Superintendence," *Judicature* 66 (1982): 109–21, 109, and Arlene Sheskin and Charles W. Grau, "Judicial Responses to Technocratic Reform," in James A. Kramer, ed., *Courts and Judges* (Beverly Hllls, Cal.: Sage Publications, 1981), pp. 225–49.

4. Between 1953 and 1979 numerous attempts were made to adopt a merit plan. See "Judicial Selection and Tenure—The Merit Plan in Ohio," *Cincinnati Law Review* 42 (1973): 255–78, and Kathleen L. Barber, "Selection of Ohio Appellate Judges: A Case Study in Invisible Politics," in John J. Gargan and James J. Cook, eds., *Political Behavior and Public Issues in Ohio* (Cleveland: Kent State University Press, 1972), pp. 157–231. Professor Barber has concluded that nonpartisan judicial elections, like other nonpartisan elections, disadvantage less affluent, less educated, and less sophisticated voters and that gubernatorial selection provides the optimum balance between judicial independence and accountability. Merit selection continues to be backed by the Ohio State Bar Association and civic groups and is opposed by organized labor. Pat Hampton, "Bar backs merit system for judges," *Columbus Post Dispatch,* Nov. 17, 1985, p. 1, col. 1. Democrats on the Celebrezze court supported the present system and one of them argues that a judge's party affiliation should appear on the general as well as primary ballot. Republican justices who participated in the bitter judicial campaign of 1984 profess to be "deathbed converts" to merit selection. In interviews, the justices showed familiarity with the arguments for and against merit selection (November 18–21, 1985, Columbus). Chief Justice Celebrezze maintains that there is no empirical evidence that appointed judges are better qualified than elected judges, and that appointed judges are more difficult to remove from office than those who are elected. "Top Judge of Ohio defends elections," *Plain Dealer,* Jan. 31, 1985, p. 12B, col. 1.

norship and other state offices.[5] The Ohio high court was dominated from the close of the Civil War to 1978 by conservative, "old stock" Republicans who fashioned the law to conform to the values and interests they shared with small town and rural Ohioans, with business and industry. Like the old Alabama court, the Ohio Supreme Court did not challenge or offend the legislature, the political forces to whom the justices owed their positions, or what it regarded as its constituencies. Attuned to their state's political culture, the justices were well aware, as Kathleen L. Barber has put it, that "Ohio political practices have tended to award and advance those decision makers whose role perceptions favor stability, continuity and avoidance of conflict."[6]

5. Political scientist Kathleen L. Barber has conducted the major research on Ohio judicial elections. "Ohio Judicial Elections-Nonpartisan Premises with Partisan Results," *Ohio State Law Journal* 23 (1971): 726–89; Barber, "Nonpartisan Ballots and Voter Confusion in Judicial Elections," paper presented at the Midwest Political Science Association Annual Meeting, 1982; Barber, "Judicial Politics in Ohio," in Carl Lieberman, ed., *Government and Politics in Ohio* (Lanham, N.D.: University Press of America, 1984), pp. 89–113. For a comparative perspective on Ohio judicial elections, see Philip Dubois, *From Ballot to Bench: Judicial Elections and the Quest for Accountability* (Austin: University of Texas Press, 1980). An appointment made by Democratic governor Michael DiSalle that did not survive a subsequent election accounted for the narrow and short-lived Democratic majority. The Democratic court, which must be considered a fluke, did little to distinguish itself from Republican dominated courts.

6. "Historically, the Ohio Supreme Court has been dominated by Republicans, who handed down conservative opinions that were hailed by big business and insurance companies. The hallways of the court are covered with oil paintings of these stern-faced elders." Sharkey and Stevens, "Frank Celebrezze," pp. 20A, 22A. The state chairman of the Ohio Democratic party described the pre-Celebrezze court as "an old boy court." "If you were graduated from the right law school and were affiliated with the right law firm and hung around the bar association, you had a good chance of becoming a judge. The court was all white males with white hair." Quoted in Lee Leonard, "Slugging it out in the Ohio Supreme Court," *Columbus Monthly*, November 1985, pp. 147–50, 148. The Republican justices who "controlled" the court ran it as a "quiet gentlemen's club." Mary Anne Sharkey, "GOP pulls upset in high court races," *Plain Dealer*, Nov. 7, 1984, pp. 1A, col. 1, 6A, col. 1.

The following illustrates the court's deferential approach: Reiterating its refusal to abrogate the doctrine of sovereign immunity, the justices reversed a lower appellate holding that would have allowed parents of the young people killed by the National Guard at Kent State University to sue the state. *Krause* v. *State*, 285 N.E.2d 736 (Ohio 1972), cert. denied, 409 U.S. 1052 (1972). *Scheuer* v. *Rhodes*, 416 U.S. 232 (1974), commenced in a federal court, held that the parents could sue. *State* v. *Lockett*, 358 N.E.2d 1062 (Ohio 1976), rev'd. as to death penalty statute, 438 N.E.2d 586 (1976) upheld a post *Furman* death penalty statute despite its

This traditional pattern was abruptly broken in 1978 when the Democrats obtained a 4-3 and subsequently a 6-1 majority on the court. Under the leadership of Frank Celebrezze, a member of a politically powerful Cleveland family that personified the coming of age of ethnic politics in Ohio, the court, as its chief proudly and publicly proclaimed, became a "peoples' court," concerned with "the little guy or gal."[7] A long line of precedent pertaining, inter alia, to restrictions on suits against state and local governments and limitations on medical malpractice claims and on the rights of tenants,

---

obvious constitutional defects. (*Furman* v. *Georgia*, 408 U.S. 238 (1972), precipitated the change in death penalty statutes.) Chief Justice O'Neill, joined by Justices Stern and William Brown, dissented in *Lockett*. For a scathing critique of *Lockett* I, in which Frank Celebrezze concurred, see Charles Black, *Capital Punishment: The Inevitability of Caprice and Mistake* (New York: Norton, 1981), pp. 138–50. *Erickson* v. *Hunter*, 233 N.E.2d 129 (Ohio 1967); rev'd., 393 U.S. 385 (1969), sustained a municipal regulation subjecting fair housing legislation to voter referendum. "Partisan advantage has been awarded in decisions about legislative reapportionment, gubernatorial eligibility and the lieutenant governor's legislative role." Barber, "Judicial Politics in Ohio." See, *State ex rel. King* v. *Rhodes*, 228 N.E.2d 653 (Ohio 1967); *State ex rel. Rhodes* v. *Brown*, 296 N.E.2d 538 (Ohio 1973); and *Maloney* v. *Rhodes*, 345 N.E.2d 407 (Ohio 1976). The facts in *State ex rel. Rhodes* v. *Brown* tellingly make the point. Republican Governor Rhodes had served two consecutive terms as governor. He was succeeded, left office, wanted to run again, and was refused permission to file by the secretary of state on grounds that Article 3, Section 2 of the Ohio Constitution holds that "No person shall hold the office of governor for a period longer than two successive terms of four years." The court ordered the secretary to accept Rhode's filing. See also Barber, "Partisan Values in Lower Courts: Reapportionment in Ohio and Michigan," *Case Western Reserve Law Review* 20 (1969): 401–21. Recent cases involving electoral disputes in which the justices divided along party lines are *State ex rel. Carter* v. *Celebrezze*, 410 N.E.2d 1249 (Ohio 1980), and *State ex rel. Morrison* v. *Board of Education*, 410 N.E.2d 764 (Ohio 1980). Barber, "Judicial Politics in Ohio."

7. Justice Celebrezze's father, Frank, was a prosecutor, safety director, and municipal judge. His uncle, Anthony J. Celebrezze, served as mayor of Cleveland, President Kennedy's secretary of Health, Education and Welfare, and as judge on the 6th Circuit Court of Appeals. Anthony Celebrezze's son and namesake served in the General Assembly (as did Justices Frank and James Celebrezze) and as secretary of state, and in 1984 he was elected state's attorney general. Tony Celebrezze, a proven vote-getter, is "regarded by many as the Ohio Democrat Party's brightest political prospect." Herb Cook, Jr., and Sharon Crook West, "The Ohio Supreme Court," *Columbus Monthly*, July 1982, pp. 51–56, 121–24, 121. For reasons that have not been made public, the two branches of the Celebrezze family do not get along. Tony Celebrezze has distanced himself politically from his first cousins, Frank and James. Cook and West, cit. Also see Charles Stella, "The Celebrezze Dynasty," *Plain Dealer*, Sunday Magazine, Apr. 24, 1983, pp. 28, 30–33. Mary Anne Sharkey, "Celebrezze is Supreme at the Court," *Plain Dealer*, Aug. 28, 1983, pp. 25A, 29A.

consumers, and workers injured during the course of employment was reversed. Virtually overnight the court became "pro-labor and highly urban"[8] in orientation.

8. Municipal immunity: *Haverlack* v. *Portage Homes, Inc.*, 442 N.E.2d 795 (Ohio 1982), and *Enghauser Mfg.* v. *Erickson Eng'g, Ltd.*, 451 N.E.2d 228 (Ohio 1983); *Adams* v. *Peoples*, 480 N.E.2d 428 (Ohio 1985); *Longfellow* v. *Newark*, 480 N.E.2d 432 (Ohio 1985); medical malpractice: *Oliver* v. *Kaiser Health Foundation*, 449 N.E.2d 438 (Ohio 1983); tenants: *Shroades* v. *Rental Homes, Inc.*, 427 N.E.2d 774 (Ohio 1981), overruled precedent established only a year earlier, *Thrash* v. *Hill*, 407 N.E.2d 495 (Ohio 1980); consumers: *Cleveland Electrical Illuminating Co.* v. *Public Utilities Commission*, 431 N.E.2d 683 (Ohio 1982), ruling that charitable donations and advertising expenses cannot be passed on to consumers. In cases involving insurance claims, the court recognized the tort of a bad faith refusal to pay, thus joining "a growing number of jurisdictions that have recognized the good faith duty to pay." *Hoskins* v. *Aetna Life Insurance Co.*, 452 N.E.2d 1315 (Ohio 1983), "Insurance Law: Tortious Liability for Bad Faith Refusal to Pay," *Akron Law Review* 17 (1984): 683. Two rulings emphasized that contracts written in ambiguous or unintelligible language would be construed in favor of the policyholder. *Suburban Community Hospital* v. *Lindquist*, 423 N.E.2d 173 (Ohio 1982), and *Adys* v. *West American Insurance Co.*, 433 N.E.2d 547 (Ohio 1982).

In *Blankenship* v. *Cincinnati Milacron Chemicals, Inc.*, 433 N.E.2d 572 (Ohio 1982), the court held that an employee covered by workers' compensation laws might sue to recover for injuries incurred as a result of an employer's "intentional tort." The case appeared to overrule at least two earlier decisions, *Bevis* v. *Armco Steel Corp.*, 102 N.E.2d 444 (Ohio 1951), and *Greenwalt* v. *Goodyear Tire and Rubber Co.*, 128 N.E.2d 116 (Ohio 1955), and was the subject of considerable commentary, e.g., "Blankenship v. Cincinnati Milacron Chemical Co.: Workers' Compensation and the Intentional Tort—A New Direction For Ohio," *Capital University Law Review* 12 (1982): 287–312; "Workers' Compensation in Ohio: Scope of Employment and the Intentional Tort," *Akron Law Review* 17 (1983): 249–59; "Blankenship v. Cincinnati Milacron Chemicals, Inc.: Some Fairness for Ohio Workers and Some Uncertainty for Ohio Employers," *University of Toledo Law Review* 15 (1983): 403–36. While the ruling caused something of a stir in Ohio, the principle established was not novel. See cases and statutes discussed in "Tort—Workers Compensation—Employer Immunity—An Employee is Not Precluded by the Ohio Workers' Compensation Laws from Enforcing A Common Law Remedy for Intentional Torts Committed by His Employers," *University of Cincinnati Law Review* 51 (1982): 682–96, 689, n. 15. A series of rulings extending workers' rights under Ohio's compensation statute followed *Blankenship*. *Jones* v. *VIP Development Co.*, 472 N.E.2d 1046 (Ohio 1984) (injured employee need not show specific intent to injure but only that employer acted despite a perceived threat of harm to others which is substantially likely to occur); *Village* v. *General Motors Corp., G.M.A.*, 472 N.E.2d 1079 (Ohio 1984) (employee may recover for a condition that develops gradually over a period of time); *State ex rel. Nyitray*, 443 N.E.2d 962 (Ohio 1983) (dependents of workers who die from work-related injuries or occupational disease eligible to receive death benefits as well as compensation that had accrued to worker up until time of death), overruling forty years of precedent, *State ex rel. Spiker* v. *Industrial Commission*, 47 N.E.2d 217 (Ohio 1943); *Baylint* v. *Arkansas Best Freight System, Inc.*, 480 N.E. 417 (Ohio 1985) (allowed cause of action for

The aptly described quiet revolution was not received quietly. The court's former clientele, including the Ohio Manufacturers' Association, the Ohio Chamber of Commerce, and insurance companies, attempted to rally public opinion against the rulings, warning that the workers' compensation decisions in particular would discourage new business and industry from entering the state and would drive out those already established. Considerable, but by no means all, editorial comment supported this view.[9] Initial legislative response was both

intentional and wrongful termination of workers' compensation payments on the part of a self-insured employer). For a summary of cases from the perspective of an Ohio justice who strongly supported these and other "prolabor" rulings, see Clifford F. Brown, "The Trend of Workers' Compensation in Ohio: Ohio Puts the Worker Back into Workers' Compensation," *Capital University Law Review* 13 (1984): 521–32. The workers' compensation rulings were not unanimous. Republican justices, often joined by Democratic Justice Ralph Locher, dissented. For a concise (and approving) summary of the dissenters' views, see Ohio Chamber of Commerce, *Labor Affairs Bulletin*, January 10, 1985. The majority's prolabor stance was further manifested by the invalidation of an ordinance that exempted a city from the state's prevailing wage law. *State ex rel. Evans* v. *Moore*, 431 N.E.2d 1369 (Ohio 1982). Justice Locher, a former mayor, dissented. Compare with *Garcia* v. *Sifrin Residential Association*, 407 N.E. 1369 (Ohio 1981), cert. denied, 407 U.S. 911 (1981). (State law that stipulated procedures for the licensing of "family" or "group" homes for the mentally retarded does not supersede local zoning laws.) "By upholding [this and similar zoning restrictions], the court granted local communities the power to override the state's professed goal of establishing community based rehabilitation centers and effectively curtailed the integration and deinstitutionalization of the mentally ill, the mentally retarded and other disadvantaged citizens." "Exclusionary Zoning of Group Homes in Ohio," *Ohio State Law Journal* 34 (1982): 167.

Workers did not prevail in all instances, e.g., *State ex rel. McArthur Lumber and Post* v. *Industrial Commission*, 452 N.E.2d 1269 (Ohio 1983); *State ex rel. Allerton* v. *Industrial Commission*, 433 N.E.2d 159 (Ohio 1982). "Whatever the impressions, claimants often lose in the Ohio Supreme Court and have lost more often than they have won. But on the significant cases, the claimants have fared well." Interview, November 18, 1985. In what was billed as a campaign speech for the election of 1986, Celebrezze "said that in 94 cases filed in the last three years the injured worker won 45 times and the employer won 49 times. That's not anti-business, unless, of course, you think we should return to the days when the court ruled for big business almost 100% of the time," Mary Anne Sharkey, "Top judge rips big business in fundraiser," *Plain Dealer*, Feb. 7, 1986, p. 2B. As this chapter later indicates, the court's activist solicitude for the economic rights of "the little guy or gal" was not matched by civil liberties activism. Quotation is from a confidential letter to one of the authors, May 24, 1983.

9. Ohio, like other states, tried to attract the General Motors Saturn plant (which eventually located in Tennessee). Democratic Governor Celeste actively wooed GM. Spokespersons for business and industry and many newspapers voiced

partisan and bipartisan. Republicans proposed revision of the workers' compensation laws so that liberal judicial construction would be
precluded. The Democratic lower house and the Republican upper
house passed and the Democratic governor signed a bill limiting
awards in suits against municipalities and other governmental bodies.[10] On the other hand, the court's new clientele, particularly
organized labor, which was credited with securing the Democratic
judicial victories, applauded, as did the plaintiffs' bar and academic
lawyers who had long urged the court to reverse precedent and
become more attuned to tort law developments occurring throughout
the nation.[11] Amid this brew Chief Justice Celebrezze himself became

fears that the court's rulings would have a deterrent effect—a charge that
Celebrezze vehemently disputed. Representative accounts of the controversy
include Joseph Rice, "Saturn may eclipse Celeste labor clout," *Plain Dealer*, Mar.
10, 1985; Mark DiVincenzo, "Business throws workers' comp-bashing party,"
Sandusky Register Mar. 31, 1985; Bob Russ, "Workers suits may hurt Ohio Saturn
Drive," *Akron Beacon Journal*, March 1, 1985. For "in-house" management
perspectives, see the Ohio Chamber of Commerce, *Labor Affair Bulletin*, Ohio
Manufacturers' Association *Newsletter*, February 22, 1985; and *Ohio Business*, April
1985. An editorial, "Workers comp rework," *Columbus Dispatch*, Apr. 15, 1985,
approvingly described two bills that would revise the state's workers' compensation laws in order to redress the balance between employer/employee interests. On
the other hand, Celebrezze's long-time critic, *The Plain Dealer*, pointed out that one
reason insurers were "upset with the court was partly because they could not lobby
the court as they could the General Assembly," Editorial, "The Leader of the
Court," Apr. 27, 1984, and expressed impatience with the "sky-is-falling rhetoric"
that greeted the compensation rulings. As if "business lobbyists hadn't noticed,
Ohio's economy had struggled and companies moved out long before the . . .
court decisions," Editorial, "New battle over workers' comp," Mar. 31, 1985, p.
18A.

    10. Joseph Rice, "Comp and culpability come under fire," *Plain Dealer*, June 30,
1985. The Ohio General Assembly has also revamped the state's workers'
compensation system. Despite signing the bill, Governor Celeste did not lose labor's
endorsement for reelection. Letter from Kathleen L. Barber, July 2, 1986.

    11. Ohio AFL-CIO, *News and Views* 35 (1985): nos. 10 and 11, April 19 and
May 3. The labor perspective tended to appear in the form of letters to the editors,
e.g., AFL-CIO President Milan Marsh, "Don't shortchange the workers," *Akron
Beacon Journal* Mar. 19, 1985, and labor lawyer J. Michael Montelone (who won
an important case, *Hamlin* v. *Snow Metal Products*, 472 N.E.2d 1046 [Ohio 1984],
"Celebrezze court shone in comp rulings," *Plain Dealer*, May 12, 1985. "Negligent
Infliction of Emotional Distress and Bystander Recovery: A New Tort and a New
Plaintiff for Ohio," *University of Toledo Law Review* 5 (1983): 273–334;
"Blankenship v. Cincinnati Milacron Chemicals, Inc.: Some Fairness for Ohio
Workers and Some Uncertainty for Ohio Employers." In 1982 the court was urged
to make the state's newly enacted comparative negligence law retroactive, Richard
A. Wise, "The Retroactive Application of Ohio's Comparative Negligence

an issue—and indeed, to the extent that opposition to various aspects of the quiet revolution was subsumed by the chief justice, Celebrezze became *the* issue.

In 1982 a feud erupted between Celebrezze and the Ohio Bar Association. It was triggered by the association's investigation of Celebrezze's announcement (almost immediately withdrawn) of his gubernatorial candidacy and its rating of James Celebrezze (the chief justice's younger brother), whose candidacy to the high court Frank Celebrezze had successfully championed, as "unqualified." In response Celebrezze withdrew the association's fifty-year-old contract to print official court documents, stripped it of its power to investigate complaints against lawyers and judges, established a disciplinary council answerable to the court, and assessed lawyers an annual fee to pay for its operation. Lawyers throughout the state, it was said, were intimidated, not daring to speak out against the court or its chief. The perception that Celebrezze personalized disagreements was strengthened when he appointed a former juvenile judge, reportedly not highly regarded by the legal community and considered a Celebrezze crony, to head the disciplinary council, when Celebrezze "loyalists" replaced court administrators and personnel who resigned or were fired, and when Celebrezze exercised his discretionary authority to

---

Statute—A Golden Opportunity," *Ohio Northern University Law Review* 9 (1982): 68–74. After initial hesitation, the court did so rule. *Wilfong* v. *Batdorf,* 451 N.E.2d 1185 (Ohio 1983), overruled *Viers* v. *Dunlap,* 438 N.E.2d 881 (Ohio 1982). Case comment refers approvingly to the court's new directions. "If mental distress damages are foreseeable and are the natural and probable consequences of the defendant's negligence, they should be recoverable. In light of both medical knowledge and the knowledge and expectations of the reasonable man, the Ohio supreme court's decisions in *Schultz* and *Paugh* are proper in bringing the law of Ohio in step with the needs of present day society," Student Project: Torts, "Administering Ohio's Newly Recognized Tort: The Negligent Infliction of Serious Emotional Distress," *Akron Law Review* 17 (1984): 631–46, discussing *Schultz* v. *Barberton Glass Co.*, 777 N.E.2d 109 (Ohio 1983), and *Paugh* v. *Hanks,* 451 N.E.2d 759 (Ohio 1983). Whatever Celebrezze's problems with the leaders of the Ohio State Bar Association, he was popular with plaintiffs' lawyers, receiving a "warm reception . . . at the monthly meeting of the Cleveland Academy of Trial Attorneys," *Plain Dealer,* Feb. 23, 1985. For commentary critical of pre-Celebrezze tort law rulings, see "The Coming of Age of Strict Products Liability in Ohio," *Ohio State Law Journal* 39 (1978): 586–620; "Judicial Adoption of Comparative Negligence in Ohio," *University of Cincinnati Law Review* 44 (1975): 811–17; "Governmental Immunity in Ohio: Common Law Doctrine or Constitutional Prohibition," *Capital University Law Review* 3 (1974): 134–42.

assign judges to hear cases in lower courts on the basis of what was widely perceived to be their fealty to him.[12]

The combination of Celebrezze's gubernatorial "candidacy," however short-lived, his propensity to surround himself with trusted

12. Accounts of the event included Cook and West, "The Ohio Supreme Court"; Richard G. Zimmerman, "The Supreme Democrat," *Plain Dealer,* Nov. 11, 1984, p. 1C; Sharkey and Ricks, "Frank Celebrezze;" Sharkey, "Celebrezze is supreme at the court" " 'Resign-to-Run' Canon Faces Test in Ohio," *American Bar Association Journal* 68 (1982): 535. Wrote one reporter, "During the past two years, Chief Justice Frank Celebrezze has routinely spoken at Democratic fundraisers though he was not an active candidate. He announced his candidacy for the governor but declined to resign his judgeship. He has allowed as many as three groups to collect money for him, including solicitations that occurred when he was not supposed to be raising money for any race. And when his political supporters became involved in cases, he declined to step down, even when his impartiality was questioned." W. Stevens Ricks, "A Law Unto Himself: Chief justice appears to ignore judicial code," *Plain Dealer,* Apr. 26, 1984. p. 27A, col. 1. Mary Anne Sharkey, "State bar loses power under Celebrezze," *Plain Dealer,* Apr. 24, 1984. In a six-page letter to members dated July 25, 1984, Ohio State Bar Association president, Frank Bazler, detailed events surrounding the organization's relations with the Ohio Supreme Court between January 1982 and July 1984. Bazler's letter was followed by another to Celebrezze in which he accused, "in an unprecedented move," the "Ohio Supreme Court of diverting lawyer registration fees intended for enforcing legal ethics to subsidize a private publisher of the court's opinions," Mary Anne Sharkey, "State bar–high court tiff heats," *Plain Dealer,* July 27, 1984. The deteriorating bar–court relationship was not helped by a news report that Louis Damiani, the court's administrator, referred to bar association officers as "skunks" conducting a "smear campaign" against Celebrezze because of his Italian heritage. (One of incoming Chief Justice Moyer's acts was to replace Damiani with Stephen W. Stover, executive director of the Ohio Ethics Committee. Gary Webb, "Top aid gets boot from court," *Plain Dealer,* Dec. 10, 1986, p. 1B, 3B, cols. 1). Damiani was responding to a charge, vehemently denied, that bar association officials made an ethnic slur against the chief justice. *Plain Dealer,* Aug. 18, 1984, 24-D. W. Stevens Ricks, "Disciplined lawyers, judges feel flogged, want day in court," *Plain Dealer,* Apr. 25, 1985, p. 20A. Celebrezze's authority to assign judges came, of course, from the Modern Courts Amendment. His exercise of that authority further illustrates that "reform" may have unintended and not always salutary effects. Carl Baar, "The Scope and Limits of Court Reform," *Justice Systems Journal* 5 (1980): 274–90. One observer of the court described the bar association's contract to print the advance sheets as a "Mickey Mouse arrangement that never should have existed in the first place." Confidential letter to one of the authors, November 7, 1985. Nor did the writer think there was good reason for the bar's authority to discipline attorneys. In most states this task is performed by special disciplinary agencies. American Bar Association, "Statistical Report Re: Public Discipline of Lawyers by Disciplinary Agencies, 1977–1981" (unpublished paper, 1982), cited in Lawrence Baum, *American Courts: Process and Policy* (Boston: Houghton Mifflin Company, 1986), p. 89.

allies, and, above all, the spectacle of a standoff between the chief justice of the state's highest court and the state's bar association, attracted almost instant media attention. Following the lead of a team of Cleveland investigative reporters, the press began what a quiet revolution sympathizer described as an "incessant drumbeat" of criticism. Captions of stories, news items, and editorials read, for example, "Celebrezze" rules "supreme at the court"; "Celebrezze assumes vast power"; "Frank Celebrezze: a law unto himself"; "Celebrezze settles debts with spite, vindictiveness"; "The chief and his 'inimies'." Comment ranged from condemnation of Celebrezze's actions ("It's the way Frank Celebrezze has used his power that makes him the most feared public official in Ohio." Celebrezze's "running the court is called sleazy") to questions about his personality ("Celebrezze is a driven, obsessive, suspicious man, inclined to believe that anyone who isn't clearly on his side must be working against him. Privately, some lawyers call him paranoid") to theories that "explained" his behavior ("Celebrezze prides himself on being part of the American success story. But, friends said, he does not feel he has gained acceptance from the WASPish legal establishment. A Cleveland judge, also an Italian Catholic, said Celebrezze's perception is correct. 'He's not Protestant, he's dark-complected and he has a funny name. That doesn't fit in with the bluenoses. You have to understand this to understand Frank Celebrezze.' . . . A friend said that Celebrezze is sensitive about his swarthy looks and small stature").[13]

The criticism of Celebrezze reached a crescendo when, after issuing a ruling that ordered utility companies to pay refunds to their customers and shortly before the judicial election of 1984, he sent the requisite refund checks out over his signature. If Celebrezze thought the gesture would assist his brother and the other Democratic candidate, he miscalculated. The opposition and the media had a field day, and both Democratic candidates were defeated by impressive margins.[14]

13. See notes 1, 7, and 12 above for representative comment, also, Editorial, "Celebrezze settles debts with spite, vindictiveness," *Journal Herald,* May 16, 1984, p. 10, and Mary Anne Sharkey, "Celebrezze longs for acceptance," *Plain Dealer,* Apr. 23, 1984.

14. *Columbus and Southern Ohio Electric Co.* v. *Public Utilities Commission,* 460 N.E.2d 1108 (Ohio 1984), and *Columbus Gas of Ohio* v. *Public Utilities Commission,* 462 N.E.2d 116 (Ohio 1984). "In the past, utility overcharges have been routinely repaid to Ohio consumers through credits on their . . . bills," "Political refunds,"

After the election, Celebrezze found himself with the narrowest of margins. The new Republican members of the court, Andy Douglas and Craig Wright, who campaigned more against the chief justice than against their opponents, continued their vociferous criticism both on and off the bench. Celebrezze responded in kind by accusing them of case-fixing in lifting a disciplinary suspension against an attorney. The Republican-dominated Senate conducted an investigation of the controversy, indicating that it intended to look into other matters as well. Calling on separation of powers, Celebrezze refused to testify at the hearings, which one newspaper, not usually sympathetic to Celebrezze, termed a "kangaroo court." Justices Douglas and Wright, who did testify, were low-keyed and disappointingly dull. The hearings, anticipated to produce fireworks, fizzled away.[15]

Columbus Citizens' Journal, Nov. 1, 1984. "Dispute Injects Politics Into Ohio Judicial Races," *New York Times*, Oct. 24, 1984, p. 15, col. 6; "Justice high: Supreme Court hopefuls spent $1 million," *Plain Dealer*, Dec. 22, 1984; Sharkey, "GOP pulls upset in high court contests," *Plain Dealer;* Mary Anne Sharkey, "Is Chief Justice Celebrezze next?," *Plain Dealer*, Nov. 8, 1984, p. 7A, col. 1. Craig Wright, who defeated James Celebrezze, won 54.5 percent of the vote. Celebrezze, as expected, won in heavily Democratic Cuyahoga County, which includes Cleveland, but by an unimpressive margin. Andy Douglas received 53 percent of the vote. The judicial races were high-profile and bitter, and they adversely affected future intracourt relations. Mary Anne Sharkey, "It's cats-and-dogs time for high court seats," "A bitter fight for high court," *Plain Dealer*, Nov. 2, 1985, pp. 25A, 32A; Jack Torry, "GOP high court candidates say Dem ads 'insult' voters," *Columbus Post Dispatch*, Nov. 8, 1984; Thomas Suddes, "Candidate's ads lash Celebrezze's 'Cleveland court'," *Plain Dealer*, Nov. 25, 1984. Interviews, November 18 and 21, 1985. In 1986 James Celebrezze was elected a domestic relations judge, *Plain Dealer*, Nov. 2, 1986, p. 5C. The major newspapers endorsed the Republican candidates. Sharkey, "GOP pulls upset." In a study of the 1984 races between James Celebrezze and between John Corrigan and Andrew Douglas, Lawrence Baum concluded: 1. "Party was an important basis for . . . decisions even though the ballot did not disclose candidates' party affiliations." 2. "[V]oters' general ideologies and the issues and arguments in the campaign seem to have affected the vote significantly. . . . While relatively few voters cited issues and ideology as the primary basis for their choice, many others cited negative views of one of the candidates and of the supreme court as a whole. And many of the citations of media information undoubtedly referred implicitly to the issues that were raised in the media." 3. "[T]he two races seemed to differ in the ways that voters perceived and responded to them. The Celebrezze–Wright race was better publicized and the negatives attached to the Democratic side were stronger in that race. As a result, issues and ideology played a larger role in that race." "Explaining the Vote in Judicial Elections: The 1984 Ohio Supreme Court Elections," *Western Political Quarterly* 40 (1987): 369.

15. Justices Douglas and Wright, commented a *Plain Dealer* editorial, "interpreted their election as sanctioning a rhetorical free-fire zone," July 15, 1985. The

Active on other fronts, however, Justices Douglas and Wright publicly announced that they had been "warned" that their office telephones had been tapped. By whom they did not say, but presumably by Celebrezze. (When their suspicions proved groundless, Justice Douglas admitted to feeling "silly" about the matter.) Despite earlier news reports that the election results had mollified Celebrezze's combativeness, the chief justice, particularly goaded by Douglas, who Celebrezze allies maintained was aiming for Celebrezze's job, continued to make good copy. One news item described an occasion when Douglas, attempting to enter a room in which Celebrezze was holding a news conference, was physically barred by Celebrezze aides and an exchange of blows was barely averted.[16]

The Douglas-Celebrezze "feud" (the bar association-Celebrezze feud constituting yesterday's news) then engaged the attention of the press. Focus shifted from Celebrezze himself to the "bickering" among the justices, with press accounts speculating upon the identities of the "peacemakers" and the "neutrals." In an article titled "Slugging it out at the Ohio Supreme Court," one commentator described a virtual battlefield. "On just one day two justices exchanged accusations of case-fixing, payoffs, lying, electronic surveillance and political orchestration. And then things got really nasty."[17] As a *National Law Journal*

---

disciplinary case concerned an attorney whom the court had indefinitely suspended from practice. Five years later the court, with the three Republicans joined by Clifford Brown, Celebrezze's closest ally, voted to reinstate. In a nine-page dissent, Celebrezze, charging that the "majority had secretly decided the case before hearing arguments," characterized the action as "silent and sinister." *Bar Association of Greater Cleveland* v. *Wilsman*, 457 N.E.2d 824 (Ohio 1984). To which Douglas responded, "I'm outraged at the chief's false accusations. This time he has gone too far," Mary Anne Sharkey, "Discipline ruling angers Celebrezze," *Plain Dealer*, July 4, 1985; the Senate hearings were requested by Douglas and Wright. Mary Anne Sharkey, "Air Celebrezze's charges, 2 ask," *Plain Dealer*, April 11, 1985; Lee Leonard, "GOP justices give low-key testimony," *Sandusky Register*, Aug. 29, 1984, p. 31A. *Plain Dealer*, Editorial, Aug. 15, 1984.

16. "Justices' phones bug-free, Ohio Bell check determines," *Plain Dealer*, July 24, 1985, p. 3A; Carol Schmidt, "Court Bickering Is Downplayed By Celebrezze," *Toledo Blade*, July 12, 1985. Interviews, November 18 and 21, 1985; Mary Anne Sharkey, "Justices' scrap sparks shoving at court door," *Plain Dealer*, July 13, 1985, p. 20A.

17. "Ohio court justices go nose to nose," *Norwalk Reflector*, July 13, 1985; "Re: Ohio Supreme Court," *Plain Dealer*, Mar. 17, 1985, pp. 1B, 2B, 7B, provided a summary of the views of and disagreements between Justices Douglas and Brown; Jim Underwood, "Only Locher maintains dignity," *News-Journal*, July 21, 1985; Mary Grace Poidomani, "Justice Andy Douglas in Center Ring," *Akron Beacon Journal*, July 30, 1985; Lee Leonard, "Slugging it out on the Ohio Supreme Court."

report brought an account of the developments to a wider, professional audience, the call for merit selection was again heard in Ohio.[18]

Whatever the experience in other states,[19] party affiliation of the justices has made a difference in Ohio. Republican and Democratic courts *have* responded to different constituencies. What was striking about the Democratic court is that for the first time in Ohio history the court became an issue. While Celebrezze himself and then the internecine warfare among the justices made arresting headlines, it cannot be overemphasized that the court's substantive output, however ignored by the average newspaper reader, was of great import to elites and interest groups, including the state's generally conservative-to-moderate newspapers.[20] We can only speculate about whether the press would have anguished as much about a Republican chief justice who engaged in "Celebrezze-like" behavior while presiding over a court composed of justices who performed their expected function of deferring to the more affluent, influential, and articulate populations in the state. This is not to say that Celebrezze did not bring many of his problems down on his own head. It is to say that he provided a more tangible target than rulings that, say, abrogated the doctrine of sovereign immunity, held manufacturers responsible for the safety of their products, required railroads to put warning lights at crossings and insurance companies to write contracts in intelligible language, allowed suits for "mental anguish," and held that employees covered by workers' compensation might sue for injuries incurred from an intentional tort committed by employers. These and similar rulings,[21] Celebrezze himself, and the eagerness of Douglas and Wright

18. Ken Myers, "Feud Erupts Among Ohio Justices," *National Law Journal*, July 29, 1985. John S. Riley, "State Bar Launches a Merit-Selection Campaign in Ohio," *National Law Journal*, June 30, 1986, p. 7. While merit selection is generally supported by Republicans, the ranks are not closed. Said one, "Instead of campaigns amongst the highways and byways currently undertaken by judges who must go out and face the citizenry, . . . factions within the Bar, political organizations, business groups, labor groups and miscellaneous self-appointed busybodies will begin a backroom struggle which is vicious and nasty beyond anything in an open campaign." Quoted in Cook and West, "Ohio Supreme Court," p. 54.

19. Malcolm M. Feeley, "Another Look at the 'Party Variable' in Judicial Decision-Making: An Analysis of the Michigan Supreme Court," *Polity* 4 (1971): 91–104.

20. Assessment of press provided in an interview, November 21, 1985.

21. For cases and discussion, see notes 8–11 supra. *Matkovich* v. *Penn Central Railroad Company*, 431 N.E.2d 652 (Ohio 1982), held that the failure adequately to warn constitutes wanton misconduct. *Knitz* v. *Minster Machine Company*, 432

to take him on combined to make a formerly invisible court highly visible.

Equally important, the court's role changed from one of legitimizing actions taken elsewhere in government and by the reigning forces in the state to one of establishing a substantive agenda. In a state whose politics have been described as "issueless," the Ohio Supreme Court was perceived as having created issues and as having drawn ideological lines.[22] Partisanship and partisanship alone provided the impetus for this radical institutional change.

Intracourt Relations: Traditional Patterns

The disputatious Celebrezze court galvanized public attention. What has been overlooked by the press is that Ohio justices have been

---

N.E.2d 814 (Ohio 1982), cert. denied 459 U.S. 857 (1982), continued the expansion of products liability concepts, holding that a "manufacturer may be liable for injuries resulting from the use of a product if the product's design makes it more dangerous than would reasonably be anticipated or if the design embodied preventable dangers. "Ohio Supreme Court Symposium," *Akron Law Review* 16 (1983): 619–703, 623. The case followed trends established in *Lonzrick* v. *Republic Steel Corporation*, 218 N.E. 185 (Ohio 1966), and *Leichtamer* v. *American Motors Corporation*, 424 N.E.2d 568 (Ohio 1981). *Knitz* and *Blankenship*, 433 N.E.2d 572 (Ohio 1982) were among a group of closely divided rulings appealed (unsuccessfully) to the U.S. Supreme Court on the ground that Celebrezze, because he had declared his candidacy for governor, was disqualified from hearing the cases. "Resign-to-Run." "When [the court] blocked Cleveland Electric Illuminating plans to charge customers from cancelled nuclear power plants, consumer advocates around the country praised the decision," Stephanie Paul, "Democrats turn court to people," *Plain Dealer*, Apr. 22, 1984. *Consumers' Counsel* v. *Public Utilities Commission*, 423 N.E.2d 820 (Ohio 1981), aff'd. mem. dec. 455 U.S. 914 (1981). The court was, of course, no more consistently proconsumer in the public utility cases than it was prolabor in the workers' compensation cases. *Office of the Consumers' Counsel* v. *Public Utilities Commission of Ohio*, 480 N.E.2d 1105 (Ohio 1985), sustained a rate increase. Justice Locher, joined by Celebrezze, dissented, basing his comments on a law review Note that discussed the "problem of deferring" to the discretion of the commission. "[R]egulators, after an extended exposure to an industry through the regulatory process, tend to sympathize with the industry point of view, despite their statutory obligation to represent the public." "Government Regulation and Monopoly Power in the Electric Utility Industries," *Case Western Law Review* 33 (1983): 264.

22. John Fenton, *Midwest Politics* (New York: Holt, Rinehart & Winston, 1966), chap. 5, "Issueless Politics in Ohio." "One reason that the court may be regarded as activist (when in reality it has been catching up with doctrines and precedent established elsewhere) is that Ohio politics are not too clearly defined. Issues are murky. There is a tendency to move to the center. . . . There are no party

disagreeing for a long time and that the court's dissent rates have been among the highest in the nation.[23] There have been no systematic patterns of division.[24] The court was as likely to split in more or less routine cases such as those involving the bases of criminal appeals, decisions made by administrative bodies, condemnation proceedings, and family law matters ("we spend an awful lot of time on tweedle-dee and tweedle-dum cases," remarked a former justice)[25] as in disputes presenting more visible and controversial policy issues such as suits against municipalities, the imposition of the death penalty, the regulation of obscenity, the validity of "fair trade" laws, districting arrangements, restrictions on the constitutionally guaranteed right to referenda, and the court's authority to determine the effective date of

---

extremes, but the court is regarded as extreme. It is not so much extreme as extreme within the context of Ohio politics." Interview, November 19, 1985.

23. Henry R. Glick and Robert W. Pruet, Jr., "Dissent in State Supreme Courts: Patterns and Correlates of Conflict," in Sheldon Goldman and Charles M. Lamb, eds, *Judicial Conflict and Consensus; Behavioral Studies of American Appellate Courts* (Lexington, Ky.: University of Kentucky, 1986), ranks Ohio sixth among all state high courts. While the dissent rate remained stable prior to the Second World War (between 14 percent and 15 percent), it rose to 34.9 percent in 1966 and 41.4 percent in 1981. Another study, which focused on a six-year time period, ranks Ohio as seventh highest. Bradley C. Canon and Dean Jaros, "State Supreme Courts—Some Comparative Data," *State Government* (1969): 260–63. Our survey of Ohio cases reveals that justices dissented in 27.6 percent of cases in 1957, 31.5 percent in 1958, 28.4 percent in 1967, 38.7 percent in 1968, 34.9 percent in 1977, and 28.1 percent in 1978.

24. While there has been considerable speculation about the reasons for dissent on state supreme courts, no definitive conclusions have been reached. Partisan divisions are considered significant, but this does not explain differences among Ohio justices. Dean Jaros and Bradley C. Canon, "Dissent on State Supreme Courts: The Differential Significance of Characteristics of Judges," *Midwest Journal of Political Science* 15 (1971): 322–346; John W. Patterson and Gregory J. Rathjen, "Background Diversity and State Supreme Court Dissent Behavior," *Polity* 9 (1976): 610–22; Glendon Schubert, "The 'Packing' of the Michigan Supreme Court," in Glendon Schubert, ed., *Quantitative Analysis of Judicial Behavior* (Glencoe, Ill.: Free Press, 1959), pp. 129–41.

25. Criminal appeals: *State* v. *Abrams*, 313 N.E.2d 823 (Ohio 1983); "State v. Abrams: Harmless Error in the Absence of the Accused," *Ohio Northern Law Review* 2 (1975): 596–600. Administrative bodies: *Mentor Lagoons, Inc.* v. *Zoning Board of Appeals*, 151 N.E.2d 533 (Ohio 1957); *Pompei Winery, Inc.* v. *Board of Liquor Control*, 146 N.E.2d 430 (Ohio 1957); *Ohio Edison* v. *Public Utilities Commission of Ohio*, 369 N.E.2d 1209 (Ohio 1977). Condemnation: *Becas* v. *Masheter*, 238 N.E.2d 548 (Ohio 1964). Family law: *Hall* v. *Rosen*, 363 N.E.2d 725 (Ohio 1977). Justice William Brown, quoted in "Brown has no regrets at retiring," *Plain Dealer*, Apr. 24, 1984, p. 11A.

the Modern Courts Amendment.[26] Nor did the dissents typically reflect sustained jurisprudential debate among the justices. Dissents were often merely registered, unaccompanied by opinions.[27] Cases that might have provided propitious occasions for the airing of diverse views and that did present significant federal questions—such as challenges to "stop and frisk" police searches, to the prosecution of the Klu Klux Klan, and to narrow definitions of "family" for zoning purposes—were denied certiorari.[28]

While monolithic and near total Republican control might theoretically have produced a higher degree of unanimity, it only generated indifference to party identification. With so few Democratic colleagues, Republicans felt no need to coalesce as Republicans. Further, the lack of party labels in general elections presumed, as a number of Ohio justices indicated, a nonpartisan and/or bipartisan ethos,[29]

26. Suits against municipalities: *Haas* v. *Akron*, 364 N.E.2d 1367 (Ohio 1977). Death penalty: *State* v. *Lockett*, 358 N.E.2d 1062 (Ohio 1976), rev'd. in part and remanded, 438 U.S. 586 (1976). Obscenity: *State* v. *Jacobellis*, 179 N.E. 777 (Ohio 1962); rev'd. 378 U.S. 184 (1964); *State* v. *Mapp*, 166 N.E.2d 387 (Ohio 1960), rev'd 367 U.S. 643 (1961). Fair trade laws, enacted to protect businesses threatened by competition, have been regularly challenged in state courts. "Counterrevolution in State Constitutional Law," *Stanford Law Review* 15 (1963): 309–330, 309; John A.C. Hetherington, "State Economic Regulation and Substantive Due Process of Law," *Northwestern University Law Review* 53 (1958): 234–37. *Olin Mathieson Chemical Corp.* v. *Ontario Store of Price Hill*, 223 N.E.2d 592 (Ohio 1967). Districting: *State ex rel. King* v. *Rhodes*, 228 N.E.2d 653 (Ohio 1967). Referenda: *State ex rel. Riffe* v. *Brown*, 365 N.E.2d 876 (Ohio 1977). "A Threat to Ohio's Referendum: State ex rel. Riffe v. Brown," *Ohio State Law Journal* 39 (1978): 158–72. Modern Courts Amendment: *Euclid* v. *Heaton*, 238 N.E.2d 790 (Ohio 1968), "startled both professional and lay observers of Ohio government. In numerous newspapers, editorial reactions approached indignation," Leslie W. Jacobs, "The Supreme Court of Ohio, 1969 Term," *Ohio State Law Journal* 30 (1969): 626–735. Such press attention to the court was rare.

27. "An annoying habit of theirs," commented a law student researcher in relation to two wrongful death decisions. *Woodward* v. *Everly*, 147 N.E. 255 (Ohio 1958), and *McCord* v. *Ohio Division of Parks and Recreation*, 375 N.E.2d 50 (Ohio 1978).

28. Stop-and-frisk: *Terry* v. *Ohio*, 392 U.S. 1 (1968). Klan's right of association: *Brandenberg* v. *Ohio*, 395 U.S. 444 (1969). Zoning: *Moore* v. *City of East Cleveland*, 431 U.S. 494 (1977). The lower court holding in *Terry* was sustained; the others were reversed.

29. Between 1950 and 1978, four Democrats served on the Ohio high court. Justice Charles Zimmerman, according to his son, "had such a low political profile that many of his Good Ol' Boy Republican friends at the Country Club wondered why his name never appeared on their Republican primary ballot, never realizing that he was a life-long Democrat." Zimmerman, "The Supreme Democrat." Justice Zimmerman was on the court for thirty-four years.

depending sometimes on the nature of the substantive questions before the court.[30] One recently retired justice wrote, "While I am a Democrat, I believe in the nonpartisan nature of the court. I never consistently voted *with* anyone." Another noted, "Not always can you depend on there being a party 'perspective.' In my case, I am a registered Republican but I tend to be more liberal on many issues than some of my Democratic colleagues." A third provided this forthright assessment:

> The majority of Republicans (Wright and Holmes) typically express views and decisions opposed to the worker, consumer, victim of tort-feasor wrongs, tenants and the average person, but on the side of the insurance industry, corporate interests, etc. (Republican Douglas excepted therefrom), but the majority of Democrats . . . granting equal justice to the worker, consumer, etc. (but Democrat Locher is excepted). Thus one Republican, Douglas, does not fit the Republican mold, and one Democrat, Locher, is more like a Republican in his thinking and views than most Republicans.

In other words, a justice's party affiliation may be relevant only for purposes of acquiring and maintaining party support for electoral purposes. Fellow partisans disagree freely on the bench even to the extent of parting company with a chief justice who holds a firm position on a case. Further, "nonpartisanship" or "bipartisanship" on the bench may be indicative of configurations within the parties. Justice Ralph Locher's independence vis-à-vis other Democratic justices reflects his long identification with the more conservative wing of the Democratic party and a power base fashioned during many years spent in Cleveland politics, including three terms as mayor.

Persistent dissent may be attributed to deficiencies in leadership; and commentary supports the view that Ohio's chief justices have not been interested in encouraging collegial deliberation or the development of common perspectives on the law. Specifically, the court has had the reputation, even when dealing with complex issues, of substituting speed for thoroughness of consideration; of announcing decisions in brief opinions issued shortly after oral argument; of relying heavily on its own precedent and paying scant attention to legal treatises, law reviews, social facts, and legal developments outside the state. References to rulings from other jurisdictions have been characterized as peremptory, providing little indication of their relevance to the case at hand. The standards applied for granting

30. Responses to questionnaire. See Appendix A.

certiorari have been unclear.[31] The impression is that of a court performing in a perfunctory and haphazard fashion, almost by rote, and of lackadaisical chief justices who are unwilling to prod their courts into providing even a modicum of legal leadership for the state.

While there is no way of knowing the extent to which dissent was personalized, there is some evidence of animosities. For example, Justice Kingsley Taft, a Republican, ran against his chief, Carl Weygandt, a Democrat who had served on the court for thirty years. One may only surmise about intracourt relations during the period between Taft's announcement of his candidacy and his electoral victory: Weygandt died shortly after his defeat, reportedly a "broken man," and Taft was later introduced by a "rather drunken lawyer as the man who killed Carl Weygandt."[32]

There are suggestions of behind-the-scenes manipulation. Celebrezze's immediate predecessor, William "Billy" O'Neill, is remembered for an easy charm and charisma that stood him in good stead during a long and varied career in public office, including his years on the bench.[33] In contrast to Celebrezze, O'Neill has been described as smooth and deft. Celebrezze supporters have countered that O'Neill was no less "political" than Celebrezze; he simply "operated in the backroom, genteel manner of Republicans . . . rather than in the more open, fisticuff manner of Democrats."[34]

31. See Thomas B. Marvell, *Appellate Courts and Lawyers: Information Gathering in the Adversary System* (Westport, Conn.: Greenwood Press, 1978), pp. 17, 98, 114, 187, 192; Robert J. Archibald, "Stare Decisis and the Ohio Supreme Court," *Western Reserve Law Review* 9 (1957): 23–25. Commentary on these tendencies is illustrative. "The notably short opinions of the Supreme Court of Ohio [in two defendants' rights cases] reveals a lack of analysis of the current and controversial issues concerning the introduction of mug shots into evidence on direct examination. . . . Furthermore, the court's opinion lacked development of the issue of whether the new rule of criminal procedure [announced previously] should be applied retroactively. . . . [T]he court's opinion will do little to aid future development of Ohio law on the issue of retroactive application of the new rules of criminal procedure." "State v. Evans: Mug Shots and Retroactivity, Ohio Supreme Court Review," *Ohio Northern Law Rev.* 1 (1979): 187. Jacobs, "The Supreme Court of Ohio."

32. Zimmerman, "The Supreme Democrat." Weygandt had been elected to the court five times. "Taft defeated Weygandt by a mere 1,775 of the 2.66 million votes cast," Dubois, *From Ballot to Bench*, p. 125. While Kingsley Taft undoubtedly benefited from a famous name he was only distantly related (if at all) to the William Howard/Robert A. line of Tafts.

33. O'Neill, former speaker of the General Assembly, state's attorney, and governor, has been described as an "exquisite politician." Interview, November 21, 1985.

34. Sharkey and Ricks, "Frank Celebrezze."

In a word, collegial relations on pre-Celebrezze courts were characterized by considerable and persistent dissent. Sources close to the court have reported unpleasantness and internal politicking. But dissent and infighting attracted no more public attention than did the court's lack of distinction. And whatever else the reputation of Ohio's chief justices, they managed to keep the court out of the public eye. This may indeed have constituted their mission.

Disagreements on earlier courts may be attributed, at least in part, to indifferent leadership; conflict on the Celebrezze court was attributed to abrasive leadership. Celebrezze's style was, of course, bound to be more forceful than that of his predecessors. He had an agenda. But his penchant for engendering controversy on and off the court, while related to judicial objectives, stemmed directly from his political ambitions and personality characteristics.

Prior to his election to the supreme court in 1972, Celebrezze's career followed patterns similar to those of other state high court judges.[35] He served as state senator, as special counsel to the attorney general, and as a trial judge. Although identified with a prominent political family, Celebrezze experienced frustrations that may well explain his later actions on the bench. His party was willing to back him for the judiciary, but for little else. He ran for the state senate without official endorsement and lost the Democratic nomination for governor to Richard Celeste. A tentative bid for the Cleveland mayoralty was short-lived; no one was eager to help him take on Carl Stokes, one of the nation's first black mayors.[36]

Celebrezze obviously wanted to make his name by attaining a high electoral post. And the governorship ultimately appeared so desirable

35. "A significant majority of state supreme court justices have held prior public office, have had prior judicial experience, and have developed more than nominal ties to the Republican or Democratic party in the state." Mary Cornelia Porter and G. Alan Tarr, "Editors' Introduction," *State Supreme Courts: Policymakers in the Federal System* (Westport, Conn.: Greenwood Press, 1982), pp. xi–xxvii, xiv. For specifics, see Walter A. Borowiec, "Pathways to the Top: The Political Careers of State Supreme Court Justices," *North Carolina Law Review* 7 (1976): 280–85; Bradley C. Canon, "Characteristics and Career Patterns of State Supreme Court Justices," *State Government* 45 (1972): 34–41; Robert A. Heiberg, "Social Background of the Minnesota Supreme Court Justices: 1858–1968," *Minnesota Law Review* 53 (1969): 901–37; Francis H. Heller, "The Justices of the Kansas Supreme Court, 1861–1975: A Collective Portrait," *University of Kansas Law Review* 24 (1975–76): 521–35.

36. Sharkey, "Celebrezze longs for acceptance"; Stella, "The Celebrezze Dynasty"; "The Ohio Supreme Court Justices: A Biographical Sketch," *Ohio Northern Law Review* 11 (1982): ix–xi, ix.

that wittingly or unwittingly he blurred the lines between what is considered acceptable and unacceptable political and judicial behavior. Thus, ruling that public utility customers should be refunded for excessive charges is hardly extraordinary; signing and distributing the refund checks is. Promoting a trusted and close relative for office is not unheard of, nor is trying to secure a seat on a court for one in whom a judge may feel confidence; combining the two practices hardly comports with notions of accepted judicial norms. Considering other career options while on the bench does not raise eyebrows; preparing for and announcing a candidacy from the bench while continuing to hear cases is considered a serious breach of judicial ethics. Seeking revenge against one's political enemies, however much deplored, falls within the rules of the game; the exercise of judicial retribution, however great the perceived provocation, does not.[37]

The son of a former (Democratic) Ohio justice has described the failure to distinguish between the values of American political and legal cultures this way: Celebrezze, like anyone elected to Ohio courts, must be a "political animal"; indeed, former chief justices "were not totally above ward politics." The example of Taft undercutting his own chief justice is illustrative, and "O'Neill, a former house speaker, attorney general and governor had enough political axes to grind (he despised [Republican Governor] Jim Rhodes) to wear out a large emery wheel." Yet, O'Neill, "once seated in the chief justice's chair at least showed," as had his predecessors, "a little style, a little grace, a little class." Celebrezze, by contrast, was described as running "the state's highest court like a Cuyahoga county ward hall . . . passing

---

37. President John F. Kennedy appointed his brother, Robert, U.S. attorney general. Chief Justice William Howard Taft, "the champion influencer," took an active role in the selection of U.S. Supreme Court justices. Henry A. Abraham, *Justices and Presidents* (New York: Oxford University Press, 1985), p. 30. Justice Arthur Goldberg, according to general speculation, was bored with the U.S. Supreme Court and eagerly accepted appointment as U.S. ambassador to the United Nations. Ohio observes Canon 7(A)(3) of the American Bar Association's Code of Judicial Conduct. "A judge should resign his office when he becomes a candidate in a party primary or in a general election for non-judicial office." Exactly when one becomes a candidate is not clear and has not been litigated. "Resign-to-run Canon Faces Test in Ohio." Lawyers who challenged Celebrezze's participating in cases after his announcement of his candidacy were summoned by Celebrezze to explain themselves, an action described by one of the justices present as an "attempt to intimidate these lawyers." Mary Anne Sharkey, "Celebrezze's Political Moves Raise Questions," *Plain Dealer*, Apr. 26, 1984. A *Plain Dealer* editorial referred to Celebrezze's calling of a "secret meeting to berate law firms that have filed motions against him." Apr. 27, 1984. An adage often attributed to the Kennedys, "Don't get mad, get even."

out measly little refunds like some Mark Hanna ward precinct pimp."[38]

Further, in his comments both on and off the bench, Celebrezze gave the impression that he was actively courting the electorate, particularly blue-collar and ethnic, Catholic voters, with appeals to their economic self-interest and traditional values. A concurrence in a worker's compensation case makes the point:

> I am troubled by the language in the dissenting opinion that workers who are intentionally chemically poisoned on the job should not be able to recover damages from their employers because the elimination of health hazards would cost two million dollars.
>
> The bottom line of this case is that prohibiting an employee from suing . . . for tortious injury would allow a corporation to "cost-out" an investment decision to kill workers. This abdication of employer responsibility as represented by the dissenters is an affront to the dignity of every single working man and woman in Ohio.[39]

Celebrezze's populism, like much American populism, contains a strong moral component. In a speech to the Akron bar association he astonished members by blaming what he called the "counterculture" for "promiscuity, prostitution and perversion" (summed up as "the three P's"), for the "revolt against marriage," for "undermining the American family," for "justifying crime," and for "opposing nuclear power plants." "Counterculture philosophies," he continued, "were pushed into our homes by the sympathetic media."[40]

Such talk can touch the deeply held convictions and fears of many American voters, and, as Celebrezze may have calculated, a gubernatorial platform based on the economic liberalism espoused by his court and on social conservatism would reach out to and cut across many constituencies and voting blocs.

The blatant politicization of the chief justiceship was what many, including those who were sympathetic to Celebrezze's judicial objectives, found particularly offensive. A newspaper editorial provided this perspective: "A chief justice—any chief justice—should lead by intellectual capacity, persuasion and example. The present chief justice has chosen a different course, that ill-becomes him and ill

---

38. Zimmerman, "The Supreme Democrat." Mark Hanna, the ultimate political boss, sponsored the presidential candidacy of William McKinley.
39. *Blankenship* v. *Cincinnati Milacron*, 433 N.E.2d 572 (Ohio 1982).
40. *Plain Dealer*, Feb. 3, 1979, p. 1A.

serves the state of Ohio."[41] The extent to which Celebrezze chose his course is arguable, for his style appeared to be part and parcel of his character. He lacked that elusive, though commonly cited quality "judicial temperament." Those who have had off-the-court dealings with him described him as mercurial; one never knew what reaction he would have—suspicion, hostility, anger, manifestations of a "siege mentality," charm and cordiality—or why.[42] On the court Celebrezze evoked animosity and bitterness; but also loyalty, sympathy, and affection. Several days' interviewing of the Ohio justices yielded further insights into the effect of Celebrezze's personality on the court. Tensions and animosities ran deep; the justices (noncombatants excepted) blamed each other for the stress and divisiveness; the justices were distressed and embarrassed by the court's public image; the crisis situation, while by no means incapacitating, was not considered conducive to the orderly conduct of judicial business; the uncertainty of whether the judicial elections of 1986 would or would not return Celebrezze to the bench exacerbated the mistrust on both sides and the anxieties of all.

More striking than the malaise that permeated his court was Celebrezze's propensity to personalize disagreements, to lash out against and humiliate those who opposed his views, and to draw lines that precluded future accommodations. Two of his opinions, accurately described as "caustic" and "sarcastic," are illustrative.[43]

In one, Celebrezze likened Justice Blanche Krupansky, one of the dissenters, to a "19th century robber baron," accusing her of not carrying out the responsibilities of a "justice of this court who is duty-bound to serve all the people of Ohio." (Justice Krupansky, who was defeated by James Celebrezze in 1982, was reportedly told by the chief justice to "shut up" during a judicial conference.) For, he continued, "even a simple perusal of the current literature, cases and commentaries would demonstrate to the casual reader, unless he were living on Fantasy Island, that toxic fumes and chemicals in the work place are genuine health hazards to many workers."[44]

41. Ibid., July 24, 1984.
42. Sharkey and Ricks, "Frank Celebrezze: A law unto himself." One of the authors, who interviewed Chief Justice Celebrezze, found him helpful, informative, open, cordial, and amusing. Requests for information always received a prompt response—either from him personally or from his office.
43. Sharkey and Ricks, ibid.
44. *Blankenship* v. *Cincinnati Milacron*, 433 N.E.2d 572, 617 (Ohio 1982). Sharkey and Ricks, ibid.

Shortly before the election that she lost, Krupansky was again targeted for an opinion that Celebrezze described as "Kafkaesque judicial alchemy." The holding that a wife could testify against her husband in a criminal trial was, said Celebrezze, "demonstrably incorrect, plainly disingenuous, intellectually dishonest and intellectually flawed." As for the reasoning, "While the majority's rhetorical treatment of the battle of the sexes from Adam and Eve to Mork and Mindy stupefies the reader for its ideological pronunciamento, it fails to analyze the critical considerations at bar."[45]

Celebrezze's hyperbole is puzzling. Krupansky did not represent serious opposition. He had the votes for quiet revolution cases and was in control of the court's administrative apparatus. He may have thought that discrediting her prior to the judicial elections would assist his brother's chances, but such reasoning assumes that voters pay attention to court opinions—which they do not. We return to aspects of his personality that, for some reasons and under some circumstances, simply took over. The perils and the consequences of this lack of control were articulated by two of his Democratic colleagues—who may well have tried to dissuade their chief from exhibiting such petulance and pyrotechnics. "I don't think these strident things back and forth are particularly helpful to anybody," chided Justice Locher. "We must not forget that the two most important words in the judiciary are 'judicial restraint'." Added Justice William Brown, "I try not to get personal. That's bad judgment. It always comes back to haunt you. The best thing to do is just dissent."[46]

Celebrezze presided over a court no more disharmonious than those of his predecessors. The differences were of degree, not kind. Dissent

45. *State* v. *Mowery*, 438 N.E.2d 897, 900 (Ohio 1982). The court relied on the traditional rule that a wife could not testify against her husband. In dissent, Krupansky took careful aim at the majority's argument that precedent was applicable in this case. "[W]hile the achievement of marital peace and harmony is undeniably a laudable goal, it is unrealistic to believe it is an attainable goal under factual situations such as presented herein. This appellee shot his wife with a shotgun in the back, shoulder and face, essentially removing a large portion of her face. At the time of trial seven operations had been performed on Mrs. Mowery's face in an attempt to alleviate the damage inflicted by her husband. It seems obvious to this court that any maritial harmony which may have existed between Mr. and Mrs. Mowery was surely destroyed by the five blasts from Mr. Mowery's shotgun," at 902.

46. Quoted in Sharkey and Ricks, "Frank Celebrezze: A law unto himself," p. 20A.

on earlier courts was unimportant because the court was unimportant. Squabbles on the Celebrezze court were important because, owing to the Celebrezze agenda, the court was important. The irony of Celebrezze's stewardship is that as his court attained prominence, his actions, so visible on so many fronts, brought the court as an institution into disrepute. During all the years, then, when Ohioans might well have questioned the quality of justice emanating from their highest court as well as its lackluster leadership, they paid no attention. But when a chief justice did provide purpose and direction, when the court issued rulings considered noteworthy and commendable, Ohioans perceived their court as a "circus."[47]

Intracourt relations during the Celebrezze years provide a conspicuous and vivid example of a common phenomenon: personal relations on small collegial bodies such as appellate courts may become difficult and acrimonious. From a public interest perspective, an important question is the extent to which tensions affect a court's conduct of its business. Equally critical is the question whether public confidence in courts may be eroded by fractious justices—courts, after all, are meant to settle, not foment, disputes.[48] While the outcome of the judicial election of 1986 did not provide complete answers to these questions, it indicated their significance.[49]

47. Editorial, *Plain Dealer*, July 15, 1985.

48. For an (undocumented) account of internecine warfare on the U.S. Supreme Court, see Bob Woodward and Scott Armstrong, *The Brethren: Inside the Supreme Court* (New York: Avon Books, 1981). Infighting on the California, Missouri, and Wisconsin supreme courts has become a matter of public attention, e.g., Preble Stolz, *Judging Judges: The Investigation of Rose Bird and the California Supreme Court* (New York: Free Press, 1981); Paul Wenske, "Dissension Rocks Missouri Justices," *National Law Journal*, May 27, 1985, pp. 1, 26–28; and Richard Kenyon, "Justice awry: Collegiality crumbles as temperaments clash," *Milwaukee Journal*, Apr. 12, 1987, pp. 1A, 18A, 19A. "Do interpersonal relations affect a court's functioning? Supreme Court Justice William Douglas argued that they make little difference, at least for the achievement of agreement. Yet there is reason to doubt Douglas's view. Good relations are likely to facilitate consensus in cases and to enhance a court's efficiency in handling its work." Baum, *American Courts*, p. 282.

49. Thomas J. Moyer, Celebrezze's Republican opponent in the election of 1986, deplored the bickering on the court and promised that his "primary responsibility [would] be to restore integrity to the office of the chief justice." Steve Meissner, "Court Hopeful says Celebrezze biased," *Plain Dealer*, Dec. 5, 1985. Another Republican candidate, Joyce J. George, said, "I think interpersonal problems are causing an inability to work together, and that may result . . . at the very least in a perception of unfairness." Thomas Suddes, "Akron judge seeks seat on Ohio top court," *Plain Dealer*, Jan. 16, 1986.

The Court and the Press

Press coverage of the Celebrezze court was unusual within the context of the history of Ohio's judiciary. Just the same, once the court engaged media attention, newsgathering and reporting and the judicial response followed fairly typical press-court patterns. State judiciaries, unlike other branches and offices of government and unlike politics generally, are not the objects of routine press attention. With the exception of a handful of metropolitan dailies, most newspapers cannot afford to employ reporters who are legal experts. They rely on staff, usually political reporters, to cover occasions when courts make what is considered "news." Consequently, since journalists and judges have little experience dealing with one another, there is mutual misunderstanding about institutional norms and responsibilities.[50] Judges take the press to task for "failing to give the public the amount and type of information it needs to critically evaluate the judiciary."

> Coverage [is] criticized as frequently superficial if not misleading or inaccurate. Journalists themselves have been criticized for being both inadequately trained in the law and in the judicial process and for therefore being unable to separate the significant from the sensational, unable to competently monitor the judiciary and unable to understand what they are observing and recording.[51]

Journalists, on the other hand, reject a "comprehensive civics course" approach, claiming that it is their function to "inform of particular events and developments" and to "emphasize noteworthy cases and problems of the court system."[52] Further, journalists complain that courts do little to provide the sort of information that would facilitate informed newsgathering and reporting.[53] One justice,

50. See generally *The Public Image of Courts* (Williamsburg, Va.: National Center for State Courts, 1978).

51. Robert E. Drechsel, *Newsmaking in Trial Courts* (New York: Longman's, 1983), p. 4. See also Dennis Hale, "The Court's Perception of the Press," *Judicature* 57 (1973): 183–189.

52. *The Public Image of Courts,* pp. 77–78.

53. For a discussion of the question of journalists' access to courts, descriptions of the manner in which some courts make an effort to keep the press informed, and guidelines for press/court relations, see M. Marvin Berger, "Do Courts Communicate," *Judicature* 55 (1972): 318–23.

echoing a standard complaint voiced by judges, chided the press for not reporting in ways that serve the public interest:

> The media coverage reflects a lack of knowledge about how the court functions and what its purposes are. This lack of knowledge is consistent, generally, with that of the general public. The real business of the Supreme Court of Ohio is not of any interest to the media and so it is barely reported. I believe the media should obtain a working knowledge of how the court functions and obtain legal advice before interpreting legal decisions. Very often a sensationalist media report of a decision does not accurately report the effect of the decision.

Ordinarily, all Ohio justices may well have shared this view. However, since the court had become so polarized, justices assessed the coverage in terms of their own positions. Some found it to be accurate and fair; others thought it distorted, biased, false, and unfair. Yet others felt that the press had blown matters out of proportion, but recognized, with resignation, that the media are more interested in disputes than in the routine conduct of the public's business. One hinted that the press had been remarkably restrained and might have revealed more. Another contended that Celebrezze was the "whipping boy" for "progressive" rulings that had offended special interests and the "conservative" press.[54]

From the press perspective, it was argued that political reporters assigned to the court lacked time to educate themselves in the law and the judicial processes; they handled the court as best they knew how, "as though it was a legislature." In addition, not only are reporters "generalists," but they address "laymen," and "cutting through legal jargon means oversimplification almost to the point of distortion." On this score the court itself was not considered helpful. Journalists felt they lacked access to the court and were not provided with information on a timely basis. For example, they were not alerted to the pathbreaking *Blankenship* workers' compensation-tort decision, the significance of which "took a while to percolate." Newspeople considered Celebrezze personally hostile to them and the court as a whole unsympathetic to the exercise of press freedoms.[55] Finally,

54. Responses to questionnaire, and interviews, November 18–21, 1985.
55. Interviews, November 18–21, 1985, and responses to questionnaire. Justice Celebrezze commented that he was weary of press emphasis on his ethnic background, religious affiliation, and looks. Interview, November 18, 1985. In

Milkovich v. *News Herald,* 473 N.E. 1190 (Ohio 1984), a bare majority held that a wrestling coach, whom a sports writer claimed had "beat the law with a big lie," was not a public figure within the meaning of post–*New York Times* v. *Sullivan* cases, 376 U.S. 254 (1964), i.e., *Gertz* v. *Welch,* 418 U.S. 323 (1974); *Time* v. *Firestone,* 424 U.S. 448 (1976); *Hutchinson* v. *Proxmire,* 445 U.S. 111 (1979); *Wolston* v. *Readers' Digest,* 443 U.S. 157 (1979). The dissenters, Justices William Brown and Locher (Democrats) and Holmes (Republican), would have relied on *Curtis* v. *Butts,* 385 U.S. 338 (1967). "The coach" was considered to be "one of the most prominent in the nation." Letter to one of the authors, Nov. 7, 1985. In *State ex rel. Dispatch Printing Co.* v. *Wells,* 481 N.E.2d 632 (Ohio 1985), the court held that a newspaper might be denied access to a police chief's personnel file, but that information that would be part of the public record must be released. Justice Holmes dissented. Justice Douglas considers himself a near-absolutist concerning freedom of expression, "stopping only at the 'shouting fire in a crowded theater' analogy." "The Founding Fathers intended speech to be free, and no matter how distasteful speech or expression may be, it is constitutionally protected." He was "salivating" in anticipation of a libel case on the docket and was critical of an earlier libel ruling, *Embers Supper Club* v. *Scripps Howard,* 457 N.E.2d 1164 (Ohio 1982), in which the court, determining that simple negligence alone constituted a basis for winning a libel judgement, misapplied the U.S. Supreme Court's *Gertz* v. *Welch* test. Interview, November 21, 1985. The Ohio high court's understanding and interpretation of post-*Sullivan* rulings was not dissimilar from those of other state appellate courts. See, for example, "State Court Reactions to Gertz v. Robert Welch, Inc.: Inconsistent Results and Reasoning," *Vanderbilt Law Review* 29 (1976): 1431–77. Where public officials were concerned, the Ohio Supreme Court adhered strictly to the *Sullivan* principles. *Bukky* v. *Painesville Telegraph and Lake Geauga Printing Co.,* 428 N.E.2d 405 (Ohio 1981). In *State ex rel. Dayton Newspapers Inc.* v. *Rauch,* 12 Ohio St. 3d 100 (1984), the court denied family members access to autopsy records of a murdered couple. "Secret government received a boost," the press indignantly reported, pointedly noting that the requested information had been "accumulated by investigators . . . paid with tax dollars. The court's unanimous ruling, while insensitive to the needs of a society to know what its government is doing, is especially objectionable because it reversed two earlier rulings that kept autopsy records open to the public. The court said the records were part of the investigative material gathered by law enforcement officials, who may need to keep them secret during the course of an investigation. On the surface, this ruling doesn't seem so bad. Why should the coroner's office release information if it looks like the investigation will be damaged? To do so could interfere with the defendant's right to a free trial or ruin the state's attempt to convict. But the . . . case doesn't come close to these problems. Dale Johnston, the convicted murderer, has already gone through the legal system. He now is in jail and on death row. The investigation is closed; there is no confidentiality to protect. Public reports are paid for with tax dollars. Thus every taxpayer has the right to know how that money is being spent. Autopsy reports include not only information about the work inside the morgue, but other facts pertaining to the case. The court's ruling makes this information off limits for reporters and the public at large. By taking its antagonistic stance, the Ohio Supreme Court has sealed off a section of government and made it less accountable." *Plain Dealer,* July 17, 1984.

Ohio newspeople were, of course, allowed considerable "access" during the notorious trial of Dr. Sam Sheppard. In the words of the U.S. Supreme Court, journalists know full well that the public is more interested in reports about "personal controversies" between judges than in coverage that reflects "sophistication and knowledge about the law." A chief justice who "does some screaming" makes good copy. "The press smelled blood," as it was succinctly put, "and went after the court."[56]

There was, in short, nothing remarkable about the press's pursuit of a story that took on the dimensions of a soap opera.[57] And given the nature of events and issues, there was nothing remarkable about the judicial response. What is noteworthy is the effect that the coverage had on the court itself. First, there is no doubt that the press played a major role in the outcome of the judicial elections in 1984 and 1986. Celebrezze's defeat in 1986 and the reinstatement of a Republican majority is attributable in no small part to media coverage and advocacy.[58]

Second, press fascination with the court's battles, however understandable, exacerbated the tensions. The press's criticism of Celebrezze provided Justices Douglas and Wright with ammunition to be fired at their chief. And some justices were not reluctant to use the press for their own purposes and as a vehicle for ad hominem attacks

---

"bedlam reigned at the courthouse during the trial and newsmen took over practically the entire courtroom." *Sheppard* v. *Maxwell*, 384 U.S. 33, 34 (1966). In addition, Sheppard's "guilt" had in effect been "determined" by inflammatory (and inaccurate) pretrial news accounts of the case. The conviction was sustained over two dissents by an abashed Ohio Supreme Court. "Murder and mystery, society and sex and suspense were combined in a case in such a manner as to intrigue and captivate the public fancy to a degree perhaps unparalleled in recent annals. Throughout the preindictment investigation, the subsequent legal skirmishes and the nine-week trial, circulation-conscious editors catered to the insatiable interest of the American public in the bizzare. . . . In this atmosphere of a 'Roman carnival' for the news media, Sam Sheppard stood trial for his life." *Sheppard* v. *Maxwell*, 135 N.E.2d 340, 342 (Ohio 1956), cert. denied, 352 U.S. 955 (1956); habeas corpus petition granted *Sheppard* v. *Maxwell*, 384 U.S. 33 (1966). On retrial, Sheppard's conviction was reversed, but he had already served twelve years in prison. *Blankenship* v. *Cincinnati Milacron Chemicals, Inc.*, 433 N.E.2d 572 (Ohio 1982).

56. Interview, November 21, 1985.

57. Joe Dirck, "Let's catch up on As the Court Turns," *Citizen-Journal*, July 18, 1985.

58. "Whatever role the media played in the race for chief justice, it was clear from the election results that voters were listening and reading. Celebrezze went from being the state's top vote-getter in 1980 to early retirement. . . . [Governor] Celeste said that the fact that Ohio's newspapers were almost unanimously opposed to Celebrezze played an important part in the campaign." Gary Webb, "Newspapers called key in defeat of Celebrezze."

against each other.[59] The press, in essence, not only recorded but became an active participant in the more unseemly aspects of the court's affairs.

Third, the press made Ohioans aware (as interest groups had long been) of the part the court plays in governance. Whatever course the court may follow, the press will likely make sure it is at least nominally aware of judicial rulings and activities; decisions with wide policy implications, such as *Blankenship*,[60] will surely not catch reporters (and their editors) by surprise again. Even if the justices preferred to return to the days when the court operated in the shadows of Ohio politics, it is unlikely that the press would cooperate.

In sum, during the Celebrezze years Ohio's fourth estate and third branch took each other's measure, and a symbiotic relationship that could affect the way each institution goes about its business may be in the making. The press will be alert to the court as news. The court, within the context of its institutional role and responsibilities, will seek to avoid negative coverage.[61] To this extent the press has shaped the court—perhaps for many years to come.

59. "The traditional decorum of Ohio's highest court was shattered again this week when an Ohio Supreme Court justice accused a colleague of attempting to incite hatred and distrust of the court in an attempt to advance his career. Justice Clifford Brown said a speech last week by fellow Justice Andrew Douglas to the Cleveland district of the Ohio State Bar Association was 'garbage' and reflected Douglas's history of political grandstanding. Douglas responded by accusing Brown of being on a faction on the court that most lawyers consider to be intimidating and unfair. . . . 'I'm disappointed in Justice Brown's comments, but given his record for such activities, I'm not surprised,' Douglas shot back. 'Obviously, I struck a nerve and I'm happy for him to be defending a system that most members of the press and most lawyers and judges know to be unfair,' Douglas said referring to the disciplinary council." Harry Stainer, "Angry Justice Brown condemns colleague Douglas' criticism," *Plain Dealer*, Feb. 15, 1985. In a telephone call to a newspaper office, Brown referred to Douglas and Wright as "flannel-mouthed flim-flammers." Bertram de Souza, "Justice Brown lashes out at freshman colleagues on the bench," *The Vindicator*, Oct. 6, 1985, p. 10A.

60. *Blankenship* v. *Cincinnati Milacron Chemicals, Inc.*, 433 N.E.2d 572 (Ohio 1982).

61. Since Ohio judges are elected, they are, in theory at least, as "beholden" to the media as they are to the public. While judicial races have seldom aroused much media interest, *Sheppard* v. *Maxwell*, 384 U.S. 33 (1966), provides evidence that Ohio judges have had occasion to be aware of the power of the press. The presiding judge and the prosecutor in the case were, at the time of the trial, a few weeks away from "hotly contested" campaigns for judgeships. "The Cleveland press quite early took the position that Sheppard was guilty, and that any investigatory action on the part of law enforcement officials pointing in any direction other than Sheppard's

Republican and Democratic Courts: Civil Rights and Liberties

The jurisprudential changes that so dramatically marked the advent of a Democratic majority on the Ohio Supreme Court were not reflected in the court's civil rights docket. The Democratic court has been no more and no less attuned to civil liberties than Republican courts and has continued to follow decisional patterns established by its immediate Republican predecessors. In family law cases, for example, the court not only has been faithful to federal precedent, but also has interpreted it imaginatively.[62] On the other hand, the Democratic court's eagerness in economic cases to discard outmoded precedent, to embrace doctrines initiated in other jurisdictions, and to innovate was not always matched when the court was provided with other sorts of policy-making opportunities. For instance, when it offhandedly rejected the admission of expert testimony on the battered woman syndrome as a defense in a homicide case the court did not take its bearings from precedent in the twenty jurisdictions that permitted the introduction of such evidence, but relied instead on a federal ruling from 1923 now largely considered irrelevant for psychiatric testimony.[63] And, in keeping with the spirit of deferential

---

guilt was an attempt to shield wealthy and influential people from the processes of the law, and thus was evidence of corruption." Alexander B. Smith and Harriet Pollack, *Criminal Justice: An Overview* (New York: Holt, Rinehart and Winston, 1980), p. 189. Three Ohio Supreme Court justices, Weygandt, Matthias, and Herbert, were up for election in 1956. This is not to say that the judges concerned succumbed to media pressure. It is to say that the Ohio press, like the press anywhere, wields considerable influence through its reporting. The judicial elections of 1984 and 1986 demonstrated that the press can defeat and elect justices. The point cannot have been lost on judicial incumbents and aspirants.

62. In *Re Byrd*, 421 N.E.2d (Ohio 1981) following *Caban v. Mohammed*, 441 U.S. 380 (1979), represented a significant departure from previous Ohio law dealing with the rights of unwed fathers. For similarly innovative rulings concerning the rights of illegitimates and men faced with alimony payments, see "Bastardy Proceedings—The Expansion of the Rights of Illegitimates—Franklin v. Julian, 283 N.E.2d 813 (Ohio 1972)," *Ohio State Law Journal* 341 (1973): 428–35; *Cherry v. Cherry*, 421 N.E.2d 1293 (Ohio 1981). These decisions followed the U.S. Supreme Court's rulings in *Levy v. Louisiana*, 391 U.S. 68 (1968); *Weber v. Aetna Casualty Co.*, 406 U.S. 164 (1972) (rights of illegitimates); and *Orr v. Orr*, 440 U.S. 268 (1979) (alimony).

63. *State v. Thomas*, 423 N.E.2d 137 (Ohio 1981). For highly critical commentary, see Elizabeth Schneider, "Equal Rights to Trial for Women: Sex Bias in the Law of Self Defense," *Harvard Civil Rights-Civil Liberties Law Review* 15 (1980):

Republican courts, the Democratic court sustained the state's school finance law against state constitutional challenge—despite the emphatically contrary examples of five other state high courts.[64]

In any case, whatever the Ohio Supreme Court's concern with protecting rights, the justices have not been pressed by their political constituencies to take an active civil libertarian role. Party leaders in Ohio may differ on economic issues but are in essential agreement on civil rights issues.[65] To the extent that Republican and Democratic justices have protected civil liberties, they have done so without obligation to keep faith with those who promoted their candidacies for judicial office.

Prior to the mid-1960s the Ohio court, like most high courts, heard

---

623–47; "State v. Thomas: The Final Blow to Battered Women?," *Ohio State Law Journal* 43 (1982): 491–511. *Frye* v. *United States,* 293 F. 1013 (1923).

64. *Board of Education* v. *Walter,* 390 N.E.2d 813 (Ohio 1979), cert. denied, 444 U.S. 1014 (1980), overruled trial and intermediate appellate court holdings. Democratic Justice Locher dissented. For a discussion of the case pending its disposition by the Ohio Supreme Court as well as an overview of other state cases and the school finance reform movement, see Norman C. Thomas, "Equalizing Educational Opportunity Through School Finance Reform: A Review Assessment," *University of Cincinnati Law Review* 48 (1979): 255–319. For a critical comment on the Ohio Supreme Court's reasoning, see "Equal Educational Opportunity and Public School Finance Reform in Ohio: Board of Education v. Walter," *Ohio State Law Journal* 41 (1980): 79–210. For the role played by the New Jersey Supreme Court in reforming the state school finance system, see chap. 5. By holding that the Texas finance scheme did not violate the Equal Protection Clause of the Fourteenth Amendment, the United States Supreme Court in effect told state courts and state legislatures that the problem was theirs to handle. *San Antonio Independent School Distrist* v. *Rodriguez,* 411 U.S. 1 (1973).

65. It has long been noted that concerns for economic justice and civil rights do not necessarily march hand in hand. Samuel Stouffer, *Communism, Conformity and Civil Liberties* (New York: Doubleday, 1955); Herbert McCloskey and Alida Brill, *Dimensions of Tolerance* (New York: Russell Sage Foundation, 1983). For the attitudes of Ohio party leaders, see Thomas A. Flinn and Frederick M. Wirt, "Local Party Leaders: Groups of Like Minded Men," *Midwest Journal of Politics* 9 (1965): 82. Democrats were found to be slightly more tolerant than Republicans on a few now largely dated issues--teacher loyalty oaths, investigations of communism, enforcement of laws against communism and film censorship. On the whole, Ohio Democrats are found in the moderate-to-conservative wing of their party, e.g., U.S. Senator John Glenn and Governor, subsequently U.S. Senator, Frank Lausche. An exception is U.S. Senator Howard Metzenbaum. Wrote one Ohio justice, "I do not detect much difference in viewpoint among Republican and Democrat members on the issue of civil liberties, criminal defendants' rights, freedom of speech, etc. In five death penalty cases in the past eight months the decisions have been unanimous, except in one case where Justice Wright dissented." Response to questionnaire.

few civil liberties issues. Except for a smattering of first amendment claims, mostly involving convictions obtained under obscenity statutes,[66] the court's constitutional docket was devoted to challenges to such governmental actions as zoning regulations, tax assessments, administrative orders, and the taking of private property. When the court did address civil liberties claims, it was generally unsympathetic. In the notorious Sam Sheppard murder case, for example, it concluded that the trial judge's willingness to permit highly questionable activities by the press and others had not denied Dr. Sheppard a fair trial.[67] In another case the Ohio court turned a deaf ear, despite prodding from the United States Supreme Court, to due process claims of witnesses bullied by a legislative committee investigating subversive activities.[68]

When, in the early 1960s, the Warren Court began to issue a series of broad, innovative decisions affecting the administration of justice in the states, the Ohio Supreme Court's response was largely negative. Chief Justice Kingsley Taft stated his opposition to *Mapp* v. *Ohio* in off-the-bench writings, predicting that the exclusionary rule would undermine public confidence in the law.[69] And although most state supreme courts readily followed the mandate of *Gideon* v. *Wainright* (1963), the Ohio court initially sought to circumscribe its effects. By "restricting habeas corpus writs, by not requiring magistrates to inquire whether defendants want, need, or can afford counsel, and by allowing waiver of the right to counsel to be presumed, the Ohio supreme court," it was charged, "abdicated its responsibility to protect constitutional rights."[70] The Ohio court's initial response to *Miranda* v.

66. A prime example is *State* v. *Mapp*, rev'd., on other grounds, 166 N.E.2d 387 (Ohio 1960); 367 U.S. 643 (1961).

67. *Sheppard* v. *Maxwell*, 384 U.S. 33 (1966).

68. *State* v. *Morgan*, 133 N.E.2d 104 (Ohio 1958), vacated for reconsideration in light of recent decisions, 354 U.S. 929 (1956), on remand, 147 N.E. 847 (1958), aff'd. in part, rev'd. in part sub nom. *Raley* v. *Ohio*, 360 U.S. 423 (1959). As Justice. Brennan noted, "[T]o sustain the judgement of the Ohio Supreme Court . . . would be to sanction the most indefensible sort of entrapment by the State—convicting a citizen for exercising a privilege which the State clearly had told him was available to him." 360 U.S. 423, 438 (1959).

69. Taft, Book Review, *Notre Dame Lawyer* 42 (1967): 589–94; "Protecting the Public from Mapp v. Ohio Without Amending the Constitution," *American Bar Association Journal* 50 (1964): 815–18. *Mapp*, 367 U.S. 643 (1961).

70. *Gideon* v. *Wainwright*, 375 U.S. 335 (1963). "The Right to Counsel Under the Sixth and Fourteenth Amendments," *Ohio State Law Journal* 24 (1964): 446, referring, inter alia, to *Doughty* v. *Saks*, 183 N.E.2d 368 (Ohio 1962), vacated and

Arizona demonstrated a further lack of sympathy for the aims of the Warren Court. In one case it upheld a conviction even though the defendant's repeated requests for counsel had been ignored. In others the court showed an unusual willingness to accept claims that confessions were voluntary and that defendants had waived their rights, leading one commentator to conclude that "if a defendant's confession had been induced by threat or promises, such as to make it involuntary according to United States Supreme Court standards, that defendant does stand a better chance of having his confession held involuntary by a federal court than by the courts of Ohio."[71]

This is not to say that the Ohio Supreme Court consistently ignored, distinguished, or circumvented directives from the United States Supreme Court; no state supreme court can do that. Thus the court followed *Mapp* in excluding evidence, and adhered to the spirit of *Gideon* by holding that the criterion for determining eligibility for state-provided counsel was not "whether the accused ought to be able to employ counsel, but whether he was in fact able to do so."[72] Over time it tempered its distaste for *Miranda,* establishing precise guidelines for police to follow in determining whether defendants had waived their rights, and refusing the implication of a waiver of the right to counsel, even though the facts of the case might have supported the state's contention.[73] On the other hand, it did anticipate the Burger Court's erosion in *Harris* v. *New York* of the *Miranda* protections, ruling two years prior to *Harris* that although previous inconsistent statements obtained in violation of *Miranda* were inadmissible, they could be used by the prosecutor to impeach the defendant's trial testimony because the privilege against self-incri-

remanded for reconsideration in light of *Gideon,* on remand, 191 N.E.2d 727, rev'd. sub nom. *Doughty* v. *Maxwell,* 376 U.S. 202 (1964). For a discussion of reactions to *Gideon,* see Stephen L. Wasby, *The Impact of the United States Supreme Court.* (Homewood, Ill.: The Dorsey Press, 1970), pp. 149–50.

71. *Miranda* v. *Arizona,* 384 U.S. 436 (1966). *State* v. *Edgell,* 283 N.E.2d 145 (Ohio 1972). For discussion of cases, see Jeffrey P. Swayman, "State v. Wellman: 'Intelligent' and 'Knowing' Waiver of Right to Counsel," *Ohio Northern Law Review* 2 (1974): 57–58. Barbara Child, "The Involuntary Confession and the Right to Due Process: Is A Criminal Defendant Better Protected in the Federal Courts than in Ohio?," *Akron Law Review* 10 (1976): 280.

72. *State* v. *Bernius,* 203 N.E.2d 241 (Ohio 1964); *State* v. *Tymico,* 325 N.E. 556, 560 (Ohio 1975), appeal dismissed, 423 U.S. 993 (1975).

73. *State* v. *Jones,* 306 N.E.2d 409 (Ohio 1974); *State* v. *Wellman,* 309 N.E.2d 915 (Ohio 1974), discussed in Swayman, "State v. Wellman."

mination does not permit the accused "to lie with impunity once he elects to take the stand to testify."[74]

In other civil liberties areas the court's record was equally mixed. First Amendment claims were sustained, for example, against the enforcement of ordinances restricting solicitations for magazine and political expression. Press access rights to public records and judicial proceedings were affirmed, in some instances presaging United States Supreme Court holdings.[75] The regulation of obscenity was another matter. The Ohio high court was decidedly uncomfortable with Warren Court holdings and failed even to observe the far more relaxed Burger Court guidelines.[76]

74. 401 U.S. 222 (1971). *State* v. *Butler,* 249 N.E.2d 818, 821 (Ohio 1969). In *Harris,* Chief Justice Burger virtually echoed the Ohio Supreme Court: "The shield provided by Miranda cannot be perverted into a license to use perjury by way of defense." 401 U.S. 222, 226. Justice Brennan, dissenting, noted that six federal appellate courts and fourteen state appellate courts did not distinguish between direct examination and impeachment, while only three appellate courts, including the Ohio Supreme Court, did so distinguish. 401 U.S. 231. *State* v. *Kassow,* 277 N.E.2d 435 (Ohio 1971), adhered to *Harris.*

75. In *Bowling Green* v. *Lodice,* 228 N.E.2d 325 (Ohio 1967), it was held that a conviction for selling a (socialist) magazine without the requisite license constituted prior restraint, following *Lovell* v. *Griffin,* 303 U.S. 444 (1938), and *Near* v. *Minnesota,* 283 U.S. 697 (1931), and distinguishing *Breard* v. *Alexandria,* 341 U.S. 622 (1951). *Peltz* v. *South Euclid,* 228 N.E.2d 320 (Ohio 1967), invalidated a zoning ordinance whose express purpose was the "elimination of political signs," further holding that the plaintiff had standing to sue despite the fact that the election was past. *Wooster Republican Printing Co.* v. *Wooster,* 383 N.E.2d and 124 (Ohio 1978), held that hospital records could be open for inspection to the extent that a patient's name, address, date of admission, and discharge could be revealed without an invasion of the patient's privacy. *State ex rel. Dayton Newspapers* v. *Phillips,* 351 N.E.2d 127 (Ohio 1976), predated *Nebraska Press Association* v. *Stewart,* 427 U.S. 539 (1976), and *State ex rel. Beacon Journal Publishing Co.* v. *Kincaid,* 384 N.E. 695 (Ohio 1976), established rights later aticulated in *Richmond Newspapers, Inc.* v. *Virginia,* 448 U.S. 555 (1980).

76. In *State* v. *Jacobellis,* 179 N.E.2d 777, (Ohio 1962), the court claiming to follow federal precedent, sustained a conviction for showing an obscene motion picture. The U.S. Supreme Court reversed on the ground that *Roth* v. *U.S.* 354 U.S. 476 (1957), had not been correctly interpreted. 378 U.S. 184 (1964). *State* v. *Mazes,* 218 N.E.2d 725 (Ohio 1966), sustained a conviction on the ground that the material in question met the U.S. Supreme Court's "utterly without redeeming social value" test' *Memoirs* v. *Massachusetts,* 383 U.S. 463 (1966), was overruled on the basis of the somewhat more stringent requirements enunciated in *Redrup* v. *New York,* 386 U.S. 767 (1967). It has been suggested that the timing of the state and federal rulings accounted for the U.S. Supreme Court's apparent willingness to sustain Ohio obscenity statutes, which, commentators agreed, did not meet

The manner in which the Democratic court responded to the claims of defendants evokes the civil liberties approaches of its Republican predecessors. In some instances it generously enforced the constitutional protections of the accused.[77] In others it moved in the opposite direction,[78] on occasion holding to a view more restrictive than that adopted by lower courts.[79] What appeared to be a one step forward two steps backward pattern aroused unfavorable comment; a ruling that allowed the introduction of hearsay evidence, earlier precedent notwithstanding, indicated an ominous "shift . . . from a due process priority to a crime control approach." "It is almost as though the Ohio Supreme Court will no longer be 'bending over backwards' to serve the rights of the criminally accused. The court's concern that 'the

---

standards enunciated in *Miller* v. *California,* 413 U.S. 11 (1973). *State ex rel. Keating* v. *Vixen,* 273 N.E.2d 137 (Ohio 1971); 301 N.E.2d 880 (Ohio 1973); vacated and remanded, 413 U.S. 905 (1973); reh. denied, 414 U.S. 881 (1973). *Sensenbrenner* v. *Adult Book Store,* 271 N.E.2d 13 (Ohio App. 1971); appeal dismissed by Ohio Supreme Court (no citation provided); vacated and remanded in light of *Miller;* earlier conviction affirmed, 301 N.E.2d 695 (Ohio 1973); cert. denied after remand, 421 U.S. 934 (1975), Brennan, Stewart, and Marshall dissenting. For critical views of the train of events and outcomes see, "Constitutional Law-Obscenity-Injunctive Proceedings against the Display or Sale of Obscene Materials," *Ohio State Law Journal* 33 (1972): 236–46, and Richard H. Harris, "Obscenity Law in Ohio," *Akron Law Review* 13 (1980): 520–39.

77. *State* v. *Roberts,* 378 N.E.2d 492 (Ohio 1978), rev'd., 448 U.S. 56 (1980), see notes 83–104 infra and accompanying text. *State* v. *Burkholder,* 446 N.E.2d 176 (Ohio 1984) held that exclusionary rule is applicable in probation revocation proceeding. Noted in *American Bar Association Journal* 70 (1984): 121–22. *State* v. *Buchholz,* 462 N.E.2d 1222 (Ohio 1984), held that *Miranda* warnings must be given prior to interrogation if incarceration is a possibility, regardless of whether the potential charge is a misdemeanor or a felony. Shortly thereafter the U.S. Supreme Court held that motorists taken into custody for traffic offenses must be advised of their rights whatever the severity of the offense. *Berkemer* v. *McCarty,* 464 U.S. 1038 (1984). Following the federal ruling, Chief Justice Celebrezze said the U.S. Supreme Court had "merely followed our lead once again." *Plain Dealer,* July 7, 1984. In *State* v. *Daniels,* 437 N.E.2d 1186 (Ohio 1982), it was held that counsel must be permitted to participate actively in *in camera* proceedings.

78. *State* v. *Jackson,* 413 N.E.2d 819 (Ohio 1980), holding that defendant in a postconviction hearing must meet high burden of proof in claiming ineffective assistance of counsel. For highly critical comment, see "State v. Jackson: Ineffective Assistance of Counsel," *Ohio Northern Law Review* 8 (1981): 577–85.

79. *State* v. *Gerwin,* 432 N.E.2d 828 (Ohio 1982), holding that an uncounseled conviction may be considered at trial for a subsequent offense; *State* v. *Moss,* 433 N.E.2d 181 (Ohio 1982), holding that statutory prohibition against double jeopardy was not violated.

criminal law will not be brought into contempt' bears out this analysis."[80]

Further, while civil liberties concern certainly assumed a place on the court's agenda, due to Warren Court prodding, other interests continued to rank higher. Chief Justice Celebrezze's account of his stewardship is illustrative. In an overview of the 1981–82 term, which he titled "Ohioans Gain Rights," three defendants' rights rulings (two of which sustained convictions), one indigents' rights decision, and seven quiet revolution cases were discussed.[81] Not included in the

80. *State* v. *Spikes*, 423 N.E.2d 1122 (Ohio 1981), overruling *State* v. *Tims*, 224 N.E.2d 238 (Ohio 1967). "State v. Spikes: Admissibility of Hospital Records in Ohio Criminal Proceedings," *Ohio Northern Law Review* 9 (1982): 163–69, quoting from *Spikes* at 1127. Most of the Ohio justices responding to the 1985 questionnaire welcomed Burger Court modification of Warren Court criminal justice rulings. "The Warren Court in some areas went too far in expanding the rights of criminals, e.g., the complicated standards for the validity of searches and seizures with or without a warrant." "The Warren Court was out in the middle of nowhere, but the Burger Court is putting things back on an even keel. There was an increase in crime due to the Burger Court and victims felt they were not getting a fair deal." One said that after law school the American Civil Liberties Union agenda was his agenda until the Warren Court "ran off on" him. Celebrezze is considered a tough law and order judge. "Frank is no liberal," remarked one of his colleagues. While appreciating "the Burger Court's willingness to recognize the practical problems of law enforcement in applying the principles established by the Warren Court," another wrote that "he was becoming increasingly concerned that the Burger Court, at the urging of a United States Attorney General, will totally erode those principles by placing them in a subordinate position to the results the court seeks to achieve by not applying them." One justice supported "some restraints on warrantless searches and seizures. The police just can't bust everyone in sight." Interview, November 18, 1985.

81. *Ohio Northern Law Review* 9 (1982): 559–62. Defendants' rights: In *State* v. *Wilcox*, 436 N.E.2d 532 (Ohio 1982), the court again refused to recognize the defense of diminished capacity. *State* v. *Geraldo*, 429 N.E.2d 141 (Ohio 1981), cert. denied, 456 U.S. 962 (1982), held that evidence obtained from a monitored telephone conversation between consenting police informant and a nonconsenting suspect was admissible. *State* v. *Daniels*, 437 N.E.2d 1186 (1982). Indigents' rights: *Anderson* v. *Jacobs*, 482 N.E.2d 419 (Ohio 1982), held that under some circumstances the state must provide free blood tests to determine paternity. Quiet revolution cases: *Shroades* v. *Rental Homes*, 427 N.E.2d 774 (Ohio 1981); *Matkovich* v. *Penn Central Trans. Co.*, 431 N.E.2d 652 (Ohio 1982); *Blakenship* v. *Cincinnati Milacron Chemicals, Inc.*, 433 N.E.2d 572 (Ohio 1982); *Adys* v. *West American Insurance Co.*, 433 N.E.2d 547 (Ohio 1982); *Parrish* v. *Walsh*, 429 N.E.2d 1176 (Ohio 1982), holding that an automobile owner may sue negligent driver of a car in which the owner is a passenger; *State ex rel. Evans* v. *Moore*, 431 N.E.2d 311 (Ohio 1982); *Cleveland Electric Illuminating Company* v. *Public Utilities Commission*, 431 N.E.2d 683 (Ohio 1982).

summary of "major cases" were holdings that invalidated an ordinance regulating the content of billboards, and one that recognized a group home for delinquent boys as a family within the meaning of zoning specifications.[82] "Rights" meant economic and societal, not individual, rights.

The similarities between Republican and Democratic courts on civil liberties issues is most strikingly manifested by reactions to the new judicial federalism.[83] In a series of six decisions, two rendered when Republicans and four when Democrats were in the majority, the Ohio court had the opportunity to develop state constitutional law along lines established by other courts. In just one instance did it respond positively.

Four cases involved defendants' rights; the first, *State* v. *Gallagher*, concerned the admissibility of a confession obtained from a defendant in custody by a parole officer who had failed to issue *Miranda* warnings. The Ohio Supreme Court ruled that the confession was inadmissible because questioning by a parole officer was inherently more coercive than questioning by police, and the confession could not thereby be considered voluntary. The court did not specify the constitutional guarantee on which it relied, observing only that the confession violated the privilege against self-incrimination provided by the Ohio and United States constitutions. The state appealed to the United States Supreme Court, urging that *Miranda* not be extended to these particular circumstances. The question arose during oral argument whether the Ohio court's ruling rested on independent state grounds—a crucial consideration in determining whether the United States Supreme Court had jurisdiction. On remand, the Ohio court replied that it had, indeed, relied on the state constitution; Supreme Court review was, perforce, foreclosed. But the Ohio court failed to

82. *Norton Outdoor Advertising Inc.* v. *Arlington Heights*, 433 N.E.2d (Ohio 1982), following, inter alia, *Virginia State Pharmacy Board* v. *Citizens' Consumer Counsel*, 425 U.S. 478 (1976), which extended First Amendment protection to certain kinds of commercial expression. *Saunders* v. *Clark County Zoning Department*, 421 N.E. 152 (Ohio 1981), appeared to overrule *sub silentio* an earlier and much criticized ruling, *Garcia* v. *Siffrin Residential Association*, 407 N.E.2d 1169 (Ohio 1980), cert denied, 407 U.S. 911 (1980). However, in *East Cleveland* v. *Board of County Commissioner*, 430 N.E.2d 465 (Ohio 1982), the court sustained enforcement of a muncipal zoning ordinance that denied a state agency permission to construct a home for the mentally retarded within a residential zone.

83. What follows draws upon Mary Cornelia Porter and G. Alan Tarr, "The New Judicial Federalism and the Ohio Supreme Court: Anatomy of a Failure," *Ohio State Law Journal* 45 (1984): 143–59. © 1984 The Ohio State University.

define the scope of the state protection, noting merely that the justices would "reach the same conclusion under the [federal] Fourteenth Amendment."[84]

The situation in *Gallagher* gave rise to a slight and, it might be argued, logical extension of *Miranda*. It was followed by a case that involved interpreting what appeared to be conflicting rulings of the Warren and Burger courts.[85] At stake in *State* v. *Roberts*[86] was whether a defendant's right to confront adverse witnesses was violated by the admission of testimony taken at a preliminary hearing from a witness later unavailable for trial. By distinguishing Burger Court precedent the Ohio court held that the defendant's rights had been violated. The United States Supreme Court reversed on the grounds that the questioning of the witness was thorough, that she was unavailable for trial, and that her testimony had met the Supreme Court's standards for indicia of responsibility. On remand the Ohio court accepted the Supreme Court's approach and conclusions.

Reversal by the United States Supreme Court need not, however, have ended the matter. The state counterpart to the federal confrontation clause reads,

> In any trial, in any court, the party accused shall be allowed to appear and defend in person and with counsel; . . . to meet the witnesses face to face . . . ; but provision may be made by law for the taking of a deposition by the accused or by the state, to be used for or against the accused, of any witness whose attendance can not be had at trial, always securing the accused means and opportunity to be present in person and with counsel at the taking of such deposition and to examine the witness face to face as fully and in the same manner as if in court.[87]

---

84. 313 N.E.2d 396 (Ohio 1974), vacated 425 U.S. 257 (1975), on remand, 348 N.E.2d 336, 338 (Ohio 1976).

85. In *Barber* v. *Page*, 390 U.S. 719 (1968), the Warren Court held that a state's failure to make a good faith effort to produce a witness for trial rendered preliminary hearing testimony inadmissible even though defendant's counsel had foregone an opportunity to cross-examine the witness at the preliminary hearing. But in *California* v. *Green*, 399 U.S. 148, 165, (1970), the Burger Court ruled that when there had been an honest effort to produce the witness, when an opportunity for cross-examination had existed at the preliminary hearing, and when the testimony bore various "indicia of reliability," the testimony was admissible.

86. *State* v. *Roberts*, 378 N.E.2d 492 (Ohio 1978); rev'd 448 U.S. 56 (1980).

87. Ohio Constitution, Art. 1, Section 10.

This clearly means, as one commentator has put it, that "preliminary hearing testimony should be admissible at trial only if the witness is dead or precluded from testifying through the connivance of defendant."[88] On remand, this provision could have been cited in support of a holding that under Ohio law, testimony taken at a preliminary hearing, no matter how reliable, simply is no substitute for testimony given at trial. But that holding would have required the invalidation of a recently enacted statute authorizing the use of hearsay evidence and would, additionally, have forced the court to overrule earlier decisions that sustained the introduction of evidence of this type against state constitutional claims.[89] Acceptance of the federal mandate in this particular case, thus, may have seemed the less troublesome alternative.

In a similar case, *State* v. *Madison,* the court following the Burger Court held that per se preliminary hearing testimony was admissible at trial—a good faith effort to produce the witness for trial had been made, and the testimony satisfied the "indicia of reliability" test. Yet in finding such testimony admissible, the Ohio Supreme Court abandoned the far more stringent *Roberts* criteria. Only (Republican) Justice Paul Brown, author of *Roberts* opinion, dissented in *Madison,* arguing that the Ohio constitution afforded greater protection than the federal Constitution and that the state constitution was violated when a defendant's opportunity to cross-examine witnesses occurred only during the preliminary hearing.[90]

In the final criminal justice case encouragement to expand state constitutional provisions came not from the highest federal court, but from a lower state court. In *State* v. *Geraldo*[91] a common pleas court held that use of a warrantless tap with the consent of a police informant violated the defendant's Fourth Amendment rights. To reach this conclusion the court rejected the precedent of *United States* v. *White,* which held that since there is no legitimate expectation of privacy in telephone conversations with police agents or informers there can be no Fourth Amendment violation when police monitor

88. "Criminal Procedure—Sixth Amendment," *University of Cincinnati Law Review* 51 (1982): 178.
89. The earlier decisions include *State* v. *Swiger,* 214 N.E.2d 717 (Ohio 1966), and *Henderson* v. *Maxwell,* 198 N.E.2d 256 (Ohio 1964).
90. 415 N.E.2d 272 (Ohio 1980).
91. No. CR 78-7059A (Lucas County C.P. Oct. 18, 1979), rev'd., No. L-79-303 (Ohio Ct. App. Oct. 3, 1980), aff'd., 429 N.E.2d 141 (Ohio 1981), cert. denied, 456 U.S. 962 (1982).

single-party consent calls, and relied instead on Ohio statutory and common law that prohibits telephone taps and recognizes an invasion of privacy tort for its violation.[92] But because Ohio had no exclusionary rule for police violation of state law,[93] it was necessary, in order to reach the desired judicial outcome, to combine state law with federal constitutional principles. Federal law, said the trial judge, "is not the sole source from which an individual's expectation of privacy may be 'legitimated'. . . . [I]t is necessary to look to state law when analyzing the legitimacy of an individual's expectation of privacy."[94] Put differently, although the United States Supreme Court in *Katz* v. *United States*[95] provided the standard for interpreting the Fourth Amendment, Ohio law provided the basis for determining that a telephone tap violated a reasonable expectation of privacy.

Although an Ohio court of appeals reversed, a dissenting judge pointed out that the Ohio General Assembly had failed to adopt legislation authorizing consent taps, thereby indicating that it intended to provide "greater protection . . . under state law than the federal government does under Federal law."[96] *Geraldo*, then, came to the Ohio Supreme Court after judges on two lower courts had pointed out with great clarity the applicability of state law to its resolution. Nevertheless, the Ohio Supreme Court, relying on *White*, upheld the legality of the tap. Although it acknowledged the United States Supreme Court's invitation to state courts to grant rights broader than those guaranteed under the federal Constitution, the court expressed its disinclination "to impose greater restrictions in the absence of explicit state constitutional guarantees protecting against invasions of privacy that clearly transcend the Fourth Amendment."[97]

The Ohio high court's failure in *Roberts*, *Madison*, and *Geraldo* to participate in the practice of the new judicial federalism had been anticipated in an earlier case that, in an experience rare for the court,

92. 401 U.S. 745 (1971). *LeCrone* v. *Ohio Bell Tel. Co.*, 201 N.E.2d 533 (Ohio App. 1963).

93. *State* v. *Lindway*, 2 N.E.2d 490 (Ohio 1936). *Cincinnati* v. *Alexander*, 375 N.E.2d 1241, 1246 n. 6 (Ohio 1978).

94. *State* v. *Geraldo*, No. CR 78-7059A, slip op. at 3.

95. 389 U.S. 347 (1967). Telephone tap on a public telephone violates Fourth Amendment's guarantee of an "expectation of privacy."

96. *State* v. *Geraldo*, No. L-79-303, slip op. at 466 (Ohio Ct. App. Oct. 3, 1980).

97. *U.S.* v. *White*, 401 U.S. 745 (1971). *Oregon* v. *Hass* 420 U.S. 714, 719 (1975). *Geraldo*, 429 N.E.2d 145.

received critical acclaim when initially decided.[98] *Forest City Enterprises* v. *Eastlake* concerned the constitutional validity of a city charter amendment whereby all zoning changes required approval both of the council and of an extraordinary majority, 55 percent, in a referendum. The amendment was precipitated by a city planning commission's recommendation that a zoning ordinance be altered to permit construction of light industry and a multifamily high-rise. The court held that the charter change, by delegating legislative power to the people, violated the due process guarantees of the federal Constitution. In support of its position, the court relied on United States Supreme Court rulings that had established the principle that "procedures for the exercise of municipal power [must] be structured so that fundamental choices among competing . . . policies are resolved by a responsible organ of government." The Eastlake charter, on the contrary, "blatantly delegated legislative authority, with no assurance that the result reached thereby would be reasonable or rational." Moreover, four members of the five-judge majority concurred separately to focus attention on the underlying issue in the case, namely, the use of zoning regulations "to perpetuate the de facto divisions in our society between black and white, rich and poor."[99]

On appeal the United States Supreme Court reversed, ruling that the referendum could not be regarded as an unconstitutional delegation of power because the electorate had only exercised a power reserved to itself. The Court thereby avoided confronting, as Justices Powell and Stevens pointed out, the "disquieting opportunities for local governmental bodies to bypass normal protective procedures for resolving issues affecting individual rights."[100] The majority supported its decision by noting that the Ohio constitution secured the right to employ referenda as a means of exercising authority reserved to the people. Although the Ohio Supreme Court had originally relied solely on federal precedent, this reference to the state constitution

98. Lawrence Gene Sager, "Insular Majorities Unabated: Warth v. Seldin and City of Eastlake v. Forest City Enterprises," *Harvard Law Review* 91 (1978): 1373–1425, 1423, described the opinion as carefully crafted. One Ohio justice remarked on a "standing joke" about the Ohio high court. Namely, that if one of its decisions was accepted for review by the U.S. Supreme Court, it was because reversal was in order. Interview November 21, 1985.

99. 324 N.E.2d 740 (Ohio 1975), rev'd. 426 U.S. 668 (1976), on remand, 356 N.E.2d 499 (Ohio 1976). Quotes are drawn from 324 N.E.2d 746, 749.

100. 426 U.S. 672, 680.

underscored the possibility that on remand it could "conform state practices to the premises of due process contained in the Ohio Constitution." This, in "reflexive obedience to the United States Supreme Court's view," it failed to do. The Ohio court stated, "[W]e perceive no state due-process constitutional questions which, under this record, we would choose to decide in a manner other than that mandated by the opinion on remand."[101]

An even more clear-cut invitation to explicate state constitutional law was extended in Zacchini v. Scripps-Howard Broadcasting Co. Here, the Ohio Supreme Court upheld the right of a television station to videotape and broadcast a human cannonball act at a county fair against the claim that it violated the performer's right to publicity. Although the court did not specifically cite the First Amendment, it relied on Supreme Court rulings to support the claim that the privilege to report matters of legitimate public interest outweighed the performer's right to control access to his act and to profit from it. The United States Supreme Court reversed on the ground that the media could not claim federal constitutional protection when they broadcast a performer's act in its entirety and without his permission. Despite ambiguities in the Ohio opinion, the majority determined that the Ohio court had relied on federal grounds, and that even if it had not, the Supreme Court would have to assume jurisdiction in order to correct the state court's erroneous interpretation of federal case law. Yet in remanding for consideration of the question of restitution to the performer, the Court pointed out that the Ohio court could, under state law, extend protection to the television station beyond that required by the First Amendment. Despite this clear invitation, the Ohio Supreme Court remanded the case to the trial court, instructing it to determine whether the Ohio constitution immunized the station from paying damages. The court's obvious reluctance to take the responsibility for issuing guidelines for consideration of the state constitutional issue prompted Justices Celebrezze, who had dissented in Zacchini I, and William Brown to file concurring opinions in which they criticized their colleagues for evading the state law issue.[102]

Roberts, Madison, Geraldo, and Zacchini II were decided by Democratic courts; Gallagher II and Eastlake II by Republican courts.

101. Sager "Insular Majorities Unabated," pp. 1423–24. The court's quotation is from 356 N.E.2d 500.

102. 351 N.E.2d 454 (Ohio 1976), rev'd. 433 U.S. 562 (1977), on remand 376 N.E. 582 (Ohio 1978).

Gallagher excepting, the rulings exemplify a failure of the new judicial federalism. For that matter, *Gallagher* should probably be included in the list; for even when the ultimate result was an expansion of defendants' rights under state law, the Ohio high court continued to insist that its decision comported with federal precedent. Whatever the merits of the individual decisions, together they point to the fact that Democratic as well as Republican courts were reluctant to consider state law an independent source of rights and concomitantly to engage in a particular and historically unique form of policy-making.

The account of the Ohio Supreme Court's response to the new judicial federalism is not intended to be disparaging. Only a few state high courts had, at that time, begun to interpret state constitutions more generously than the United States Supreme Court interpreted the federal Constitution. Even fewer would persist in their course in face of the Burger Court majority's growing hostility toward the new trend, particularly when the Court insisted upon imposing rigid and altogether unrealistic requirements concerning the state law's "independence" of federal law. The Burger Court's remands to its Ohio counterpart were but a foretaste of what was to come when other state courts, more inclined to protect civil rights than the Ohio court, held that state constitutions went beyond the minimal protections guaranteed by the United States Supreme Court.[103] In short, the Ohio high court, lacking a traditional regard for individual rights, needed help rather than discouragement from the United States Supreme Court: for the United States Supreme Court, without compromising its standards, could have given the Ohio high court the incentive to develop state constitutional law. *Gallagher* could have gone unques-

---

103. An initial attempt to identify courts that have most frequently availed themselves of the opportunities provided by the new judicial federalism is found in G. Alan Tarr and Mary Cornelia Porter, "Gender Equality and Judicial Federalism: The Role of State Appellate Courts," *Hastings Constitutional Law Quarterly* 9 (1982): 926, n. 50. For the difficulties encountered by state courts in interpreting state civil liberties protections, almost de novo, as it were, and the concomitant necessity of referring to federal precedent, see "Developments in the Law—The Interpretation of State Constitutional Rights," *Harvard Law Review* 95 (1982): 1324–1502, 1356–67, and Robert C. Welsh, "Whose Federalism? The Burger Court's Treatment of State Civil Liberties Judgments," *Hastings Constitutional Law Quarterly* 10 (1983): 819–75. U.S. Supreme Court rulings that continued the trend of discouraging the development of state constitutional law include *Florida* v. *Casal,* 462 U.S. 637 (1983), *South Dakota* v. *Neville,* 459 U.S. 553 (1983), and *Michigan* v. *Long,* 463 U.S. 1032 (1983).

tioned. Express consideration of the state constitution could have been urged in the *Eastlake* remand. The *Zacchini* lecture to the Ohio court about its misapplication of federal precedent was at best gratuitous. And while one cannot claim with certainty that the Ohio Supreme Court's experiences in *Gallagher, Eastlake,* and *Zacchini* influenced the ultimate outcome in *Roberts* or the *Madison* and *Geraldo* holdings, it is reasonable to surmise that a cause-and-effect relationship may have existed.

The Ohio high court, then, can hardly be faulted for not pursuing the new judicial federalism after the reception accorded its early and hesitant efforts.[104] The point is that the bolder Democratic court was as uncertain as to the course to be followed as its more self-effacing Republican predecessor. This, in turn, harks back to the Ohio high court's long-standing ambiguity about its responsibility to protect individual rights.

Ohio Supreme Court Elections: Plus ça Change?

Ohio's "semipartisan" judicial selection system is the creature of the Progressive movement, two earlier systems, legislative and partisan selection, having been deemed as compromising judicial independence and integrity.[105] The new system, however, was quickly perceived as encouraging judicial candidates to appeal to the voters on the basis of publicity rather than on their fitness for office. Between

104. One Ohio justice had this observation about the new judicial federalism: "While I believe the U.S. Supreme Court should recognize the independence of state constitutions, I also think that the Burger Court is avoiding what I think is its duty to take the lead judicially to insure that the United States Constitution remains the primary and controlling legal document in the country. I do not think that the development of state constitutional law should be an excuse for the U.S. Supreme Court to avoid perplexing civil liberty issues, nor should it result in fragmentation between the states on basic issues. No, I am not satisfied that the U.S. Supreme Court takes seriously the attempts by state courts to use 'independent and adequate state grounds.' This is another area where I believe the court is result-oriented. The court will accept 'independent and adequate state ground' determinations if it would prefer not to reach the merits of the constitutional issue, but will find a way around it when it wants to address the question." Response to questionnaire.

105. Unless otherwise designated, the material in this section relies on Kathleen L. Barber, "Selection of Ohio Appellate Judges," "Ohio Judicial Elections," "Nonpartisan Ballots" and "Judicial Politics." Perusal of Sherrod Brown, secretary of state, *Ohio Election Statistics 1983–84,* which covers general and primary election outcomes, 1940–84, provides evidence of the significance of Ohio's "political names" in races for a variety of statewide offices.

the late 1930s and the 1970s second and third generations of reformers futilely attempted to institute merit selection, eventually failing even to acquire enough support to put the proposal for the necessary constitutional amendment on the ballot.

Under the system of nomination by partisan primary and election by nonpartisan ballot the pattern of Ohio appellate court elections remained stable from the end of the Second World War to the late 1970s. In a state in which the parties have traditionally been highly competitive, the appellate judiciary was predominately one-party; between 1960 and 1980, for example, two-thirds of the judges were Republican. Republican hegemony was reflected by more frequent competition in Republican than in Democratic judicial primaries and by the failure of appointed Democrats to win subsequent elections. (Appointment to the appellate bench in Ohio has not been, as elsewhere, an assured means of accession; Republican appointees also lose elections, but not as routinely.) Whatever the fortunes of the parties in elections for national, statewide, and local offices, there has been little correlation between the outcomes of judicial and other elections. Republican candidates for appellate court seats were virtually inoculated against the effects of Democratic victories and ran well ahead of fellow partisans running for other offices. General elections for Ohio's appellate courts have been insulated from trends in the state and the nation as well. Politically, Ohio appellate judges have inhabited a safe, self-contained universe.

The explanation for the phenomenon, according to Kathleen Barber, is the nonpartisan ballot. Participation in and outcomes of nonpartisan judicial elections faithfully replicate those of nonpartisan elections for other offices. While "voter fatigue" is common enough in most judicial elections, it is voters with the greatest interest and endurance who will mark ballots that lack the clues that party provides—namely, the more affluent, the better educated, and, by virtue of these characteristics, Republican party identifiers.

Nonetheless, given the vagaries of voter preference when party provides no guidance, Republicans and Democrats—especially the latter—have relied upon name recognition and ethnicity to trigger voter response. Political names such as Taft, Herbert, O'Neill, Sweeney, Corrigan, Celebrezze, and Brown (especially Brown: twelve Browns have been among the sixty candidates who have run for the Ohio Supreme Court between 1960 and 1980) show up regularly on judicial as well as other ballots. Ohio's notorious "name game" in supreme court elections has sometimes had bizarre and unintended results. Browns have run against Browns (in one supreme court race three Browns were running) and O'Neills against O'Neills. Republicans deserted a Republican Corrigan on the not unreasonable premise that an Irish name denoted a Democrat, while Democrats turned their backs on a Democratic Brown on the assumption that Browns were Republicans. On the other hand, Frank Celebrezze's first, very successful run for the supreme court may well be attributed to voter belief that he and his distinguished uncle, federal judge, former secretary of Health, Education and Welfare, and Cleveland mayor Anthony J. Celebrezze, were one and the same. If this was indeed the case, Frank Celebrezze's party calculated well in supporting his candidacy.

While seats on Ohio's highest bench have been ardently sought and intensely fought over, voter interest in primary as well as general judicial elections has been even more modest than is usual throughout the states. One reason for public indifference to judicial elections is that the contests are dull. Judicial candidates are forbidden by state law, time-honored practice, or state high court promulgations from campaigning in the normal sense. Consequently, as an irritated Ohio newsperson put it, all the information judicial candidates may provide for the electorate is "name, rank and serial number."[106] And media inattention to judicial elections (reporters have had nothing, after all, of interest to report) has reinforced a climate of nonconcern and indifference.

Incumbents have not been able to count on automatic reelection; in 1972 three sitting justices were voted out of office. Expenditures for judicial campaigns have been nominal. Republicans have outspent Democrats, and incumbents, feeling disadvantaged by the strictures against running on their "records" and fearing defeat, have sometimes outspent their opponents. The correlation between expenditures and electoral strength has not been ascertained. Organizations and interest groups endorsed judicial candidates much as they do other candidates. Business and industry (and bar associations) backed Republicans, organized labor the Democrats.

Between 1978 and 1986 the patterns and practices discussed above were appreciably altered. In 1976 two Democrats, William A. Sweeney and Ralph S. Locher, were elected to the court. Sweeney won handily, Locher barely.[107] Their victory has been attributed to the

---

106. James Neff, "Judging the Judges," *Plain Dealer*, Sept. 19, 1985, p. 17A, col. 1.

107. Brown, *Ohio Election Statistics*, p. 265.

role of organized labor; according to one participant-observer, the possibility of establishing a judicial beachhead, especially as union power declined, became increasingly appealing: "Labor found it could elect a governor when Rhodes was not running and could also make legislative gains from time to time. However, since elected politicians come and go, labor lawyers and unions decided they would achieve their goals more effectively if they could elect sympathetic judges to the Ohio Supreme Court. Everyone was surprised that it worked."[108]

But other factors were equally significant. William Sweeney was possessed of a "good" name; Ralph Locher, three-time Cleveland mayor and protégé of Governor Frank Lausche, was a well-known politician and a seasoned campaigner. Republicans, as far as the court was concerned, had been asleep at the switch. Taking high court elections for granted, they concentrated on races for governor and the legislature. And the name game as well as ethnic identity, as witnessed by Frank Celebrezze's succeeding victories[109] and James Celebrezze's initial, though short-lived, electoral success, continued to favor Democrats.

The judicial elections of 1984 were unlike those previously experienced in Ohio. Media coverage was extensive, editorial support lopsidedly favored the Republican candidates and undoubtedly (in conjunction with unfavorable comment on Frank Celebrezze) had considerable effect on the electoral outcomes. Candidates Douglas and Wright (as contrasted with candidate Corrigan and incumbent-candidate James Celebrezze) went on the attack, aided along the way, however belatedly, by a federal court's modification of sections of the Ohio supreme court's Code of Judicial Conduct that prohibited judicial candidates from criticizing their opponents and their opponents' records. Expenditures for the four races far surpassed those of previous elections, with Republicans outspending their Democratic opponents by a large margin. By the time the voters went to the polls, more information—provided by the media, interest groups, and

---

108. Interview, November 19, 1985.

109. Celebrezze was first elected by a 71,934 vote margin in 1972 to fill an unexpired term. In 1974 he won by 374,451 votes, and in 1978 he won by 79,343 votes. In 1980, running against a black woman, Sara J. Harper, he led the Democratic ticket and won by an impressive 806,199 votes, carrying all of the state's eighty-eight counties. In 1972, 1974, and 1978 he was the only Democrat among the high court candidates to be elected. Brown, *Ohio Election Statistics,* pp. 281, 255.

television advertising—about judicial candidates had been made available than ever before.[110]

As the election of 1986 drew near, both Democratic and Republican partisans, including powerful interest groups, claimed that their party needed a majority in order to, respectively, maintain faith with Ohio's working men and women or to save the state from the sorts of rulings that would lead to fiscal ruin. Democrats, with the governorship and other state offices at stake, were said to wish the "Frank problem" would somehow disappear, while warning of the vast resources the Republicans would pour into court races. Republicans, with an eye to the union vote, which through the years provided them with significant support, talked less of workers' compensation-tort rulings and more of returning "dignity" to the state's highest bench.[111]

On the other hand, it appeared for a while that the controversies

110. "Ohio has never seen the likes of this four-candidate race for the Ohio Supreme Court," wrote an Ohio columnist. "It may never again. The campaign has been a standout in judicial annals because of the bending or breaking of many heretofore sacrosanct rules . . . that made judicial contests about as exciting as watching ice melt." Duane St. Clair, " 'The Chief' may have last word in bitter court race," *Columbus Post-Dispatch*, Nov. 4, 1984, p. 4C, col. 1. "Normally," wrote another, "the race for the Supreme Court is a yawner. Lawyers get excited about it. Judges are thrilled. But most people would be hard pressed in an election to name the candidate for the Supreme Court." Jack Torry, "Ohio chief justice's actions help GOP more than Dems," *Citizen-Journal*, Oct. 13, 1984, p. 5. Sharkey, "It's cats-and-dogs time for high court seats," and "GOP pulls upset in high court races." "In judicial races the public is treated like an enemy from whom candidates should keep useful knowledge. This gag rule was lifted, at least in part, by a recent finding of U.S. District Judge Robert Duncan in Columbus. He held that judicial candidates can criticize their opponents and their opponents' record and their administration of a court so long as the criticism is based on fact and is not misleading. Editorial, "No more Mr. Nice Guy," *Plain Dealer*, Sept. 27, 1984, p. 24A. In 1984 the Republicans took a page from labor's book and conducted a vigorous campaign. Some labor leaders were not enthusiastic about the candidacies of James Celebrezze and John Corrigan in 1982 and 1984 ("A couple of turkeys they were stuck with"), but in the interest of "not making Frank mad" lodged no protest. Interview November 19, 1985.

111. Joe Dirk, "Let's catch up on As the Court Turns." Frank Celebrezze's candidacy would, some feared, threaten his cousin Tony Celebrezze's reelection for state's attorney. Mary Anne Sharkey, "A fine political name is laid to waste," *Plain Dealer*, July 14, 1985; Mary Anne Sharkey, "Get 'cha '86 GOP scorecards heah!" *Plain Dealer*, May 12, 1985. Despite such fears, Tony Celebrezze won handily. Amidst speculation that Justice Douglas was behind the move (vigorously denied), a Democrat announced that he would challenge Celebrezze in the primary. Mary Anne Sharkey and Joseph Rice, "Jefferson County prosecutor taking on Justice Celebrezze," *Plain Dealer*, Oct. 6, 1985.

that had swirled about the court had subsided. Celebrezze, while not ducking, did not seek fights; his State of the Judiciary address in 1985, for example, was temperate and well received. The state bar association, its position substantially vindicated, had less cause to view the chief justice with alarm. James Celebrezze had been roundly defeated in 1984 and a committee of the American Bar Association investigated and made recommendations, later partially adopted by a divided court, concerning the disciplining of Ohio's lawyers and judges. A policy change that mitigated the bar association's unhappiness about the loss of its printing contract was initiated (over the opposition of Celebrezze and his closest ally, Clifford Brown) by the court. And, as was pointed out by an active participant in the Celebrezze/Ohio Bar Association battle, normal relations were, in late 1985, being quietly reestablished.[112]

Given these circumstances, and the fact that Celebrezze's opponent, appellate judge Thomas J. Moyer, was considered to be a dull and unprepossessing candidate, it appeared as though Celebrezze would win reelection. Bar association and newspaper endorsement of Celebrezze's opponent in the Democratic primary were shrugged off by Celebrezze, particularly after an easy victory, and the anticipated bar/press support of Moyer in the general election was apparently not

112. Frank D. Celebrezze, "State of the Judiciary Address," presented to the Ohio Judicial Conference, Annual Meeting, September 5, 1985, Columbus. The chief justice "was given high marks by the judges on hand for delivering an intelligent and constructive speech, without the rabble-rousing comments of the past. Some court observers believe that intense Republican criticism of the chief is backfiring, and that Justice Celebrezze, by fighting back only when attacked, is getting sympathy from Ohioans." Joe Hallett, "Statehouse Notebook," *Toledo Blade,* Sept. 8, 1985, p. 3A. Contributing to the general amiability of the occasion, "Justice Andy Douglas was the first on his feet to lead a standing ovation. . . . Queried by reporters after his speech, the chief justice said, 'I have not participated in any squabble. . . . My tenure as chief justice has been under intense scrutiny and nothing dishonest or illegal has ever been discovered. I'm not very smart and I'm not very good looking, but I am honest.' " Ibid. The revisions of the disciplinary system were described as a "compromise," and the chief justice–elect, Thomas J. Moyer, "has called for more extensive changes." Editorial, "Dealing with bad judges, lawyers," *Plain Dealer,* June 7, 1986, p. 14A; Gary Webb, "Laying down the new law: New top judge wants to free court from lawyer discipline," *Plain Dealer,* Nov. 7, 1986, pp. 1A, 2A. The vote on the disciplinary rules was along party lines, with the Republicans complaining that the changes were merely "cosmetic," "with ultimate authority either directly or vicariously in the hands of the chief justice," Mary Anne Sharkey, "Judging lawyers," *Plain Dealer,* June 4, 1986. Mary Anne Sharkey, "High court ends printing spat with Ohio's bar by 5-2 vote," *Plain Dealer,* Jan. 18, 1985, pp. 1A, 16A. Interview November 21, 1985.

considered sufficiently crucial to offset what was considered to be Celebrezze's support in heavily Democratic Cuyahoga County. Further, the dismal campaign waged by former governor James Rhodes against incumbent governor Richard Celeste did not bode well for Republicans generally. Polls taken in July showed Celebrezze leading Moyer by twenty-eight points.[113] In October the *Plain Dealer* and the

113. Reporters for *Plain Dealer*, the Cleveland paper that had taken the lead in attacking Celebrezze's management of the court, were distinctly unimpressed with the Moyer campaign. One referred to him as a "virtual unknown" who "ran what could most charitably be described as a modest campaign," Webb, "Newspapers called key in defeat of Celebrezze." Mary Anne Sharkey, one of Celebrezze's most vociferous media critics, acknowledged that Moyer "did not run an impressive campaign," "Everyone won something last Tuesday," *Plain Dealer*, Nov. 9, 1986, p. 3D: Moyer's "soft-spoken demeanor," it was reported, "reminded some people of Mr. Rogers, the children's television showhost," Gary Webb, "Moyer vows to end brawling on Supreme Court," *Plain Dealer*, Nov. 9, 1986, pp. 1B, 6B. After the election the Republicans, it was suggested, wished they had nominated a person who would be a more impressive chief justice, telephone interview, November 17, 1986. "A special commission of the Ohio State Bar Association . . . gave top ratings to two Republicans and one Democrat for the Ohio Supreme Court and a not recommended rating to Chief Justice Frank D. Celebrezze who declined to appear before it for an interview," "State Bar Panel pans Ohio chief justice," *Plain Dealer*, Mar. 27, 1986, p. 21A; "Celebrezze aid blasts Ohio bar," *Plain Dealer*, Apr. 1, 1986, 5B. The Bar Association of Greater Cleveland gave Celebrezze "the second lowest rating among judges seeking re-election," John F. Hagan, "Top Judge gets 36% approval," *Plain Dealer*, Feb. 13, 1986, p. 26A. Editorial, "Stern, Ford for high court," *Plain Dealer*, Apr. 21, 1986.

Celebrezze's primary opponent was Stephen M. Stern, a county prosecutor who was, according to *Plain Dealer*, "the target of a 1984 disciplinary probe after he criticized a Celebrezze-backed judge in a court brief." Editorial, "Stern, Ford for high court." Stern ran against the Celebrezze court's brand of judicial activism, charging that Celebrezze's claims about a "peoples' court" put the chief justice in the category of a "lobbyist" rather than a judge, Thomas Suddes, "Celebrezze court of primary interest," *Plain Dealer*, Apr. 20, 1986, p. 36A. In the primary Celebrezze received 70.9 percent of the Democratic vote, Thomas Suddes, "Celebrezze easily nominated to court," *Plain Dealer*, May 7, 1986, p. 2B. (Celebrezze's Cuyahoga County margin in the general election was 2,835 votes, Governor Celeste's was 218,843, and Tony Celebrezze's (for state's attorney) was 193,048. Brown, *Official Report Statewide Summary Sheet, General Election, November 4, 1986.*

"A prominent GOP strategist said the only time the Rhodes campaign was in a race was when its campaign bus was stopped for speeding . . . ," Brent Larkin and Mary Anne Sharkey, "Rhodes fades; other races take over the spotlight," *Plain Dealer*, Oct. 19, 1986, p. 1A. Celeste received 60.60 percent of the vote, *Official Report*, Joseph Rice, "Celebrezze leads challenger by 28 points, pollsters report," *Plain Dealer*, July 3, 1986. Celebrezze's "strongest area was Cleveland" [the source of Democratic strength in Cuyahoga County], where his support was measured at 74 percent compared to Moyer's 10 percent, ibid.

Akron Beacon Journal published allegations that "mob-linked" union political action committees (PACs) contributed to Celebrezze's campaign fund and that the reversal of the arson conviction of union leader Chester Liberatore (whose organization had reportedly provided similar support through the years) was due to Celebrezze's persuading Justice Clifford Brown to switch from his original position in the case. Following these reports, the supreme court race began to capture significant interest, eclipsing other statewide contests.[114]

114. The *Plain Dealer* "broke" the tainted union money story. Gary Webb, "Mob-linked group donate to chief justice," *Plain Dealer*, Oct. 12, 1986, pp. 1a, 16A, cols. 1; "Officials detail mob-laborers link," ibid., p. 16A, col. 1; "Criminals contributed to laborers' political funds," ibid. Celebrezze reportedly received $15,500 from the PAC funds of Locals 310 and 860 of the Laborers' International Union of North America, $5,000 of which was "funnelled through another PAC before it was given to Celebrezze." Other elected officials, including James Celebrezze, reportedly received donations from the same sources, ibid., col. 3. The *Plain Dealer* revelations made reference to the arsonist case ("In 1982 Celebrezze cast a tie-breaking vote against convicting Liberatore of arson. State records show that five days later a Celebrezze campaign fund was given $5,000—money that came from Liberatore's union PAC and followed indirect path into the chief justice's campaign coffers. Just over two years earlier, Celebrezze had freed Liberatore from jail after two lower courts had ordered him imprisoned pending appeal of that arson conviction.") The *Akron Beacon Journal* picked up on the *Liberatore* case. Mary Grace Poidomani, "Switched vote freed union leader," Oct. 26, 1986. Brown denied that Celebrezze had persuaded him to change his vote, pointed out that other justices had changed positions, and that the only way the *Akron Beacon Journal* could have obtained its information was by Douglas "and two other Republican judges leaking private information" to the reporter. Gary Webb, "Charges fly again on Liberatore court vote," *Plain Dealer*, Oct. 26, 1986. *State* v. *Liberatore*, 433 N.E.2d 561 (Ohio 1982). Shortly before and after the tainted money and *Liberatore* charges, the press carried accounts of "dirty trick" tactics by Celebrezze forces, of Celebrezze's accepting campaign money from relatives and his appointees, of Moyer's acceptance of donations from questionable sources, of Celebrezze's "political" plane trips made at taxpayers' expense, of "fraudulent" campaign advertisements and of television and radio "blitzes." For representative news stories see Gary Webb, "2 candidates for top court crying foul," *Plain Dealer*, Oct. 26, 1986, pp. 1A, col. 1, 10A, col. 1; Gary Webb, "Appointees kin donate to chief justice," *Plain Dealer*, Mar. 30, 1986; Gary Webb, "Chief justice's plane trips cost taxpayers $13,800," *Plain Dealer* (no date provided in clipping); "Chief justice challenges foe over contributions," *Plain Dealer*, Oct. 17, 1986, p. 8A; "Campaign mailings for Moyer ok'd," *Plain Dealer*, Oct. 24, 1986, p. 7B; Thomas Suddes, "Ad blitzes on TV heat up races," *Plain Dealer*, Oct. 28, 1986, p. 4B; Gary Webb, "Chief justice's foe is irked by radio show," *Plain Dealer*, Oct. 29, 1986, pp. 1A, 12A; Thomas Suddes, "Dem says judge's ad is fraudulent," *Plain Dealer*, Oct. 30, 1986, p. 6B; Thomas E. Suddes, "Supreme court race is hottest in years," *Plain Dealer*, Oct. 19, 1986, p. 11A; Roger K. Lowe, "Race for chief justice heats up," *Columbus Post*

Despite Celebrezze's denials about the "mob role" in his campaign and Brown's defense of his position in the *Liberatore* case, Celebrezze steadily lost ground. His opponent called for a probe of Celebrezze as well as his resignation pending an investigation; state's attorney Tony Celebrezze maintained that an investigation was in order. Newspapers had further grist for their mills, not that they would have endorsed Celebrezze in any case. Between mid-October and election day 1986 the media, as in 1984, kept the pressure on Celebrezze, adding, from time to time, to the mob role story and airing the complaints of the Republican candidates. The only defense of Celebrezze appeared in letters to the editors; the *Liberatore* story was, for the most part, accepted as one more example of the (predictably) egregious behavior of Celebrezze (and Clifford Brown). Celebrezze gave the impression of being under siege, emerging from time to time to attack the media as the source of his troubles. Moyer, capitalizing on the mob-linked donations charges became increasingly aggressive; shortly before election day the race was considered too close to call; the day after the election Moyer's electoral strength was considered "surprising."[115]

Dispatch, Oct. 19, 1986, p. 6B; Jackie Jadrnak, "Chief justice role overshadows bids for governorship," *Cincinnati Enquirer*, Oct. 26, 1986, p. F2; Steve Luttner, "Opponent keeps pressure on chief justice," *Plain Dealer*, Oct. 29, 1986; Thomas Suddes, "Candidates present diverse views to voters: Controversy dogs chief justice; challenger gets tough," *Plain Dealer*, Oct. 26, 1986, p. 10A.

115. Gary Webb and Mary Anne Sharkey, "Chief Justice denies mob role in contributions," *Plain Dealer*, Oct. 15, 1986, pp. 1A, 16A; "Celebrezze says he would back probe of his funds," (no source provided on copy of news story sent to one of the authors); "Justice Clifford Brown criticizes story on decisions," letter to editor, *Beacon Journal*, Nov. 11, 1986; Gary Webb, "Opponent seeks probe of Celebrezze union ties," *Plain Dealer*, Oct. 14, 1986, p. 1A; Gary Webb, "Foe wants chief justice off court now," *Plain Dealer*, Oct. 18, 1986, p. 1B; Gary Webb, "Attorney general supports probe of Ohio chief justice," *Plain Dealer*, Oct. 16, 1986, p. 1A; Editorial, "End the insult—elect Moyer," *Plain Dealer*, Oct. 22, 1986, p. 6B. "Every major newspaper in Ohio emphatically endorsed Moyer over Celebrezze," Gary Webb, "Moyer takes lead over Celebrezze," *Plain Dealer*, Nov. 5, 1986, pp. 1A, 2C; Gary Webb, "Mob-linked funds aid Democratic hopefuls," *Plain Dealer*, Oct. 24. 1986, p. 2B; Gary Webb, "Union PAC gifts appear camouflaged," *Plain Dealer*, Oct. 30, 1986; "High court delay riles candidate," *Columbus Post Dispatch* (no date provided); Konrad A. Fuetter, letter supporting Celebrezze, *Plain Dealer*, Oct. 28, 1986; union newspapers defended Celebrezze, e.g., Editorial, "Who Ordered the 'Hit' on Frank Celebrezze," *Cleveland Citizen*, Oct. 24, 1986, issue no. 4619; "Vote by chief justice may not have been the deciding one," *Columbus Post Dispatch*, Oct. 19, 1986 (questioning whether Celebrezze's vote in the *Liberatore* case should be given any more weight than those of other justices who voted with him); for an attack on Justice Brown, see Editorial, "On the Road Again," *Toledo Blade*, Aug. 4,

While we may present only educated guesses about the jurisprudential consequences of the election, we venture that the Moyer court
will neither advance nor repudiate the quiet revolution. In the first
place, the new chief justice is considered a cautious moderate who
would be no more inclined to precipitously reverse than to precipitously create new precedent. After all, one of the tenets of
judicial restraint is to follow precedent—or at least to distinguish
or slowly erode precedent on a case-by-case basis. Indeed, a new
coalition on the Celebrezze court had commenced the process of gradually retreating from earlier positions in a narrow class of workers'
compensation rulings.

In the second place, Moyer will not be able to count on solid
partisan support any more than his predecessors did. Justices Holmes
and Wright are "regarded as extremely conservative," while the
"maverick," somewhat "quirky" "populist" Republican Douglas
could "ironically" "turn out to be labor's best friend on the court."
Should Moyer be inclined to move slowly away from some quiet
revolution precedent he will need to count from time to time on the
support of Democrats Locher, Sweeney, and Herbert Brown. Locher
has established a record of a moderate-to-conservative. Sweeney,
considered more a Celebrezze loyalist than an ideologue, might, it has
been suggested, accommodate himself to the dominant force on the
court. Herbert Brown is for the most part an unknown quantity, and
his campaign, except for putting distance between him and Celebrezze, was unrevealing. He is said to have been the only Democrat in
the large Columbus law firm in which he worked and from which he
took a two-year leave to write a novel; he is considered to be a strong
civil libertarian, a "moderate" on economic issues, and an "egghead"
whose judicial performance will resemble that of independent-
minded U.S. Supreme Court Justice John Paul Stevens. Furthermore, Moyer is faced with two justices, Wright and Douglas, who

1986, p. 14. "Celebrezze's campaign has been long on saturation advertising and
short on personal contact with the press. His campaign schedule, for example, is a
well-kept secret," Suddes, "Candidates present diverse views to voters." Steve
Luttner, "Opponents keep pressure on chief justice," *Plain Dealer,* Oct. 30, 1986;
Chief justice is blasted on campaign donations," *Plain Dealer,* Oct. 19, 1986;
Thomas Suddes, "Chief justice blasted in foe's TV message," *Plain Dealer,* Oct. 22,
1986, p. 2B; Gary Webb, "Moyer surprisingly strong in defeat of Celebrezze," *Plain
Dealer,* Nov. 5, 1986, p. 1A. The authors appreciate the assessments of the race
given by newspersons in telephone interviews, October 20 and November 17,
1986.

have become accustomed to attacking their chief openly and vociferously—granted that Moyer is not the target Celebrezze was, but Wright and Douglas have sought the limelight: nothing in their records suggests that they enjoy anonymity. To avoid the risk of offending either of them, Moyer will have to steer something of a middle course.[116]

In the third place, the supreme court election results cannot, whatever the claims of businesses and organizations opposed to many Celebrezze court rulings, be interpreted as a vote against the quiet revolution. Republican Justice Holmes, despite his minority position on the Celebrezze court, his incumbency, and the Moyer sweep, won by only a 1 percent margin. Republican candidate Joyce George, who joined Holmes in criticizing the Celebrezze court majority "for far reaching decisions they said came closer to legislating than interpreting the law," lost.[117]

The election of 1986 was more intense and more widely publicized

116. The assessment of Moyer came from an interview, November 22, 1985. The new trend in workers' compensation cases focused on the system of retrying cases decided by the Ohio Industrial Commission. A switch in Justice Douglas's position accounted for the 4-3 majorities. "Court pulls back on workers' comp," *Columbus Post Dispatch,* Aug. 21, 1986, p. 9F. The positions of Justices Holmes, Wright, and Douglas appeared in Webb, "Moyer vows to end brawling on Supreme Court." For Locher, see a collegial view given in an interview, note 30 and accompanying text. Sources for Herbert Brown include Jackie Jadrnak, "4 vie for Supreme seats," *Cincinnati Enquirer,* Oct. 26, 1986, p. F2, col. 1; Webb, "2 candidates for top court crying foul;" Suddes, "Celebrezze court of primary interest;" telephone interview, November 17, 1986. At his first press conference following the election, Moyer conceded that he might have problems in turning down the "volume on the court" and "controlling the other justices." Webb, "Moyer vows to end brawling on Supreme Court." It was taken for granted that Moyer's leadership would result in an end to the internal bickering on the court, the replacement of Celebrezze appointees on the administrative staff, rapprochement with the bar association concerning lawyer discipline, the establishment of an independent body to review disciplinary cases involving judges, and an audit of a Celebrezze-established "private" fund accruing from an annual fee for practicing law in Ohio. Editorial, "Fresh Air for High Court," *Toledo Blade,* Nov. 14, 1986, p. 8.

117. Holmes received 1,326,736 votes and his opponent, Francis Sweeney, 1,293,364. Sweeney's strength may—or may not—be attributed to his good political name or the possibility that voters confused him with sitting Justice A. William Sweeney, who was not running for election. For a discussion of candidate George, see Jadrnak, cit. note 116 supra. George, an appellate judge, lost by less than 1 percent of the vote—a loss which may or may not be attributed to the fact that her opponent bore the magical name of Brown. *Official Report, Statewide Summary Sheet, General Election,* November 4, cit, note 113 supra.

than the one held two years earlier, in which Celebrezze was (ostensibly) not a candidate. Whether Celebrezze would have lost without the mob money stories can only be a matter of conjecture. However, given the media's—particularly the *Plain Dealer's*—opposition to Celebrezze, it is perhaps not unlikely that another approach would have been found to be equally effective. Be that as it may, the coverage was not edifying, presenting little, if any, discussion of the Celebrezze court's work. That was left to the candidates, who either defended or attacked the tort, workers' compensation, and liability rulings in broad and vociferous terms. Whatever the merits of the arguments on both sides, the tone of the campaign was shrill and vituperative; and the media had much to do with creating that tone.[118]

The effect of this sort of campaign on the judiciary as an institution was a matter of some concern to the president of the Ohio State Bar Association and the chief justice—elect. The former warned, "[I]f we have to go through one of these things every two years, my fear is that the public soon won't trust the judges." Moyer said, "[T]his campaign is a good example of why we need merit selection." On the other hand, the judicial elections of 1986 evoked features of earlier elections: incumbency was not an assurance of election, the effects of money were problematical, the outcomes of supreme court races did not reflect the outcomes of other statewide races. The name game continued to be played, and Republicans took control of the court.[119]

118. Celebrezze stressed his prounion record, his "peoples' court," and warned of the bad times that prevailed before Democrats took control of the court. "The issue is pretty obvious to anyone that's seen any part of this election campaign—are we going back to an open court system or are we going back to the days when the court belonged to a privileged few when vested interest groups more or less decided which cases were going to be heard by the court and who used the court for their own purposes." Moyer stressed that he would "run a court devoid of partisan politics that will interpret the law, not promote the personal views of individual justices." He also charged that "some plaintiffs walk into Celebrezze's court with the deck stacked against them because of Celebrezze's implied ideology," Suddes, "Candidates present diverse views." Referring to the statewide Ohio elections of 1986, one newspaper castigated the candidates' negative television advertisements but maintained that "newspapers and some electronic media in Ohio and elsewhere did try to report the substance as well as the slanders of the campaign of 1986." As the editorial indicated, the election campaigns of 1986 throughout the nation were among "the dirtiest in recent years." "Muddy, Muddier, Muddiest," *Toledo Blade*, Nov. 17, 1986, p. 10.

119. The bar association president was quoted in Gary Webb, "Moyer takes lead over Celebrezze," *Plain Dealer*, Nov. 5, 1986, pp. 1A, 2C. For the Moyer quote, see Gary Webb, "Laying down the new law." The Ohio State Bar Association had rated

With Frank Celebrezze off the scene, judicial elections in Ohio could revert to more familiar patterns.

In our study of the Ohio Supreme Court, we have focused on a number of idiosyncratic factors that would have little bearing in a study of other state high courts—media coverage of the court, for example, the personality of the chief justice, and intracourt relations. Nonetheless, generalizations may be drawn and some lessons may be learned from the Ohio experience.

First, while a court may undergo radical change in several respects, it may also continue to follow traditional paths. That is, an institution may develop characteristics that are not easily altered. From a jurisprudential perspective, the Ohio court, despite the quiet revolution, persisted in its cautious, almost minimalist approach to civil liberties. From a political perspective, a change from Republican to Democratic control had virtually no impact on the manner in which the court conducted its business. Ohio justices went on exercising considerable independence vis-à-vis their colleagues, no matter their party affiliation.

Second, as has long been observed by students of the United States Supreme Court, the personality and leadership style of a chief justice may have a profound effect on collegial relationships and, thereby, on the court's work.[120] To whatever extent other justices may instigate quarrels, the point is that the chief justice is responsible for establishing the atmosphere in which a court works, and a lack of harmony leading to difficult working relationships will be attributed to a failure of leadership.

Third, the media, with the exception of a handful of newspapers

---

Celebrezze as "not recommended" and Moyer as "highly recommended." Suddes, "Candidates present diverse views." Commenting on the Ohio elections in general, Governor Celeste argued that candidates should spend less money and more time discussing issues. Celebrezze and Moyer spent approximately the same amount, $1.7 million and $1.3 million, respectively. The other four supreme court candidates spent no more than $300,000, "Celeste ponders a lid on campaign spending," *Plain Dealer*, Dec. 14, 1986. For discussion of earlier elections, see notes 105–06 supra and accompanying text.

120. See, for example, Lawrence Baum, *The Supreme Court* (Washington, D.C.: Congressional Quarterly Press, 1981), pp. 137–40, and David J. Danelski, "The Influence of the Chief Justice in the Decisional Process of the Supreme Court," in Sheldon Goldman and Austin Sarat, eds., *American Court Systems* (San Francisco: W. H. Freeman, 1978). For Chief Justice Earl Warren's massing a unanimous court in *Brown* v. *Board of Education*, 347 U.S. 483 (1954), see Richard Kluger, *Simple Justice* (New York: Knopf, 1976), pp. 678–99.

and reporters, are not equipped to handle courts. And courts, in turn, with fewer exceptions, are even less prepared to handle the press. Ordinarily this failure of communication is of no great consequence. However, when for whatever reason a court becomes news, run-of-the-mill misunderstandings may result in rancor on both sides. Further, as this chapter illustrates, the public, heretofore mostly ignorant about judicial functions and processes, may be made aware of the third branch only through sensationalist accounts of possible skulduggery in high places. The result is that the press, not having taken the time or not having cared about educating readers about courts, presents an erroneous and distorted view of the third branch and its purposes. The *Plain Dealer,* for example, which for the most part approved of the quiet revolution, devoted little space to the business of courts in general and to the debate over the legitimacy of judicial activism. Instead the newspaper concentrated on the short-comings of the chief justice whose court had brought much Ohio law into the twentieth century.[121] More sophisticated and in-depth cover-age—once reporters had put the court on their beats—would have provided the Ohio electorate with more information upon which to base their decisions.

Fourth, the Ohio experience highlights the tensions that exist between the concepts of judicial independence and judicial accounta-bility. By way of comparison, in California the electoral defeat of the controversial and equally embattled chief justice, Rose Bird, centers attention on an identical opposition. Ohio and California have different judicial selection systems, the former leading more toward accounta-bility and the latter toward independence. Yet in both states the combination of a series of rulings (in California, pro-defendant criminal decisions and pro-"underdog" civil decisions) and ad homi-

121. *Plain Dealer* reporters coined the phrase "quiet revolution," and in their initial exposé of Celebrezze, presented coverage and discussion of the court's major rulings. Sharkey and Ricks, "Frank Celebrezze: A law unto himself." Following Celebrezze's defeat and his decision, which overruled the majority, to hear thirty important cases during the court's lame-duck session, the *Plain Dealer,* gave credit where it thought credit due ("[T]he Celebrezze court generally has been progres-sive, shaking the dust out of Ohio's legal system in keeping with national trends in the law and court administration"), while predicting that Celebrezze would be remembered for his mistakes rather than his accomplishments ("To paraphrase Shakespeare, the good Celebrezze did will be interred with the boners he pulled along the way: petty personal attacks in court opinions and in public; paranoia about real or imagined opponents, and apparent ethical conflicts from questionable campaign donations") Editorial, "Supreme haste" (no date provided), p. 18A.

nem campaigns against chief justices (led in California by conservative-to-right-wing ad hoc organizations and in Ohio by the press, which indirectly aided the cause of interest groups opposed to the quiet revolution) resulted in the unusual defeats of incumbent chief justices.[122] This is not to deny that Celebrezze and Bird themselves were to a large measure responsible for the public images that led to their downfalls; that the Democratic party in both states provided little, if any, support, testifies to both chiefs' lack of political finesse. It is to say that it is relatively easy for powerful interest groups, well-financed organizations, and a hostile press to bring down justices who lead populist and/or civil libertarian courts. Courts have come to view their mission as protecting those least able to fend for themselves in the economic, social, and political system.[123] And the frenetic supreme court races of 1986 in Ohio and California suggest that

122. California justices are nominated by the governor, must be approved by at least two of three members of a commission on judicial appointments, and face voters in retention elections in the first gubernatorial election following their appointment and again at the end of their first terms. Following that, justices serve for a twelve-year term and are eligible for any number of terms thereafter. Bird narrowly won in the retention election of 1978 and, as predicted, was resoundingly defeated in 1986, the first time a chief justice had been defeated in California. In Ohio, Justice Kingsley Taft defeated Chief Justice Carl Weygandt (see note 32 and accompanying text above). In North Carolina Chief Justice Rhoda B. Billings was defeated by a Democratic opponent, Justice James G. Exum, who "managed to defuse aggressively partisan advertisements" by a conservative Republican group. Anthony Paonita, "Voters in 3 States Reject Chief Justices," *The National Law Journal,* Nov. 17, 1986, pp. 3, 16. For the question of judicial independence and accountability in general and as it relates to Bird in particular, we have drawn upon John H. Culver and John T. Wold, "Rose Bird and the politics of judicial accountability in California," *Judicature* 70 (1986): 81–98, which also makes the comparison with Celebrezze. For samplings of the *Los Angeles Times*'s thorough and thoughtful coverage of the Bird court and the retention election (in which two other Democratic justices, Joseph Grodin and Cruz Reynoso, went down to defeat with Bird), see Frank Clifford, "Lone Justice," *Los Angeles Times Magazine,* Oct. 5, 1986, pp. 13–17; 42–43, and "Stature of Honored Court Tested Amid Bird Debate," Sept. 14, 1986, pp. 1, 34.

123. For classic statements of the antimajoritarian position of courts, see Chief Justice Harlan Fiske Stone's renowned *Carolene Products* footnote, *U.S.* v. *Carolene Products Co.,* 304 U.S. 144, 152, footnote 4 (1938), and Justice Robert Jackson's opinion in *West Virginia State Board of Education* v. *Barnette,* 319 U.S. 624 (1943). Following the judicial elections of 1986 in California, defeated justice Reynoso remarked, "Judges, consciously or subconsciously, will have to worry about whether their opinions are making powerful political or economic interests in this state unhappy." Bob Egelko, "Vote politicized High Court, Reynoso says," *Los Angeles Times,* Nov. 22, 1986.

judges who offend enormously influential groups and institutions may become visible—and highly vulnerable—targets. While in some respects the issues in the Ohio and California judicial elections were quite different, the concerted and sustained efforts to replace both chief justices indicate that the concept of judicial independence may, under the right set of circumstances, become subservient to the concept of judicial accountability.

In the fifth place, our study of Ohio's high court demonstrates that while partisan affiliation does make a difference in a court's substantive output, the effects of returning a court to its "normal" majority need not necessarily be far-reaching or long-lasting. We have indicated that incoming chief justice Moyer will steer and moderate a middle course. Further, the Ohio Democratic party and the labor unions, having in the recent past "taken" the court and at present still retaining three out of seven seats, may well have the opportunity to reassume control. Indeed, justices on the Celebrezze court anticipated that the court will for many years seesaw between Republican and Democratic control. In addition, the Moyer court did not commence its first term with a mandate to revert to the jurisprudential status quo, but only to go about its business in a more seemly fahion. Ohio's voters were far more impressed, it would seem, by questionable donations to the Celebrezze campaign (which served mostly to remind them of earlier controversies that had started to fade from view) than by Moyer's self-effacement and calls for judicial self-restraint.

Finally, we demonstrate here, as in the chapters on the Alabama and New Jersey courts, that chief justices, given some leeway in the environment in which they operate, may turn a court around. Judicial reform was the vehicle by which Howell Heflin and Arthur Vanderbilt, chief justices of the Alabama and New Jersey courts, respectively, created entirely new supreme courts. Frank Celebrezze's partisan ideology, not institutional change, spurred the change on Ohio's high court. And so while describing the Ohio high courts as old and new is not entirely accurate, it is appropriate, in placing the court in its historical context, to speak in terms of the periods that preceded, included, and followed the Celebrezze court and its quiet and, we would venture, largely accepted revolution.

FIVE

NEW JERSEY:
THE LEGACY OF REFORM

Since World War II the New Jersey Supreme Court has assumed a role of leadership in the development of legal doctrine, thereby earning for itself a national reputation for activism and liberal reformism. Its rulings in tort law have, according to one survey, stamped it as the most innovative state high court in the field.[1] Its decisions on school finance and on the "right to die" have attracted nationwide attention and established important precedents for other state tribunals.[2] Several of the court's less publicized recent decisions, such as those admitting the battered woman defense in homicide cases and safeguarding the right of reporters to protect their sources, attest to its continuing willingness to address controversial issues and to entertain novel legal claims.[3] With its ruling on exclusionary zoning in 1983, the New Jersey court became the first state supreme court to venture into the field of "institutional litigation."[4] Taken altogether, the

1. Bradley C. Canon and Lawrence Baum, "Patterns of Adoption of Tort Law Innovations: An Application of Diffusion Theory to Judicial Doctrines," *American Political Science Review* 75 (December 1981): 978, table 2. See also Lawrence Baum and Bradley C. Canon, "State Supreme Courts as Activists: New Doctrines in the Law of Torts," in Mary Cornelia Porter and G. Alan Tarr, eds., *State Supreme Courts: Policymakers in the Federal System* (Westport, Conn.: Greenwood Press, 1982), pp. 97–99.

2. School finance: *Robinson* v. *Cahill* I, 303 A.2d 273 (N.J. 1973), and *Robinson* v. *Cahill* VII, 339 A.2d 193 (N.J. 1975). Right to die: *In re Quinlan*, 355 A.2d 647 (N.J. 1976), and *In re Conroy*, 486 A.2d 1209 (N.J. 1985).

3. Battered woman defense: *State* v. *Kelly*, 478 A.2d 364 (N.J. 1984); reporter's privilege: *Maressa* v. *New Jersey Monthly*, 445 A.2d 376, cert. denied, 459 U.S. 907 (1972), and *Resorts International* v. *NJM Associates*, 445 A.2d 395, cert. denied, 459 U.S. 907 (1982).

4. *Southern Burlington County N.A.A.C.P.* v. *Township of Mount Laurel*, 456 A.2d 390 (N.J. 1983). This decision is usually referred to as *Mount Laurel* II because of the earlier decision with the same title at 336 A.2d 713, cert. denied, 423 U.S. 808 (1975).

picture that emerges is of a court that has eagerly embraced opportunities to promulgate policy for the state and doctrine for the nation, confident of its own abilities and of the legitimacy of the activist posture it has adopted.

It was not always so. The same survey of tort law innovation that ranked the New Jersey court first in the postwar era placed it thirty-fourth in the period before 1945, and as late as 1950 one commentator lamented that New Jersey was lagging behind other states in the reform of tort law.[5] For a long time too, its constitutional rulings revealed little interest in assuming an independent role in doctrinal development. Throughout the 1950s, for example, the New Jersey Supreme Court echoed the U.S. Supreme Court in its willingness to authorize restraints on the freedoms of speech and association in order to safeguard national security.[6] When faced with issues on which the Supreme Court had not ruled, the New Jersey court during the 1950s characteristically upheld governmental action against constitutional challenge, as exemplified by its rulings rejecting the exclusionary rule and upholding a state statute that mandated daily Bible-reading in the public schools.[7] Even when violations of constitutional rights seemed clear, the New Jersey justices showed considerable reluctance to act. In 1949, for example, the New Jersey court reversed a lower court and upheld the practice of giving priority to whites in filling an emergency housing project for veterans, even though this effectively excluded blacks from occupancy, at least in the short run.[8] And in 1957 it ignored the state constitution's guarantee of a speedy trial by sanctioning a criminal trial conducted twenty-eight years after arraignment and thirty-three years after indictment.[9] Instead of assuming leadership in the protection of civil liberties, the New Jersey Supreme Court was at best a follower of the U.S. Supreme Court's initiatives and, when the Court announced expansive views of individual rights, at times a rather reluctant follower.

5. Canon and Baum, "Patterns of Adoption," p. 978, table 2. The negative assessment of the New Jersey Supreme Court's record in tort law is found in Abraham Glasser, "An Evaluation of New Jersey Tort Law Doctrines: The 1948–1949 Decisions," *Rutgers Law Review* 4 (January 1950): 424–26.

6. See *Thorp* v. *Board of Trustees of School for Industrial Education*, 79 A.2d 462 (N.J. 1951), and *Eggers* v. *Kenny*, 104 A.2d 10 (N.J. 1954).

7. Exclusionary rule: *State* v. *Alexander*, 83 A.2d 441 (N.J. 1951), and *Eleuteri* v. *Richman*, 141 A.2d 46 (N.J. 1957); Bible-reading: *Doremus* v. *Board of Education*, 75 A.2d 880 (N.J. 1950).

8. *Seawell* v. *MacWithey*, 67 A.2d 309 (N.J. 1949).

9. *State* v. *O'Leary*, 135 A.2d 321 (N.J. 1957).

Thus, like the Alabama Supreme Court, the New Jersey high court has undergone a major transformation during the postwar era. In New Jersey this movement has been from relative passivity to liberal activism and from obscurity to national prominence. But what are the nature and scope of these changes, and why did they occur? How have they affected the court's relations with federal courts, with other state supreme courts, and with other branches of New Jersey government? To begin to answer these questions, we turn first to the establishment of the modern New Jersey Supreme Court in 1947 and to the contributions of its first chief justice, Arthur Vanderbilt.[10]

The Emergence of the New Jersey Supreme Court

Through his support of judicial reform and his service as chief justice, Arthur Vanderbilt fundamentally reshaped—one might even say created—the New Jersey Supreme Court. New Jersey, of course, had a state high court before it ratified its current constitution in 1947, and Vanderbilt himself did not even attend the convention that drafted the document. Once installed as chief justice in 1948, he had to contend with a set of judges who had served under the old constitution and did not fully share either his vision or his aims. Nevertheless, Vanderbilt provided impetus and direction to the movement for judicial reform in the state, and, as chief justice, he secured the gains of the reform movement, gave the court stature, and ensured it the independence it needed to play a major role in the governance of the state. Despite the obvious differences, the comparison that springs to mind is with John Marshall, who—like Vanderbilt—assumed the leadership of a relatively moribund court and transformed it.

THE CREATION[11]

Medieval features which England developed centuries ago in her judicial system still flourish in New Jersey, although it is more than a quarter

10. For excellent general treatments of the emergence of the New Jersey Supreme Court as an active participant in policy making, see Stanley H. Friedelbaum, "Constitutional Law and Judicial Policy Making," in Richard Lehne and Alan Rosenthal, eds., *Politics in New Jersey*, rev. ed. (New Brunswick: Rutgers University Press, 1979), and Richard Lehne, *The Quest for Justice* (New York: Longman, 1978).

11. An extensive literature has developed on the process of judicial reform in New Jersey. Among the most useful works are Bennett M. Rich, *The Government and Administration of New Jersey* (Newark: T. Y. Crowell, 1957); Richard J. Connors,

century since the mother country abolished them.—Charles H. Hartshorne (1905)[12]

If you want to see the common law in all its picturesque formality, with its fictions and its fads, its delays and uncertainties, the place to look for them is not London, not in the Modern Gothic of the Law Courts in the Strand, but in New Jersey. Dickens, or any other law-reformer of a century ago, would feel more at home in Trenton than in London.—Denis W. Brogan (1943)[13]

That the New Jersey courts prior to 1947 should have resembled medieval English tribunals is hardly surprising, for the state's courts were in large part modeled on those very bodies. The system of courts established under the state's original constitution in 1776 retained the legal institutions that had been established in 1704, and these reflected the legal structures and practices found in England during that period. Perhaps the most noteworthy instance of this borrowing from the mother country was the establishment of separate courts for law and equity, a feature that survived in New Jersey until 1947.

When a new constitution was ratified in 1844—it would continue in operation until 1947—it retained most features of the state's original judicial system. This constitutional continuity did not, of course, preclude all institutional change: additional courts were gradually established by the New Jersey Assembly to meet legal needs created by an expanding population, intrastate migration, and urbanization. Indeed, as of 1947, seventeen separate classes of courts were operating in the state, frustrating all attempts to impose system and uniformity and creating a jurisdictional maze for unwary litigants.

The Process of Constitutional Revision in New Jersey: 1940–1947 (New York: National Municipal League, 1970); Joseph Harrison, "Judicial Reform in New Jersey," *State Government* 22 (October 1949): 232–36, 247–48; Eugene C. Gerhart, *Arthur T. Vanderbilt: The Compleat Counsellor* (Albany, N.Y.: Q Corporation, 1980); and Arthur T. Vanderbilt II, *Changing Law: A Biography of Arthur T. Vanderbilt* (New Brunswick: Rutgers University Press, 1976). In addition, of course, much can be learned by examining the extensive writings of Vanderbilt himself. A useful introduction to these writings is Fannie J. Klein and Joel S. Lee, eds., *Selected Writings of Arthur T. Vanderbilt,* 2 vols. (Dobbs Ferry, N.Y.: Oceana Publications, 1965).

12. Quoted in Carla V. Bello and Arthur T. Vanderbilt II, *Jersey Justice; Three Hundred Years of the New Jersey Judiciary* (Newark: Institute for Continuing Legal Education, 1978), p. 23.

13. Denis W. Brogan, *The English People: Impressions and Observations* (New York: Knopf, 1943), p. 108.

Admittedly, neither outdated legal institutions nor incoherence in institutional design was unique to the New Jersey court system: many other states had, like New Jersey, added new courts in ad hoc fashion during the nineteenth and early twentieth centuries. Yet the shortcomings of "Jersey justice" were so severe that the American Judicature Society, the nation's preeminent organization supporting judicial reform, felt compelled to nominate New Jersey's as "the nation's worst court system."[14]

In such a system, one would hardly expect a distinguished supreme court, and the Court of Errors and Appeals, which served as the state's high court until 1947, in no way belied expectations. The problems with the old court can be traced in part to defects in institutional design that prevented the court from keeping abreast of its work and acting cohesively. For one thing, the court had sixteen members— some wags described it as "a little larger than a jury, a little smaller than a mob"—and the unwieldy size of the body undoubtedly contributed to the court's lack of cohesion. So too did the court's composition. The old court consisted of the chancellor of the Chancery Court (the state's intermediate appellate court for equity cases), the chief justice and eight associate justices of the Supreme Court (the intermediate appellate court for law cases), and six "lay" members, usually lawyers, for whom service on the court was only a part-time responsibility. Because members of the Court of Errors and Appeals did not sit on appeals of their own decisions, the composition of the court varied from case to case. Even more important, because the court drew its membership from other courts and from busy practitioners, the judges could not devote full attention to their responsibilities on the high court.

The effects of these structural defects on the quantity of the court's work can be seen by comparing the output of the Court of Errors and Appeals to that of the postreform New Jersey Supreme Court. The new court in its first year disposed of 50 percent more appeals than the old court had in the preceding year and did so in 74 percent less time from date of argument to date of decision.[15] The effects on the quality of the old court's work, although less susceptible to measurement, were probably just as great.

14. "New Jersey Goes to the Head of the Class," *Journal of the American Judicature Society* 31 (1948): 131.

15. Kiester, "Faster Justice in Your Courts," *Parade, Sun-Star Ledger* (Newark, N.J.), December 9, 1956, p. 9, quoted in Gerhart, *Arthur T. Vanderbilt*, p. 79.

Yet it was not only structural problems that accounted for the failures of the Court of Errors and Appeals. During the first half of the twentieth century governors increasingly gave precedence to partisan political considerations in selecting those who would serve on the court, and thus the court ceased to attract the most able lawyers in the state, with predictable effects on the quality of its work. The nadir of this development was probably the appointment to the court of Frank Hague, Jr., son of Jersey City's politically powerful mayor, in 1938. At the time of his appointment Frank Jr., only twenty-eight, had been practicing law for only a short time because it had taken him five tries to pass the state bar exam. Asked to explain the appointment, the governor responded, "I knew it would please his daddy."[16]

Given the manifest deficiencies of New Jersey's judicial system, it is not surprising that efforts to reform it long antedated the adoption of the new constitution in 1947. As early as 1887, the *New Jersey Law Journal* "wearily exhorted the Bar back to the fray, to rally behind a new amendment to the Judicial Article."[17] These reform initiatives ultimately failed, and with the passage of time the organized bar became progressively more resigned to, perhaps even comfortable with, the state's judicial system. In 1926, for example, the New Jersey Bar Association rejected a proposal from its Committee on Law Reform for a complete restructuring of the state's judicial system. By the early 1940s, according to Vanderbilt, "but two judges were interested affirmatively in a new constitution" and "of the 8,000 lawyers in New Jersey, not more than ten percent were interested affirmatively."[18] Vanderbilt's estimate is borne out by the reception accorded the judicial article crafted by the convention in 1947: both the chief justice and the chancellor appeared before the convention to speak against the proposed article, and not a single county bar association endorsed it.

This combination of public apathy and opposition from the bar underscores Vanderbilt's achievement. Beginning in 1930, following his appointment as the initial chairman of the New Jersey Judicial Council, the advisory body on legal reform that he headed for a decade, he issued a series of reports documenting the defects and

16. Vanderbilt, *Changing Law*, p. 72.
17. Nicholas C. English, "State Courts: New Jersey Reorganizes Its Judicial System," *American Bar Association Journal* 34 (1948): 12, n. 1.
18. Arthur T. Vanderbilt, "New Jersey Courts Under the New Constitution," *Pennsylvania Bar Association Report* 56 (1950): 510, 511.

inequities of New Jersey's judicial system and calling for fundamental structural reforms. These reports had little immediate effect—Justice Dayton Oliphant, who had served as chancellor of the old Court of Chancery, scoffed that the Judicial Council "never accomplished a damn thing."[19] Just the same, the work of the council strengthened Vanderbilt's commitment to judicial reform, stimulated interest in reform among some key members of the bar, and prompted the development of a consensus among reformers. Thus when in 1941 Governor-elect Charles Edison proposed a constitutional convention, the outline for a restructured judicial system was readily available.

This effort at constitutional revision also failed, as New Jersey voters rejected the proposed constitution at the polls in 1944. Opposition to the constitution was led by Mayor Hague, who (quite accurately) viewed it as an attempt to undermine his political power. The proposed judicial article, which Vanderbilt helped to draft, excited little opposition, although its requirement of ten years' legal experience before a candidate could be considered for appointment to the state's appellate bench would have precluded the appointment of Frank Hague, Jr., and its elimination of lay judges from the state's high court removed patronage opportunities.[20] Learning from this defeat, delegates to the constitutional convention of 1947 sought to accommodate Hague's forces and avoid partisan divisions, a strategy that secured Hague's support for the proposed constitution and ensured its ratification.

Although a stroke sidelined Vanderbilt just before the constitutional convention met, the judicial article that emerged clearly bears his imprint. This was hardly coincidental. The members of the Committee on the Judiciary freely borrowed from the recommendations of the Judicial Council and from the judicial article of the constitution of 1944 in designing the new judicial article. Moreover, several members of the committee were Vanderbilt allies: its chairman, Dean Sommer, was a lifelong associate of Vanderbilt, and its most influential member, vice-chairman Nathan Jacobs, was a former colleague in Vanderbilt's law firm and a strong advocate of judicial reform. And

19. Quoted in Sidney M. Wolinsky, *Arthur T. Vanderbilt: The Amending Hand* (Senior thesis, Woodrow Wilson School of Business and International Affairs, Princeton University), p. 56.

20. Rich, *Government and Administration of New Jersey,* p. 21.

according to some accounts, Vanderbilt was in frequent telephone contact with committee members throughout the convention.[21]

Not all of Vanderbilt's prescriptions for reforms were accepted. Bowing to political pressures, the convention voted to retain county courts,[22] and although the constitution gave rule-making authority to the supreme court, it did so "subject to law," a condition that Vanderbilt opposed in a letter to the committee. (This provision would spark a major controversy during Vanderbilt's tenure as chief justice.) Nevertheless, the judicial article did eliminate the division of law and equity, consolidate judicial structures, create a seven-member supreme court, and centralize managerial authority in the chief justice's hands. Given Vanderbilt's contributions to the development of the new judicial system, it came as no surprise when Governor Driscoll appointed him as chief justice of the reconstituted supreme court.

INSTITUTIONALIZATION

When Vanderbilt assumed the office of chief justice, he was determined to assert managerial control over New Jersey's courts and to make them more efficient. Time and again in speeches and articles he had preached the importance of introducing business methods and sound administrative practices in the courts, and administrative and procedural concerns dominated his tenure on the bench.[23] Prior to 1947, each of New Jersey's various courts had operated autonomously, developing its own rules and procedures. Vanderbilt's first priority was to standardize judicial procedures by promulgating rules of procedure modeled on the Federal Rules of Civil Procedure.[24]

21. Accounts vary on how much contact Vanderbilt had with committee members during the convention. Nathan Jacobs has denied being in telephone contact, but other committee members have disputed this claim (Wolinsky, *Vanderbilt,* p. 82). The two biographies of Vanderbilt also offer contrasting views—compare Vanderbilt, *Changing Law,* p. 162, with Gerhart, *Arthur T. Vanderbilt,* p. 152. The discrepancy is ultimately unimportant, for as Gerhart observes, "Vanderbilt's real influence, however, on the Judiciary Committee, had been exercised long before 1947" (p. 152).

22. New Jersey's trial courts were unified and the county courts abolished by constitutional amendment in November 1978. See New Jersey Constitution, Article 11, Section 6.

23. Gerhart, *Arthur T. Vanderbilt,* pp. 206–11.

24. Vanderbilt had supported the adoption of the Federal Rules of Civil Procedure while he was serving as president of the American Bar Association and had participated in drafting the Federal Rules of Criminal Procedure.

Another long-standing problem was delay in the courts. The solution, Vanderbilt believed, was to highlight instances of delay and to enlist judicial energies in remedying them. To do so, he required that each judge submit to the Administrative Office of the Courts a weekly report listing work accomplished and undecided cases.

Because these and other changes met with resistance from many New Jersey judges, who resented intrusions on their autonomy, Vanderbilt had to devote considerable effort to persuasion and arm-twisting.[25] His impatience with delay and his enthusiasm for court statistics became legendary. He personally reviewed the weekly reports from each court, and judges who failed to keep current could expect a call from the chief justice demanding an explanation. His work on New Jersey's rules of procedure and other projects likewise required constant attention—for example, he completely revised New Jersey's rules of procedure only five years after their initial adoption. He was also forced to fight a continuing battle with political forces in the state legislature that sought to assert legislative control over judicial rule-making, a battle that culminated in Vanderbilt's most controversial decision, *Winberry* v. *Salisbury*.[26]

Winberry offered the New Jersey Supreme Court its first opportunity to determine whether it or the state legislature would exercise ultimate control over the rules of judicial procedure. In seeking to revise the procedural rules established by the high court, the New Jersey Assembly had insisted that because the constitution of 1947 gave the supreme court its rule-making power "subject to law," the legislature could override the court's exercise of that power through statutory enactments. Speaking for five members of the court, Chief Justice Vanderbilt rejected this interpretation of the phrase, holding that

> The only interpretation of "subject to law" that will not defeat the objective of the people to establish an integrated judicial system and which will at the same time give rational significance to the phrase is to construe it as the equivalent of substantive law as distinguished from pleading and practice. . . . The phrase "subject to law" . . . serves as a continuous reminder that the rule-making power as to

25. Vanderbilt himself estimated that "my administrative duties take a full third of my time." Address before the Advertising Club of New Jersey, Newark, N.J., May 2, 1951, quoted in Vanderbilt, *Changing Law*, p. 176.

26. *Winberry* v. *Salisbury*, 74 A.2d 406, cert. denied 340 U.S. 877 (N. J. 1950).

practice and procedure must not invade the field of the substantive law as such. While the courts necessarily make new substantive law through the decisions of specific cases coming before them, they are not to make substantive law wholesale through the exercise of the rule-making power.[27]

In sum, so long as the supreme court confined its rule-making to procedural matters, its exercise of this power was not subject to control by the legislature.

Vanderbilt's opinion was vehemently attacked. In refusing to join the chief justice's opinion, Justice Case observed that it was not necessary to construe the constitutional provision in order to resolve the case. More important, Vanderbilt's interpretation flew in the face of constitutional history. In its report to the convention, the Committee on the Judiciary had expressly indicated that it considered "subject to law" to mean subject to legislation.[28] And Vanderbilt himself, in his letter to the convention objecting to inclusion of the phrase, had interpreted it the same way.[29] Thus although Vanderbilt's position may have secured the independence of the judiciary and promoted better administration of the courts, it more closely resembled a usurpation than a faithful interpretation of the constitution.

Winberry is in many ways an instructive case for understanding the New Jersey Supreme Court. First, it showed the court reaching out to address a politically explosive issue rather than deciding the case on narrow grounds. This willingness, even eagerness, to confront controversial questions is consistent with Vanderbilt's more general understanding of the judicial role—in both opinions and extrajudicial writings, he categorically rejected the standard canons of judicial restraint.[30] And his influence here has been decisive: what Vanderbilt preached and practiced became orthodoxy for the New Jersey Su-

27. 74 A.2d 406, 410 (N.J. 1950).

28. The Judiciary Committee's report to the constitutional convention stated that "this Court [New Jersey Supreme Court] was given the power to make rules . . . subject to the overriding power of the legislature with respect to practice and procedure." Quoted in Gerhart, *Arthur T. Vanderbilt*, p. 240.

29. The latter is reprinted in Gerhart, *Arthur T. Vanderbilt*, App. A.

30. A representative case, in which Vanderbilt expressly rejects judicial restraint, is *State* v. *Otis Elevator Co.*, 95 A.2d 715, (N.J. 1953); see also *Doremus* v. *Board of Education of Hawthorne*, 75 A.2d 880 (1950). Vanderbilt's major off-the-bench statement on judicial restraint is found in *The Doctrine of the Separation of Powers and Its Present-Day Significance* (Lincoln, Neb.: University of Nebraska Press, 1953), pp. 134–40.

preme Court.[31] Second, *Winberry* showed the justices to be largely
united as they addressed an issue with implications for the court's
institutional position.[32] This movement toward a common position
cannot be attributed solely to Vanderbilt's leadership, for he was
unable to marshal the court in some other cases about which he felt
deeply. Rather, it exemplifies the justices' particular sensitivity to the
institutional position of their court and their tendency to coalesce
when announcing a highly controversial decision.[33] Third, despite
Vanderbilt's dubious argument in *Winberry*, the important thing is
that he prevailed. Following the decision, the press and bar almost
universally supported the court; and in the face of this sentiment,
opponents of the decision in the New Jersey Assembly were forced to
shelve plans for a constitutional amendment and accept the decision.
The lesson was clear: the reforms of 1947 and thereafter had raised
the stature of New Jersey's courts and created a reservoir of public and
elite support on which the New Jersey Supreme Court could draw.

THE VANDERBILT LEGACY

By 1957, when Chief Justice Vanderbilt died suddenly of a heart
attack, he had largely completed his task of modernizing the state's
judicial system. New Jersey's courts enjoyed an unaccustomed national stature, and the state basked in its reputation for judicial
progressivism. The news of Vanderbilt's death brought a nationwide
outpouring of praise for the man and his accomplishments. Representative of the tributes was the comment of Justice William J. Brennan,
Jr., who had served with Vanderbilt before being elevated to the U.S.

31. See, for example, *Home Builders League of New Jersey, Inc.* v. *Township of
Berlin,* 405 A.2d 381 (N.J. 1979), and *State* v. *Allen,* 373 A.2d 377 (N.J. 1977).

32. In *Winberry* Justice Clarence E. Case concurred in the result, although he
would not have reached the constitutional issue—he claimed that the court was
"swerved by the impulse to find a way of reaching a desired result" (74 A.2d 420).
Justice Harry Heher dissented without opinion in the case.

Chief Justice Vanderbilt made immediate efforts to rally the court behind the
position he had staked out in *Winberry,* and when the court unanimously did so in
George Siegler Co. v. *Norton,* 86 A.2d 8 (N.J. 1952), Justice Heher was assigned the
opinion of the court. For a post-*Winberry* ruling that seems to broaden the New
Jersey Supreme Court's rule-making power even further, see *Busik* v. *Levine,* 307
A.2d 571 (N.J. 1973).

33. Among the New Jersey Supreme Court's unanimous decisions in controver-
sial cases are *Robinson* v. *Cahill,* 303 A.2d 273 (N.J. 1973); *Southern Burlington
County N.A.A.C.P.* v. *Township of Mount Laurel,* 336 A.2d 713 (N.J. 1975), and 456
A.2d 390 (N.J. 1983); and *In re Quinlan,* 355 A.2d 647 (N.J. 1976).

Supreme Court: "He is one of the very great judges of our time. His contribution toward the improvement of judicial administration and substantive law are an imperishable moment to this legacy."[34] Former governor Driscoll added, "New Jersey has lost a great citizen whose contributions to our educational, political, and judicial systems will long be remembered, respected, and, I hope, protected in years ahead."[35]

What is most striking about these comments is their ready identification of New Jersey's judicial system with Vanderbilt: he had succeeded in transferring his personal reputation and stature to the judicial system he had designed. The effect of this transfer was to safeguard his work and provide "breathing space" for its continuation. After his death, criticisms of New Jersey's courts would appear as attacks on Vanderbilt and his work, challenges to their decisions as undermining his aim of a strong, independent judiciary that deserved to be "protected in years ahead." Yet Vanderbilt did more than insulate the state's courts from political attack. He furnished an example and an implicit challenge, namely, how to live up to the tradition of judicial progressivism that he had founded and personified. As current chief justice Robert Wilentz put it, the "experience of that reform is so strong, and its meaning so clear, that it still moves us substantially in New Jersey."[36]

Although Vanderbilt initiated fundamental institutional and procedural changes, they were not accompanied by similarly dramatic transformations of the substantive law. Several factors account for this. For one, despite his commitment to reform Vanderbilt was no radical, as his Republican affiliation and prior service as president of the American Bar Association attest. Furthermore, both by background and inclination, Vanderbilt's reformist bent was procedural rather than substantive. And even if his desire for reform had encompassed major changes in the law, the need to establish the new judicial system on a firm foundation was his first priority. That he is most remembered for *Winberry* v. *Salisbury,* a decision vindicating the independence of the New Jersey Supreme Court, underlines this point. Last, even if Vanderbilt had had the opportunity and inclination to reform the substantive law of the state, he might not have

34. Quoted in Gerhart, *Arthur T. Vanderbilt,* p. 296.
35. Ibid.
36. Quoted in Peter Buchsbaum, "The Courts: The 1947 'Revolution'," *New Jersey Reporter* (November 1982), p. 33.

succeeded in carrying the rest of the court with him. Indeed, his most eloquent appeal for a less precedent-bound approach to the common law occurred in solitary dissent, as a majority of the justices clung to a more conservative approach.[37]

In retrospect, however, it is easy to trace the connection between Vanderbilt's accomplishments and the major initiatives in legal reform that have characterized the New Jersey Supreme Court since the early 1960s. Reflecting on the meaning of the "revolution" of 1947, Chief Justice Robert Wilentz observed that it produced a "refusal to accept rules that bear no present relationship to the needs of society" and a willingness to subject legal doctrine to "more penetrating analysis based on the social realities of the time."[38] Yet more appears to be involved. Vanderbilt's reforms had catapulted the court to national prominence and created an expectation of continuing leadership. Since Vanderbilt had already preempted the field of administrative reform, legal modernization through doctrinal initiatives became the logical focus. In addition, by affording the New Jersey court broad discretion in granting review, the constitution of 1947 allowed it to control the size and substance of its docket. During the period since the adoption of the constitution, the New Jersey Supreme Court has consistently decided fewer cases per year than the U.S. Supreme Court. This in turn has affected the court's interpretation of its responsibilities. As Chief Justice Joseph Weintraub observed of the court in 1976, "its major concern is with the 'institutional' aspect of the appellate process which, simply stated, includes a creative responsibility for making law."[39] Furthermore, by raising the reputation of the state's courts, Vanderbilt's reforms increased the attractiveness of serving on the state's high court, a fact reflected in the caliber of judges recruited in the post-1947 era. In sum, Vanderbilt's reforms promoted the creation of a court with the inclination, ability, and opportunity to play a major national role.

37. See, for example, his dissent in *Fox* v. *Snow,* 76 A.2d 877 (N.J. 1950).

38. Quoted in Buchsbaum, "The 1947 'Revolution', " p. 33.

39. Joseph Weintraub, "Justice Frederick W. Hall: A Tribute," *Rutgers Law Review* 29 (1976): 499. This is consistent with the interview data reported by Henry R. Glick, who noted that over half (four out of seven) of the justices of the New Jersey Supreme Court described themselves as "Law-makers"; two took an intermediate position, categorized by Glick as "Pragmatists"; and only one described himself as a "Law-interpreter." *Supreme Courts in State Politics* (New York: Basic Books, 1971), p. 46, table 2–3.

The New Jersey Supreme Court and the U.S. Supreme Court

Although the New Jersey Supreme Court has not regularly defied the rulings of the U.S. Supreme Court, relations between the two in the era since World War II have often been marked by considerable tension. As early as 1950, the New Jersey Supreme Court refused to adopt the Supreme Court's interpretation of the Establishment Clause of the First Amendment, construing the Court's rulings in a manifestly disingenuous manner in order to sustain statutes mandating daily Bible-reading in the state's public schools and permitting daily recitation of the Lord's Prayer.[40] On other occasions as well, the New Jersey court has sought to protect the interests of the state at the expense of fidelity to federal rulings or, at least, to shift the onus of invalidation to the Supreme Court.[41]

More important than these instances of evasion, however, has been the New Jersey court's overall approach to Supreme Court rulings. During the 1960s, the New Jersey Supreme Court frequently found itself at odds with the Warren Court's rulings on the rights of defendants, and it used the leeways available to it to limit the effect of those rulings, while campaigning for a different interpretation of the constitutional protections for defendants' rights. In the 1970s and early 1980s, changes in the composition of both courts led to new differences in perspective, as the New Jersey justices rejected the conservative thrust of the Burger Court's rulings and relied on their state constitution to afford greater protection to civil liberties. Since the early 1960s, then, the New Jersey court has viewed the U.S. Supreme Court's rulings with a skeptical eye, ever willing to challenge the wisdom of the Court's pronouncements and to exploit legitimate opportunities for advancing its own conceptions of good judicial policy.

THE WEINTRAUB COURT VERSUS THE WARREN COURT

With its ruling in *Mapp* v. *Ohio* (1961) that evidence obtained as a result of unconstitutional searches and seizures was inadmissible at

40. *Dormeus* v. *Board of Education*, 75 A.2d 880 (N.J. 1950). For an elaboration of how this ruling departs from U.S. Supreme Court precedents, see G. Alan Tarr, *Judicial Impact and State Supreme Courts* (Lexington, Mass.: Lexington Books, 1977), pp. 40–42.

41. See, for example, *City of Philadelphia* v. *State*, 348 A.2d 505 (N.J. 1975), reversed, 437 U.S. 617 (1978).

trial in state courts, the U.S. Supreme Court signaled the start of a decade-long revolution in American criminal justice.[42] Its rulings during the 1960s imposed new obligations on state courts by incorporating various guarantees of the federal Bill of Rights. At the same time they expanded the scope of protection under those guarantees. Although all states were affected by these changes, the potential disruption was greatest in those states in which the judges had neither anticipated the rulings in their own decisions nor developed comparable protections for defendants' rights under their state constitutions.

New Jersey unquestionably fit into this category. Although twenty-two states had adopted the exclusionary rule prior to *Mapp*, New Jersey was not among them, having reiterated its rejection of the rule only three years earlier.[43] Its position on the right to counsel and on warnings for defendants likewise lagged behind not only the U.S. Supreme Court's rulings of the 1960s but also the positions of several other state supreme courts.[44] This failure to develop constitutional protections for the rights of the accused reflected the court's determination not to interpret those protections in a way that might jeopar-

42. *Mapp* v. *Ohio*, 367 U.S. 643 (1961). The Warren Court's transformation of constitutional law pertaining to the rights of defendants is discussed in chapter 1.

43. *Eleuteri* v. *Richman*, 141 A.2d 46 (N.J. 1958). Earlier cases in which the New Jersey Supreme Court rejected the exclusionary rule include *State* v. *Alexander*, 83 A.2d 441 (N.J. 1951), cert. denied, 343 U.S. 908 (1952); *State* v. *Merra*, 137 A.2d 575 (N.J. 1927); and *State* v. *Lyons*, 122 A. 758 (N.J. 1925). In contrast, twenty-two states had adopted the exclusionary rule on their own prior to *Mapp*. See Bradley C. Canon, "Testing the Effectiveness of Civil Liberties Policies at the State and Federal Levels: The Case of the Exclusionary Rule," *American Politics Quarterly* 5 (1977): 57.

44. On the New Jersey Supreme Court's willingness to admit confessions, even if obtained in violation of the court's rule requiring speedy arraignments, see, inter alia, *State* v. *Bunk*, 73 A.2d 249 (N.J. 1950), and *State* v. *Pierce*, 72 A.2d 305 (N.J. 1950). For an example of the New Jersey court's continued adherence to the "totality of circumstances" approach to providing counsel in noncapital cases, see *State* v. *Cynowski*, 92 A.2d 782 (N.J. 1953). Prior to *Malloy* v. *Hogan*, 378 U.S. 1 (1964), and *Griffin* v. *California*, 380 U.S. 609 (1965), the New Jersey Supreme Court allowed trial court comment on defendants' failure to testify. As the court noted, New Jersey was one of "only a small minority of states" permitting such comment, but "we are satisfied that the rule accords with common sense and justice" (*State* v. *Corby*, 145 A.2d 289, 293 [1958]). After the Supreme Court rulings, the New Jersey court complied with the Court's mandates—see *State* v. *Dent*, 241 A.2d 833 (N.J. 1968).

dize the safety of the community. Indicative of the court's sentiments is the statement of Chief Justice Vanderbilt in *State* v. *Tune:*

> Thus, although we are ever alert to protect the rights of the individual accused, we must also remember that the people of this State must also be protected. In weighing the rights of the individual and those of the State, we must not be carried away in our desire to protect the individual accused to such an extent that the safety of the public is jeopardized.[45]

This was not an isolated instance. As one commentator complained in 1958 after reviewing the New Jersey Supreme Court's rulings, "The Bill of Rights continues to be a weak document because our Supreme Court continues to be overly concerned with the efficiency of the administration of law enforcement."[46]

What is surprising is how little immediate effect the Warren Court's rulings had on the perspective and performance of the New Jersey Supreme Court. The New Jersey court's rulings on searches and seizures are particularly revealing. Between 1962 and 1973 the Weintraub Court decided sixty cases involving the validity of searches and seizures under the Fourth Amendment.[47] In fifty-one of the sixty cases, the court denied motions to suppress the incriminating evidence.[48] In sixteen of the eighteen cases the New Jersey court heard

---

45. *State* v. *Tune,* 98 A.2d 881, 888 (1953). At another point in the opinion, Chief Justice Vanderbilt quoted Judge Learned Hand to the same effect: "Our dangers do not lie in too little tenderness to the accused. Our procedure has always been haunted by the ghost of the innocent man convicted. It is an unreal dream. What we need to fear is the archaic formalism and the watery sentiment that obstructs, delays, and defeats the prosecution of crime." Ibid. at 885–86, quoting *United States* v. *Garsson,* 291 F. 646, 649 (D.C.S.D. N.Y. 1923).

46. C. Willard Heckel, "Annual Survey of the Law of New Jersey: Constitutional Law," *Rutgers Law Review* 13 (1958): 27.

47. For a listing of these cases, see John B. Wefing, "Search and Seizure—New Jersey Supreme Court v. United States Supreme Court," *Seton Hall Law Review* 7 (1976): 777, n. 21. Also useful for understanding the New Jersey Supreme Court's position are Bradley C. Canon, "Reactions of State Supreme Courts to a U.S. Supreme Court Civil Liberties Decision," *Law & Society Review* 8 (1973): 109–34; "Judicial Federalism: Rights of the Accused in New Jersey," *Rutgers Law Review* 23 (1969): 530–68; and Dominick A. Mazzagetti, "Chief Justice Joseph Weintraub: The New Jersey Supreme Court 1957–1973," *Cornell Law Review* 59 (1974): 197–220.

48. See Wefing, "Search and Seizure," p. 780, n. 26. Thus lawyers and judges were often heard to quip that in New Jersey the Bill of Rights contained one less amendment than in other jurisdictions. Ibid., p. 773, n. 4.

on appeal from state intermediate appellate courts, it reversed the lower court and upheld the police searches.[49] Although Chief Justice Weintraub clearly provided intellectual leadership on the court, authoring more Fourth Amendment opinions than any other justice, what is remarkable is the court's unity of perspective: of the sixty search-and-seizure decisions from 1962 to 1973, all but two were decided unanimously.[50]

State v. *McNair* exemplifies how the Weintraub Court dealt with Warren Court rulings on search and seizure.[51] At issue in the case was the legality of a warrantless search by police officers of McNair's three-room store, including a locked closet, conducted at the time that he was arrested. A New Jersey intermediate appellate court ruled the search unconstitutional, relying on the U.S. Supreme Court's decisions in *Chimel* v. *California* (1969) and earlier cases, which had restricted the scope of searches incident to arrest.[52] In reversing the appellate court, the Weintraub Court distinguished *McNair* from *Chimel*, noting that the police in *Chimel* conducted a "general exploratory search" of a home, whereas the present case involved a more limited search of a store. Perhaps recognizing the limited usefulness of this distinction, particularly since *Chimel* had restricted searches incident to arrest to areas within the control of the arrested person, the New Jersey Supreme Court stressed that *Chimel* was not controlling, since the Supreme Court had not made it retroactive and the arrest had occurred eighteen days prior to the decision. Denying the applicability of *Chimel* enabled the court to employ the "reasonability" standard that had been endorsed by the Supreme Court prior to that ruling and to uphold the search on that basis.[53]

The New Jersey Supreme Court's response to *Escobedo* v. *Illinois*

49. Ibid., pp. 780–81.
50. The two departures from unanimity themselves underline the level of consensus on the Weintraub Court. The first dissent, which occurred in *State* v. *Hutchins*, 202 A.2d 678 (N.J. 1964), hinged upon the propriety of a judge's instructions to a jury rather than the search-and-seizure issue. The other dissent was written by a temporarily assigned judge in the last search-and-seizure case decided by the Weintraub Court, *State* v. *Sheffield*, 303 A.2d 68, cert. denied, 414 U.S. 876 (1973).
51. 285 A.2d 553 (N.J. 1972).
52. *Chimel* v. *California*, 395 U.S. 752 (1969); *Preston* v. *United States*, 376 U.S. 364 (1964); and *Agnello* v. *United States*, 269 U.S. 20 (1925).
53. For examples of the U.S. Supreme Court's earlier approach in such circumstances, see *Rabinowitz* v. *United States*, 339 U.S. 56 (1950), and *Harris* v. *United States*, 371 U.S. 145 (1947), both of which were cited by the New Jersey court in *McNair* at 285 A.2d 558.

(1964) and *Miranda* v. *Arizona* (1966) exhibited a similar pattern.[54] Prior to *Escobedo*, the New Jersey court had employed a "voluntariness" standard in determining whether confessions were admissible in evidence, and it had been reluctant to characterize confessions obtained in the absence of physical force as involuntary.[55] After *Escobedo* the court continued to employ the voluntariness standard, insisting that its rulings were unaffected by *Escobedo*. Moreover, in those cases that directly raised the right-to-counsel issue, the court read *Escobedo* narrowly—unless a suspect specifically requested access to counsel and the police refused the request, the New Jersey court held, *Escobedo* did not apply.[56] In the wake of *Miranda*, which spelled out the constitutional requirements for interrogations in considerable detail, the New Jersey court again attempted to dilute the effect of the Supreme Court's ruling. It rejected the notion, first of all, that *Miranda* applied to the retrial of pre-*Miranda* cases, even if such retrials were commenced after *Miranda* was announced.[57] It also restricted the applicability of *Miranda* to criminal trials of adults, permitting statements obtained in violation of its guidelines to be used in other forums, such as juvenile court proceedings.[58] In those cases

54. *Escobedo* v. *Illinois*, 378 U.S. 478 (1964), and *Miranda* v. *Arizona*, 384 U.S. 436 (1966). For a useful survey of state supreme court reactions to these decisions, see Neal T. Romans, "The Role of State Supreme Courts in Judicial Policymaking—Escobedo, Miranda, and the Use of Judicial Impact Analysis," *Western Political Quarterly* 27 (1974): 38–59.

55. See, for example, *State* v. *Bunk*, 73 A.2d 249 (1950), and *State* v. *Pierce*, 72 A.2d 305 (1950).

56. For an example of the continued use of the voluntariness standard after *Escobedo*, see *State* v. *Taylor*, 217 A.2d 1 (N.J. 1966). Indicative of the New Jersey court's narrow reading of *Escobedo* in clearly applicable situations is *State* v. *Blanchard*, 207 A.2d 681 (N.J. 1965). When the United States Court of Appeals for the Third Circuit (encompassing New Jersey) concluded in *United States ex rel. Russo* v. *New Jersey*, 351 F.2d 429 (3d Cir. 1965), that the applicability of *Escobedo* did not depend upon a request for counsel, Chief Justice Weintraub countered by instructing New Jersey prosecutors and lower courts to ignore the ruling, and the New Jersey court subsequently did so itself in decisions such as *State* v. *Ordog*, 212 A.2d 370 (N.J. 1965), cert. denied, 384 U.S. 1022 (1966). The intercourt conflict is discussed in Mazzagetti, "Chief Justice Weintraub," p. 205. n. 31.

57. *State* v. *Vigliano*, 232 A.2d 129 (1967). See also *State* v. *Zucconi*, 235 A.2d 193 (N.J. 1967), and *State* v. *Moe*, 235 A.2d 678 (N.J. 1967). Neal Romans found that seven of the fourteen states that confronted this issue permitted the use of *Miranda* at retrial. See Romans, "Role of State Supreme Courts," pp. 53–54.

58. Romans, "Role of State Supreme Courts," p. 55. The New Jersey Supreme Court ruled, for example, that *Miranda* was not applicable to the questioning of juveniles in *State in the Interest of R. W.*, 279 A.2d 709 (N.J. 1971), and *State in the Interest of S. H.*, 293 A.2d 181 (N.J. 1972). In the latter case, the court indicated that

where *Miranda* clearly applied, it sought to narrow the effects of the decision.

State v. *Barnes* illustrates the Weintraub Court's approach.[59] The police officers in *Barnes*, after obtaining an arrest warrant, stopped Barnes's car and then arrested and handcuffed her. During the course of searching her car after the arrest, the police came across some stolen checks on the floor and—without giving the *Miranda* warnings— asked her whose they were. The defendant's response that they were hers was admitted in evidence against her, and she appealed her conviction, contending that *Miranda* was clearly applicable. The New Jersey Supreme Court, however, unanimously sustained her conviction. Although admitting that the defendant was in custody, the court ruled that the officer's question did not amount to "custodial interrogation," which would trigger the *Miranda* requirements, because it was not part of a series of questions and thus not interrogation. In addition, the court noted that the question did not have the effect of focusing guilt upon her. To reach this conclusion, the court had to adopt an extremely narrow interpretation of *Miranda* and subsequent decisions of the Supreme Court, an interpretation it justified by reference to the very voluntariness standard that *Miranda* was designed to replace.[60] As Justice Proctor put it in his opinion for the court:

> We do not believe that the holdings in the three United States Supreme Court cases cited above should be spun so finely that the defendant's answer in this case cannot be used against her. In our efforts to protect a defendant's essential *privilege not to be coerced into self-incrimination*, we cannot strain to bar as well those inculpatory statements which so clearly are not the product of *inherently coercive police practices.*[61]

The unsympathetic reception that the Weintraub Court accorded to the Warren Court's rulings on the rights of defendants hardly distin-

---

interrogation of juveniles must be conducted "in accordance with the highest standards of due process and fundamental fairness" (at 185). For a critique of this decision as inconsistent with the U.S. Supreme Court's mandate in *In re Gault,* 387 U.S. 1 (1967), see "Constitutional Law—Miranda Warnings to Juveniles in New Jersey: The Worst of Both Worlds Revisited," *Rutgers Law Review* 26 (1973): 358–82.

59. 252 A.2d 398 (N.J. 1969).

60. In addition to *Miranda,* see the Supreme Court's decisions in *Orozco* v. *Texas,* 394 U.S. 324 (1969), and *Mathis* v. *United States,* 391 U.S. 1 (1968).

61. *State* v. *Barnes,* 252 A.2d 398, 402. Emphasis added.

guished it from other state supreme courts.[62] What was unusual, however, was the character and tone of the court's disagreement. Although acknowledging its responsibility to follow relevant precedents of the Supreme Court, the New Jersey court did not hesitate to criticize the clarity of the Court's opinions and their failure to provide adequate direction to lower courts.[63] Nor did it merely follow the approach used by other state supreme courts to erode Supreme Court rulings, circumscribing their effects while professing adherence to their mandates. Rather, it directly attacked the Warren Court's due process model of criminal justice, which emphasized freedom from governmental intrusion and redress against governmental violations of rights, urging instead a crime control model, which promoted use of all reliable evidence to determine factual guilt and thereby secure society against lawbreakers.[64] By propounding this position it sought to enter into a dialogue with the Supreme Court and to persuade it to change or reconsider its course.[65] The picture that thus emerges is of an independent-minded and self-assured court, willing not merely to

62. Canon, "Reactions of State Supreme Courts," and Romans, "Role of State Supreme Courts," document short-term responses to the Supreme Court's *Mapp* and *Miranda* rulings. For a more general survey, see Charles Johnson and Bradley Canon, *Judicial Policies: Implementation and Impact* (Washington, D.C.: Congressional Quarterly Press, 1984).

63. The general phenomenon of state courts criticizing the U.S. Supreme Court's rulings is surveyed in Bradley C. Canon, "Organizational Contumacy in the Transmission of Judicial Policies: The *Mapp, Escobedo, Miranda,* and *Gault* Cases," *Villanova Law Review* 20 (1974): 58–77. Yet the Weintraub Court's criticism appears unusually sharp and pointed. Thus in *State v. Funicello,* 286 A.2d 55, 60, cert. denied, 408 U.S. 942 (1972), Chief Justice Weintraub wrote: "Among the first demands upon the State is the protection of the citizen from criminal attack in his home, in his work, and in the streets. The citizen looks to the State judiciary for fair and effective prosecution of violators of the criminal law. Yet, although the State Supreme Court is thus charged with the responsibility for that result, its power to lay down the rules has been shifted to the Federal Supreme Court by a run of its decisions over the past 12 years or so. Those decisions were not compelled by 'my copy' of the Constitution or its history. Surely the Federal Supreme Court would not have been derelict if it had left the final power where it had reposed for almost 200 years."

64. These two models of criminal justice are discussed in Herbert L. Packer, *The Limits of the Criminal Sanction* (Stanford, Cal.: Stanford University Press, 1968).

65. Lobbying of the U.S. Supreme Court by state supreme courts suggests a dialogue rather than a hierarchical arrangement. The intricacies of such a dialogue are explored in Daniel Kramer and Robert Riga, "The New York Court of Appeals and the U.S. Supreme Court, 1960–1976," in Porter and Tarr, *State Supreme Court.* See also chapter 1 above, pp. 14–19.

curtail the effects of the Supreme Court's rulings but also to put forth its own views on the proper development of constitutional law.

THE PASSING OF THE WEINTRAUB COURT

Chief Justice Weintraub's retirement in 1973 marked the end of an era in the New Jersey Supreme Court's relations with the U.S. Supreme Court. Four other members of the Weintraub Court had already left the bench over the preceding two years, and another would follow in the next year.[66] These changes in judicial personnel affected, first of all, the New Jersey court's mode of operation. When Richard Hughes assumed the office of chief justice a few months after Weintraub's retirement, he brought to the position a new style of leadership.[67] Weintraub had served as the court's intellectual leader, establishing preeminence by the force of his opinions; Hughes concentrated instead on building consensus and on inculcating an awareness of political realities without necessarily seeking to impose his own jurisprudential views on his fellow judges. Indicative of this change are the opinion-writing practices of the two chief justices: whereas Weintraub wrote more opinions of the court than any other justice, Hughes during the 1975–76 term voted with the majority in 95 percent of the cases but wrote the opinion of the court in only one of them.[68] (The appointment of Chief Justice Wilentz in 1979 prompted some shift back toward Weintraub's style of leadership.)

66. Between 1971 and 1974, the following members of the Weintraub Court left the bench: Vincent S. Haneman, John J. Francis, C. Thomas Schettino, Haydn Proctor, and Joseph Weintraub. Their replacements included Worrall F. Mountain, Mark A. Sullivan, Pierre P. Garven, Morris Pashman, and Robert L. Clifford.

67. Following Chief Justice Weintraub's retirement, Pierre Garven was appointed chief justice, but he died in office less than two months later and was succeeded by former governor Richard J. Hughes.

68. On Chief Justice Weintraub's opinion writing, see John J. Francis, "Joseph Weintraub—A Judge for All Seasons," *Cornell Law Review* 59 (1974): 187. On his leadership of the court, see Milton D. Cornford, "Joseph Weintraub: Reminiscences," *New Jersey Law Journal* 96 (1973): 1205, 1210. On Hughes's record of assigning opinions to other justices, see "The 1976–1977 New Jersey Supreme Court Term," *Rutgers Law Review* 31 (1978): 369, table II. On his leadership style more generally, see Richard Lehne, *The Quest for Justice* (New York: Longman, 1978), pp. 130–31. For a seminal discussion of court leadership styles that has obvious application to Weintraub and Hughes, see David J. Danelski, "The Influence of the Chief Justice in the Decisional Process," in Walter F. Murphy and C. Herman Pritchett, eds., *Courts, Judges, and Politics,* 4th ed. (New York: Random House, 1986).

The court's changes in personnel likewise affected the court's substantive output. Perhaps the most noteworthy appointment from this perspective was that of Justice Morris Pashman in 1974, whose record on the court led commentators to describe him as "the William O. Douglas of New Jersey" and "the most liberal man who's been on the court since the formation of the present system in 1948."[69] Yet if Pashman was more liberal than most of his colleagues on the court, they for the most part shared his generally positive assessment of the Warren Court's rulings. Thus just as personnel changes on the United States Supreme Court were creating a body more sympathetic to the Weintraub Court's perspective on criminal justice and more conservative in its overall orientation, the New Jersey Supreme Court was becoming increasingly committed to pursuing an activist, liberal course. The rediscovery of state constitutional law and state bills of rights thus offered an opportunity for the New Jersey court to promote its own conception of good constitutional policy, and the court made the most of this opportunity.

THE NEW JERSEY SUPREME COURT AND THE NEW JUDICIAL FEDERALISM

Although the New Jersey Supreme Court embraced the new judicial federalism and relied on the state's constitution to announce rulings that earned it the title of "the most innovative [court] in the country,"[70] its development of civil liberties law under the New Jersey Constitution was in many ways distinctive. Most of the initial proponents of the new judicial federalism viewed it as a means of circumventing rulings of the Burger Court that curtailed the rights of defendants, and many of the early decisions relying on state bills of

---

69. The former quote is attributed to Frank Astin, counsel to the New Jersey American Civil Liberties Union, and the latter to fellow justice Worrall Mountain. See Rick Sinding, "Conscience of the Court," *New Jersey Reporter* 12 (November 1982): 15–18. Not all assessments of Pashman were positive; one lawyer suggested that "Pashman does not know what legislatures are for except to raise judicial salaries, and, since they do not do that fast enough, he would really like to take that function away from them too." Quoted in Lehne, *Quest for Justice*, p. 134. For reviews of Justice Pashman's jurisprudence, see "Morris Pashman: Humanitarian Jurist," *Rutgers Law Journal* 14 (1982): 135–74, and "Justice Morris Pashman: A Symposium," *Rutgers Law Review* 35 (1983): 200–37.

70. This plaudit is from Professor Yale Kamisar of the University of Michigan Law School, quoted in Bruce S. Rosen, "A Bold Court Forges Ahead," *National Law Journal* (November 5, 1984), p. 38.

rights had that character.[71] Less a coherent theory than a mode of evasion, the new judicial federalism offered those courts an opportunity to reject selected rulings of the Burger Court while generally relying on the federal Constitution for the protection of individual rights.

The Hughes Court's embrace of the new judicial federalism, however, had little to do with the rights of defendants. It is true that in *State* v. *Johnson* (1975) the New Jersey Supreme Court held that the state constitution required the prosecution to prove that a defendant, in authorizing a search, had knowingly waived the right to refuse consent, thereby affording greater protection than the Burger Court had in *Schneckloth* v. *Bustamonte*.[72] And in that case Justice Sullivan asserted that despite the virtually identical language of New Jersey's constitutional guarantee and the Fourth Amendment, the court had the "right to construe our State constitutional provision in accordance with what we conceive to be its plain meaning."[73] Yet in no other case did the Hughes Court rely on the state constitution to afford greater protection to criminal defendants than was available under the federal Constitution. Moreover, on at least two occasions it aligned itself with controversial rulings of the Burger Court in upholding convictions, despite the claims of dissenters that the cases involved violations of defendants' rights under the state constitution.[74] Even when the court did rule in favor of defendants in a search-and-seizure case, it based its ruling on the Fourth Amendment, despite Justice Pashman's plea in a concurring opinion that it rely on the state constitution.[75]

More recently, the Wilentz Court has shown more willingness to

---

71. See, in particular, the series of articles by Donald E. Wilkes, Jr., and the cases cited therein: "The New Federalism in Criminal Procedure: State Court Evasion of the Burger Court," *Kentucky Law Journal* 62 (1974): 421–51; "More on the New Federalism in Criminal Procedure," *Kentucky Law Journal* 63 (1975): 873–94; and "The New Federalism in Criminal Procedure Revisited," *Kentucky Law Journal* 64 (1976): 729–52. The initial article providing impetus for recourse to state constitutions is "Project Report: Toward an Activist Role for State Bills of Rights," *Harvard Civil Rights-Civil Liberties Law Review* 8 (1973): 271–350.

72. *State* v. *Johnson,* 346 A.2d 66 (N.J. 1975); *Schneckloth* v. *Bustamonte,* 412 U.S. 218 (1973).

73. 346 A.2d 66, 68, n. 2.

74. See, for example, *State* v. *Kleinwaks,* 345 A.2d 793 (N.J. 1975), and *State* v. *Miller,* 337 A.2d 36 (N.J. 1975). In *Miller* the New Jersey Supreme Court endorsed the U.S. Supreme Court's ruling in *Harris* v. *New York,* 401 U.S. 232 (1971), a decision rejected by numerous other state supreme courts.

75. *State* v. *Ercolano,* 397 A.2d 1062 (N.J. 1979). See also *State* v. *Slockbower,* 397 A.2d 1050 (N.J. 1979).

afford protections to defendants not available under the federal Constitution. Thus in *State* v. *Alston* (1981) the New Jersey Supreme Court "respectfully part[ed] company with the Supreme Court's view" and ruled that the New Jersey Constitution afforded the defendant standing to challenge the legality of a search that uncovered illegal weapons.[76] And in *State* v. *Hunt* (1982) the court concluded that defendants' private telephone toll-billing records were protected under the state's constitutional right to privacy and struck down their seizure without a search warrant.[77] Nonetheless, it should be noted that in *Alston* the Wilentz Court, while recognizing that the defendant had standing to challenge an officer's search of another person's vehicle which yielded incriminating evidence, reversed the lower court and admitted the gun into evidence. In *State ex rel. T.L.O.* (1983), which involved the admissibility of evidence obtained during a warrantless search by school officials of a student's purse and school locker, an issue never previously considered under either the state or federal constitutions, the New Jersey court altogether ignored the state constitutional guarantee and based its ruling of inadmissibility on the Fourth Amendment.[78] Moreover, in other cases, it has rejected defendants' state constitutional claims and upheld stringent state criminal legislation.[79] This suggests that enlarging defendants' rights has not been a major priority for either the Hughes or Wilentz courts.

The New Jersey court's rulings cannot be understood either as an attempt to vindicate a particular conception of the relationship between federal and state constitutional law. In *State* v. *Hunt* Justice Alan Handler, in a concurring opinion, listed seven criteria for determining when to diverge from the rulings of the U.S. Supreme Court and to base the court's decisions on the state constitution.[80] In *State* v. *Williams* the New Jersey Supreme Court unanimously adopted

76. 440 A.2d 1311 (N.J. 1981).

77. 450 A.2d 952 (N.J. 1982).

78. 463 A.2d 934 (N.J. 1983).

79. See, for example, *State* v. *Hodge*, 471 A.2d 389 (N.J. 1984), and *State* v. *Roth*, 471 A.2d 370 (N.J. 1984).

80. The criteria Justice Handler suggested in *Hunt* (450 A.2d 965–67) included (1) "Textual language"—whether the state provision grants rights not expressly granted by the U.S. Constitution or is so different that it is open to interpretation on an independent basis; (2) "Legislative history"—whether such history reveals an intention that would support an independent reading of the provision; (3) "Preexisting state law"; (4) "Structural differences"—the conclusions to be drawn from such differences as the state constitution's character as a limit on the sovereign power; (5) "Matters of particular state interest or local concern"; (6) "State traditions"; and (7) "Public attitudes"—distinctive attitudes of the state's citizenry.

a modified version of the Handler criteria.[81] Some justices, however, have challenged the notion that certain conditions must be fulfilled before one consults the state constitution.[82] Moreover, the very generality of the criteria endorsed in *Williams*—two of the criteria, for example, are "important cases" and "structural differences"—means that the New Jersey court retains broad discretion as to when to rely on the state constitution. And a survey of the court's rulings after *Williams* found "an inconsistent application by the court of the Handler criteria and an apparent arbitrariness as to when to conduct a review under the state constitution."[83]

Even if Handler's criteria cannot predict when the court will or will not rely on the state constitution, they do reflect the justifications that the court has offered for its recourse to state protections of individual rights. Of these, the three most important are differences in the language of the state constitution, differences in state traditions, and the different institutional positions of the New Jersey Supreme Court and the U.S. Supreme Court. Thus the New Jersey court cited textual differences in relying on the state constitution to strike down discrimination against women by private employers, to mandate state funding of therapeutic abortions, to strike down the system of school finance in the state, and to protect free speech against private abridgement.[84] It recognized the concern for privacy rights underlying state constitutional protections in striking down a fornication statute and protecting the right to terminate life-support systems, and it emphasized the state's particular concern for health in the abortion-funding case.[85] The New Jersey court noted that the concerns about federalism that might limit the Supreme Court's intervention did not bar it from becoming involved in issues of school finance and exclusionary

81. 459 A.2d 641 (N.J. 1983). The three additional criteria are (1) the "absence of a definite Supreme Court determination" of the legal issue; (2) the importance of the case; and (3) the "public's interest" in the case. Ibid., at 650–51.

82. See, for example, Justice Morris Pashman's concurring opinion in *Hunt*, at 959. For a fellow justice's agreement that the court must "make more predictable the recourse to and the results of state constitutional law analysis," see Stewart G. Pollock, "State Constitutions as Separate Sources of Fundamental Rights," *Rutgers Law Review* 35 (1983): 708.

83. "The New Jersey Supreme Court's Interpretation and Application of the State Constitution." *Rutgers Law Journal* 15 (1984): 499.

84. *Peper* v. *Princeton University Board of Trustees*, 389 A.2d 465 (N.J. 1978); *Right to Choose* v. *Byrne*, 450 A.2d 925 (N.J. 1982); *Robinson* v. *Cahill*, 303 A.2d 273 (N.J. 1973) and *State* v. *Schmid*, 423 A.2d 615 (N.J. 1980).

85. *State* v. *Saunders*, 381 A.2d 333 (N.J. 1977); *In re Quinlan*, 355 A.2d 647 (N.J. 1976); *Right to Choose* v. *Byrne*, 450 A.2d 925 (N.J. 1982).

zoning, nor did concerns about justiciability prevent it from vindicating privacy rights or the rights of suspects.[86]

What is striking about these rationales is how little they partake of reaction to the rulings of the U.S. Supreme Court. Instead of viewing the state constitution as a last resort against disfavored decisions of the Supreme Court, the New Jersey court has undertaken to pursue its own constitutional course. It has not altogether ignored Supreme Court decisions: in *Quinlan* and *Saunders* the New Jersey court noted that its rulings were consistent with the general direction of the Supreme Court's decisions, and in *Robinson* it reviewed the Court's failure to strike down Texas's reliance on the property tax for school finance before turning its attention to the relevant state provision. Nevertheless, the focus has not been on Washington but on New Jersey, on developing an independent body of state constitutional law rather than on tying its analysis to the views of either the majority or dissenters on the Burger Court. And thus far the results have been impressive.

Despite shifts in doctrine and personnel, then, the relations between the New Jersey Supreme Court and the U.S. Supreme Court have been marked by a continuing tension. Since the late 1950s at least, the New Jersey Supreme Court has sought to chart its own constitutional direction and to establish its own body of constitutional law. During the Weintraub era, this entailed efforts to restrict the effect of Warren Court decisions and to persuade it to give greater attention to the need for effective law enforcement. For the Hughes and Wilentz courts, it meant using the potentialities of the new judicial federalism to devise doctrine more consistent with the language of the state constitution and the perceived needs of the state. Yet whether the court pursued its constitutional vision by circumventing the Supreme Court or by acting independently of it, what shines through is the New Jersey court's confidence in its own views and its unwillingness to defer to the expertise or stature of the U.S. Supreme Court.

The New Jersey Supreme Court and State Government

State supreme courts interact not only with federal courts but also with other governmental institutions in the state. Like the United

---

86. *Robinson* v. *Cahill*, 303 A.2d 273, 282 (N.J. 1973); *Southern Burlington County N.A.A.C.P.* v. *Township of Mount Laurel*, 336 A.2d 713 (N.J. 1975); *In re Quinlan*, 355 A.2d 647 (N.J. 1976); and *State* v. *Alston*, 440 A.2d 1311 (N.J. 1981).

States Supreme Court, which umpires the federal system, they too must resolve conflicts over the allocation of powers between various levels of government. They are also intimately involved in the day-to-day operations of state government, overseeing the actions of the state's administrative agencies, resolving disputes about the mechanics of government, and deciding interbranch conflicts. In addition, they may actively participate in determining state policy by invalidating enactments, placing items on the agendas of other branches of government, or enunciating their own policies. The New Jersey Supreme Court's reputation for liberal activism derives from its activity in this last sphere. But a full understanding of the court's role in state policy-making requires consideration of how it relates to other governmental institutions in all three areas.

THE NEW JERSEY SUPREME COURT AND THE DECLINE OF HOME RULE

To understand the New Jersey Supreme Court's role in allocating power between state and local governments, one must begin with New Jersey's hallowed tradition of home rule. New Jersey residents have historically identified with their local governments, an attitude reinforced by the strength of local party organizations and the absence of statewide media that might impart a broader perspective. One commentator on New Jersey politics has described the home rule tradition as "the dominant force behind public life," noting that "it would be difficult to overstate its importance in explaining the political, social, and economic development of the state."[87] One obvious consequence of this orientation has been the devolution of considerable policy-making authority to local government.

Both directly and indirectly, the New Jersey Supreme Court has worked against this tradition of localism and for more centralized policy making. Although Chief Justice Vanderbilt was forced to compromise with the forces of localism in structuring the judicial system (a situation since altered by constitutional amendments), the Constitution of 1947 did vest the rule-making power in the supreme court, and successive chief justices have vigorously wielded this power to centralize control over the courts and to promote uniformity in their operations. Even more significant are the court's rulings in cases involving the powers of local government. When conflicts have arisen

    87. Maureen Moakley, "New Jersey," in Alan Rosenthal and Maureen Moakley, eds., *The Political Life of the American States* (New York: Praeger, 1984), p. 222.

between the state and local governments, the New Jersey Supreme Court has characteristically favored the claims of the state.[88] Other decisions have also undermined the forces supporting localism. Among these were the court's rulings on reapportionment, especially *Scrimminger* v. *Sherwin* (1972), which curtailed the power of county political organizations by mandating that county boundaries need not be considered in drawing up state legislative districts.[89] The New Jersey Supreme Court's pathbreaking rulings on school finance and exclusionary zoning have also impinged on home rule by requiring the state to assume responsibility for meeting constitutional requirements in these areas. Ruling that the state had a constitutional obligation to ensure a "thorough and efficient education" for all students, *Robinson* v. *Cahill* in effect required the state to assume a larger role in funding elementary and secondary education.[90] In *Mount Laurel* I it held that the zoning power, which was delegated to local communities by the state, must be exercised in a manner consistent with the public interest and in particular must not be used by communities to exclude the poor.[91] When localities refused to accept this mandate and the state failed to act, *Mount Laurel* II made use of a previously ignored plan for the development of the state to impose the court's own requirements and threatened affirmative judicial decrees against communities that failed to meet their obligations.[92] One of the (perhaps predictable) effects of this extraordinary ruling was to stimulate the other branches of state government to address themselves to the problems raised by the court's decision.

THE INVIGORATION OF STATE GOVERNMENT

The court has sought not only to centralize power at the state level but also to promote its vigorous exercise. Thus, unless confronted by

88. See, for example, *Board of Education of Elizabeth* v. *City Council of Elizabeth*, 262 A.2d 881 (N.J. 1970), and *In the Matter of the Application of the Board of Education of Upper Freehold Regional School District*, 430 A.2d 905 (N.J. 1981).

89. 291 A.2d 134 (N.J. 1972).

90. 303 A.2d 273 (N.J. 1973). Reactions to *Robinson* in the state are discussed below.

91. *Southern Burlington County N.A.A.C.P.* v. *Township of Mount Laurel*, 336 A.2d 713 (N.J. 1975). For a discussion of the actual effects of *Mount Laurel* I, see G. Alan Tarr and Russell S. Harrison, "Legitimacy and Capacity in State Supreme Court Policymaking: The New Jersey Court and Exclusionary Zoning,"*Rutgers Law Journal* 15 (1984): 514–20, 530–34.

92. *Southern Burlington County N.A.A.C.P.* v. *Township of Mount Laurel*, 456 A.2d 390 (N.J. 1983).

claims that rights were violated, it has consistently construed constitutional restraints in such a way as to sustain the actions of state
government. For example, despite an express constitutional mandate
that the separation of powers be maintained, it has approved broad
delegations of power to the executive branch.[93] And in rejecting a
constitutional challenge to a state bond issue, it emphasized its
concern that "public progress and development . . . not be stifled and
that public problems with their ever increasing complexity . . . be
met and solved."[94] In addition, it has accorded a presumption of
legality to the actions of administrative agencies and permitted them
broad discretion in meeting their responsibilities.[95] It has likewise
construed collective bargaining statutes for state employees very
narrowly in order to safeguard the managerial prerogatives of the state
and promote effective government.[96]

This concern for effective management suggests another theme in
the court's jurisprudence, namely, its support of the state's executive
branch. The fact that New Jersey has a competitive, two-party system
has often resulted in divided control of state government, fueling
interbranch conflict. When such conflicts have occurred, governors,
whatever their party affiliation, have generally prevailed; and the
rulings of the state's supreme court have played a role in this
gubernatorial domination of New Jersey government.[97] As we have

93. See, for example, *Ward* v. *Scott,* 93 A.2d 385 (N.J. 1952); *Boller Beverages
Inc.* v. *Davis,* 183 A.2d 64 (N.J. 1962); and *New Jersey General Assembly* v. *Byrne,*
448 A.2d 438, 447 (N.J. 1982).

94. *New Jersey Association on Correction* v. *Lan,* 403 A.2d 437, 447 (N.J. 1979).

95. See, for example, *New Jersey Association of Health Care Facilities* v. *Finley,* 415
A.2d 1147 (N.J. 1980), and *Cole National Corp.* v. *State Board of Examiners,* 271 A.2d
421 (N.J. 1970). However, in giving administrative agencies broad discretion, the
New Jersey Supreme Court has sought to retain some power to intervene when it
finds the administrative action unjust. See *Monks* v. *New Jersey State Parole Board,*
277 A.2d 193 (N.J. 1971), and *State* v. *Kunz,* 259 A.2d 895 (N.J. 1969); for
commentary on these and related cases, see Bruce D. Greenberg, "New Jersey's
'Fairness and Rightness' Doctrine," *Rutgers Law Journal* 15 (1984): 927–54.

96. See, for example, *In re Paterson Police Benevolent Association,* 432 A.2d 847
(N.J. 1981), and more generally, Jeffrey B. Tener, "New Jersey Supreme Court
Interprets 1974 Amendments to New Jersey Employer-Employee Relations Act,"
Rutgers-Camden Law Journal 11 (1980): 177–230.

97. The unusual strength of the governor in New Jersey politics is documented
in Moakley, "New Jersey," pp. 232–35, and in Alan Rosenthal, "The Governor,
the Legislature, and State Policy Making," in Richard Lehne and Alan Rosenthal,
eds., *Politics in New Jersey* (New Brunswick: Rutgers University Press, 1979).

noted, the court has supported the executive branch on such issues as the delegation of legislative power and the authority of executive-branch agencies. When governors have adopted broad constructions of constitutional powers such as the item veto, the court has sustained those interpretations, and it has been vigilant to protect executive power against legislative encroachments such as the legislative veto.[98] Taken altogether, the New Jersey Supreme Court's resolution of interbranch disputes has augmented the powers of an already power-ful state executive.

POLICY INITIATIVES

Although the New Jersey Supreme Court's policy initiatives have encompassed several issue areas and taken various forms, they fall into two analytic categories. One set of innovative rulings, including the court's tort law reforms (to be discussed later in the chapter) and its decisions on the right to die, involves either realms of undisputed judicial responsibility or intricate and sensitive moral issues. Although the other branches of state government have at times disputed the justices' conclusions, the legitimacy of the court's involvement has been acknowledged and its leadership often gratefully accepted.[99] Thus these rulings have not precipitated conflict over intra-governmental relations or the judicial role.

Other initiatives of the court have involved such complex and contentious policy areas as reapportionment, school finance, and

98. On the item veto, see *Karcher* v. *Kean,* 479 A.2d 403 (N.J. 1984); on the legislative veto, see *New Jersey General Assembly* v. *Byrne,* 448 A.2d 438 (N.J. 1982), and *Enourato* v. *New Jersey Building Authority,* 448 A.2d 449 (N.J. 1982). For a general perspective, see L. Harold Lewinson, ''The Decline of the Legislative Veto: Federal/State Comparisons and Interactions,'' *Publius* 17 (1987): 115–32.

99. Indicative of the political branches' relief at the court's ruling in *In re Quinlan* is their decision not to appeal the decision, despite the unprecedented character of the issue and the excellent chances of review by the U.S. Supreme Court.

The New Jersey Supreme Court's rulings in tort law reform and in *Quinlan* most closely resemble what we have denominated ''complementary policymaking,'' that is, ''[r]ulings that either aid state legislative goals or relieve state legislatures of the onus of taking politically awkward stands,'' See Mary Cornelia Porter and G. Alan Tarr, ''Editors' Introduction,'' in Porter and Tarr, *State Supreme Courts,* p. xvii–xviii.

For an article that depicts the *Quinlan* ruling as consistent with the New Jersey Supreme Court's tendency to expand administrative authority, see Michael Nevins, ''New Jersey's 'Right-to-Die' Cases: A View from the Ring,'' *American College of Physicians Observer* (March 1986): 13–16.

zoning.[100] Because the court's rulings have overturned established policies, they have brought it into conflict with the political authorities responsible for those policies. Because the issues in these cases could not be resolved through a single decree, they have required protracted judicial oversight over the formulation of policy. And because resolution of these issues in line with the court's rulings has required policy shifts with statewide implications, the court's rulings have almost inevitably exacerbated tensions between the court and other branches of government and raised questions about the legitimacy of judicial involvement. It is to this second category of policy initiatives that we now turn.

Reapportionment[101]

Under the constitution of 1947 the New Jersey state legislature resembled the federal model—in the Senate each county had equal representation, and in the General Assembly each had a single representative, with the remaining seats apportioned according to population. In 1960, however, representation in the Assembly did not accurately reflect the distribution of the state's population, because a legislative deadlock had prevented reapportionment since 1941. This problem was not unique to New Jersey—in several states legislative majorities had ignored the mandates of their constitutions to reapportion—but judges had characteristically declined to intervene, insisting that apportionment was a "political question" and thus not appropriate for judicial resolution.[102]

In *Asbury Park Press, Inc.* v. *Woolley* (1960), however, the New Jersey Supreme Court rejected the counsels of judicial restraint and unanimously endorsed the contention of several taxpayers that the

100. The New Jersey Supreme Court's rulings on reapportionment, school finance, and zoning fit into the categories of "innovative policymaking" and "agenda-setting policymaking," discussed in Porter and Tarr, "Editors' Introduction," *State Supreme Courts,* pp. xvi–xvii.

101. Background on the reapportionment controversy in New Jersey is presented in Alan Shank, *New Jersey Reapportionment Politics* (Cranbury, N.J.: Associated University Presses, 1969), and in Friedelbaum, "Constitutional Law," pp. 211–13.

102. The U.S. Supreme Court concluded that legislative apportionment was a "political question" in *Colegrove* v. *Green,* 328 U.S. 549 (1946). For a discussion of the reluctance of state courts to intervene in disputes about apportionment prior to 1960, see Robert G. Dixon, Jr., *Democratic Representation: Reapportionment in Law and Politics* (New York: Oxford University Press, 1968), pp. 105–07, 117–18. The New Jersey Supreme Court itself had previously refused to get involved in reapportionment disputes—see *Botti* v. *McGovern,* 118 A. 107 (1922).

failure to reapportion violated the state constitution.[103] The court noted various approaches to correcting the violations but delayed a remedial decree pending remedial action by the legislature. When the legislature seemed reluctant to act, the court issued an ultimatum, establishing a deadline for compliance and threatening imposition of a judicially devised plan if the deadline was not met.[104] This threat proved effective—a few hours before the deadline, the legislature adopted its own reapportionment plan.

The U.S. Supreme Court's ruling mandating a "one-man-one-vote" apportionment of state legislatures brought the reapportionment issue back before the New Jersey court. Once again the justices resorted to agenda-setting policy making, combined with deadlines and threats of sanctions, to spur legislative action on the issue.[105] Throughout the protracted litigation, the court, ever mindful of "political implications and legislative prerogatives," steadfastly refused to impose its own solution and maintained pressure to "coax the more appropriate organs of government into the proper action."[106] This strategy eventually succeeded with the adoption in 1974 of an apportionment plan that met federal standards.

School Finance

Historically, elementary and secondary education has been viewed as a local responsibility. As a result, expenditures for education have depended largely on the financial resources and funding efforts of school districts, a system that has led to substantial disparities in expenditures among districts within individual states. In the 1960s litigants began to challenge these intrastate inequalities in school finance, basing their claims primarily on the Equal Protection Clause of the federal Constitution. In 1971, while New Jersey's lower courts were considering the constitutionality of the state's reliance on local

103. 161 A.2d 705 (N.J. 1960).

104. Shank, *Reapportionment Politics*, pp. 168–84.

105. *Reynolds* v. *Sims*, 377 U.S. 533 (1964).

106. The continuing interaction between the judiciary and political officials is reflected in the New Jersey Supreme Court's major reapportionment rulings: (1) *Jackman* v. *Bodine*, 205 A.2d 713 (N.J. 1964); 205 A.2d 735 (N.J. 1964); 209 A.2d 825 (N.J. 1965); 231 A.2d 193 (N.J. 1967); 232 A.2d 419 (N.J. 1967); 252 A.2d 209 (N.J. 1969); 262 A.2d 389 (N.J. 1970); (2) *Scrimminger* v. *Sherwin*, 291 A.2d 134 (N.J. 1972); and (3) *Davenport* v. *Apportionment Commission of New Jersey*, 308 A.2d 3 (N.J. 1973); 319 A.2d 718 (N.J. 1974). The quotations are drawn from Mazzagatti, "Chief Justice Joseph Weintraub," pp. 214, 220.

property taxes to finance its educational system, the California Supreme Court invalidated a similar system of school finance as a violation of federal and state guarantees of equal protection.[107] The optimism that this ruling generated among advocates of finance reform was short-lived, for two years later in *San Antonio* v. *Rodriguez* the U.S. Supreme Court, in refusing to strike down Texas's system of school finance, effectively short-circuited federal constitutional challenges to interdistrict disparities.[108]

Rodriguez was decided after the New Jersey Supreme Court had already heard oral argument in *Robinson* v. *Cahill*, the challenge to New Jersey's system of school finance.[109] Less than two weeks later, the New Jersey Supreme Court announced its ruling. Like their colleagues on the U.S. Supreme Court, the New Jersey justices rejected equal protection attacks on the existing system of school finance. However, this did not conclude the court's constitutional inquiry. The court conducted a thorough historical review of the constitutional provision requiring the state to provide a "thorough and efficient" education to all children and determined that the existing system failed to satisfy the state's constitutional obligation.[110] Because the court did not employ an equal protection rationale for its ruling, it did not mandate equal expenditures in all school districts. Nevertheless, the ruling clearly indicated that the state had to monitor more closely the provision of education at the local level and had to increase substantially its financial support for elementary and secondary education. This in effect put the school finance issue—and, almost inevitably, the issue of a state income tax as a means of generating the necessary revenues—on the legislative agenda.

The legislative response came slowly and begrudgingly; not until the court ordered the state's schools closed were funds appropriated for a new state program for education. The delay and opposition that greeted the court's ruling can be attributed, at least in part, to the political situation in the state.[111] For policy direction on major issues,

107. *Serrano* v. *Priest*, 487 P.2d 1241 (Cal. 1971).

108. *San Antonio Independent School District* v. *Rodriguez*, 411 U.S. 1 (1973).

109. *Robinson* v. *Cahill*, 303 A.2d 273 (N.J. 1973).

110. The relevant provision of the New Jersey Constitution states, "The legislature shall provide for the maintenance and support of a thorough and efficient system of free public schools for the instruction of all the children in this state between the ages of five and eighteen years." (Art. VIII, Sec. 4, Para. 1)

111. The analysis in this and the succeeding paragraph draw heavily on Lehne, *The Quest for Justice*, chaps. 3–5.

New Jersey has relied on its governors. However, for almost a year after *Robinson* the incumbent governor was William Cahill, who—having been denied renomination in the Republican primary two months after the decision—lacked the political muscle for effective leadership. Only with the accession of Governor Brendan Byrne in 1974 did the court find a consistent ally in its reform efforts. Yet given the complex issues raised by the court's ruling, gubernatorial leadership was essential to avoid deadlock in the legislature. It was no easy matter to define a "thorough and efficient" education and determine how it might be accomplished. Even more difficult was the task of creating an acceptable plan for distributing state funding and devising a viable tax package. Further complicating the situation was legislators' reluctance to institute a new tax and particularly a state income tax, a reluctance buttressed by the perception that Cahill's defeat in the primary was in part due to his endorsement of an income tax.

The New Jersey Supreme Court's inconsistent posture during the protracted litigation also contributed to the eventual confrontation. Shortly after its initial ruling, the court's membership changed dramatically, and the new justices lacked experience in dealing with the legislature. This inexperience might account for the court's willingness to grant a nine-month extension when its initial deadline for action ran out, which was interpreted as signaling a wavering judicial commitment. Four months later, perhaps stung by criticism of the extension, the court seemed to reverse course, threatening to redistribute school aid if the legislature failed to act. Yet when a school bill was passed that only partially fulfilled the court's mandate, the court—albeit with a notable lack of enthusiasm—upheld it against constitutional challenges. At the same time, it warned that its acceptance of the legislation was premised on the timely passage of funding for the bill. When efforts to secure funding stalled, the court ordered that after July 1 no further funds be expended under the constitutionally impermissible system. A week after the state's schools closed, the legislature passed the necessary tax legislation to reopen them.

Several aspects of the court's involvement are striking. First is the court's self-confident determination to pursue an independent course, which was particularly striking given the Supreme Court's recent ruling in *Rodriguez* and its identification in that case of the difficulties attending judicial oversight of school finance. Second is the court's ability to intervene forcefully on a highly contentious policy issue without political reprisal. Whereas activist rulings of the California

Supreme Court have been followed by constitutional amendments and efforts to remove justices, no serious campaign against the court followed the ruling in *Robinson,* and a last-minute suit in federal court to prevent the closing of the state's schools was unsuccessful.[112] Third is the limited success of the court's agenda-setting approach in resolving the school finance issue. Because of political factors outside its control and its own irresoluteness, the court eventually was forced to precipitate a crisis in order to get legislative action. Moreover, the legislation it eventually endorsed only partially met its goals, as evidenced by renewed litigation challenging the state's system of school finance.[113]

Zoning

The development of the suburbs, particularly in the period since 1945, has exacerbated racial and economic segregation in urban areas. According to some critics, this residential segregation reflects more than the operation of individual preferences and market forces. Through the adoption of restrictive zoning ordinances, they charge, suburban communities have prevented the construction of low-cost housing, with the effect—and frequently the intention—of excluding the poor and racial minorities. Although restrictive zoning regulations have been challenged as a denial of equal protection of the laws, federal courts have rejected the broad argument that they are discriminatory and have refused to strike them down. On the other hand, the

112. In 1972 California voters approved an amendment to the state constitution reinstating the death penalty, which had been struck down in *People* v. *Anderson,* 483 P.2d 880 (Cal. 1972), and in 1982 they approved a broad "victims' rights" amendment, which circumscribed judicial efforts to afford defendants' rights unavailable under the federal Constitution. As mentioned in chapter 4, Chief Justice Rose Bird barely survived her retention election in 1978 and was defeated for reelection in 1986. For background on the political tribulations of the California Supreme Court, see Preble Stolz, *Judging Judges* (New York: Free Press, 1981); James M. Fischer, "Ballot Propositions: The Challenge of Direct Democracy to State Constitutional Jurisprudence," *Hastings Constitutional Law Quarterly* 11 (1983); and John H. Culver and John T. Wold, "Rose Bird and the Politics of Judicial Accountability in California," *Judicature* 70 (1986): 81–89. On the federal court's refusal to block the closing of New Jersey's schools, see Lehne, *The Quest for Justice,* pp. 156–59.

113. For an assessment of the short-term impact of *Robinson,* see Lehne, *The Quest for Justice,* chap. 6. The more recent challenge to New Jersey's system of school finance is *Abbott* v. *Burke,* 495 A.2d 376 (N.J. 1985).

New Jersey Supreme Court has held since 1975 that exclusionary zoning violates the New Jersey Constitution.[114]

In *Mount Laurel* I, its first case involving exclusionary zoning, the New Jersey Supreme Court concluded that since the zoning power was a state power, albeit one that had been delegated to municipalities, it—like all state powers—had to be exercised in pursuance of the general welfare. Thus zoning ordinances designed to provide parochial advantages at the expense of state citizens beyond municipal borders were unconstitutional. Although it identified various types of regulations that had an exclusionary effect, the court did not rule them illegal per se. Instead, it merely declared that every developing municipality

> must, by its land use regulations, presumptively make realistically possible an appropriate variety and choice of housing. More specifically, it cannot foreclose the opportunity of [the poor] for low and moderate income housing and its regulations must affirmatively afford that opportunity, at least to the extent of the municipality's fair share of the present and prospective regional need therefor.[115]

Although the court's ruling sought to place zoning reform on the agenda of municipalities throughout the state, it failed to clarify their obligations under the state's constitution. Nowhere did the court's opinion define what municipalities were "developing," how "regional need" was to be ascertained, or how a municipality's "fair share" was to be calculated. This lack of precision slowed voluntary compliance and gave reluctant municipalities (and they were the majority) an excuse for inaction. Subsequent rulings, rather than resolving the outstanding issues, seemed to suggest a judicial retreat from *Mount Laurel.*[116] The statewide pattern of delay and evasion that followed the court's ruling led one commentator to conclude that on

114. The leading federal case is *Warth* v. *Seldin,* 422 U.S. 490 (1975). The initial New Jersey ruling is *Southern Burlington County N.A.A.C.P.* v. *Township of Mount Laurel,* 336 A.2d 713 (N.J. 1975).

115. 336 A.2d 713, 724.

116. The most important of these rulings are *Oakwood at Madison, Inc.* v. *Township of Madison,* 371 A.2d 1192 (N.J. 1977); *Pascack Association, Ltd.* v. *Washington Township,* 379 A.2d 6 (N.J. 1977); *Fobe Associates* v. *Borough of Demarest,* 379 A.2d 31 (N.J. 1977); and *Home Builders League* v. *Township of Berlin,* 405 A.2d 381 (N.J. 1981).

the eve of *Mount Laurel* II, "the New Jersey Supreme Court's war on exclusionary zoning . . . was clearly in disarray."[117];

In *Mount Laurel* II the New Jersey high court abandoned its agenda-setting approach and moved aggressively to provide what it termed "a realistic opportunity for housing, not litigation." To clarify municipalities' obligations under the *Mount Laurel* doctrine, the justices seized upon an obscure plan for development in the state as an authoritative guide for determining communities' "fair share" of low-cost housing and specified in detail the sorts of affirmative steps that local governments had to take in order to provide it. To ensure that communities would not ignore their ruling, the justices created an incentive for private parties to monitor compliance by authorizing trial judges to award "builders' remedies" to developers who success-fully challenged exclusionary ordinances. To "put some steel" into the *Mount Laurel* doctrine, the justices empowered the judges, when faced with municipal inaction, to undertake the revision of local ordinances to bring them into conformity with constitutional standards. The model proposed for lower-court emulation in this regard was the federal courts' development of remedial decrees in institutional litiga-tion.[118]

Perhaps in anticipation of the controversy the ruling would create, Chief Justice Wilentz attempted at great length to justify the court's extraordinary intervention in local policy making.[119] His efforts were unavailing—the reaction to the court's ruling was overwhelmingly negative.[120] Legislators from both parties attacked the decision, Gover-nor Thomas Kean denounced it as "communistic," and local officials offered even less temperate comments. Although some municipalities entered into *Mount Laurel* settlements or voluntarily initiated changes in their zoning and housing policies, many bided their time, hoping to avoid action or to place the onus for it on the courts. This inaction,

117. John M. Payne, "From the Courts," *Real Estate Law Journal* 12 (1983): 85.
118. *Southern Burlington County N.A.A.C.P.* v. *Township of Mount Laurel*, 456 A.2d 390 (N.J. 1983).
119. Chief Justice Wilentz's justification for the court's interventionist approach is analyzed in Tarr and Harrison, "Legitimacy and Capacity in State Supreme Court Policymaking," pp. 526–42.
120. Prime sources for the effects of *Mount Laurel* II, as well as for analysis of the Fair Housing Act of 1985, are two articles—Alan Mallach, "Blueprint for Delay," and Jerome Rose, "Caving In to the Court"–in *New Jersey Reporter*, (October 1985): pp. 20–27; 29–33. For a more anecdotal assessment, see Anthony DePalma. "New Jersey's Struggle with Fair Housing," *New York Times*, December 1, 1985: EY 8.

together with over one hundred suits by developers and landowners seeking builders' remedies in the two years after the ruling, created the potential for judicial domination of land-use decisions in the state and prompted a response by the state legislature.

Even political officials who were sympathetic to the court's objectives agreed that judges should not formulate local zoning policy. To head off a constitutional amendment reversing *Mount Laurel*, liberal lawmakers introduced a bill to transfer responsibility for zoning reform from the courts to a state-level agency. This legislation, after extensive revision to meet the objections of Governor Kean and other opponents of *Mount Laurel*, was enacted in 1985.[121] Although it did acknowledge the state's responsibility to address the housing needs of the poor, the Fair Housing Act challenged the court's ruling in *Mount Laurel* II on several essential points. First, the law largely eliminated the judiciary from superintending the reform of local zoning ordinances by authorizing the creation of a Fair Housing Council, requiring that most exclusionary zoning cases be transferred to it and giving a "presumption of validity" to municipal housing plans approved by the council, so that they could be overturned only by "clear and convincing evidence." Second, the act reduced the level of low-cost housing that municipalities are obliged to provide by eliminating reliance on the plan for state development, narrowly defining the housing needs of the poor, allowing suburban municipalities to "buy out" part of their obligations, and expressly denying that municipalities had an obligation to help finance affordable housing. Third, it countenanced delay in undertaking action to meet municipal obligations to provide housing by placing a one-year moratorium on future court-ordered builders' remedies and by allowing municipalities to defer action until five months after the Fair Housing Council had held statewide hearings and devised guidelines for housing plans.

Faced with this challenge to the position it had taken in *Mount Laurel* II, the New Jersey Supreme Court in *Hills Development Co.* v. *Township of Bernards* put the best possible face on the legislation and upheld it as constitutional.[122] Acknowledging that the legislature had partially eliminated the use of builders' remedies, the court insisted

---

121. The Fair Housing Act, S. 2046, S. 2334, 1985 N.J. Laws. For further analysis of the law, see Jerome G. Rose, "New Jersey Enacts a Fair Housing Law," *Real Estate Law Journal* 14 (1986): 195–217; and Harold A. McDougall, "From Litigation to Legislation in Exclusionary Zoning Law," *Harvard Civil Rights-Civil Liberties Law Review* 22 ((1987): 623–63.

122. 510 A.2d 621 (N.J. 1986).

that only the goals of *Mount Laurel* and not the means it had authorized were of "constitutional dimension."[123] Although the court noted that implementation of the law might produce some delay in meeting those goals, it concluded that this delay was more than offset by the "legitimacy" that the legislature's involvement gave to those goals, the potential for public acceptance and voluntary compliance that it created, and its consequent long-term effectiveness.[124]

The most striking feature of the opinion of the court was its explicit discussion of the controversy that its rulings on exclusionary zoning had generated and of its relations with the legislature. The New Jersey Supreme Court noted that governmental officials and the general public had criticized both its ruling in *Mount Laurel* II and its alleged desire to control public policy. The court insisted that these criticisms were based on a fundamental misapprehension of its objectives. *Mount Laurel* II was designed to stimulate action by the legislature and should be understood as "the strongest possible entreaty to the Legislature, asking for legislation on the subject."[125] All along, the court maintained, it had been mindful of the strong deference owed to legislative action, as was evident in "our exercise of comity today," that is, its deference to the legislature's solution for the problem of exclusionary zoning and its recognition of the legislature's substantial occupation of the field of zoning reform.[126] Taken altogether, the court's opinion in *Bernards* was a virtual paean to judicial modesty.

Examination of the New Jersey Supreme Court's experience in *Mount Laurel*, particularly in comparison with its initiatives in reapportionment and school finance, highlights its strengths and weaknesses as a policy innovator and clarifies its position in the governance of the state. First of all, the court's initiatives have succeeded only when it has been able to enlist allies of substantial political strength. In mandating reapportionment, for example, the court was able to count on support from the federal courts, which after *Reynolds* v. *Sims* backed efforts to establish "one man, one vote," and from those areas of the state that expected to benefit from redrawn legislative districts. To the extent it was able to reform school finance, the court benefited from Governor Byrne's aggressive efforts to secure the aims of *Robinson* and

123. 510 A.2d 621, at 643.
124. 510 A.2d 621, at 644.
125. 510 A.2d 621, at 642; see also at 654.
126. 510 A.2d 621, at 655.

from urban districts' hopes for greater funding. In *Mount Laurel,* however, the court had no significant political allies. The federal courts had demonstrated their unwillingness to invalidate exclusionary zoning, the other branches of state government were hostile to the form and substance of the court's intervention, and local communities felt threatened by the sense that they no longer controlled decisions about future development. Meanwhile, the presumed beneficiaries of *Mount Laurel* did not rally to the court's support. As one commentator put it, "Suburban housing opportunities, particularly future opportunities that do not exist even today, are not a priority issue for the urban poor."[127]

This in turn suggests that the New Jersey Supreme Court, like other courts, ultimately depends for its success on public opinion.[128] Thus it may be noted that when the court employed an agenda-setting approach to land-use reform, its ruling was widely ignored, and when it adopted a more aggressive approach, both the legitimacy of its intervention and its capacities as a policymaker were attacked. Yet the situation is not so simple. Although the court's ruling was virulently attacked, its apparent threat to impose unacceptable changes in local zoning policies did motivate the New Jersey legislature to devise its own policy, which expressly recognized the state's responsibility to address the housing needs of the poor. Indeed, one commentator has even lamented that the Fair Housing Act is "a legislative embodiment of the *Mount Laurel* decision with a vengeance."[129] Although this conclusion seems to overstate the case, the court's ability to stimulate legislative action addressing the concerns raised in its opinion, despite the almost universal condemnation of the decision, demonstrates its influence over policy making.

Finally, in assessing the implications of the *Mount Laurel* experience, one must note that the New Jersey Supreme Court has emerged relatively unscathed from the controversy its ruling generated. Whereas controversial rulings by other state high courts have led to constitutional amendments overturning the decisions and to political retribution, no amendment to override *Mount Laurel* has been ratified,

127. Mallach, "Blueprint for Delay," p. 27.
128. The classic formulation of the limits of judicial power, particularly when exercised contrary to public opinion, is Alexis de Tocqueville, *Democracy in America,* ed. J. P. Mayer (Garden City, NY: Doubleday, 1969), p. 157.
129. Rose, "Caving In to the Court," p. 31; see also McDougall, "From Litigation to Legislation," pp. 650–63.

and no more general threat to the court's powers or independence has materialized. Despite the clear opportunity to send a message to the court that was offered by the expiration of the terms of Chief Justice Robert Wilentz (author of the court's opinion in *Mount Laurel* II) and Justice Stewart Pollock, Governor Kean renominated both justices, and both were confirmed by the Senate.[130] And as our survey of the New Jersey Supreme Court's rulings on tort law reveals, the reaction against *Mount Laurel* has not deterred the court from addressing controversial issues and charting new policy directions. The New Jersey court's willingness to continue to exercise leadership and its ability to do so without political repercussions, perhaps more than anything else, reveal the position that the court has achieved in the political life of the state.

The New Jersey Supreme Court and the Common Law

I am constrained to dissent from the views of the majority of the court . . . because their opinion involves a view of the judicial process, which, if it had been followed consistently in the past, would have checked irrevocably centuries ago the growth of the common law to meet changing conditions and which, if pursued now, will spell the ultimate ossification and death of the common law by depriving it of one of its most essential attributes—its inherent capacity constantly to renew its vitality and usefulness by adapting itself gradually and piecemeal to meeting the demonstrated needs of the time.[131]

This protest against an excessive reliance on precedent in construing the common law is drawn from a dissent by Chief Justice Vanderbilt. The court majority, in a per curiam opinion, responded by emphasizing the judge's duty to adhere to established common law principles and the availability of the legislature as the preferred avenue for legal change. There was nothing particularly novel in these sentiments—a quick survey of the Reports would yield dozens of decisions rejecting changes in the common law in the name of legal stability and judicial

130. The relevant comparison here is with California, the other state supreme court that has achieved a national reputation for policy innovation. See Stolz, *Judging Judges,* and Culver and Wold, "Rose Bird." On the politics of the reappointment of Chief Justice Wilentz, see Peter Buchsbaum, "The Courts," *New Jersey Reporter* (September 1986), p. 34.

131. *Fox* v. *Snow,* 76 A.2d 877, 878 (N.J. 1950).

restraint. However, few of these decisions would come from New Jersey. Instead, at least in the period since 1958, the New Jersey Supreme Court has eagerly adopted—and frequently initiated—changes in the common law.[132] Its rulings in products liability have radically altered the legal relationship between manufacturer and consumer in New Jersey by redefining the standard for determining liability, eliminating barriers to recovery, and restricting various affirmative defenses traditionally employed in such litigation. As one lawyer specializing in defending products liability cases put it during an interview, "The main thing we do is take out our wallet and ask how much?" In other tort law areas as well, the New Jersey court "has been unusually willing to overrule traditional doctrines to support tort plaintiffs."[133] And outside the field of tort law, it has displayed considerable ingenuity in adapting common law principles to new conditions and new uses. Taken altogether, the New Jersey Supreme Court's rulings in this field of traditional judicial activity reflect its overall commitment to assertive judicial involvement in defining public policy for the state.

PRODUCTS LIABILITY[134]

Although Chief Justice Vanderbilt gave initial expression to the need for a continuing judicial scrutiny of common law doctrine, it was Justice John Francis's opinion in *Henningsen* v. *Bloomfield Motors Inc.* (1960) that vaulted the New Jersey court to the forefront of tort law reform.[135] The facts of the case were not disputed: Mrs. Henningsen, whose husband had recently purchased an automobile from Bloomfield Motors, had suffered injuries in a crash caused by a failure in the car's steering. Yet if the court adhered to established common law principles, she was effectively barred from recovery. The dealer was not liable because his liability extended only to injuries caused by

132. The tenor of the court's rulings prompted one commentator to observe that "[t]he law of tort, in New Jersey as elsewhere, has settled down to a relatively stable existence." See "Annual Survey of the Law of New Jersey, 1953–1954," *Rutgers Law Review* 9 (1954): 157.

133. Baum and Canon, "State Supreme Courts as Activists," p. 99.

134. Among the sources that have proved useful in tracing the reform of products liability law in New Jersey are "Strict Products Liability in New Jersey: A Survey," *Rutgers Law Review* 32 (1979); Richard A. Epstein, *Modern Products Liability Law* (Westport, Conn.: Quorum Books, 1980); and W. Page Keeton, Dan B. Dobbs, Robert E. Keeton, and David G. Owen, *Prosser and Keeton on the Law of Torts*, 5th ed. (St. Paul: West, 1984).

135. 161 A.2d 69 (N.J. 1960).

his own negligence and to other obligations he voluntarily incurred through contractual agreements, such as warranties of product safety and serviceability. And under the doctrine of privity, the manufacturer was liable only for injuries to parties with whom it had a direct contractual relationship (it had no such relationship with the Henningsens).[136]

In his opinion for a unanimous court, Justice Francis rejected the privity requirement and insisted that negligence was not the appropriate standard for determining liability. In support of these contentions, Francis first of all emphasized that other courts had developed exceptions to the privity requirement and that this accorded with a more general movement toward holding manufacturers responsible for the injuries that their products caused. Yet he took the court a giant step further along the path. When manufacturers promote a product and place it into the stream of trade, he maintained, the product is accompanied by an implied warranty that it is reasonably suitable for use. Furthermore, the public interest in consumer safety requires that manufacturers not use contractual provisions limiting their liability to escape responsibility for injuries caused by defective products. Thus the court concluded that Mrs. Henningsen was entitled to recover for her injuries.

The court's doctrine of implied warranty was soon superseded by the doctrine of strict liability, under which manufacturers were liable for personal injuries and other damages resulting from defects in their products.[137] Despite this, *Henningsen* remains a landmark decision. Nationally, it served as a catalyst for reform, prompting "the most rapid and altogether spectacular overturn of an established rule in the entire history of the law of torts."[138] Through its influence on section

136. Although *Henningsen* was the first case to reject the doctrine of privity, earlier decisions had circumscribed its effect and provided justification—and perhaps even guidance—to the New Jersey court. See *Henningsen,* 161 A.2d 69, 76–78, 81–83.

137. The California Supreme Court adopted the standard of strict liability in *Greenman* v. *Yuba Power Products, Inc.,* 377 P.2d 897 (Cal. 1963), and the New Jersey Supreme Court expressly adopted the standard of strict liability, citing the California court's ruling, in *Santor* v. *A & M Karagheusian, Inc.,* 207 A.2d 305, 312 (N.J. 1965). By 1968 the court was referring to "the now well-recognized doctrine of strict liability in tort." See *Rosenau* v. *City of New Brunswick,* 238 A.2d 169, 176 (N.J. 1968).

138. William L. Prosser, "The Fall of the Citadel," *Minnesota Law Review* 50 (April 1966): 793–94. Richard Epstein, who is critical of the decision, nonetheless terms it "the one case that more than others inaugurated the modern age of products

402A of the American Law Institute's Restatement (Second) of Torts, it also indirectly affected developments in tort law even in those states that did not expressly endorse it.[139] Commentators have traced its influence on myriad other areas of law outside the products liability field.[140]

Within this state, *Henningsen's* effects were just as great. It decisively influenced the New Jersey Supreme Court's future development of products liability law, which may be viewed as an attempt to work out the full implications of the ruling. More generally, it committed the court to evaluating established common law doctrines in the light of current conceptions of societal needs, an approach that was to become the hallmark of the New Jersey court's common law jurisprudence.[141]

The continuity of the New Jersey Supreme Court's commitment to consumer protection through products liability law, apparent throughout its post-*Henningsen* rulings, is particularly clear in its rulings expanding the range of entities subject to strict liability and restricting the defenses available to them. Over time, the court has held lessors, builders, providers of services, and sellers of used goods to strict liability standards.[142] Even companies that did not themselves

---

liability" (*Modern Products Liability,* p. 50). See also, more generally, James T. Croyle, "An Impact Analysis of Judge-Made Products Liability Policies," *Law & Society Review* 13 (1979): 949–67.

139. *Restatement (Second) of Torts,* sec. 402A (1965). For discussion of this important and influential delineation of the elements of strict products liability, see Epstein, *Modern Products Liability Law,* chap. 6.

140. See, for example, Epstein, *Modern Products Liability Law,* p. 53, n. 12, where he recounts as "but one example of its versatility" its use in *Javins* v. *First National Realty Corp.,* 428 F.2d 1071 (D.C. Cir. 1970) to "support the judicial determination that an implied warranty of habitability is to be read into the terms of the standard apartment lease, even where such warranty is expressly negatived by the terms of the lease itself."

141. Indicative of the continuing influence of *Henningsen* is the New Jersey Supreme Court's observation in *Schipper* v. *Levitt & Sons, Inc.,* 207 A.2d 314, 324 (N.J. 1965): "Law as an instrument for justice has infinite capacity for growth to meet changing needs and mores; nowhere was this better illustrated than in *Henningsen.*"

142. Strict liability was extended to lessors in *Cintrone* v. *Hertz Truck Leasing & Rental Serv.,* 212 A.2d 769 (N.J. 1965); to builders in *Schipper* v. *Levitt & Sons, Inc.,* 207 A.2d 314 (N.J. 1965); to providers of services in *Newmark* v. *Gimbel's, Inc.,* 258 A.2d 697 (N.J. 1969); and to sellers of used goods in *Realmuto* v. *Straub Motors, Inc.,* 322 A.2d 440 (N.J. 1974). For discussion of these cases, see "Strict Products Liability," pp. 28–35. More recently, however, the New Jersey Supreme Court in *Spring Motors Distributors, Inc.* v. *Ford Motor Co.,* 489 A.2d 660 (N.J. 1985), overruled a lower appellate court and denied a tort remedy to commercial buyers

manufacture the defective products might nonetheless be liable: in 1981 the court held successor corporations strictly liable for injuries caused by products manufactured by corporations that they had acquired, and in 1984 it refused to block a damage suit against pharmaceutical companies based on the theory of "industry-liability."[143] In addition, the court has severely restricted the defenses that can be asserted in products liability cases. Under court doctrine, for example, only plaintiffs' voluntary assumption of a known risk—and not their mere carelessness or inadvertence—permits the defense of contributory negligence.[144] And, departing from the position of most jurisdictions, the court has rejected the "state-of-the-art defense," holding companies liable even for injuries resulting from dangers that were not scientifically discoverable at the time that the product was sold.[145]

OTHER TORT LAW DEVELOPMENTS

The New Jersey Supreme Court's rulings in products liability cases reflect a more general orientation toward facilitating recovery by injured plaintiffs. The justices have tended to interpret procedural requirements, such as time restrictions on commencing suits, flexibly in order to prevent defendants from escaping liability for their acts of negligence.[146] They have also expanded the responsibilities of landlords to tenants, doctors to patients, and social hosts to third parties injured by their guests, often acting earlier and reaching farther than

---

who suffered an economic loss from defective products but did not suffer any personal injury or property damage. Yet even here the court at the same time abolished the applicability in the state of the Uniform Commercial Code's vertical privity requirement in order not to foreclose all opportunity for recovery.

143. On the liability of successor corporations, see *Ramirez* v. *Amsted Industries, Inc.*, 431, A.2d 811 (N.J. 1981), and *Nieves* v. *Bruno Sherman Corp.*, 431 A.2d 826 (N.J. 1981). For the court's refusal to block a claim of industry liability, see *Salomon* v. *Eli Lilly and Co.*, 484 A.2d 320 (N.J. 1984).

144. *Suter* v. *San Angelo Foundry & Machine Co.*, 406 A.2d 140 (N.J. 1979); *Cepeda* v. *Cumberland Engineering Company, Inc.*, 386 A.2d 816 (N.J. 1978); *Bexiga* v. *Havir Manufacturing Corp.*, 290 A.2d 281 (N.J. 1972); and *Maiorino* v. *Weco Products Co.*, 214 A.2d 18 (N.J. 1965).

145. *Beshada* v. *Johns-Mansville Products Corp.*, 447 A.2d 539 (N.J. 1982). For a critical analysis as well as a review of the rulings in other jurisdictions, see "Defeat for the State-of-the-Art Defense in New Jersey Products Liability: *Beshada* v. *Johns-Manville Products Corp.*," *Rutgers Law Journal* 14 (1983): 953–75.

146. See, e.g., *Fernandi* v. *Strully*, 173 A.2d 277 (N.J. 1961), and *New Market Poultry Farms, Inc.* v. *Fellows*, 241 A.2d 633 (N.J. 1968).

other jurisdictions.[147] In allowing actions for new torts such as wrongful life, wrongful birth, negligent invasion of consortium, and prenatal injuries, they have significantly expanded the grounds of potential liability.[148]

The New Jersey court has likewise promoted recovery by plaintiffs by abrogating various immunities from tort liability. Thus in 1958, acknowledging the persuasiveness of Wiley Rutledge's "devastating opinion" in *Georgetown College* v. *Hughes,* the court followed the lead of four other state courts and abandoned charitable immunity.[149] In 1970 the New Jersey court abrogated the doctrine of sovereign immunity.[150] And after a decade of intracourt debate, highlighted by several extended scholarly dissents by Justice Nathan Jacobs, the court in 1970 abandoned the doctrines of interspousal immunity and interfamilial immunity in personal injury litigation.[151]

147. The seminal case on landlord liability is *Braitman* v. *Overlook Terrace Corp.,* 346 A.2d 76 (N.J. 1975); for more recent developments, see "New Jersey Case Comments: *Trentacost* v. *Brussel:* An Extension of the Landlord's Implied Warranty of Habitability." *Rutgers Law Review* 33 (1981): 1157–70, and Edward Chase and E. Hunter Taylor, Jr., "Landlord and Tenant: A Study in Property and Contract," *Villanova Law Review* 30 (1985): 571–699. On physicians' responsibilities, see *Anderson* v. *Somberg,* 338 A.2d 1 (N.J. 1975), and *Evers* v. *Dollinger,* 471 A.2d 405 (N.J. 1984). In *Kelly* v. *Gwinnel,* 476 A.2d 1219 (1984), the court extended liability to social hosts for injuries inflicted in automobile accidents by their guests, to whom they served liquor, knowing that they were intoxicated and would be driving.

148. On wrongful life, see *Procanik* v. *Cillo,* 478 A.2d 755 (N.J. 1984); on wrongful birth, see *Berman* v. *Allan,* 404 A.2d 8 (N.J. 1979), and *Schroeder* v. *Perkel,* 432 A.2d 834 (N.J. 1981); on negligent invasion of consortium, *Ekalo* v. *Constructive Services Corp.,* 215 A.2d 1 (N.J. 1965); and on prenatal injuries, *Smith* v. *Brennan,* 157 A.2d 497 (N.J. 1960).

149. *Collopy* v. *Newark Eye and Ear Infirmary,* 141 A.2d 276 (N.J. 1958). The more general influence of Rutledge's opinion in *Georgetown College* v. *Hughes,* 130 F.2d 810 (1942), is assessed in Lawrence Baum and Bradley C. Canon, "State Supreme Courts as Activists: New Doctrines in the Law of Torts," in Porter and Tarr, eds., *State Supreme Courts,* p. 87.

150. *Willis* v. *Department of Conservation,* 264 A.2d 534 (N.J. 1970).

151. *Immer* v. *Risko,* 267 A.2d 481 (N.J. 1970), abolished interspousal immunity in suits involving automobile-related negligence. *Small* v. *Rockfield,* 330 A.2d 335 (N.J. 1974), permitted interspousal actions for egregious marital torts. *Merenoff* v. *Merenoff,* 388 A.2d 951 (N.J. 1978), made civil redress available for all injuries negligently inflicted by a spouse who was involved in activity that created a substantial risk of harm. *France* v. *A.P.A. Transport Corp.,* 267 A.2d 490 (N.J. 1970), eroded parent-child immunities.

As early as 1960, Justice Jacobs was persuasively arguing for the abolition of interfamilial immunities—see, e.g., his dissent in *Hastings* v. *Hastings,* 163 A.2d 147 (N.J. 1960). Nonetheless, as one commentator put it, the New Jersey Supreme

NEW WINE IN OLD BOTTLES

The New Jersey Supreme Court's common law policy making has not been restricted to those substantive areas, such as products liability, that every state high court must address. At times it has resuscitated and reinterpreted traditional common law principles in order to pursue new aims. A case in point is *State* v. *Shack,* in which the New Jersey Supreme Court, eschewing constitutional arguments, overturned a conviction for trespassing on the basis of a common law right of access for union organizers attempting to counsel migrant workers housed on the property of their employer.[152] Even more dramatic are the court's rulings involving the "public trust doctrine." Under this doctrine, land covered by navigable waters (which includes rivers, tidal waters, and tide beds) belongs to the sovereign, who has an obligation to use it for the public interest. Traditionally, this was understood to require making lakes, rivers, and coastline available to the public for such commercial purposes as navigation, travel, and fishing. In 1972, however, the New Jersey Supreme Court, emphasizing that the doctrine was not "fixed or static," went beyond this traditional understanding, ruling that it also afforded the public a right to use the tidelands for recreational purposes; and it struck down a shore community's use of discriminatory fees to discourage the use of its public beaches by nonresidents.[153] Spurred by the efforts of the Office of the Public Advocate, the court built upon this reinterpretation of the public trust doctrine in subsequent cases, recognizing the public's right to gain access to and to use the dry sand owned by a quasi-public beach club.[154]

Court's abolition of interspousal tort immunity proceeded by "judicial erosion through piecemeal recognition that the immunity doctrine breeds inconsistencies and arbitrary distinctions." See: "Interfamilial Tort Immunity in New Jersey: Dismantling the Barrier to Personal Injury Litigation," *Rutgers Camden Law Journal* 10 (1979): 683.

152. 277 A.2d 369 (N.J. 1971).

153. *Borough of Neptune City* v. *Borough of Avon-by-the Sea,* 294 A.2d 47 (N.J. 1972).

154. *Matthews* v. *Bay Head Improvement Association,* 471 A.2d 355, cert. denied 469 U.S. 821 (1984); *Van Ness* v. *Borough of Deal,* 393 A.2d 571 (N.J. 1978); *Hyland* v. *Borough of Allenhurst,* 393 A.2d 579 (N.J. 1978). For a discussion of the Public Advocate's role in the *Bay Head* and *Deal* cases, see: "The Public's Right to Cross and to Use Privately Owned Upper Beach Areas," *Seton Hall Law Review* 15 (1985): 348–49, 356–57, and Martin A. Bierbaum, "On the Frontiers of Public Interest

This brief account permits several conclusions about the New Jersey Supreme Court's common law jurisprudence. Most obviously, the court has shown an unusual willingness to take the lead in pioneering change in the common law. For example, in eliminating the privity requirement in *Henningsen*, rejecting the state-of-the-art defense in *Beshada*, extending liability to social hosts for injuries suffered in accidents caused by their intoxicated guests in *Gwinnell*, and transforming the public trust doctrine in *Avon-by-the-Sea*, the court not only established new law for the state but adopted positions that had not previously been endorsed by any other court. And in imposing strict liability in *Santor* and eliminating charitable immunity in *Collopy*, it aligned itself with the small minority of courts that had introduced changes in long-established principles.

This willingness to initiate change in turn reflects the court's acceptance of the legitimacy of judicial creativity in elaborating the common law. Although the court's pioneering rulings at times created divisions on the court, what is noteworthy is that the intracourt debate has focused on the substance of the rulings rather than on the propriety of judicial initiation of legal change. In part, this might be attributed to the distinctive character of tort law—as the court put it in *Falzone* v. *Busch*, "We are dealing with torts, where there can be little, if any, justifiable reliance and where the rule of *stare decisis* is admittedly limited."[155] Yet even in tort law, few other courts have been quite so willing to acknowledge the "historical power and duty of the judiciary to correct its own errors" and to abandon doctrines that no longer "represent current notions of rightness and fairness."[156] Moreover, the court's rulings in other fields of the common law reveal a similar willingness to evaluate doctrines in the light of current societal needs. The justices' unabashed acceptance of their responsibilities as "policy-makers" appears to have freed them from the institutional constraints felt by their colleagues on other courts.[157]

Yet because the New Jersey Supreme Court has been in the forefront of tort law reform, it has been unable to present its initiatives

---

Law: The New Jersey State Department of the Public Advocate—The Public Interest Advocacy Division," *Seton Hall Law Review* 13 (1983): 488.

155. 214 A.2d 12, 17 (N.J. 1965).

156. *Collopy* v. *Newark Eye and Ear Infirmary*, 141 A.2d 276, 278–79 (N.J. 1958); *Schipper* v. *Levitt & Sons, Inc.*, 207 A.2d 314, 324 (N.J. 1965).

157. Glick, *Supreme Courts in State Politics*, p. 41, table 2–3.

as merely the application of established law. This has presented a problem for the court, since as Justice Alan Handler has noted, "the legitimacy of the judiciary must be self-evident in its product."[158] The court's response to the problem of legitimacy has taken three forms. First, where possible, it has attempted to demonstrate the continuity of its decisions with its own previous rulings or with those of other courts. The court's citation in *Henningsen* of other rulings that circumscribed the doctrine of privity is a prime example. Second, insofar as it has lacked legal precedent for its rulings, the court has sought support in nonjudicial legal sources. Thus one survey noted that the New Jersey Supreme Court exceeded all other state supreme courts in its citation of articles in law reviews.[159] Third, the court has justified its use of such sources by emphasizing the courts' responsibility to keep the common law abreast of current societal conditions and needs. For if the court is to fulfill its policy-making responsibilities, it must rely on the best evidence about those conditions and the best arguments about those needs.

This does not mean that the court's initiatives have escaped challenge. After its abrogation of charitable immunity, for example, the New Jersey Assembly adopted legislation reinstituting it in a limited set of cases.[160] And after its ruling extending the responsibilities of social hosts, several legislators introduced legislation to overturn the decision. Yet such legislative involvement was not unexpected, and at times it was specifically invited: the court's prospective abrogation of sovereign immunity in *Willis* clearly invited legislative action.[161] Thus in the field of the common law, as in the best of its constitutional jurisprudence, the New Jersey Supreme Court's initiatives have produced dialogue rather than dominance.[162]

158. Alan Handler, "A Matter of Opinion," *Rutgers Law Journal* 15 (1983): 5.

159. Robert A. Kagan, Bobby D. Infelise, and Robert R. Detlesfen, "American State Supreme Court Justices, 1900–1970," *American Bar Foundation Research Journal* (1984): 405.

160. The New Jersey legislature's limited reinstitution of charitable immunity is found at N.J.S.A. 2A:53A–7. The furor created by *Kelly* v. *Gwinnell* is reviewed in Bruce S. Rosen, "A Bold Court Forges Ahead," *National Law Journal*, Nov. 5, 1984, p. 40. A more general response to the court's tort law rulings is the New Jersey Tort Claims Act of 1972, N.J.S.A. 59:1–1 *et seq.*

161. See *Willis* v. *Department of Conservation*, 264 A.2d 534, 541.

162. For a general discussion of the nature of this dialogue between judges and legislators, see Robert E. Keeton, *Venturing to Do Justice: Reforming the Private Law* (Cambridge: Harvard University Press, 1969), chaps. 1–6.

The New Jersey Supreme Court: Independence and Activism

Our analysis confirms the New Jersey Supreme Court's reputation for activism, innovation, and independence. In its relations with the U.S. Supreme Court, the New Jersey court has quite consciously pursued an independent course. Although they have rarely challenged the Court's authority directly, the justices in Trenton have declined to defer to its judgment and have exploited the leeways available to them to pursue their own constitutional vision. Despite the inevitable tensions inherent in partially hierarchical relations between two strong courts, the New Jersey court's independence has served the state and the nation well, exemplifying the potential advantages of a system of judicial federalism.

In its relations with other branches of state government, the New Jersey Supreme Court has attempted to combine active participation in the determination of state policy with appropriate deference to the prerogatives of elected officials. Through its rulings enhancing state governmental power, it has sought to equip officials to deal with the policy problems confronting the state. Through its prospective overruling of precedent in tort law, it has invited the legislature to enter into a dialogue on policy development. And through its reliance on agenda-setting policy making, it has sought to mandate attention to pressing problems and to establish parameters for their solution without foreclosing the exercise of discretion and political judgment.

This attempt to reconcile a concern for substantive outcomes with a concern for the locus of decision making has not been altogether successful. On the one hand, as the response to the court's rulings on school finance and exclusionary zoning illustrates, reliance on political officials for the development of policy has, perhaps inevitably, endangered—or at least compromised—the achievement of judicial objectives. On the other hand, judicial formulation of policy has strained the capacities of the court, exposed it to political attack, and threatened to erode its authority. Like other activist courts, then, the New Jersey Supreme Court has been forced to come to grips with the tension between its substantive and process concerns; and as the court addresses itself to new policy issues, this tension will likely continue to affect its relations with other institutions of state government.

The New Jersey Supreme Court's willingness to assess legal doctrine in the light of current conditions and to pioneer change in constitutional law and in the common law is the prime factor affecting its relations with other state supreme courts. As studies of tort law reform and of citation patterns reveal, the court's reputation for innovation and craftsmanship has prompted other courts to look to its decisions for guidance, although they have not always been willing to follow New Jersey's lead.[163] In deciding cases, the New Jersey court has relied most heavily on the rulings of other "national-reputation" courts, such as the California Supreme Court. Its opinions have characteristically included as well extensive citations from other courts throughout the nation.[164] This high citation rate does not necessarily indicate, however, that those courts have exerted great influence on the New Jersey court's rulings. In fact, because it has frequently sought to introduce doctrinal changes, it has often found itself without immediately applicable precedent from other states and been forced to rely on its analysis and on extrajudicial writings. In part, then, the extensive citations reflect the court's style of opinion writing.[165] In part, too, as in *Henningsen*, they have served to provide a sense of continuity despite the court's innovations. In sum, by self-consciously assuming a leadership role, the New Jersey court has provided direction for less adverturesome or ambitious courts, while remaining quite self-reliant in deciding the cases that come before it.

Yet what explains the posture that the court has adopted in its relations with other legal and political actors? Three interrelated contextual factors have undoubtedly been important. First, the New Jersey Supreme Court's discretionary jurisdiction has afforded it the opportunity to devote thoughtful attention to a limited number of important cases each term. Certainly a comparison of the current supreme court with the old Court of Errors and Appeals supports the

163. See, for example, Canon and Baum, "Patterns of Adoption," p. 978, table 2; Gregory A. Caldeira, "On the Reputation of State Supreme Courts," *Political Behavior* 5 (1983): 89, table 1; and Lawrence Friedman, Robert Kagan, Bliss Cartwright, and Stanton Wheeler, "State Supreme Courts: A Century of Style and Citation," *Stanford Law Review* 33 (1981): 805, 806–07. Pioneering decisions of the New Jersey court that have not been followed by other courts include its rulings on the state-of-the-art defense (*Beshada*), social host liability (*Gwinnell*), and exclusionary zoning (*Mount Laurel*).

164. In one sampling of opinions, the New Jersey Supreme Court averaged more than twenty citations to rulings of other courts in the period since 1948. Friedman et al., "Century of Style and Citation," p. 800.

165. Friedman and his associates reported that during the 1960–70 period, the New Jersey court had the longest average opinion-length of the courts they studied. See "Century of Style and Citation," p. 784, n. 29.

proposition that a manageable caseload is a necessary, though not sufficient, condition for judicial statesmanship. Second, New Jersey has recruited a number of exceptionally able justices for its high court, justices who have been willing to reexamine existing doctrines, tackle new issues, and participate creatively in directing the course of legal development. Third, litigants have brought before the New Jersey court the types of cases that offer opportunities for judicial creativity and policy making. To some extent, of course, as the Canon-Baum study of innovation in tort law has shown, the procession of cases coming to a court is serendipitous.[166] However, to some extent a court's rulings, by communicating a willingness to address certain issues or a sympathy to certain claims, may invite further litigation. Thus the range of tort cases appealed to the New Jersey court reflects in part its propensity to rule in favor of plaintiffs, and its rulings on privacy rights and on the new judicial federalism more generally its willingness to develop state constitutional protections. In addition, the accessibility of judicial redress may also affect the range of issues that the court addresses. The New Jersey court's rulings on standing, political questions, and similar issues have clearly facilitated litigation of policy disputes. Even more crucial has been the creation of the Office of the Public Advocate in 1974, which has institutionalized public interest litigation. The Public Advocate was the driving force behind the exclusionary zoning and public trust litigation, and its secure funding and wide discretion virtually ensure that policy issues will continue to come before the court.[167]

Important as these factors are, they have not been decisive. To understand the New Jersey Supreme Court and its place in state governance and national legal development, one must consider the court's own conception of its role in state and nation. This in turn directs attention to the efforts of Chief Justices Vanderbilt and Weintraub. Vanderbilt, by virtue of his reformist efforts and his personal stature, helped to create a distinctive legal culture in the state, giving the supreme court a national reputation and securing its

166. Canon and Baum, "Patterns of Adoption."

167. See, generally, Bierbaum, "Frontiers of Public Interest Law," and "The Private Attorney General and the Public Advocate: Facilitating Public Interest Litigation," *Rutgers Law Review* 34 (1982): 350–77. In *Home Builders League of New Jersey, Inc.* v. *Township of Berlin*, 405 A.2d 381 (N.J. 1979), and *Township of Mount Laurel* v. *Department of the Public Advocate*, 416 A.2d 886 (N.J. 1980), the New Jersey Supreme Court announced rulings favorable to the Department of the Public Advocate, and these have facilitated the initiation of public interest litigation.

SIX

STATE SUPREME COURTS IN PERSPECTIVE

The Alabama, Ohio, and New Jersey supreme courts have exhibited a considerable diversity of behavior and perspective, with significant differences apparent among the courts and with major changes occurring on individual courts over time. The Alabama and New Jersey supreme courts each underwent fundamental transformations within the course of a few years. The Ohio Supreme Court, while retaining its partisan character throughout the period, changed dramatically when a Democrat majority attained control in the late 1970s. As these changes occurred, so too did the courts' relationships with political authorities within the state and their interactions with other state and federal courts. To analyze these patterns of uniformity and variation, continuity and change, we turn first to a discussion of the courts' institutional identities.

Institutional Identity

THE MEANING OF INSTITUTIONAL IDENTITY

Our account of the political and legal development of the Alabama, Ohio, and New Jersey supreme courts documents the distinctiveness of each court and the persistence of certain intracourt continuities over time. Each court has developed its own understanding of its responsibilities—its particular jurisprudential orientation and attitude toward legal change, its relationship to other political and legal institutions, and its pattern of intracourt interaction. These continuities permit one to refer to, for example, the Ohio court's tradition of partisanship and the New Jersey court's continuing commitment to reformist activism. This orientation toward judicial responsibilities and toward the court's function, which is internalized by the members of a court and reflected in their actions, we refer to as the court's institutional identity.

Although the term *institutional identity* may be unfamiliar, students of politics have often acknowledged that governmental bodies develop distinctive patterns of operation. Congressional scholars, for example, have observed such patterns in comparative studies of the two houses of Congress and of various congressional committees.[1] So have students of bureaucracy in analyzing bureaucratic behavior.[2] Most important for our purposes, judicial scholars studying the United States Supreme Court have long distinguished between various "courts," such as the Warren Court, the Burger Court, and the New Deal Court.[3] Underlying those distinctions is the assumption that each "court" develops its own characteristic orientations and decisional patterns and that an understanding of the Supreme Court requires elaboration of how those orientations and patterns have changed over time. At times, as the distinction between the Warren and Burger courts suggests, these changes in institutional identity may reflect changes in court personnel. At other times the transformations have occurred without significant personnel changes—the "switch in time" of 1937 is a prime example—although subsequent personnel changes may solidify the shift in institutional identity. Thus, in focusing on the institutional identities of state supreme courts, we are systematically applying a mode of analysis that has long been implicit in studies of other governmental bodies and of changes over time on the U.S. Supreme Court.

STABILITY AND CHANGE IN INSTITUTIONAL IDENTITY

State supreme courts—and, indeed, courts more generally—can develop consistent institutional identities more readily than other

1. The pathbreaking study was Donald R. Matthews, *U.S. Senators and Their World* (Chapel Hill: University of North Carolina Press, 1960). Studies identifying the special character of various congressional committees include Richard F. Fenno, Jr., *The Power of the Purse* (Boston: Little, Brown, 1966); George Goodwin, Jr., *The Little Legislatures* (Amherst: University of Massachusetts Press, 1970); and Richard F. Fenno, Jr., *Congressmen in Committees* (Boston: Little, Brown, 1973).

2. The classic account is Anthony Downs, *Inside Bureaucracy* (Boston: Little, Brown, 1966).

3. The works in this genre are legion. For a recent contribution, see Vincent Blasi, ed., *The Burger Court: The Counter-Revolution That Wasn't* (New Haven: Yale University Press, 1983). Other major examples include C. Herman Pritchett, *The Roosevelt Court: A Study in Judicial Politics and Values, 1937–1947* (New York: Macmillan, 1947); C. Herman Pritchett, *Civil Liberties and the Vinson Court* (Chicago: University of Chicago Press, 1954); and Bernard Schwartz, *Super Chief Earl Warren and His Supreme Court: A Judicial Biography* (New York: Columbia University Press, 1983).

governmental bodies can. A comparison of courts with legislatures indicates why this is so. For one thing, the process of judicial recruitment tends to elevate persons who are prepared to accept a court's prevailing patterns and norms and to conform their behavior to them. Since positions on the bench are reserved to the legal fraternity, new justices already share with the other members of the court a common set of professional norms to which they have been socialized in the course of their legal education and subsequent practice of law. Among these norms, significantly, are a respect for precedent and for incremental rather than radical change in the law, both of which serve to promote continuity in the court's jurisprudential posture. By contrast, members of legislative bodies, because they are more diverse in background and life experience, are less likely to share common perspectives, and they are not subject to professional norms mandating legal continuity.

Related to this are the perceptions of the judicial role that prospective judges hold prior to their elevation to the bench. The functions of courts are clearer and more circumscribed than those of legislatures, and those seeking judicial posts, by virtue of their professional experience, often have more immediate knowledge of court operations. Thus potential judges tend to have a clear understanding of their state supreme courts and of the requirements of the judicial role. For example, as Henry Glick has noted, "the nonpartisan values operating on the New Jersey court would be visible to political activists and anticipated by potential court appointees."[4] In contrast, previous exposure to the legislative process is not a prerequisite for election, and new legislators have at times admitted that they attained office with a totally inadequate understanding of the norms and standards governing legislative work.[5] The greater foreknowledge of candidates for judicial office serves an important screening function—because the legal norms and perspectives of the state supreme court are more accessible, those unsympathetic to judicial role requirements tend to eliminate themselves from consideration. Consequently, those who do seek judicial office are generally those with a willingness to conform to prevailing modes and requirements.[6]

Courts are also in a better position than legislatures to maintain

4. Henry R. Glick, *Supreme Courts in State Politics* (New York: Basic Books, 1971), p. 106.

5. See generally William K. Muir, Jr., *Legislature: California's School for Politics* (Chicago: University of Chicago Press, 1982).

6. See Glick, *Supreme Courts*, chap. 5.

their institutional identity despite the influx of new members. Judicial terms are lengthy, and turnover on courts usually staggered, so the incoming justice is typically the only new member of an ongoing institution with established patterns of behavior and perspective. This in turn facilitates the process of socialization. In addition, sitting justices possess important resources for promoting adherence to the court's norms. Because legislators can pursue a variety of aims, only some of which require the cooperation of other members, they can to some extent insulate themselves from pressures to conform to institutional norms.[7] On the other hand, the aims that a judge can legitimately pursue are much more circumscribed. For most justices, elevation to the high court is the culmination of a political career rather than a step on the career ladder, so their sights are focused on the work of the court rather than beyond it. (The Ohio Supreme Court, of course, provides a conspicuous counterexample.) Moreover, all judicial decisions are collegial decisions, and therefore effectiveness on the court depends upon influence among one's fellow justices. To the extent that one is dependent upon one's colleagues, however, they can exact conformity with the court's norms of behavior and perspective as the price of success. This in turn provides a strong incentive to subscribe to the norms of the court.

A final factor should also be mentioned. Courts are small groups that function through the close continuing interaction of their members.[8] Usually the greater the interaction within a group, the greater the mutual influence. Moreover, the necessity of working together over time is both an incentive for collegiality and a subtle mechanism for enforcing conformity to institutional norms. Indeed, on many courts collegiality and intracourt cooperation have emerged as important standards governing judicial behavior.[9]

These factors, taken together, help explain why courts develop

---

7. For a representative discussion, see Fenno, *Congressmen in Committees*, chap. 1.

8. The seminal work on courts as small groups—a work that informs our analysis of state supreme courts—is Walter F. Murphy, *Elements of Judicial Strategy* (Chicago: University of Chicago Press, 1964).

9. Glick, *Supreme Courts*, pp. 104–106. The authors' discussions with New Jersey justices have confirmed that the norm of consensualism still prevails on the court. Accounts of other courts suggest that many justices attach great importance to intracourt collegiality. See, for example, Edward N. Beiser, "The Rhode Island Supreme Court: A Well Integrated Political System," *Law & Society Review* 8 (1974): 167–86.

institutional identities and maintain them over time. Yet the notion of institutional identity is also compatible with the pattern of change that we have discovered on, for example, the Alabama and New Jersey supreme courts. Because of their legal character, it is natural to think of courts as changing slowly and gradually. In fact, however, the movement from the "old" to the "new" court in Alabama and from the prereform to postreform court in New Jersey took place in the space of a few years. Furthermore, these changes took the form of self-conscious transformations, repudiations of the courts' past orientation and rulings and the adoption of alternative perspectives on their responsibilities. New justices were recruited who both clearly understood the norms that had prevailed on the courts and sought seats on the bench in order to change them—in short, to establish a new institutional identity. Interestingly, the small size of state supreme courts, which helped them sustain their institutional identities, also facilitated the exertion of strong leadership to change them. Later in the chapter we shall discuss in detail how and why the changes in institutional identity occurred. For now, the primary point is that the pattern of change on the three courts we studied confirms the crucial importance of understanding them in terms of their institutional identities.

THE INSTITUTIONAL IDENTITIES OF STATE SUPREME COURTS

Our discovery that the Alabama, Ohio, and New Jersey supreme courts have developed distinctive institutional identities directs attention to several key questions concerning state supreme courts. First, what are the different institutional identities found among state supreme courts? Second, in what respects do the courts' institutional identities differ, and in what respects are they similar? Third, how do courts develop their distinctive identities, and how do they maintain them over time? Fourth, how do courts change their institutional identities, and what factors promote such changes?

One prefatory comment seems appropriate. The initial chapters of this book surveyed the various factors that might affect how state supreme courts interact with other legal institutions and participate in governance. Yet as we shall see, our case studies suggest that the same factors can, depending on circumstances, produce either uniformity or variation, continuity or change. This seeming paradox, which is more apparent than real, testifies to the crucial significance of contextual factors in determining the roles played by a supreme court in its state and nationally. More precisely, intrastate factors interact with broader legal and political factors and mediate their effects on state supreme courts. How this occurs will become apparent in the comparative analysis of the Alabama, Ohio, and New Jersey, supreme courts.

Uniformity and Variation

ISSUES BEFORE THE COURTS

Variations among state supreme courts might reflect in part the subject matter of the cases they act upon. More specifically, it has been suggested that the range of issues a court addresses depends on the jurisdiction it is assigned, in particular its mandatory jurisdiction, and on the number of cases it hears. Although Alabama, Ohio, and New Jersey have all established intermediate appellate courts, the jurisdiction and caseloads of their supreme courts differ markedly. Whereas the Alabama Supreme Court is obliged to hear appeals in a variety of minor cases, such as boundary disputes, the Ohio Supreme Court exercises considerable discretion in case selection, and the New Jersey Supreme Court is virtually a "cert. court." And whereas the Alabama and Ohio courts decide over two hundred cases each year, the new Jersey Supreme Court rules in fewer than half that number. Yet these differences have had little effect on the types of issues that have come before the three courts. Each of the courts has been called upon to resolve disputes about the extent and allocation of state governmental power. Each has also addressed a range of private-law controversies arising under the statutory or common law of the state, involving issues in tort law, family law, contract law, and the like. Last, each has heard a large number of criminal law appeals, which have often involved constitutional claims by defendants. A moment's reflection suggests that this similarity in caseload composition is not surprising. Because state supreme courts are primarily concerned with state law, and because the law in all states must regulate certain basic areas of state responsibility, the same subjects recur in state after state.[10] Thus

10. The case data we collected for the Alabama, New Jersey, and Ohio supreme courts bear this out. For national data for a single year, see Burton M. Atkins and Henry R. Glick, "Environmental and Structural Variables as Determinants of Issues in State Courts of Last Resort," *American Journal of Political Science* 20 (1976). For patterns over time, see Robert A. Kagan, Bliss Cartwright, Lawrence M. Friedman, and Stanton Wheeler, "The Business of State Supreme Courts, 1870–1970," *Stanford Law Review* 30 (1977): 121–56.

the legal function served by state supreme courts is more crucial than jurisdiction or "gatekeeping" in determining the composition of their caseloads.

The similarity in caseload composition among the three supreme courts extends beyond broad subject matter categories: many of the same issues were litigated and many of the same doctrinal claims advanced in the three states. The rulings of sister courts, both state and federal, operating through what we have labeled vertical judicial federalism and horizontal judicial federalism, account for much of this uniformity. For example, once the New Jersey Supreme Court rejected the privity requirement in *Henningsen* and the California Supreme Court adopted the strict liability standard in *Yuma Power*, plaintiffs in products liability cases in other states, purely out of self-interest, were bound to argue that their courts should follow a similar course.[11] When these arguments were presented to the Alabama, Ohio, and New Jersey supreme courts during the 1960s, the latter two responded by adopting the strict liability standard, and the Alabama court by rejecting it, a position it later abandoned.[12] Similarly, the Alabama and New Jersey supreme courts confronted arguments that suits for wrongful life should be permitted, a position they all initially rejected, although the New Jersey Supreme Court has since reversed its position on the issue.[13] As these examples suggest, arguments for doctrinal innovation do not necessarily prevail in the short run, or even in the long run. However, the respectability that doctrinal changes gain through their acceptance by sister courts requires a state supreme court to hear the cases in which they are proposed and to give the changes serious consideration.[14]

11. *Henningsen* v. *Bloomfield Motors*, 161 A.2d 69 (N.J. 1960), and *Greenman* v. *Yuma Power Products Co.*, 377 P.2d 897 (Cal. 1963).

12. The New Jersey Supreme Court endorsed the strict liability standard in *Santor* v. *A & M Karagheusian, Inc.*, 207 A.2d 305 (N.J. 1965); the Alabama Supreme Court in *Casrell* v. *Altec Industries, Inc.*, 335 So.2d 128 (Ala. 1976); the Ohio Supreme Court in *Lonzrick* v. *Republic Steel*, 218 N.E.2d 185 (Ohio 1966).

13. In *Procancik* v. *Cillo*, 478 A.2d 755 (N.J. 1984), the New Jersey Supreme Court became the third court to recognize wrongful life as a cause of action. Its earlier decision denying such a cause of action, *Gleitman* v. *Cosgrove*, 227 A.2d 689 (N.J. 1967), had been the leading wrongful life case nationally. The tort was rejected as a cause of action in Alabama in *Elliot* v. *Brown*, 361 So.2d 546 (Ala. 1978). Thus far there has been no case raising this claim under Ohio law.

14. A perfect example of this is the development of litigation on sovereign immunity in Alabama, notwithstanding the bar to recovery in the state's constitution. See chapter 4.

The judicial reform of tort law during the 1960s and 1970s supplies the clearest instances of intercourt influences on caseload composition. However, the phenomenon extends beyond the common law. The Warren Court's expansion of the rights of defendants during the sixties, for example, dramatically affected the caseloads of all state high courts, including those of Alabama, Ohio, and New Jersey. Equally dramatic were the effects on state courts' caseloads produced by the rediscovery of state bills of rights and the emergence of the new judicial federalism. Although the renewed reliance by litigants on state constitutional guarantees originated in California, it quickly spread to New Jersey in the early 1970s, where it led to landmark rulings on school finance and exclusionary zoning. But it did not long remain limited to national "lighthouse courts." By the late seventies litigants were bringing appeals under the state constitution to the Ohio Supreme Court, and by the 1980s the same thing was happening in Alabama. Although the Alabama and Ohio supreme courts were not as receptive to such claims as New Jersey's had been, substantive claims and doctrinal approaches pioneered in a few states within a relatively short time became part of the caseload mix of supreme courts throughout the nation. Moreover, the nationwide reemergence of state constitutional law ensured that litigants in most states would advance state constitutional claims and that state courts would treat them seriously.

Despite the considerable congruence in the composition of state supreme courts' caseloads, political and legal differences among the states have had some influence on the issues they address. On occasion, differences in caseload composition have resulted from a judicial hostility to a class of litigants, which deters them from bringing cases in the state's courts. The Alabama Supreme Court's animus against black litigants prior to the 1970s presents the most egregious example of this. This hostility led black plaintiffs, whenever the choice was available, to pursue their claims of discrimination or of other rights violations in the federal courts. When there was no recourse to the federal courts, they tended not to initiate suit rather than to litigate in the Alabama courts or, as defendants, not to appeal adverse decisions to a court that they perceived as predisposed to reject their claims.

A more common influence on caseload composition has been the state supreme court's record of receptivity to specific types of claims—put simply, sympathy begets and hostility deters litigation and appeals. Thus the New Jersey Supreme Court's receptivity to products liability claims has encouraged plaintiffs to file such claims and to appeal adverse rulings to it. Similarly, the Democratization of the Ohio Supreme Court prompted workers to file workers' compensation cases and to appeal them to the court, just as the conservatism of the court prior to Democratic ascendancy had deterred them from filing and had encouraged employers to appeal unfavorable rulings. The influence of this factor extends beyond merely the number of cases appealed to the court. For by its rulings a state supreme court establishes what is a viable claim in the state and thereby affects as well the substance of the claims it receives and the timing of litigation raising them. For example, for a long time the Ohio Supreme Court's rulings discouraged litigation based on a broad interpretation of work-related injuries, but in the wake of personnel changes during the late 1970s, the court's greater receptivity to workers' claims prompted plaintiffs to appeal cases where recovery depended on extending the margins of the concept.[15]

Examination of the New Jersey Supreme Court's record in products liability cases reveals the operation of an additional factor as well. By its rulings in *Henningsen* and subsequent cases, the court signaled its sympathy for consumers in products liability suits and its willingness to overturn long-standing precedent to vindicate their claims. This encouraged potential litigants in products liability cases to bring suits challenging established doctrines, such as the state-of-the-art defense, and presenting novel claims, such as industry liability. It also prompted litigation to extend the court's principles to new areas, such as landlord-tenant relations, and to undermine other established tort law doctrines, such as interfamilial immunity. Canon and Baum's research on the spread of tort law innovation confirms the importance of the court's reputation for progressivism: although the order in which states adopted reforms varied as a result of the vagaries of litigation, certain states, with New Jersey in the lead, pioneered innovations or to adopt them early on.[16] Thus even if horizontal

15. A summary of the Ohio Supreme Court's rulings, from the perspective of a Democratic justice, is Clifford F. Brown, "The Trend of Workers' Compensation in Ohio: Ohio Puts the Worker Back into Workers' Compensation," *Capital University Law Review* 13 (1984): 521–32.

16. Bradley C. Canon and Lawrence Baum, "Patterns of Adoption of Tort Law Innovations: An Application of Diffusion Theory to Judicial Doctrines," *American Political Science Review* 75 (1981): 975–87; and Lawrence Baum and Bradley C. Canon, "State Supreme Courts as Activists: New Doctrines in the Law of Torts," in Mary Cornelia Porter and G. Alan Tarr, eds., *State Supreme Courts* (Westport, Conn.: Greenwood Press, 1982), pp. 97–102.

federalism ensures that almost all states will sooner or later address most of the same issues, a court's receptivity to particular types of claims and its overall willingness to innovate affect whether it addresses those claims sooner rather than later, or—in the case of some more marginal claims—whether it addresses them at all.

This analysis suggests that courts send signals to litigants—more particularly, to their attorneys—about the likely success of various claims. Yet although courts can encourage litigation in particular areas, they are, as one commentator has wryly observed, like unreliable clocks, which must be shaken to be started.[17] Whether such shaking occurs depends on whether the attorneys in a state heed and act on the signals they receive. Thus a complex pattern of reciprocal influence operates. In New Jersey the aggressiveness of the private bar and the Public Advocate has created opportunities for the supreme court to exert leadership by bringing novel claims before it and by quickly following up on legal developments in other states. At the same time, the New Jersey court's receptivity to such claims has encouraged innovative legal arguments and prompted groups to pursue their aims through the courts. Similarly in Ohio, the labor bar reacted quickly to the supreme court's new receptivity to workers' claims, and the court's rulings reinforced expectations of success. And in Alabama, the plaintiffs' bar has responded to the court's newfound willingness to consider reforms in tort law.

POLITICAL CULTURE AND LEGAL CULTURE

During the twentieth century various factors, among them the nationalization of state politics and the professionalization of state judiciaries, have served to mitigate the differences among the political and legal cultures of the American states.[18] In the postwar era the pace

17. Quoted in Donald L. Horowitz, *The Courts and Social Policy* (Washington, D.C.: Brookings, 1977), p. 38.

18. On the nationalization of state politics, see Donald E. Stokes, "Parties and the Nationalization of Electoral Forces," in William N. Chambers and Walter Dean Burnham, eds., *The American Party System: Stages of Political Development* (New York: Oxford University Press, 1967), and Frank Sorauf, *Party Politics in America* (Boston: Little, Brown, 1980); for a somewhat different assessment, see William Claggett, William Flanigan, and Nancy Zingale, "Nationalization of the American Electorate," *American Political Science Review* 78 (1984): 77–91. The professionalization of state judiciaries, exemplified by the elimination of lay judges and by the movements for court unification and the merit selection of judges, is discussed in Henry R. Glick and Kenneth N. Vines. *State Court Systems* (Englewood Cliffs, N.J.: Prentice-Hall, 1973).

of this movement has quickened, particularly in southern states such as Alabama, which had prided themselves on their rather perverse exceptionalism.[19] Still, differences persist among state supreme courts. This diversity in part reflects the continuing resilience of state political and legal traditions.[20] As long as these differences remain, political culture and legal culture will continue to operate as forces for diversity as well as for uniformity, affecting judicial attitudes and behavior and promoting interstate variation among supreme courts. Furthermore, although national norms define the parameters within which action should occur, they do not necessarily specify the form that it should take. Thus, even in states with roughly comparable political or legal cultures, broad leeways for action remain, and considerable intercourt variation is possible. The dual character of the norms guiding state supreme court justices also promotes interstate diversity. Because a state's political culture and its legal culture may create conflicting expectations of appropriate behavior, variation among state supreme courts may arise from whether their members seek to conform their conduct to legal cultural or political cultural norms.

The contrast between the Ohio and New Jersey supreme courts underlines the importance of a court's choice between allegiance to legal cultural or political cultural norms. Similar in terms of demographic mix, party competitiveness, urbanization, and industrialization, Ohio and New Jersey also share a common (individualistic) political culture.[21] Therefore one might well expect their courts to be similar, and indeed, prior to 1947, in many respects they were. Today, however, the Ohio and New Jersey supreme courts are poles apart jurisprudentially. Whereas the state's political culture continues to exert a decisive influence on the Ohio Supreme Court, the New Jersey Supreme Court has largely insulated itself from the prevailing political culture in the state and created a distinctive state legal culture.

The great achievement of Chief Justice Vanderbilt was to reorient the New Jersey Supreme Court to legal cultural norms and to insulate the court from the influence of the political realm. To do this, Vanderbilt—and his successors—encouraged a commitment to legal professionalism on the court and a perception within the state that the court's distinctive character and its national stature within the legal

19. See Daniel J. Elazar, *American Federalism: A View from the States,* 3d ed. (New York: Harper & Row, 1984), pp. 14–23 and tables 1.2 and 1.3.
20. Elazar, *American Federalism,* chap. 5.
21. Data on these features are presented in chap. 2, table 2.

community justified its autonomy from the ordinary politics of the
state. *Winberry* v. *Salisbury* provided the crucial early test of the court's
ability to maintain its autonomy from political interference and
thereby pursue its chosen legal course.[22] The court's victory in
Winberry both confirmed and enhanced its position as a legal body
separated from political strife. Internally, the court's insulation from
political pressures and its commitment to legal professionalism have
meant the elimination of partisan divisions on the court, the absence
of strong personal antipathies—or at least of their expression in
judicial opinions—and the development of a norm of intracourt
consensualism.[23] Externally, through its leadership in doctrinal development and legal reform, the New Jersey Supreme Court has sought
to enhance its national legal reputation. The court's legal stature has
served to increase its distance from political forces in the state and to
justify its insulation from them. It has also helped to convince other
elements of the political system that although the court's rulings have
had major policy consequences, they did not justify compromising the
court's independence. This national reputation and insulation from
partisan politics in turn have made service on the court more
attractive and have facilitated the recruitment of highly qualified
jurists to the court.

In contrast, the Ohio Supreme Court—like other political institutions in the state—has responded to clientele concerns throughout the
postwar period. The political parties' domination of recruitment has
resulted in elevation to the bench of partisans whose perspectives and
rulings complemented those of their fellow partisans in the other
branches of state government. In routine cases the justices have
generally pursued a moderate-to-conservative course, following pre-

22. 74 A.2d 406, cert. denied 340 U.S.877 (N.J. 1950).
23. Discussions with members of the New Jersey Supreme Court, the court's
unanimous opinions in controversial cases, and the general tenor of opinions when
the justices have not agreed all support this assessment. The court's relatively low
dissent rate is all the more remarkable in light of its history of relatively high dissent
prior to 1947 and the presence of various factors (e.g., high urbanization, the
existence of an intermediate court of appeals) usually associated with high dissent.
On the New Jersey Supreme Court's dissent rates over time, see Glick and Vines,
State Court Systems, p. 79, table 5-2. On the factors contributing to dissent on state
supreme courts, see Bradley C. Canon and Dean Jaros, "External Variables,
Institutional Structure, and Dissent on State Supreme Courts," *Polity* 4 (1970):
185–200.

cedent, and although rarely leading, usually eventually following the path pioneered by more adventuresome courts. However, when issues with partisan implications have arisen, legal-cultural norms have not been sufficient to prevent efforts to secure political advantage, and thus throughout the postwar era, the Ohio Supreme Court has remained an arena for the continuation of partisan politics. During the court's Republican era, for example, the justices were reluctant to abandon tort law doctrines that protected business and adopted restrictive positions in workers' compensation cases. With the accession of a Democratic majority, the court's rulings changed dramatically. Eschewing *stare decisis,* the justices proclaimed their agenda as protecting "the little guy and gal" and swiftly proceeded to modify or abandon many of the tort law and workers' compensation rulings of their predecessors. This, in turn, escalated partisan conflict on a court on which the justices had frequently divided. Put simply, political cultural norms that endorsed the use of political power for group advantage have guided the behavior of justices once they were elevated to the court.

The contrast between the old and new courts in Alabama is likewise instructive. The old court saw itself in political terms as an element in the state governmental phalanx seeking to protect the state's system of racial subordination against outside interference. Thus, when called upon by state officials, it compliantly armed them with rulings that legitimated their illegal actions. On its own it sought to maintain the system of racial subordination by consistently ruling against black litigants and civil rights organizations. Having decided to favor state interests over legal requirements in this realm, it carried that disdain for the national legal community and its norms over into other areas. This can be seen in the court's cavalier attitude toward disposing of its work, its obsequious refusal to seek adequate procedural rules modeled on the federal rules, and its inattention to precedent and legal developments beyond its borders.

The creation of the new court in Alabama, on the other hand, was an attempt to restore the legal respectability of the Alabama Supreme Court. By the mid-1960s, when Howell Heflin began his efforts to reform the state's court system, the battle for segregation had largely been lost, and the Alabama court's posture was at best obsolescent, at worst an embarrassment before the national legal community. When an avowed segregationist decided to run for chief justice, promising no more than a continuation of the court's failed efforts, Heflin opposed him under the banner of legal professionalism. Once elected, he successfully utilized his position to lead efforts to bring the state's court structure into conformity with the accepted standards of the legal profession. His success as a legal reformer in the face of political opposition was both a declaration of independence for the Alabama Supreme Court and a crucial first step in improving the court's tarnished national reputation. In his position as chief justice, Heflin likewise sought to bring the court's rulings back to the legal mainstream and legal respectability, a process aided by the recruitment of new justices similarly committed to legal professionalism and amenable to national decisional trends. This is not to say that the Alabama court, like its New Jersey counterpart, became a pioneering court. Rather, it became transformed into what might be called a mainstream court. Thus in tort law it moved to adopt reforms and follow doctrinal leads that were well established in other states. It also sought to give consideration, again like many other courts, to state constitutional claims. If it did not seek to make waves, nonetheless it sought—and succeeded—in developing a record that would earn the respect of the national legal community. Thus Heflin's achievement, like Vanderbilt's, was the replacement of political norms with legal norms as the guiding standards for the state's highest court.

Nonetheless, as the Alabama and New Jersey courts illustrate, adherence to legal cultural norms does not necessarily produce similar courts. The differences between the two courts in turn point to the opportunities for states to develop distinctive institutional identities even within the confines of legal cultural norms. Indeed, the ongoing debates within the legal community on judicial activism, doctrinal innovation, *stare decisis,* and the appropriate level of deference to political authorities testify to the range of permissible behavior within the American legal culture.[24] Moreover, legal cultural norms are not unchanging. The decisions and opinions of activist courts, such as the New Jersey Supreme Court and the United States Supreme Court, have served to redefine somewhat the range of permissible behavior, and as other courts have followed their lead, mainstream courts such as Alabama's have followed suit. Thus some courts have helped to

24. The literature here is enormous. For excerpts from many of the classic discussions of these issues, see William Lockhart, Yale Kamisar, and Jesse Choper, *The American Constitution,* 5th ed. (St. Paul: West, 1981). A collection of recent articles is Stephen Halpern and Charles Lamb, eds., *Supreme Court Activism and Restraint* (Lexington, Mass.: Lexington Books, 1982).

redefine national legal cultural norms in the course of defining their own state legal cultures.

Our analysis has examined uniformity and variation among state supreme courts in terms of the opportunities they have for divergence, as reflected in differences in the range of issues coming before them, and the uses that they have made of those opportunities. Our main conclusion is that state supreme courts have considerable discretion in developing their institutional identities. Because state supreme courts have common responsibilities for the development of state law and the application of federal constitutional law, the range of cases they confront is quite similar. Moreover, the same specific issues recur in state after state, as litigants draw upon the successful arguments of attorneys in other states and upon the pioneering rulings of more adventuresome courts. To the extent that there are differences in the claims presented to state supreme courts and in the sequence in which courts confront them, these differences reflect the willingness of private or public counsel to advance the claims. This willingness depends in large measure upon perceptions of how receptive the court will be to such claims. Instead of being merely passive, state supreme courts, through their response to the opportunities presented them, affect what opportunities they will have.

This directs attention to how political culture and legal culture affect state supreme courts. As we have noted, some variation among state supreme courts reflects differences in the states' political and legal cultures. Equally important, however, have been judicial decisions to conform to political or legal norms. States such as New Jersey and Ohio, which have similar political cultures, may have very different courts. Even within a single state like Alabama, a decision to adhere to legal rather than political norms can transform a state supreme court. Thus, although both political culture and legal culture can influence a court's institutional identity, to a considerable extent state high courts actively shape their institutional identities by determining how they will respond to these factors.

This becomes even clearer when one focuses on those courts that draw direction from their state's legal culture. Although state legal cultures are all subspecies of the national legal culture, important interstate variations may occur when national norms are either vague or controversial. Yet the institutions that play the leading role in developing state variants within the interstices of the national legal culture are state supreme courts. Thus state supreme courts participate in devising the very norms that will govern their behavior.

Continuity and Change

Change on state supreme courts has had a dual aspect. The evolution of American law and society has affected, directly and indirectly, the development of state supreme courts throughout the nation. Although the pace and extent of change may have varied somewhat from court to court, the process of change has been gradual and its overall direction uniform. Yet not all change on state supreme courts has had this gradual and uniform character. Despite the force of institutional conservatism and legal factors such as judicial role conceptions and *stare decisis,* various state supreme courts—among them the Alabama, Ohio, and New Jersey supreme courts—have undergone dramatic transformations within relatively short periods. These latter realignments, each distinctive in its own way, underline the importance of intrastate factors, both alone and in conjunction with national developments, in promoting change on state supreme courts and influencing its direction.[25] In this section we explore the sources and character of the changes that have occurred on the Alabama, Ohio, and New Jersey supreme courts.

THE NATIONAL LEGAL CONTEXT AND ITS INFLUENCE

Significant changes have occurred over time in the sorts of cases appealed to state supreme courts and in the justices' approach to those cases.[26] One survey of the dockets of selected state supreme courts, for example, has revealed that in the hundred years from 1870 to 1970 the business of state high courts gradually shifted from commercial to noncommercial cases, from disputes involving contracts and property law to issues in torts and criminal law.[27] Various legal scholars have also concluded that in addressing those issues, state supreme court justices, like other judges, have been affected by the changes in the styles of judicial decision making that had gained favor nationally.[28]

25. The term *realignment* has been used to suggest the similarity to the notion of *realigning elections* drawn from the literature on presidential elections. In each instance, what is suggested is a sharp discontinuity following a period of *stasis* or gradual change. For discussion of the concept, see Walter Dean Burnham, *Critical Elections and the Mainsprings of American Politics* (New York: Norton, 1970).

26. This section draws heavily on the framework and background provided by Kagan et al., "Evolution of State Supreme Courts," and Kagan et al., "Business of State Supreme Courts," esp. pp. 152–56.

27. Kagan et al., "Business of State Supreme Courts."

28. See Karl Llewellyn, *The Common Law Tradition* (Boston: Little, Brown, 1960); Grant Gilmore, *The Ages of American Law* (New Haven: Yale University

Research has also shown that the outcomes in cases before state supreme courts have also shifted somewhat, as the justices have come to view their roles less conservatively: "They seem to be less concerned with the stabilization and protection of property rights, more concerned with the individual and the downtrodden, and more willing to consider rulings that promote social change."[29]

Various national developments—social, legal, and political—help to account for these changes. To some extent the evolution in the business of state supreme courts has mirrored changes in the broader society—as social and economic conditions have changed, so too have the sorts of disputes that have arisen and thus the range of cases coming before state supreme courts. To take an obvious example, the invention and widespread use of the automobile have spawned a mass of litigation and have had a major impact on the dockets of state supreme courts. It is something more than coincidence that the New Jersey Supreme Court's rejection of the doctrine of privity occurred in the context of a dispute over an automobile accident. Similarly, the changing relations between men and women in America have raised new legal issues and fueled demands that courts rethink established principles in the light of new conditions and attitudes. And as we have seen, the Alabama, Ohio, and New Jersey supreme courts—like their counterparts in other states—have all been involved in this endeavor. From 1965 to 1974 these three courts all overruled established precedent to recognize a wife's right to recover for negligent loss of consortium.[30] During the 1980s both the New Jersey and Ohio courts considered, albeit with different results, the "battered-woman defense" in homicide cases.[31] And all three courts have had to consider whether to continue to employ the "tender years doctrine" in the light of changing views on child custody.[32]

Changes in substantive legal doctrine have also promoted changes

---

Press, 1977); and Roscoe Pound, *The Formative Era of American Law* (New York: Peter Smith, 1950).

29. Kagan et al., "Business of State Supreme Courts," p. 155.

30. Alabama: *Swartz* v. *United States Steel Corporation,* 304 So.2d 881 (Ala. 1974); Ohio: *Leffler* v. *Wiley,* 239 N.E.2d 2235 (Ohio 1968), and *Clouston* v. *Remlinger Oldsmobile-Cadillac, Inc.,* 258 N.E.2d 230 (Ohio 1970); and New Jersey: *Ekalo* v. *Constructive Services Corporation,* 215 A.2d 1 (N.J. 1965).

31. New Jersey: *State* v. *Kelly,* 478 A.2d 364 (N.J. 1984); Ohio: *State* v. *Thomas,* 423 N.E.2d 137 (Ohio 1981).

32. See the discussion in G. Alan Tarr and Mary Cornelia Porter, "Gender Equality and Judicial Federalism: The Role of State Appellate Courts," *Hastings Constitutional Law Quarterly* 9 (1982): 942–50, 963–69, table E.

in the business of state supreme courts. The United States Supreme Court, through its authoritative interpretation of federal law, has played a decisive role here. Most obviously, the Court's rulings during the 1960s expanding the rights of defendants in state criminal prosecutions—particularly its extension of the exclusionary rule to the states and its requirement of counsel for indigent defendants—promoted challenges to rights violations. Like other states, Alabama, Ohio, and New Jersey experienced a rapid increase in criminal appeals to their high courts. In addition, doctrinal innovations at the state level have also had a major impact on the business of state supreme courts. Among the most important rulings have been those transforming the notions of fault and injury in tort law and, by removing immunities and other barriers to suit, creating new causes of action at common law. Clearly the New Jersey Supreme Court has played an active part here, whereas the Alabama and Ohio courts have more frequently been in the position of responding to initiatives from beyond their borders.

State supreme courts' approach to legal issues has also changed over time, largely in response to national shifts in patterns of legal thought and changes in legal culture. One such shift occurred in response to the criticisms of the Legal Realists.[33] By demonstrating that judicial decision making is not and cannot be merely deductive, the Realists directed attention to the policy considerations underlying judicial rulings. Their critique increased courts' self-consciousness about judicial involvement in policy making and prompted more forthright consideration of the policy implications of judicial decisions. Commentators have characterized the shift in various ways: Karl Llewellyn, for example, has spoken of a movement from the Formal Style, which developed in the late 1800s, back to the Grand Style, and Grant Gilmore of a movement from the Age of Faith to an Age of Anxiety prompted by the collapse of Langdellian jurisprudence.[34] However, whatever the formulation, these commentaries share the notion that courts have developed an approach to decision making that is less deductive and more instrumentalist. The New Jersey Supreme Court has been unusually forthright in recognizing

33. For a summary of the views and influence of the Legal Realists, see Wilfrid E. Rumble, Jr., *American Legal Realism: Skepticism, Reform, and the Judicial Process* (Ithaca: Cornell University Press, 1968).

34. Llewellyn, *Common Law Tradition*, pp. 35–45, and Gilmore, *Ages of American Law*, pp. 68–69, and—generally—chap. 2–4.

and eager in embracing its policy-making role, as shown by its common law jurisprudence in general and its approach to the reform of tort law in particular.[35] However, this shift in approach also characterizes the rulings of the Alabama and Ohio supreme courts.[36] For example, both courts have critically examined whether charitable immunity and governmental immunity in fact serve the purposes for which they were established and have rejected the denial to wives of recovery for negligent invasion of consortium because it was inconsistent with contemporary notions of gender equality.[37]

A second shift has resulted from the activist rulings of the United States Supreme Court expanding and safeguarding individual rights. Whatever state courts' opinion about the defensibility of particular rulings, the Court's overall approach has served as a model for state courts in interpreting federal constitutional guarantees and in resuscitating their state bills of rights. Thus the New Jersey Supreme Court's privacy rulings reflect approaches pioneered by the federal courts. Even less adventuresome courts, like the Alabama and Ohio courts have, in elaborating state or federal constitutional guarantees, typically relied on the Supreme Court for inspiration and for constitutional doctrine.[38] As a result, the Supreme Court's approach to considering rights claims has been incorporated into the jurisprudence of state supreme courts.

JUDICIAL REFORM

The nationwide movement for judicial reform made significant inroads in Alabama, New Jersey, and Ohio, as in most other states, during the postwar period, and their judicial systems underwent important reforms. In Alabama and New Jersey, the triumph of the judicial reformers precipitated a fundamental transformation in the institutional identities of the states' supreme courts. The ratification of

35. Among the New Jersey Supreme Court's clearest expressions of this are the rulings and opinions in *Henningsen* v. *Bloomfield Motors,* 161 A.2d 69 (N.J. 1960); *Immer* v. *Risko,* 267 A.2d 481 (N.J. 1970); *State* v. *Shack,* 277 A.2d 369 (N.J. 1971); and *Borough of Neptune City* v. *Borough of Avon-by-the-Sea,* 294 A.2d 47 (N.J. 1972).

36. See Llewellyn, *The Common Law Tradition,* pp. 148–53, 162–67, 484–89.

37. See cases and discussions in chapters 3, 4, and 5.

38. For examples from the Alabama Supreme Court, see *Peddy* v. *Montgomery,* 345 So.2d 631 (Ala. 1977); *Pierce* v. *State,* 296 So.2d 218 (Ala. 1974); and *McKinney* v. *State,* 296 So.2d 228 (Ala. 1974). For examples from the Ohio Supreme Court, see *State* v. *Madison,* 415 N.E.2d 272 (Ohio 1980); and *Zacchini* v. *Scripps-Howard Broadcasting Co.,* 351 N.E.2d 454 (Ohio 1976), rev'd. 433 U.S. 562 (1977), on remand, 376 N.E.2d 582 (Ohio 1978).

the Modern Courts Amendment apparently had no such effect in Ohio.[39] Analysis of the contrasting experiences of these states thus suggests how and why judicial reform may serve as a catalyst for broader change.

Important similarities mark judicial reform in Alabama and New Jersey. In both states the initiative and impetus for reform came from attorneys who, although clearly major legal figures, did not hold judicial positions: Howell Heflin was at the outset a plaintiffs' attorney with prior service as president of the state bar association; Arthur Vanderbilt was a law school dean and former president of the American Bar Association. In both states the reformers initially confronted indifference and/or opposition from the state bench and from powerful political leaders, which led them to circumvent the legal establishment and involve the broader public in reform efforts—Vanderbilt through his reports and speeches, Heflin through the citizens' group he organized. In both states too, leadership in the reform cause provided an avenue to the chief justiceship, so that the reform leaders were able to offer direction to the high court in the immediate aftermath of reform. Heflin's election apparently signaled a public endorsement of a professionalized judiciary (as well as a repudiation of the state's segregationist past), and he was therefore able to use his position as chief justice to complete the task of reforming the Alabama judiciary. For Vanderbilt, appointment as chief justice climaxed a successful campaign for judicial reform, secured with the adoption of the constitution of 1947. Finally, in both states the appointment of the reformers as chief justices was accompanied by other significant changes in the composition of the state supreme courts: from 1971 to 1977, the years of Heflin's tenure, six new justices were added to the court, and in New Jersey ratification of the constitution of 1947 led to the reconstitution of the old supreme court, with two new justices appointed thereafter during Vanderbilt's tenure.

The reform experience in Ohio lacked the political drama and broad public involvement found in Alabama and New Jersey. Although judicial reform had long been urged by "good government" groups, it was not until the 1960s that the state bar association, by publicizing caseload pressures on the courts, was able to secure passage of a reform package. The Modern Courts Amendment streamlined the

---

39. See chapter 4 above.

state's judicial system, extended the supreme court's supervision over lower courts, and rescinded the "all-but-one" rule for invalidating enactments on constitutional grounds. As implemented by Chief Justice William O'Neill, reform served largely to centralize administrative control over the Ohio courts in the hands of the chief justice.[40] However, it did not restrict the political parties' involvement in judicial selection, nor did it work any drastic changes in the jurisdiction, workload, or composition of the state supreme court. Thus whatever its contribution to judicial administration, judicial reform in Ohio neither introduced nor promoted significant change on the Ohio Supreme Court.

Whereas judicial reform in Ohio reflected the success of an elite interest group promoting changes that would benefit its members, the politics of reform in Alabama and New Jersey was very different. Howell Heflin and Arthur Vanderbilt personified judicial reform in their respective states. It might thus be tempting to endorse the "great man" view of history and attribute the success of the reform efforts in these states to the personal qualities displayed by their leaders. And, in fact, there is much truth to this view. In addition, however, a variety of factors outside the control of the reform leadership were also crucial to reform efforts. Clearly, the institution of judicial reform in a large number of states since 1950 reflects not the simultaneous emergence of a set of strong leaders but the developing strength of a nationwide consensus for reform. Complementing this national receptivity to reform were developments within individual states that either promoted reform or removed obstacles to its success. In Alabama, for instance, Howell Heflin benefited from the decline of race as a polarizing issue and the emergence of concern about the state's national reputation, both of which permitted a critical examination of the state's court system. Had he championed judicial reform a decade earlier, it is safe to say that he would have failed. Similarly in New Jersey, concern about the state's outmoded judicial system, which Vanderbilt himself helped to stimulate by documenting its inefficiencies and injustices, made the public receptive to judicial reform. Nonetheless, Vanderbilt succeeded only when his desired reforms were tied to the campaign for a new constitution and for a more general reform of state government.

40. See Arlene Sheskin and Charles W. Grau, "Judicial Responses to Technocratic Reform," in James A. Cramer, ed., *Courts and Judges*, vol. 15 (Beverly Hills: Sage Criminal Justice System Annuals, 1981).

Yet if the national movement for judicial reform succeeded in Alabama, Ohio, and New Jersey, the source and character of reform leadership in the states was crucial to the pace, form, and consequences of judicial reform. In Ohio, the leadership for reform came from elements of the legal establishment who viewed their task as largely ameliorative. As a result, the aims and effects of reform were limited. Judicial reform was seen not as a reflection of a general dissatisfaction with the state's judicial system nor as an occasion for remaking the institutional identity of its high court, but rather as a means to introduce administrative rationality to the courts and facilitate their operation. Indicative of this narrow focus and of the source of reform leadership was the emphasis in Ohio on centralizing managerial responsibility in the state's supreme court. By contrast, in Alabama and New Jersey the movement for reform was led by "outsiders," who championed administrative and structural reform as part of a broader effort to give a new direction to the state's courts. The identification of Heflin and Vanderbilt with efforts for reform increased their prominence and stature in the state and helped them attain the chief justiceship. On the state supreme court, they were able to use their position to ensure the successful implementation of reform and to lead the court in new directions. Their example and their success affected judicial recruitment, encouraging lawyers who were committed to the reform objectives to seek elevation to the high court, thereby securing what Heflin and Vanderbilt had begun. Thus, although the movement for judicial reform enjoyed considerable success nationwide, its effects on state supreme courts varied, depending on the character and objectives of the reform leadership.

COURT COMPOSITION

It is a truism of politics that what government does largely depends on who governs. Underlying this statement is a theory about political change: changes in those who hold office are what produce changes in governmental outputs. As the history of the American presidency shows, when a single officeholder wields governmental power, change in the occupant of the office can have dramatic effects. However, when power is exercised by a large multimember institution, such as a legislature, changes in the body's composition—and thus in governmental policy and practice—are likely to be more gradual. Courts fall somewhere in between executives and legislatures. On the one hand, they are multimember institutions, on which tenure tends to be long and turnover staggered. Indeed, almost all state supreme courts have experienced extended periods in which their membership has remained static. On the other hand, periods of virtually no turnover can be followed by rapid and sizable shifts in judicial personnel as retirements and deaths produce a series of vacancies on a court. Moreover, because court membership is so small, simultaneous replacement of a relatively few justices—or even, in some instances, a single justice—can have a significant impact. To what extent, then, can the transformations of the Alabama, Ohio, and New Jersey supreme courts be attributed to changes in court composition?

The recent history of the Ohio Supreme Court illustrates how changes in court composition can produce shifts in institutional outputs. Throughout the postwar era both the Democratic and Republican parties have nominated candidates for the state's high bench, who have then run without party labels in the general election. Whatever the Democrats' success statewide, they had little success in electing their adherents to the Ohio Supreme Court—from 1950 to 1978, only four Democrats were elected to the high bench, and only in 1959–60 did the Democrats (thanks to a gubernatorial appointment) hold a majority on the court. In the late 1970s, however, organized labor in Ohio—stymied elsewhere in the political system and hoping to recoup its sagging fortunes—targeted the supreme court and poured money and other resources into judicial races. With the Republican party apparently caught napping in 1978, the Democrats won the two seats necessary to control the court. The new majority, albeit a narrow one, took little time translating electoral results into rulings favorable to labor and consumers. Once alerted, the Republicans began a sustained counterattack, ousting James Celebrezze from the court in 1984 and taking aim at restoring a Republican majority in the elections of 1986.

The passing of the Weintraub Court in New Jersey during the early 1970s stands in sharp contrast to the Ohio experience. From 1971 to 1974 six new justices were appointed to the New Jersey Supreme Court. Despite this turnover, the court continued much as before. The Hughes Court endorsed and extended the innovative approach to tort law pioneered by Chief Justice Weintraub. The Weintraub Court's record of intervention in sensitive policy areas, such as reapportionment and school finance, was matched by the Hughes Court, which carried the school finance initiative to eventual resolution and attacked exclusionary zoning. Only in the area of criminal law and defendants' rights can one find significant discontinuity, and even here the Weintraub and Hughes courts were united in their determination to follow an independent course rather than merely defer to the United States Supreme Court. The New Jersey experience demonstrates that a rapid turnover in court membership is not a sufficient condition for fundamental jurisprudential shifts or changes in institutional identity.

The changes in institutional identity in Alabama and New Jersey point to a more complex relationship between shifts in court composition and judicial outputs. When Arthur Vanderbilt became chief justice of the New Jersey Supreme Court, his colleagues on the court had all served as judges under the old constitution. When vacancies occurred on the court, justices were appointed who were his allies in the struggle for reform and shared his perspective. Eventually the new justices would undertake the pioneering rulings in tort law and other areas that have solidified the court's reputation for progressivism and activism. Yet even prior to these rulings, Vanderbilt had by his reforms and his leadership already reoriented the court and established its national reputation. And by giving it new stature and direction, he had already made service on the New Jersey court more attractive, ensuring that qualified jurists would be eager to serve on it. Thus Vanderbilt's accession to the court and his example were decisive, and subsequent changes in the overall composition of the court, although important, were more a consequence than a cause of the change in the court's institutional identity.

A similar pattern emerged in Alabama. The election of Howell Heflin as chief justice and his leadership of judicial reform marked a watershed for the Alabama Supreme Court. Certainly Heflin's reorientation of the court was aided by the retirement of several sitting justices, some of whom might not have jumped had they not been pushed. Yet the quality and character of the candidates who replaced them testifies to the influence on judicial recruitment of Heflin's example and of his vision for the court. By the time Heflin left the Alabama Supreme Court, to be succeeded by an early ally in the fight for reform, he had supplied the direction and impetus for change, and it remained to the new justices largely to work out the implications of what Heflin had begun. Thus the relatively rapid shift in the overall composition of the Alabama Supreme Court reflected and secured, rather than caused, the change in the court's institutional identity.

In sum, our analysis suggests that multiple personnel changes on a court are neither necessary nor sufficient to produce changes in institutional identity or judicial outputs. Whereas in Ohio such personnel changes were crucial, the reconstitution of the New Jersey Supreme Court in the early 1970s had little impact, and the transformation of the institutional identities of the Alabama and New Jersey courts preceded such shifts. The context, both intrastate and intracourt, within which the judicial turnover takes place seems decisive in determining its effects. However, if one focused on the chief justiceship rather than on more general shifts in personnel, then one could conclude that changes in court composition were decisive in all three states. Indeed, even in Ohio, where electoral success brought a Democratic majority to the court, the accession of Frank Celebrezze to the chief justiceship had important implications for what the new majority would accomplish. Thus the change in a single justice on the state supreme court, particularly when it involves the elevation of a forceful chief justice with a clear agenda, can transform a court.

The supreme courts in Alabama, Ohio, and New Jersey not only evolved gradually in response to national legal influences but underwent their own distinctive changes in the postwar era. No single factor can account for the extraordinary changes we have found. In Alabama, what was decisive was the conjunction of a well-mounted reform effort and a change in the overall climate of Alabama politics. In Ohio, the decisive factor was political in a narrow sense: Ohio politics changed not at all, but a different political party gained control of the state supreme court. Given the absence of (or limited effectiveness of) legal restraints, the new justices—like their predecessors— used judicial rulings as an extension of partisan conflict, or at least as a way of rewarding clientele groups. In New Jersey, what was decisive was a fundamental shift in legal culture, initiated by Chief Justice Vanderbilt and solidified under Chief Justice Weintraub, that has given the state an appellate judiciary insulated from narrow partisan politics but emboldened to make an important and distinctive contribution to the political life of the state.

Despite the diversity of factors that contributed to change, the important point is that in each state groups or individuals succeeded in transforming the court's institutional identity or reorienting its decisions. In contrast to the common perception of courts as slowly evolving bodies, we found that as institutions supreme courts were not only capable of rapid and fundamental changes but in fact seemed ripe for the plucking. A variety of factors—among them the courts' limited membership, low visibility, and independence from direct constituency or partisan pressures in decision making—might account for this. Whatever the causes, the fact that these radical transformations occurred on three very different courts suggests that other state supreme courts are likewise susceptible to similar major shifts.

State Supreme Courts in a National Perspective

Thus far our conclusions have been based primarily on evidence from the Alabama, Ohio, and New Jersey supreme courts, and our generalizations have in large part been limited to those courts. However, in speaking of national factors that promote change or in noting the general susceptibility of state supreme courts to efforts to transform them, we necessarily raise the twin questions of representativeness and generalizability. To what extent are the experiences of the three state supreme courts we have studied representative of the experiences of other state supreme courts? To what extent can we generalize from the Alabama, Ohio, and New Jersey supreme courts to state high courts nationwide?

The diversity we uncovered in our three case studies cautions against a precipitous rush to broad pronouncements. If these courts have shown such variation in institutional identity and jurisprudence, there is reason to believe that equally significant differences will be found among the supreme courts of other states. This underlines our repeated assertion that there is no such thing as a typical state supreme court. Nevertheless, with this proviso in mind, we can offer some observations about the likely representativeness of the Alabama, Ohio, and New Jersey courts.

ALABAMA

The old court in Alabama seems to have been in many respects representative of southern supreme courts prior to 1970. The membership of southern high courts was typically drawn from reactionary elements of the white elite.[41] When racial equality emerged as an

41. See Bradley C. Canon, "Characteristics and Career Patterns of State Supreme Court Justices," *State Government* 45 (1972): 34–41; Bradley C. Canon, "The Impact of Formal Selection Processes on the Characteristics of Judges—Reconsidered," *Law & Society Review* 6 (1972): 579–93; and Kenneth N. Vines, "The Selection of Judges in Louisiana," in Kenneth N. Vines and Herbert Jacob, eds., *Studies in Judicial Politics*, vol. 8 of Tulane Studies in Political Science (New Orleans, 1962).

issue, the justices supported state efforts to maintain segregation, and throughout the South black litigants fared badly when they came before the state high courts.[42] Even when race was not an issue, southern justices tended to line up behind the largely conservative political forces prevailing in the state.[43] And as a rule, southern supreme courts lagged behind those in other regions in responding to national developments in tort law and constitutional law.[44]

In Alabama the impetus for judicial reform and for a change in the supreme court's institutional identity came from a desire to restore the court's respectability in the eyes of the national legal community. The enfranchisement of black voters and other regional political developments that effectively ended resistance to the struggle for racial equality created an environment conducive to such an endeavor not only in Alabama but throughout the South. There is some evidence that other southern high courts have followed a course similar to Alabama's. First of all, several southern states have—like Alabama—undertaken to bring their judicial systems in line with nationally accepted standards regarding the organization and operation of courts. During the 1970s six southern states adopted major structural and administrative reforms designed to create more unified judicial systems.[45] During the same period six also for the first time established state court administrative offices to promote a more efficient administration of justice.[46] Several southern states also joined the national

42. Kenneth N. Vines, "Southern State Supreme Courts and Race Relations," *Western Political Quarterly* 18 (1965): 5–18.

43. For a case study that dramatizes this, see Kenneth N. Vines, "Political Functions of a State Supreme Court," in Vines and Jacob, *Studies in Judicial Politics*.

44. On tort law, see Bradley C. Canon and Lawrence Baum, "Patterns of Adoption of Tort Law Innovations: An Application of Diffusion Theory to Judicial Doctrines," *American Political Science Review* 75 (1981): table 3, p. 979, and pp. 983–85. On constitutional law, see inter alia Bradley C. Canon, "Reactions of State Supreme Courts to a U.S. Supreme Court Civil Liberties Decision," *Law & Society Review* 6 (1972): 109–34: and Vines, "Southern State Supreme Courts."

45. See Larry Berkson and Susan Carbon, *Court Unification: History, Politics, and Implementation* (Washington, D.C.: National Institute of Law Enforcement and Criminal Justice, 1978), p. 46, table 3–1. The states are Alabama, Florida, Georgia, Louisiana, South Carolina, and Virginia. During the 1980s Mississippi has also taken steps to unify its judicial system.

46. *Book of the States, 1984–85* (Lexington, Ky.: Council of State Governments, 1985), p. 163, table 7. The states are Alabama, Florida, Georgia, Mississippi, South Carolina, and Texas.

movement toward adoption of new court rules modeled on the Federal Rules of Civil Procedure.[47]

Whether changes have occurred, as in Alabama, in the sorts of persons elevated to southern high courts is more difficult to determine. Demographic changes provide the most obvious indicator of such changes, and, as in Alabama, blacks and women have begun to be named to southern high courts.[48] The substantive rulings of other southern supreme courts have also paralleled Alabama's. No southern state has continued the pattern of defiance of federal courts. In addition, southern supreme courts have moved to adopt various reforms in tort law, although some southern courts were prominent in the reform movement even prior to 1970, and the steps taken represent judicial catch-up rather than innovation.[49] This suggests that other southern supreme courts have, like Alabama's, sought primarily to enter the legal mainstream rather than to assume a leadership role in national legal development. While hardly conclusive, the fact that no southern supreme court has been in the forefront of the movement to resuscitate state bills of rights tends to bear this out.[50]

47. For an analysis of the new rules in one southern state, see Walter Cox and David Newbern, "New Civil Procedure: The Court That Came in from the Code," *Arkansas Law Review* 33 (1979): 1–90. More generally, see Robert J. Sheran and Barbara Issacson, "State Cases Belong in State Courts," *Creighton Law Review* 12 (1978): 49–50, and works cited therein.

48. Women have served on southern supreme courts since 1970 in Alabama, Arkansas, Mississippi, and North Carolina. In 1984 blacks were serving on the supreme courts in Alabama, Arkansas, Florida, and North Carolina.

49. Canon and Baum, "Patterns of Adoption." According to their computations, the Louisiana Supreme Court ranked second nationally in the postwar period in tort law innovation.

50. This is confirmed by an analysis of the findings of early articles describing the new judicial federalism. In a series of articles on the new judicial federalism and defendants' rights, Donald Wilkes found the courts in seven states offered greater protection than the federal courts, but none of those courts was a southern supreme court. See Donald Wilkes, "The New Federalism in Criminal Procedure: State Court Evasion of the Burger Court," *Kentucky Law Journal* 62 (1974): 421–51; Wilkes, "More on the New Federalism in Criminal Procedure," *Kentucky Law Journal* 63 (1975): 873–94; and Wilkes, "The New Federalism in Criminal Procedure Revisited," *Kentucky Law Journal* 64 (1976): 729–52. A. E. Dick Howard discovered that five courts offered greater protection in the area of religion, three in the area of education, and six in the area of personal autonomy, but none of these were southern supreme courts. See "State Courts and Constitutional Rights in the Day of the Burger Court," *Virginia Law Review* 62 (1976): 874–944.

Some commentators have suggested that this situation is now changing. See, for example, "Tennessee Judicial Activism: Renaissance of Federalism," *Tennessee Law*

Finally, the fact that the Alabama Supreme Court's search for legal respectability has led it to adopt national legal standards as its own deserves repeated emphasis. One may well speculate that in aligning itself with those standards, it is representative of a wider range of courts nationally than either the Ohio or New Jersey courts. Although firm conclusions on this matter must await further research, this possibility—given the deviant character of the old court—underlines the potential for substantial change in the institutional identity of a state supreme court over time.

OHIO

The Ohio Supreme Court has not aspired to a pioneering role in legal development or seized opportunities for leadership when they presented themselves. On the other hand, neither has it attempted to maintain idiosyncratic legal positions in the face of national legal trends. Rather, the court has been content to remain in what might be termed the legal mainstream, eventually adopting doctrinal developments and innovations as they gained acceptance nationwide. Yet this has not prevented intense intracourt conflict over the pace of legal change. The Ohio justices have frequently divided, particularly when confronting issues of economic liberalism or conservatism. In doing so, they have mirrored the divisions between the Republican and Democratic parties in the state, which have been tied, respectively, to business and labor interests. Thus in marked contrast to their counterparts in New Jersey, the Ohio justices have not sought to insulate themselves from the prevailing political conflicts in the state but rather have continued them on the court. Consequently, the creation of a Democratic majority on the court after a long period of Republican ascendancy had a pronounced effect on the court's rulings.

Partisan conflict on a supreme court is certainly not unique to Ohio. Several studies have documented connections between state justices'

Review 49 (1981): 135–59. And a few southern courts have occasionally relied on their state bills of rights—see, for example, *State* v. *Hernandez,* 410 So.2d 1381 (La. 1982); and *State* v. *Hudson,* 185 So.2d 189 (N.C. 1976). However, with the exception of the Florida Supreme Court's rulings on search and seizure, discussed below, surveys of state court rulings and affording greater protection of individual rights than are available under federal rulings did not reveal a great upsurge of activity among southern supreme courts. See "Developments in the Law—The Interpretation of State Constitutional Rights," *Harvard Law Review* 95 (1982): 1324–1502; and Ronald K. L. Collins, "Rebirth of Reliance on State Charters," *National Law Journal,* March 12, 1984, pp. 25–32.

partisan affiliations and their voting behavior.[51] Moreover, studies of the Michigan Supreme Court during the 1950s reveal a pattern of events that closely parallels what transpired in Ohio.[52] Throughout the decade, the Michigan court divided along partisan lines, particularly on economic issues pitting business against labor. Thus the Michigan justices—like the Ohio justices—replicated the divisions between the Republican and Democratic parties in the state. In the late 1950s, the election of new justices gave the Democrats control over the Michigan Supreme Court, and, as in Ohio, the shift in the balance of partisan forces prompted immediate and substantial changes in the court's rulings.

Yet if the Ohio Supreme Court is not unique in reflecting the partisan cleavages in the state, neither is it characteristic of state supreme courts generally. Indeed, the available evidence, although fragmentary, seems to suggest that most state high courts do not resemble the Ohio and Michigan supreme courts. For one thing, intracourt conflict along party lines depends on the presence of a competitive party system that elevates adherents of both parties to the bench. This eliminates those states whose internal politics and state

51. Studies that have addressed the influence of party affiliation on judicial behavior include Philip L. DuBois, *From Ballot to Bench* (Austin: University of Texas Press, 1980); Glendon Schubert, *Quantitative Analysis of Judicial Behavior* (New York: Free Press, 1959); David Adamany, "The Party Variable in Judges' Voting: Conceptual Notes and a Case Study," *American Political Science Review* 63 (1969): 57–73; Edward N. Beiser and Jonathan J. Silberman, "The Political Party Variable: Workmen's Compensation Cases in the New York Court of Appeals," *Polity* 3 (1971): 263–80; Malcolm M. Feeley, "Another Look at the 'Party Variable' in Judicial Decision-Making: An Analysis of the Michigan Supreme Court," *Polity* 4 (1971): 91–104; Stuart S. Nagel, "Political Party Affiliation and Judges' Decisions," *American Political Science Review* 55 (1961): 843–50; and Sidney Ulmer, "The Political Party Variable in the Michigan Supreme Court," *Journal of Public Law* 11 (1962): 352–62.

52. See Schubert, *Quantitative Analysis of Judicial Behavior*, pp. 129–42; Adamany, "The Party Variable in Judges' Voting"; Kathleen L. Barber, "Partisan Values in the Lower Courts: Reapportionment in Ohio and Michigan," *Case Western Reserve Law Review* 20 (1969): 401–16; Feeley, "Another Look at the 'Party Variable' "; Ulmer, "Political Party Variable"; and S. Sidney Ulmer, "Leadership in the Michigan Supreme Court," in Glendon Schubert, ed., *Judicial Decision-Making* (Glencoe, Ill.: Free Press, 1963). For an account of another court which changed dramatically following personnel shifts, see John Patrick Hagan, "Policy Activism in the West Virginia Supreme Court of Appeals," *West Virginia Law Review* 89 (1986): 149–65.

benches are dominated by a single party.[53] In addition, such intracourt conflict depends upon a judicial propensity for division rather than unanimity. Although unanimity may at times mask significant disagreements that are expressed through divergent unanimous decisions, the fact remains that few state supreme courts manifest the level of dissent found in Ohio.[54]

In addition, although partisan competitiveness in a state is associated with the level of dissent on state supreme courts, intracourt conflict need not reflect partisan divisions.[55] This is true even on issues pitting business against labor in states where the political parties are closely tied to those groups. Thus David Adamany found that the Wisconsin Supreme Court did not divide along party lines in workers' compensation cases during the 1960s, and Edward Beiser and Jonathan Silberman's historical analysis of workers' compensation litigation in the New York Court of Appeals revealed that party affiliation rarely accounted for alignments on the court.[56] Contrasting the Wisconsin and Michigan supreme courts, Adamany suggested that "the constituencies of Michigan supreme court justices are highly partisan and those of Wisconsin supreme court justices are bipartisan. This would be an adequate explanation of the sharp differences in the role that party plays in the decisional process of the two states."[57] Although the Ohio justices identify with partisan constituencies, it seems likely—especially given the movement away from direct parti-

---

53. See Francis G. Lee, "Party Representation on State Supreme Courts: 'Unequal Representation' Revisited," *State and Local Government Review* 11 (1979): 48–52. Thus a recent study of the relationship between partisan affiliation and judicial voting behavior began by excluding all the southern states because they were one-party systems. See DuBois, *From Ballot to Bench.*

54. For data on dissent rates on state supreme courts, see Dean Jaros and Bradley C. Canon, "Dissent on State Supreme Courts: The Differential Significance of Characteristics of Judges," *Midwest Journal of Political Science* 15 (1971): 322–46; Canon and Jaros, "External Variables, Institutional Structure, and Dissent on State Supreme Courts"; and John W. Patterson and Gregory J. Rathjen, "Background Diversity and State Supreme Court Dissent Behavior," *Polity* 9 (1976): 610–22.

55. On the relation between party competitiveness and dissent rates on state supreme courts, see Canon and Jaros, "External Variables, Institutional Structure, and Dissent on State Supreme Courts."

56. On dissent on the Wisconsin Supreme Court, see Adamany, "The Party Variable in Judges' Voting." On dissent on the New York Court of Appeals, see Beiser and Silberman, "The Political Party Variable."

57. "The Party Variable in Judges' Voting," p. 69.

san participation in judicial selection—that this is a minority perspective.

Even the state supreme court that most resembles the Ohio Supreme Court has shown a marked difference in jurisprudential outlook. For one thing, the Michigan Supreme Court has indicated a much greater readiness to adopt tort law innovations, ranking seventh on the Canon/Baum index during the postwar period.[58] This might conceivably be explained by the election of a Democratic majority on the Michigan court at a time when the Republicans continued to control the Ohio Supreme Court. Not so easily explained, however, are the differences between the two courts on civil liberties issues. Whereas the Ohio court has not shown a particular sensitivity to civil liberties concerns, even during the period of Democratic ascendancy, the Michigan Supreme Court has actively participated in the development of state civil liberties law.[59] This greater propensity to innovate, to take the lead in legal development, in turn raises further questions about how representative the Ohio Supreme Court really is.

NEW JERSEY

If the Alabama and Ohio supreme courts are characteristic of two sets of courts, the New Jersey Supreme Court seems to exemplify a third—the activist, "lighthouse" courts that have assumed a leadership role in national legal development. Several state supreme courts have developed reputations for innovation and leadership in specific areas of the law: for example, the Oregon and Washington supreme courts in state constitutional law, and the Kentucky and Louisiana supreme courts in tort law.[60] However, in terms of overall influence,

58. Canon and Baum, "Patterns of Adoption," p. 978, table 2.

59. Illustrative cases include *People* v. *Beavers*, 227 N.W.2d 511 (Mich. 1975); *People* v. *Secrest*, 321 N.W.2d 368 (Mich. 1982); *People* v. *Cooper*, 247 N.W.2d 866 (Mich. 1976); *People* v. *Jackson*, 217 N.W.2d 22 (Mich. 1974); and *People* v. *Bloss*, 228 N.W.2d 384 (Mich. 1975).

60. Under the leadership of Justice Hans Linde, the Oregon Supreme Court has adopted the "first things first" approach of addressing issues of state law, including state constitutional law, before looking to federal constitutional provisions. The rulings of the Oregon court, together with Linde's many speeches and publications extolling the new judicial federalism, have encouraged other states either to adopt a similar approach or to give greater attention to their state constitutions. Illustrative cases include *State* v. *Kennedy*, 666 P.2d 1316 (Or. 1983); *Sterling* v. *Cupp*, 625 P.2d 123 (Or. 1981); and *State* v. *Lowry*, 667 P.2d 996 (Or. 1983). Justice Linde's writings include "Without 'Due Process': Unconstitutional Law in Oregon," *Oregon*

national reputation, and innovation, the only court comparable to the New Jersey Supreme Court—and perhaps even paramount to it—is the California Supreme Court.

The similarities between the California and New Jersey supreme courts are readily apparent. The California Supreme Court has viewed itself as a national leader in legal development, and the citation patterns of other supreme courts indicate that its ascendancy is widely recognized. Not only is it the most frequently cited state supreme court, but the citation level exceeds what might be expected on the basis of state population, urbanization, and other standard predictors of citation patterns.[61] Like its New Jersey counterpart, the California Supreme Court has established a record of leadership in tort law reform.[62] For example, under the persistent urging of Justice (later Chief Justice) Roger Traynor, probably the most influential common law jurist of the contemporary era, the California Supreme Court became the first court to impose strict liability in products liability cases and the first to abrogate both sovereign and municipal immu-

---

Law Review 49 (1970): 133–87, and "First Things First: Rediscovering the States' Bills of Rights," *University of Baltimore Law Review* 9 (1980): 379–96.

The Washington Supreme Court has actively sought to develop state constitutional law, and Justice Robert Utter of the Washington court has emerged as a leading exponent of state constitutional jurisprudence. Illustrative cases include *State* v. *Ringer*, 674 P.2d 1240 (Wash. 1983); *State* v. *Chrisman*, 676 P.2d 419 (Wash. 1984); and *Alderwood Associates* v. *Washington Environmental Council*, 635 P.2d 108 (Wash. 1981). An overview of Washington constitutional law is found in "Symposium: The Washington Constitution," *University of Puget Sound Law Review* 7 (1984): vi–484. For a sampling of Justice Utter's views, see his "Freedom and Diversity in a Federal System: Perspectives on State Constitutions and the Washington Declaration of Rights," *University of Puget Sound Law Review* 7 (1984): 491–525; and "Swimming in the Jaws of the Crocodile: State Court Comment on Federal Constitutional Issues When Disposing of Cases on State Constitutional Grounds," *Texas Law Review* 63 (1985): 1025–50.

Louisiana and Kentucky ranked second and third in tort law innovation since 1945. See Canon and Baum, "Patterns of Adoption," p. 978, table 2. Representative rulings include *Williamson* v. *Garland*, 402 S.W.2d 80 (Ky. 1966); *Haney* v. *City of Lexington*, 386 S.W.2d 738 (Ky. 1964); and *Mullikin* v. *Jewish Hospital Association*, 348 S.W.2d 930 (Ky. 1961).

61. Gregory A. Caldeira, "On the Reputation of State Supreme Courts," *Political Behavior* 5 (1983): 89, table 1, and passim; and Gregory A. Caldeira, "The Transmission of Legal Precedent: A Study of State Supreme Courts," *American Political Science Review* 79 (1985): 178–93.

62. According to Canon and Baum, California ranked fourth in tort law innovation since 1945—see "Patterns of Adoption," p. 978, table 2.

nity, that is, governmental immunity from suit at both the state and municipal levels.[63] Recent rulings, such as its recognition of a cause of action for wrongful birth, reflect a continuing commitment to tort law innovation.[64] In addition, like the New Jersey Supreme Court, the California Supreme Court has been willing to take the lead in policy initiation and to announce rulings requiring major policy shifts by other branches of state government. For example, in 1971 it invalidated California's system of school finance, and in 1976 it ruled that the state constitution mandated governmental efforts, including busing, to remedy de facto segregation in the state's public schools.[65] Furthermore, the California court has been a leader in interpreting state constitutional provisions to protect rights beyond those recognized by the United States Supreme Court. Relying on the state bill of rights, it has (in addition to its rulings on school finance and school desegregation) recognized gender as a "suspect classification" for equal protection analysis, given an expansive interpretation to freedom of speech, invalidated the death penalty as "cruel or unusual punishment," and staked out a position on the rights of defendants that frequently puts it at odds with Burger Court rulings.[66]

Yet despite the similarities in their rulings and activism, the two courts operate in widely divergent contexts and in rather dissimilar

63. Strict liability: *Greenman* v. *Yuma Power Products Co.*, 377 P.2d 897 (Cal. 1963), adopting a position first urged by Justice Traynor in a concurring opinion in *Escola* v. *Coca Cola Bottling Co.*, 150 P.2d 436 (Cal. 1944); abrogation of sovereign and municipal immunity: *Muskopf* v. *Corning Hospital District*, 359 P.2d 457 (Cal. 1961). Justice Traynor's contributions to the development of tort law are discussed in G. Edward White, *The American Judicial Tradition: Profiles of Leading American Judges* (New York: Oxford University Press, 1976), chap. 13.

64. *Turpin* v. *Sortini*, 643 P.2d 954 (Cal. 1982).

65. School finance: *Serrano* v. *Priest*, 487 P.2d 1241 (Cal. 1971); school desegregation: *Crawford* v. *Board of Education*, 551 P.2d 28 (Cal. 1976).

66. Gender: *Sail'er Inn* v. *Kirby*, 485 P.2d 529 (Cal. 1971); freedom of speech: *Robins* v. *Pruneyard Shopping Center*, 592 P.2d 341 (Cal. 1979); capital punishment: *People* v. *Anderson*, 483 P.2d 880 (Cal. 1980); rights of defendants: *People* v. *Disbrow*, 545 P.2d 272 (Cal. 1976), *People* v. *Brisendine*, 531 P.2d 1099 (Cal. 1975), *People* v. *Pettingill*, 578 P.2d 108 (Cal. 1978), and *People* v. *Bustamonte*, 634 P.2d 927 (Cal. 1981). One civil libertarian has described the California Supreme Court as "the most consistent, articulate, and principled of the state courts in advancing the new federalism." See Donald E. Wilkes, Jr., "The New Federalism in Criminal Procedure in 1984: Death of the Phoenix?" in Bradley D. McGraw, ed., *Developments in State Constitutional Law* (St. Paul: West, 1985), p. 171. For a somewhat different assessment, see Mary Cornelia Porter, "State Supreme Courts and the Legacy of the Warren Court: Some Old Inquiries for a New Situation," in Porter and Tarr, eds., *State Supreme Courts.*

fashions. Whatever the popularity of particular rulings, the New Jersey Supreme Court has been able to rely on its legal reputation and its stature within the state to shield it from efforts to undermine its integrity or compromise its independence. During the Traynor era, the professional reputation of the supreme court created a similar situation in California. "In the fifties and beyond, controversial judicial decisions [were] defended by a broad spectrum of politicians on the ground that what the courts ordered was the law and deserved support even if the substance of a decision was distasteful."[67] Over time, however, as the California Supreme Court "became identified with the liberal side of the political spectrum," its apparent politicization eroded the diffuse support it had enjoyed among political elites and the state's citizenry, and "political leaders tended to defend particular decisions only if they agreed with the result."[68] As a result, it became vulnerable to political attack. Constitutional amendments were adopted to overturn specific rulings on capital punishment, busing, and the rights of defendants.[69] The justices were accused of delaying announcement of an unpopular ruling until after an election in which Chief Justice Rose Bird was on the ballot, and the resulting public investigation, at which they were called upon to justify their actions, further damaged the court's reputation.[70] In 1986 Chief Justice Bird—together with several of her colleagues on the high court—succumbed to determined efforts to deny them reelection and give the incumbent Republican governor an opportunity to reshape the California Supreme Court.[71]

---

67. Preble Stolz, *Judging Judges* (New York: Free Press, 1981), p. 82.

68. Ibid.

69. Amendments to the California constitution were adopted to reinstate the death penalty (Art. I, sec. 27 [1972]), to bring the state's responsibilities for desegregation in line with federal requirements (Art. I, sec. 7 [1979]), and to overturn a host of decisions extending the rights of defendants (Art. I, sec. 28 [1982]).

70. As it was, Chief Justice Bird received only 51.7 percent of the vote, thereby almost becoming the first justice to lose a retention election in the fifty-one years California has had the system. For discussions of this investigation from widely different perspectives, see Stolz, *Judging Judges*, and Betty Medsger, *Framed: The New Right Attack on Chief Justice Rose Bird and the Courts* (New York: Pilgrim Press, 1983).

71. Six of the seven justices of the California Supreme Court were on the ballot in 1986. For an overview and analysis of the election results, see John T. Wold and John H. Culver, "The Defeat of the California Justices: The Campaign, the Electorate, and the Issue of Judicial Accountability," *Judicature* 70 (1987): 348–55.

Commentators have disagreed about the causes of the California Supreme Court's fall from grace, attributing it variously to a decline in the court's performance and professionalism,[72] to the unprincipled politics of the radical right,[73] or—more generally—to the development of civil liberties "absolutism" in a state characterized by strong populist traditions and ideological polarities.[74] Whatever the persuasiveness of the various explanations, they all point to the inability of the California Supreme Court to present itself and its rulings as above politics and to insulate itself from political conflicts in the state. This difficulty became particularly acute as the court adopted a strongly civil libertarian stance on the rights of defendants and other issues. Other courts that have sought to expand civil liberties—and particularly the rights of defendants—under state bills of rights have encountered similar problems. Following a series of rulings by the Florida Supreme Court restricting searches by the police, for example, the Florida electorate amended the state constitution to prohibit state courts from granting protection beyond that secured by the Fourth Amendment.[75] In similar fashion, following a series of decisions by the Massachusetts Supreme Judicial Court striking down the death penalty, voters approved an amendment reinstating capital punishment in the state.[76] When the Maryland Court of Appeals construed a state statute to suppress confessions when there was a delay in taking the arrestee before a magistrate, the legislature quickly enacted a law

72. See, for example, Stolz, *Judging Judges.*

73. See, for example, Medsger, *Framed.*

74. This position is presented in Thomas C. Dalton, *The State Politics of Judicial and Congressional Reform* (Westport, Conn.: Greenwood, 1985), chap. 4.

75. The relevant Florida rulings include *Grubbs* v. *State,* 373 So.2d 905 (Fla. 1979); *Norman* v. *State,* 379 So.2d 643 (Fla. 1980); *State* v. *Sarmiento,* 397 So.2d 643 (Fla. 1981); and *State* v. *Dodd,* 419 So.2d 333 (Fla. 1982). The 1982 amendment to Article I, Section 12 stated that the right against unreasonable search and seizure "shall be construed in conformity with the 4th Amendment to the United States Constitution, as interpreted by the United States Supreme Court." For a discussion of the rulings and the amendment, see Wilkes, "New Federalism in Criminal Procedure in 1984," pp. 175–79.

76. The relevant Massachusetts rulings include *Commonwealth* v. *O'Neal,* 339 N.E.2d 676 (Mass. 1975); *Opinion of the Justices,* 364 N.E.2d 184 (Mass. 1977); and *District Attorney* v. *Watson,* 411 N.E.2d 1274 (Mass. 1980). The amendment to Article 26 of the Massachusetts Constitution states that "[n]o provision of the Constitution, however, shall be construed as prohibiting the imposition of the penalty of death." For discussion of the decisions and the amendment, see Wilkes, "New Federalism in Criminal Procedure in 1984," pp. 179–82.

overturning the ruling.[77] And even when rulings have not been overturned, state supreme courts have confronted serious difficulties in "secur[ing] the authority necessary to legitimize their policies."[78]

The contrast between these courts and the New Jersey Supreme Court highlights the latter's distinctive character. Some rulings of the New Jersey court have been unpopular, and the court's strategic retreat from *Mount Laurel* II may signal a recognition that it had acted imprudently. Despite this, the New Jersey justices have managed to play an active, even aggressive, part in the governance of the state and to take a leadership role in legal development without destroying the court's reputation for professionalism and nonpartisanship. The political problems that other activist courts have encountered reveal how unusual it is to be able to combine activism with insulation from politics. Moreover, the fall from grace of the California Supreme Court, which in the 1950s and 1960s enjoyed the same stature and independence that now characterize the New Jersey court, suggests that this combination is difficult to maintain. Yet whatever the California example may portend for the future of the New Jersey Supreme Court, for now at least the court must be viewed as unique among activist supreme courts.

In pointing out distinctive aspects in the institutional identity of the New Jersey Supreme Court, we return once again to some basic themes of the entire work. State supreme courts play important roles in the governance of their states and in the overall system of American federalism. Yet the roles they play are not the same in each state nor in individual states over time. Rather, what is most impressive is the diversity that marks their relations with the federal courts, with other state supreme courts, and with political institutions within their states. Appreciation of this interstate diversity—and of the national and intrastate factors contributing to it—is the crucial first step for understanding state supreme courts.

77. The Maryland legislature in 1981 enacted a statute—Act of May 19, 1981, ch. 577, 1981 Md. Laws 2326—overturning the Maryland Court of Appeals's ruling in *Johnson* v. *State*, 384 A.2d 709 (Md. 1978). The legislation and ruling are discussed in Wilkes, "New Federalism in Criminal Procedure in 1984," pp. 169–71.

78. Dalton, *State Politics of Judicial and Congressional Reform*, p. 134, and—more generally—pp. 129–34.

APPENDIX A

Porter/Tarr Questionnaire
Justices of the Alabama Supreme Court, March 1982
Justices of the Ohio Supreme Court, November 1985

1. How do you deal with a U.S. Supreme Court decision with which you disagree?
2. Do you feel that it is proper for you to express your disagreement?
3. Do you believe that the U.S. Supreme Court responds to expressions of concern or disagreement from state supreme courts?
4. There has been much comment about the Warren Court's "revolution" and the Burger Court's "counterrevolution" as pertains to the rights of defendants? Would you agree with this characterization of the trends in decisions? Are you more comfortable with the Warren or the Burger court's criminal justice directives?
5. Do you welcome the Burger Court's invitation to state courts to use state constitutions to protect civil liberties? Are you satisfied that the Court *has* taken seriously the attempts by state supreme courts to base decisions on the "independent and adequate state ground"?
6. When issues are raised under the state and the U.S. constitutions, on which do you tend to base your rulings? What factors determine which you will reply upon?
7. Do you think that attorneys, especially in civil liberties cases, are, have been, or should be arguing for decisions based upon the state constitution?
8. Do you perceive federal district courts as intruding in matters more properly left to your jurisdiction and the elected branches of government (habeas corpus petitions, litigant demands for social and economic change)?

9. Would you welcome the abolishment/modification of the federal diversity jurisdiction?

10. Do you often look to the precedent of courts in other states in deciding cases? Are there some state high courts that are particularly helpful? Why?

11. Since becoming a member of the court, how has your caseload changed both in terms of number and types of cases? What has produced these changes?

12. What do you think are the most important types of cases your court has decided since you have been on the bench? Over the past ten years?

13. Some commentators have suggested that courts are playing a much more prominent role in governing than in the past. Would you say this is true of your court? In what ways?

14. There have been substantial changes in the common law since World War II mostly, but not entirely as a result of judicial decision. How has your court responded to these changes? Do you believe that courts should take the lead in making such changes? To what extent do you think that courts should adhere to precedent and leave the initiative for change to the legislature?

Justices of the Ohio Supreme Court Only

15. What sorts of changes pertaining to the Ohio judiciary would you like to see enacted? For example, court organization, court funding, the authority of the Supreme Court, modes of selecting and disciplining judges, modes of disciplining lawyers? Anything else?

16. The membership of the Supreme Court of Ohio has been predominately Republican for many years. Why, in your view, has this been so? To what do you attribute the recent strong Democratic gain and the current narrow Democratic majority? Do you think that one or the other party will again dominate the court, or that the party margins will be narrow, or that party dominance will seesaw throughout the foreseeable future?

17. A number of studies have indicated that party preference/affiliation is influential in judicial outcomes. Do you agree? Would you say that on some issues (workers' compensation, for example) there is a "Democratic" or a "Republican" judicial perspective; but on other issues (e.g., civil liberties, including defendants' rights, freedom of speech) party affiliation is irrelevant?

18. The Supreme Court of Ohio has received wide media attention. Do you think, on the whole, that the coverage has been fair and reported in ways that serve the public interest? Do you think the media have focused on the style at the expense of the substance of the judicial decision-making processes? State high courts are only infrequently accorded much interest by the media. What, in general, do you think should be the media's responsibility in reporting on state judiciaries?
19. Please feel free to make any further comments/observations/suggestions.

INDEX